Fragmenting Work

Blurring Organizational Boundaries and Disordering Hierarchies

Edited by
MICK MARCHINGTON
DAMIAN GRIMSHAW
JILL RUBERY
HUGH WILLMOTT

OXFORD
UNIVERSITY PRESS

OXFORD

UNIVERSITY PRESS

Great Clarendon Street, Oxford OX2 6DP

Oxford University Press is a department of the University of Oxford.
It furthers the University's objective of excellence in research, scholarship,
and education by publishing worldwide in

Oxford New York

Auckland Bangkok Buenos Aires Cape Town Chennai
Dar es Salaam Delhi Hong Kong Istanbul Karachi Kolkata
Kuala Lumpur Madrid Melbourne Mexico City Mumbai Nairobi
São Paulo Shanghai Taipei Tokyo Toronto

Oxford is a registered trade mark of Oxford University Press
in the UK and in certain other countries

Published in the United States
by Oxford University Press Inc., New York

© Oxford University Press, 2005

The moral rights of the author have been asserted
Database right Oxford University Press (maker)

First published 2005

British Library Cataloguing in Publication Data

Data available

Library of Congress Cataloguing in Publication Data

Data available

ISBN 0-19-926223-3 (hbk)

ISBN 0-19-926224-1 (pbk)

Typeset by Newgen Imaging Systems (P) Ltd., Chennai, India
Printed in Great Britain
on acid-free paper by Biddles Ltd., King's Lynn, Norfolk

ACKNOWLEDGEMENTS

Writing a book based on a long and extensive research project inevitably involves many people and far too many to name individually. Without the cooperation and support of managers, workers, and union representatives from all the organizations that took part in the project across the eight case study networks, we would not have been able to pull together the data. We are extremely grateful to all those who gave their time so willingly and who were so open in their discussions with us. When the project started we were all employed in the Manchester School of Management at UMIST, and we are especially thankful to colleagues there for making it such a good environment in which to work. By the date of submitting the manuscript several people had moved on to other universities, and by the time the book is published, neither UMIST nor MSM will be in existence following the merger with the Victoria University of Manchester.

Major acknowledgement must be made to the Economic and Social Research Council (ESRC) for its financial support, which allowed us to appoint research staff to work alongside those of us already at UMIST. The project, 'Changing Organizational Forms and the Reshaping of Work', ran from May 1999 to April 2002 under grant number L212252038 as part of the much wider Future of Work programme. The UMIST project was coordinated by Mick Marchington and the remainder of the research team was Jill Rubery, Hugh Willmott, Jill Earnshaw, Damian Grimshaw, Irena Grugulis, John Hassard, Marilyn Carroll, Fang Lee Cooke, Gail Hebson, and Steven Vincent. The whole group contributed to the final manuscript, but responsibility for putting this book together fell to the four editors, each of whom made a significant contribution to the final shape of the book. In order to recognize this, we have put the authorship for Chapters 1 and 12 in alphabetical order rather than try to differentiate between our respective contributions. Several secretaries at UMIST (Helen Anderton, Helen Dean, Lindsay Endell, and Mary O'Brien) and at Cambridge (Katherine Webster, Jacqueline Damant) were involved in keying in changes for the book and tidying up drafts. Rory Donnelly and Jane Suter helped us put together the references, and Mary O'Brien organized the final push to get the complete manuscript to the publisher.

ACKNOWLEDGEMENTS

We wish to mention two other people who were involved with the project and, in a sense, dedicate this book to them. First is Peter Nolan, who was the Director of the ESRC Future of Work Programme and who gave constant support, as well as providing opportunities for us to disseminate our findings and ideas to various bodies, but in particular The Cabinet Office. Second is John Goodman CBE, who was one of the original applicants for the grant, but who moved aside soon after it got underway and eventually retired from full-time academic work as the project neared completion. Not only was John influential in relation to this project, he also played a major part in bringing most of us to UMIST in the first place and in developing the research culture which was so central to the philosophy of the Manchester School of Management, and is—we hope—reflected in this book.

Mick Marchington, Damian Grimshaw,
Jill Rubery, and Hugh Willmott
December 2003

CONTENTS

BOXES

TABLES

FIGURES

ABBREVIATIONS

AC	Appeal Cases
ACR	Arms' length Contractual Relations
AEEU	Amalgamated Engineering and Electrical Union (now part of Amicus)
ALG	Association of London Government
APEX	Association of Professional, Executive, Clerical, and Computer Staff
ATL	Association of Teachers and Lecturers
AT&T	American Telephone & Telegraph Company
BCC	British Ceramics Confederation
CERAM	Ceramics industry research and technology organization
CATU	Ceramics and Allied Trades Union
CCT	Compulsory Competitive Tendering
CIA	Chemicals Industries Association
CRE	Commission for Racial Equality
CSA	Customer Services Advisor
CSR	Customer Services Representative
CWU	Communication Workers Union
EI	Employee Involvement
EOC	Equal Opportunities Commission
EU	European Union
EVA	Economic Value Added
EWCA	England and Wales Court of Appeal
FE	Further Education
GMB	General Municipal and Boilermakers' Union
HMSO	Her Majesty's Stationery Office
HRM	Human Resource Management
ICL	International Computers Limited
ICR	Industrial Cases Reports
ICT	Information and Communication Technology
IdeA	Improvement and Development Agency

IPA	Involvement and Participation Association
IPPR	Institute for Public Policy Research
IRLR	Industrial Relations Law Reports
JCC	Joint Consultative Committee
KIF	Knowledge Intensive Firm
KPI	Key Performance Indicator
LEA	Local Education Authority
LFS	Labour Force Survey
LGA	Local Government Association
NASUWT	National Association of Schoolmasters and Union of Women Teachers
NEDO	National Economic Development Office
NFSP	National Federation of Sub-postmasters
NHS	National Health Service
NMW	National Minimum Wage
NQT	Newly Qualified Teacher
NUMAST	National Union of Marine Aviation and Shipping Transport
NUT	National Union of Teachers
OCR	Obligational Contractual Relations
OECD	Organization for Economic Cooperation and Development
OPSR	Office of Public Services Reform
PCS	Public and Commercial Services Union
PFI	Private Finance Initiative
PPP	Public–Private Partnership
PSA	Patient Service Assistant
SPV	Special Purpose Vehicle
TGWU	Transport and General Workers Union
TUC	Trades Union Congress
TUPE	Transfer of Undertakings (Protection of Employment)
UNISON	The largest trade union for public service workers

CONTRIBUTORS

Marilyn Carroll is Research Associate in the European Work and Employment Research Centre at the University of Manchester.

Fang Lee Cooke is Senior Lecturer in Employment Studies at the University of Manchester.

Jill Earnshaw is Chair of Employment Tribunals and previously Senior Lecturer in Employment Law and Dean at the University of Manchester, Institute of Science and Technology.

Damian Grimshaw is Senior Lecturer in Employment Studies at the University of Manchester.

Irena Grugulis is Professor of Employment Studies at Bradford University.

John Hassard is Professor of Organizational Analysis at the University of Manchester.

Gail Hebson is Research Associate in the European Work and Employment Research Centre at the University of Manchester.

Mick Marchington is Professor of Human Resource Management at the University of Manchester.

Jill Rubery is Professor of Comparative Employment Systems at the University of Manchester.

Steven Vincent is Lecturer in Human Resource Management and Industrial Relations at the University of Leeds.

Hugh Willmott is Diageo Professor of Management Studies at the University of Cambridge.

1

Introduction: Fragmenting Work Across Organizational Boundaries

DAMIAN GRIMSHAW, MICK MARCHINGTON, JILL RUBERY,
AND HUGH WILLMOTT

1.1 Introduction

The claim that 'organizational forms are changing and new forms are emerging' is a popular mantra of contemporary commentaries on organization, management, and society. Bureaucracies, commentators confidently affirm, are being dismantled and replaced by looser, networked organizational forms and processes. Boundaries between organizations are becoming blurred as activities are contracted-out or franchised. Organizations are forming partnerships based on strong-trust client–supplier relationships. In short, organizations, it is said, are becoming increasingly integrated into dynamic networks connected by time–space compressing information and communication technologies. Competitive survival is now sought by acting in more connected and concerted ways to secure outcomes that are beneficial to all parties. Examples of organizations identified as 'networks' are Japanese kieretsu systems of business organization comprising strategic alliances and cross-shareholdings between suppliers and distributors; networks developed by small and medium-sized enterprises to compete against larger firms; dispersed global corporations that are seen to resemble webs more than pyramids; inter-agency public sector teams drawn from diverse organizations; and computerized communication networks within and between organizations, including 'virtual' organizations.

Accompanying this transformation, it is claimed, the historical tendency towards the internalization of employment relationships within hierarchies is being reversed. Organizations are now nurturing their core competencies and purchase whatever they need from a network of skill and service providers—in the form of agency and self-employed, non-unionized contract and contingent workers—as well as from specialist in-sourcing companies. Closely linked to this picture is the idea that work is becoming more individualized and insecure, but also less regimented and more empowering as employees enjoy greater opportunities to develop their 'soft' (e.g. teamwork) skills in addition to their technical expertise, thereby improving their employability.

Some consequences of these projected changes for the quality of life—extra pressures, long working hours, and added insecurities—are only just beginning to be taken seriously, with, for example, campaigns about the problems of work–life balance. In response, employment policies are being revised to provide individualized packages, rather than the standardized, collective arrangements associated with the 'old' or bureaucratic forms of organization and employment relations. In the present context, Castells (1996: 279) has claimed, 'Never was labor more central to the process of value-making. But never were the workers (regardless of their skills) more vulnerable to the organization, since they had become lean individuals, farmed out in a flexible network whose whereabouts were unknown to the network itself'. We find substance as well as hype in such assertions. In the name of right-sizing, delayering, and concentrating upon core competencies, the outsourcing of services continues to expand, both at the high end of services provision (IT, accountancy, human resources) and at the low end (catering, security, cleaning). Stimulated by these developments, new companies have been set up, or existing firms redesigned, to specialize in various kinds of 'facilities management'. Associated with these changes, there is increasing interest in establishing long-term relations with suppliers; evidence of firms linking up into regional networks to strengthen their mutually dependent competitive position; and, especially in the United Kingdom, a proliferation of interest in public–private partnerships. Simultaneously, there are changes in employment from the dominance of a single employer model to the emergence of a more complex inter-organizational employment nexus where there are multiple employers and clients.

In the context of blurred boundaries and fragmented activities, the established, textbook ideas of an organization as a discrete entity, and of the employment relationship as a clear-cut contract of service with a single employer, becomes difficult to sustain. In practice, it is often unclear where one organization ends and another begins, and staff are placed in multiple employment relationships where obligations as well as identifications and allegiances are negotiable rather than stable. The blurring of boundaries is generally accompanied by an increase in uncertainty and ambiguity in employment relations. In such circumstances, the identities of the organization, the employer, and the worker can become destabilized, with attendant risks of disaffection as well as opportunities to develop alternative allegiances through trusting relations. Not surprisingly, such relationships involve overt and suppressed conflicts as well as pragmatic elements of cooperation.

This book presents findings based upon eight case studies of inter-organizational forms, involving interviews with about 450 managers and workers from nearly sixty employing organizations across the different sites of employment—the supplier, the client, the franchiser, the franchisee, the public purchaser, and the private provider. Our empirical material is extensive and grounded, but it is not claimed to be 'representative' of some, larger population. Nevertheless, our research does provide a counterbalance to the excessive, hyped interest in 'new' organizational forms involving high tech or exceptionally successful organizations, since we focus upon a range of private and public sector organizations, most of which rarely find their way into business or academic literatures that are dominated by a focus upon 'high tech' and the so-called leading edge organizations. Our cases include examples of long-term supply relations, international outsourcing, franchising, and public–private partnerships. We focus principally upon processes of *fragmentation* and *the blurring of boundaries* as organizations introduce changes that increase their immediate dependence upon other organizations with the intention of reducing risk, acquiring knowledge and facilitating learning, raising profitability, and/or cutting costs while also improving product/service quality. Such changes frequently involve the development of *hybrid* elements within established organizational forms, rather than their transformation into 'new' forms or 'networks'. Similarly, our evidence points to complex and contradictory arrangements that decompose bureaucracy without being, in any meaningful sense, 'post bureaucratic'.

Our research is intended to contribute to contemporary debates on changes in work organization and 'the future of work' by reconnecting the analysis of organizations with the study of employment and work, as well as by situating the study of employment within the context of changing forms of organization. There is an urgent need to bring together these fields of study; as Child and McGrath observe, the effect of new and changing organizational forms on employment relations is one of the 'great unknowns' (2001: 1144). Studies with a similar focus tend to start from a position that interprets evidence of fragmentation and disintegration as a necessary or inevitable part of twenty-first-century capitalism associated with the rise of new information and communication technologies or new globalized systems of competition. In contrast, we argue that the forces leading to fragmentation have as much to do with the political context as with changes in technologies or production and market requirements. Indeed, we conceive of such changes as an articulation of political preferences and negotiations, rather than the outcome of impersonal forces. As a consequence, we believe that our research can contribute as much to understanding why there may be limits to fragmentation and disintegration as to an explanation of their presence and extensiveness. We continue this introductory chapter with a consideration of popular commentary on 'new' organizational forms.

1.2 Blurring organizational boundaries: modernization or disintegration?

Corporate executives, under a variety of pressures to improve competitiveness, have been attracted to the promise of reducing costs and improving services by 'reengineering' processes, including the outsourcing of previously vertically integrated activities. Project-based organization and market mechanisms—internal as well as external—have been commended and embraced as a means of speeding responsiveness to business opportunities and competitive pressures—with the consequence that extended sets of relationships with suppliers and customers have developed. In the public sector, politicians have been attracted to novel ways of financing and operating public services that promise to improve services without substantially raising taxes. Here, too, more extended and complex relationships have been forged in an effort to supplement hierarchical control with ostensibly more cost-effective and flexible means of service delivery—notably, by contracting out services to the private sector. It is these arrangements that are frequently characterized as 'networks' that, it is claimed, present a 'modern alternative' to 'markets' and 'hierarchies' as forms of economic organization.

Such 'modernization' is linked in popular discourse to enhanced efficiency, associated with introducing 'professional management', redesigning business processes to improve access to new technologies, and with changing the wage–effort relationship in employment through eliminating 'unproductive work'. It is also anticipated that these changes will transform the traditional practices of organizing work and employment. By making the boundaries between organizations more fluid, it is argued, workers will experience greater freedom and empowerment in defining more flexible and fulfilling career paths which are not restricted to the confines of a single organization. In the public sector, a particularly determined case for modernization is made, based on the belief that the bureaucratic and monopolistic form of state organization has to be shaken up and infused with the vitality, innovation, and commercial 'nous' that comes from operating in a competitive, private sector environment (Box 1.1). In both private and public sectors the modernization thesis is tightly bound up with the use of business process reengineering to streamline activities and thereby maximize 'economic value added' (Knights and Willmott 1999).

Box 1.1. Networks as modernization? The case of public–private partnerships

Amidst the boom of the professional services organizations in the UK, the Capita Group plc has been one of the star performers . . . According to Capita, outsourcing provides real benefits to an organization because it introduces clearer definitions of customer requirements and heightens focus on service delivery standards . . . The five-year contract for IT facilities management and finance services with Mendip County council in Somerset is a good example: the £2.8 million per year contract is the widest-ranging local government facilities management contract let in the UK to date, and covers services such as revenue collection, housing benefit administration, IT support, accountancy, treasury management, printing and electoral registration. After almost four years of contract operation, Capita has been able significantly to improve service performance, including lower cost of support services, higher revenue collection rates, and a coordinated and planned approach to reinvestment in IT for support services. (Domberger 1998: 88)

Box 1.2. Business process outsourcing and EVA

'Business process outsourcing', often involves the transfer of in-house staff to a contractor which undertakes to re-engineer the work of existing staff. This trend is intimately linked with the application of a new focus on 'economic value added'—EVA:

> Financial markets have always demanded efficient use of capital to some degree. However, capital efficiency gained new power in the 1990s thanks partly to the Economic Valued Added (EVA) formula designed at Stern Stewart the consulting firm. This put pressure on managers not only to increase profits but also to take account of the amount of capital invested in the business and the cost of servicing it. 'It used to be that the more you had on your balance sheet, the better. Since the logic of EVA took hold it has been all about getting things off your balance sheet', says Peter Keen, a consultant and author. Business Process Outsourcing specialists—such as Flextronics and Selectron in manufacturing; Accenture, PwC and e-Peopleserve in human resources; and UPS and Federal Express in logistics— aim to deliver cost savings by designing processes more efficiently than their clients could achieve. Companies as diverse as Dell, Cisco and Wal-Mart have shown that competitive advantage can come from outsourcing of manufacturing and logistics. (*Financial Times*, 18 April 2002)

Resources should be retained in-house only if this is where they can be most productively utilized (Box 1.2).

Other popular accounts of change, in contrast, are coloured by a media focus upon 'disasters' and 'disintegration'—when, for example, cowboy sub-contracting occurs within public–private partnerships. Fiascos and failures are seized upon by those who are ideologically opposed to governance by market discipline and the argument is made, with selective evidence, that such episodes are typical and inevitable. In many cases, popular concern stems from an assault on the kinds of entitlements and rights that citizens have grown to expect: immediate access to public health care, schools staffed with sufficient teachers, and transport systems that are safe.

The difficulties surrounding the privatization and subsequent de-privatization of the British rail network illustrate what can happen when companies lose control over outsourced activities—in this case, essential maintenance of track (Box 1.3)—with catastrophic consequences for passenger safety and the severe delays and lengthened travel times arising from speed restrictions and track repairs. Other news stories have documented the way citizens' entitlements to a range of government services have been disruptive and restricted, including the issuing of passports and driving licences, the payment of housing benefits and child benefits, and security checks on school teachers. Andrew Pinder, government e-envoy has accused IT companies of lying to the government about capabilities and of being 'crap suppliers' that deliver 'incompetent workmanship'. Peter Gershon, head of the Office of Government Commerce, whose job is to deliver better value from government procurement, said: 'Every day we are faced

Box 1.3.   Losing control over outsourcing: the case of Railtrack

Railtrack was the company established to manage the railway infrastructure as a consequence of the privatization of the UK railway industry. Railtrack outsourced track maintenance to around twelve prime contractors in a successful effort to take out costs and increase the company's profitability. The success of the company, as measured by its meteoric share price movement and the rapid, profitable growth of its contractors, deflected attention from the confusion regarding the degree to which around 2,000 subcontractors used by the prime contractors were responsible for safety issues. Ultimately, Railtrack lost control over its complex web of contractors; one of which was alleged to have issued an internal memo that ordered workers not to cut out faulty sections of track because they were 'not practical or cost effective' to fix (*The Guardian*, 30 October 2000). Following a series of fatal accidents attributable to poor track maintenance, Railtrack went into receivership and its assets and activities were effectively transferred back into an unusual type of public ownership called Network Rail. Since then, there has been a greater preparedness to acknowledge a need to replace track in order to address the 4,000 mile backlog that had accumulated during the previous 12 years. This culminated in a decision by Network Rail to axe its private contracts for railway maintenance (*The Guardian*, 24 October 2003).

with suppliers who make exorbitant claims about the performance of their products and we are bitterly disappointed' (*Financial Times*, 17 April 2002). Similar problems of IT outsourcing have also emerged, with perhaps less publicity, in the private sector: for example, the double debiting of mortgage payments from more than 100,000 Abbey National customers has been attributed to external IT suppliers (*Financial Times*, 1 November 2002).

Stories of disintegration and disaster contrast strongly with the 'modernization' view which maintains that consumers will become the beneficiaries of changes that streamline and upgrade established, in-house provision. There is no simple way of adjudicating between these divergent perspectives. Providing an account of change that is universally regarded as balanced, unbiased, and objective is a chimera. It is not just the difficulty of getting to 'the heart of the matter', and for respondents to talk openly about it. More fundamentally, findings and discussions on 'work', 'organization', and 'employment' are theoretically informed and politically charged. Any account of changes in employment and work organization that one group (e.g. employees who have been transferred to a contractor) regards as comparatively accurate and impartial invariably appears biased, insufficiently qualified, or ideologically motivated to another group (e.g. the employer of the transferred staff). Where research findings are not ignored or shelved, they are necessarily interpreted and valued in different ways, and thus become a weapon or a menace for those with an interest in them. We do not bemoan this fate but, rather, note its inescapability. The value of research resides in developing ideas, collecting evidence, and interpreting findings in ways that can inform and enrich public understanding(s) of key issues. Our task is to illuminate the nature and effects of such changes, and to challenge some of the less nuanced, hyperbolic claims about their significance and value—negative as well as positive.

One way of making some sense of the current process of change is to place these developments within the orbit of the 'financialization' of the private and public sectors. Financialization points to the dominance of financial calculations in the process of determining how organizations should be structured (Froud et al. 2000). The focus is upon how to reap immediate financial benefits—increased stock values or a containment of taxation increases—rather than the medium to long-term implications of such calculations. In the private sector, the doctrine of economic value added (EVA) (see Box 1.2) prompts companies to minimize and narrow capital invested by outsourcing non-core activities to other specialist companies for whom these activities are 'core'. In the public sector, 'financialization' takes the form of minimizing the immediate cost of investing in the rebuilding of its services—for example, by leasing them from the private sector, a stratagem that is welcomed by the private sector as an opportunity for profitable expansion and avoids the potential fall-out from tax rises and/or currency devaluation.

The emphasis upon EVA is part and parcel of a move from 'retain and reinvest' to 'downsize and redistribute' (Lazonick and Sullivan 1996). In principle, contracting out of services holds out the prospect of companies concentrating on their core competencies while reducing staffing costs and obligations without detriment to the level of service provision. This, in turn, attracts capital providers who anticipate that other investors will seek out companies committed to EVA disciplines. The claimed benefits of this philosophy may, however, prove difficult to realize in practice where peripheral functions remain critical for ensuring the timely delivery of products and services. Short-term gains in cost reduction may be offset by subsequent increases in costs—both transactional, if contract penalties are invoked, and real, if additional services not specified in the contract have to be provided.

It may be believed that poorly rewarded workers are non-strategic or 'expendable'. Yet, these workers—such as dispatchers at airports or customer service representatives in call centres—can be critical for the delivery of services to customers and the reputation of the organizations. Hazards are particularly great in the public sector where invoking penalty clauses may not solve the problem of how to deliver essential public services. The agents responsible for innovations in service delivery—the consultants, executives, and politicians—celebrate their promised benefits without paying much attention to their practical implementation, unintended consequences, or negative effects. Their careers, credibility, and election prospects are invested in commending these changes, so there is a strong tendency to conflate their operation with the anticipated advantages of their introduction; and to interpret any deviation from predicted gains as an aberration rather than as an endemic feature of such arrangements. Many politicians and managers can also anticipate moving on to new pastures before the full impact of their modernizing efforts is registered or evaluated.

We can find comparable contradictory perspectives when we turn to popular accounts of the impact of this process of change on the experience of employment. The modernization thesis suggests that staff experience improved working conditions as a consequence of opportunities for injections of new investment to provide state of the art technology and management systems. In the debate on modernization of the public sector, the private sector human resource techniques of performance management and reward are presented as offering opportunities for self-development, in contrast to the restrictive traditional public sector career and pay structures (see Box 1.4).

The contrary perspective of disintegration and disorder bemoans how, as business activities are arranged across organizational boundaries, former employment hierarchies are disordered, complicating the relationship between different sets of managers and different groups of workers. Such problems are, perhaps, most apparent in the case of temporary agency workers for whom the agency is legally the employer, not the client organization (e.g. the call centre, factory, hospital, or school where they work), despite the fact that the agency has no control over the work process. Being remote from the place of employment, the agency is in no position to determine the performance of the worker or the circumstances in which grievance and disciplinary issues may arise. This ambiguity means that agencies often fail to take responsibility for providing health and safety information to their employees (see Box 1.5); if an agency worker has an accident then it is not clear whether the client organization or the agency is liable. Greater use of inter-organizational linkages results in situations where workers with different employers work alongside each other, often doing very similar work, but receive differential terms and conditions.

For individual workers, the impact of organizational change on their experience of employment depends both on their enactment of the context and the

---

Box 1.4. Positive career prospects in new organizational forms

Sasha Marley, 28, a business and European studies graduate, began her career with an administration role in the computer systems department of what was then the Department of Social Security. Within months, her job was outsourced to the IT specialist Steria, with whom she has stayed, and she says she 'couldn't have been more delighted'. 'I saw it as a good opportunity to move to a commercial organisation and because I had exactly the same terms and conditions as I'd had in the Civil Service, and was even working in the same office, I had no real worries about the implications', she says. Steria, says Marley, offered extra responsibility and faster career progression: 'Because of my own experience, I can identify with people who say that they are desperately worried about job security and I can reassure them that it can actually be good for your career in the long run'. (*The Times*, 6 November 2002)

Box 1.5.   The health and safety of agency workers

Mel Draper, Head of the Health and Safety Executive's policy division, argues that

> although most recruitment agencies and host employers claim to exchange information . . . the fact remains that a poor level of awareness of health and safety legislation exists. As a result temps may not be issued with safe and comfortable work stations . . . they may not be using computers with glare-free screens . . . they may not be warned about fire exits and danger spots around the building . . . And, crucially, they may not know at whom to direct their frustration when they find themselves confronted with these situations in an unfamiliar office. (*The Guardian*, 16 October 2000)

Box 1.6.   Outsourcing and the clash of working cultures

Even when outsourced services do perform well, tensions arise that can have a bad effect on public services. Envy is at the root of many, particularly where 'retained' (i.e. public-sector) and 'transferred' (i.e. outsourced) staff work alongside one another in the same building. One staff group gets a performance bonus; the other does not. One cadre of managers races around in leased cars while others still have years outstanding on their car loans. Issues of integrity arise where bonuses earned by private sector managers depend explicitly on cost cutting. (*Sunday Times*, 15 September 2002)

---

significance they attach to particular aspects of the employment relationship. More positive evaluations can be expected where a transfer to a services provider means that an activity traditionally regarded as peripheral to the operation of the previous company is core business for the new employer. The benefits may include improved opportunities for skill development or career enhancement. The current expansion of companies providing a range of outsourced services may offer rapid promotion prospects through opportunities to work on a variety of contracts and to move up newly constructed hierarchies to manage client contracts. On the other hand, even where job transfers may not appear to undermine job security, employees may still feel a strong sense of betrayal by employers who 'sell' their workforce to another supplier. In the private sector, a report by Steria (itself a significant player in the outsourcing business) based upon interviews with 120 IT staff, concludes that 60 per cent of private sector staff felt that they were 'badly treated' by their original employer during the transition phase, with 66 per cent reporting that they felt or continue to feel anxiety about their own position (*Financial Times*, 26 September 2002—see also Box 1.6). Transfers from the public sector run the additional risk that staff may continue to resent the dilution of a public service ethos and associated symbolic rewards as valued servants to the community.

In this section we have considered popular accounts of new organizational forms. One set of views paints a picture of private and public corporations turning to contracting as a timely and legitimate means of cutting costs and upgrading services in the name of 'modernization'. Other commentaries suggest that a blurring of boundaries can contribute to increased risks and adverse consequences for all the parties involved—not just workers, citizens, and consumers but also managers and shareholders. Whatever the outcome, proliferation of inter-organizational linkages—franchising, temporary work agencies, public–private partnerships, and outsourcing—and the fragmentation of work all point in the same direction of a blurring of organizational boundaries and a disordering of employment hierarchies. In the next section, we consider the academic literature on fragmentation in more detail.

1.3   Fragmentation in organization and employment studies

Academic debates that have both analysed and, indeed, possibly contributed to the contemporary trend towards the fragmentation of organizations and work have tended to focus either on the changing nature of employment relations, otherwise known as the 'flexibility' debate, or on the development of inter-organizational relationships, including the 'network firm' debate. This division reflects a wider divergence among academics specializing in 'employment studies' and others specializing in 'organization studies'. Our contention is that this polarization of the 'employment' and 'organization' dimensions of work has been unhelpfully restrictive. There is a need to develop a more integrated analysis in order to appreciate the full implications of fragmentation for the employment relationship and to grasp the significance of the employment relationship in shaping inter-organizational relations.

From integration to fragmentation?

In discussing the fragmentation of organizations and employment relations it is important to remember that the boundaries of an 'organization' are in many respects defined by the extent of the internalized employment relationship. New institutionalists (e.g. Williamson 1985) have accounted for the degree of internalization by an exploration of transaction costs. Internalization, they argue, is favoured where the transaction costs of an open-ended employment contract—in which an employer exercises authority over workers within customary and legal limits—are assessed to be lower than the detailed specification of the tasks in a contract for self-employed workers or a subcontracting company (see, also, Simon 1976).

   This rational–economic explanation contrasts with the approach of radical political economists who explain the development of hierarchical forms of economic governance as a means of connecting and coordinating the latently tense and conflictual interests of employers (capital) and employees (labour) in the production process so as to ensure a disciplined output of profitable goods and services (e.g. Marglin 1974). The value of internalization of employment for the employer, radical political economists contend, is that it brings recalcitrant labour, including those with craft skills, under more effective control. The managerial agents of capital secure greater pliability and higher productivity in return for a guarantee of regular work and regular wages.

A third approach, associated with labour market segmentation theory, (e.g. Rubery 1978; Wilkinson 1983; Jacoby 1984) identifies the degree of internalization as an outcome of a more complex dynamic involving contingent and politico-economic factors. Overarching theories of capital–labour struggles are viewed as excessively deterministic and simplistic. Instead of capital operating as a unified force against labour, individual employers are conceived to harness the cooperation of labour in the very process of inter-capitalist competition. The internalized employment relationship is, thus, understood to emerge out of struggles within as well as between the buyers and sellers of labour, rather than as something imposed upon workers by an all-powerful capital and its omniscient agents. This analysis can be considered to have resonances with the post-structuralist view that interests are organized within—rather than given by—social relations, including relationships of employment (Burawoy 1985; Laclau and Mouffe 1985). The struggle is not between pre-existing protagonists where each of the parties is deemed to be fully knowledgeable of where its interests reside and fully capable of calculating how to secure their fulfilment. Instead the historical internalization of employment is interpreted through the process of identity and interest formation.

Since the 1980s, analyses of capitalist development have shifted their focus from the benefits of internalization to those of vertical disintegration. In this new phase of capitalism, the discourse is one of concentrating on core competences and removing the 'fat' associated with (overblown) forms of bureaucratic governance. This shift has coincided with an interest in the so-called 'post-Fordist' network production systems, such as those developed in the industrial districts of northern Italy and by major Japanese corporations (e.g. Brusco 1982; Piore and Sabel 1984; Dore 1986; Sayer 1986). The prospering of these developments suggests that alternative forms of organization (districts or clusters of firms, strategic alliances, and cross-shareholdings between suppliers and distributors) are congruent with contemporary economic conditions and demands, including the use of fast changing technologies, a shortening of product life cycles and the increasing importance for developed countries of competing in high value-added medium-sized markets.

For neoclassical economists, the internalized model is no longer seen as cost-effective in a context of rapid changes in knowledge and skills where organizations value rapid access to knowledge both inside and outside their boundaries. Individuals also benefit from the move away from internalization as it is not in employees' best interests to be 'bonded' to, or institutionalized within, an organization when they can benefit from developing and diversifying their human capital across a variety of employment settings.

An alternative explanation posits change in the configuration of market and production systems towards a more competitive and world order. This new configuration, it is claimed, no longer allows national capital to secure an acceptable rate of return through internalization that offers comparatively favourable, but costly, conditions of service for many employees. In this post-Fordist world, labour has become de-collectivized as many union strongholds in mature industries have been replaced by feminized industries where, in general, expectations of good employment conditions are less entrenched. In a world where corporatist settlement has been widely supplanted by an individualistic ethos, new organizational and employment arrangements are being forged for managing new sources of uncertainty (e.g. with respect to variations in the quantity and composition of demand rather than exigencies of labour supply) while sustaining profitable growth. Not only has the power of organized labour diminished, but also the emergence of new forms of labour supply—in particular the integration of women into the wage economy—has provided further opportunities for the diversification of forms of employment and contracts based on the notion of contingent rather than continuously employed labour.

These arguments have been used to explain both change within organizational boundaries—where multi-skilling and flexible deployment strategies have been used to minimize down time, handovers and other porosities in the labour process—and change in inter-capital relations. The corporatist concern for cooperation with labour is increasingly associated with an (outmoded) model of capitalism where profit in the service of private wealth is accumulated by imposing hierarchical discipline over an extensive and integrated workforce in return for relative security of employment and promotion prospects. The new model largely takes for granted the self-discipline of workers (secured through a pervasive erosion and devaluation of solidaristic working class traditions, fuelled by consumerism and individualism). Discipline is secured, instead, through the 'whip' of the market, in the form of the potential loss of contacts that connect networked organizations, and often the provision of (temporary) workers within them, combined with the reincarnation of more flattened forms of hierarchy within suppliers of specialist services. As a distillation of this trend, financialization weakens any concern to internalize and harness the skills of the workforce. This 'hollowing out of capital' is associated with a model of capitalism that unashamedly seeks out short-term profits (the 'no long term' in Sennett's (1998) terminology). Instead of reciprocity in the form of job security, career progression, and pension provision being valued as assets, permanent employees with expectations may be seen as expensive liabilities.

Analysis of the internalization of employment and the development of vertically integrated production systems developed to a large extent simultaneously. That is to say, in very different forms of analysis, the rise and size of the vertically integrated organization is related to the benefits of directly managing the employment relationship. The same cannot be said for discussions of vertical disintegration of organizations. Literature on organizational forms, primarily associated with the projected rise of a networked society, has been abstracted from issues of employment. In the parallel discussion of flexible employment systems, moves towards fragmentation of the organization have been noted as an important element, but more attention has been paid to the diversity of employment contracts than to locating these employment relationships within networks of inter-organizational relations. In the following sections, we selectively review the respective literatures on new organizational forms and employment flexibility. The concerns are explored more fully in Chapters 2 and 3, and their interconnections are a focus of the empirically based Chapters 4–11.

The changing organizational forms debate

The post-Fordist debate in the organization literature has been based on an assumption that organizational forms are changing. Here, the concept of 'network' has been widely invoked to support and illustrate the understanding that organizational forms are emerging in response to the connectivity supplied by information and communication technologies and the intensification of competitive pressures associated with the neoliberal dismantling of barriers to processes of trade globalization. Powell writes (1990: 303–304):

In network forms of resource allocation, individual units exist not by themselves, but in relation to other units. These relationships take considerable effort to establish and sustain, thus they constrain both partners' ability to adapt to changing circumstances. . . . Expectations are not frozen, but change as circumstances dictate. A mutual orientation—knowledge which the parties assume each has about the other and upon which they draw in communication and problem solving—is established. In short, complementarity and accommodation are the cornerstones of successful production networks.

Networks, it is claimed, are supplementing and displacing more established—'market' and 'hierarchical'—forms of economic organization. The concept of 'network' is commended because the established analytical tools of 'market' and 'hierarchy' fail to grasp the increasing reliance upon horizontal rather than vertical exchanges that are accompanied by a weakening of boundaries within and between organizations as risks and resources are pooled through collaborative arrangements (e.g. strategic alliances, partnership, industrial networks). More specifically, the concept of 'network' is invoked to highlight the existence of synergies between organizational units and the possibility of managing their transactions on the basis of mutuality and trust rather than impersonal contract or administrative fiat (see Table 1.1).

Network organizational forms are understood to embody and facilitate more agile, combinable, project-oriented, and permeable structures. Associated with 'the networked organization' are changes in work patterns and

Table 1.1.   Stylized comparison of forms of economic organization

	Market	Hierarchy	Network
Normative basis	Contract-property rights	Employment relationship	Complementary strengths
Means of communication	Prices	Routines	Relational
Methods of conflict resolution	Haggling—resort to courts for enforcement	Administrative fiat—supervision	Norm of reciprocity—reputational concerns
Mixed forms	Contracts as hierarchical documents	Market-like feature: profit centres, transfer pricing	Multiple partners; formal rules

Source: Adapted from Powell (1990: 300).

employment practices that include empowerment, customer-facing redesign, teamworking, real-time information sharing, and organizational learning.

A tricky feature of much writing on 'new' or 'changing' forms of organization is a conflation of prescription with analysis. It is frequently difficult to untangle whether innovations are being widely implemented or merely celebrated. All too often there is an attempt by aspirant business and policy gurus to distil complex, emergent, uneven processes into a seductive sound bite—such as 'the network form' or 'the boundaryless organization'. More sceptical analysts have argued that the contemporary transformation of organizational forms is overstated. Barley and Kunda (2001: 77–78) argue:

The claim that organizations are suddenly 'becoming networks' and that these networks are not hierarchical is overstated . . . any organization can be depicted as a network . . . organizations have always been networks. Furthermore, network analysts have shown that hierarchy is a property of a network's structure, not something that a network replaces. Within most organizations there is a reliance on the kind of 'informal' mechanisms and connections, based on the principles of cooperation, reciprocity and trust, that have come to be most closely associated with the 'network' form. These mechanisms are forged within as well as outside organizational borders and act as lubricants, in place of the old bureaucratic tool of administrative fiat. Indeed it is only when 'markets' and 'hierarchies' are conceptualized as impersonal and abstracted from the social media of their enactment that the relations now identified as 'networks' do not appear in view.

Theoretically, the impulse to identify networks as distinctive forms of organization stems from conceiving of organizations as integrated entities, representing a discrete production function. If, instead, organizations are imagined as *combinations of value chains* (activities that add value between suppliers and customers) comprising distinct but interrelated business processes, 'networks' can be regarded as fundamental rather than novel. If there is anything 'new' about the 'network' form, it is probably the increase in (reengineered)

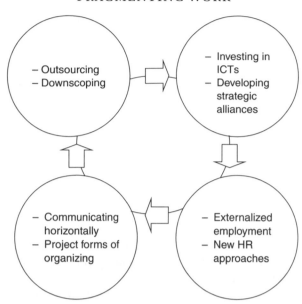

Fig. 1.1. The dynamics of vertical disintegration

cross-functional, temporary project working within organizations and the decomposition of vertically integrated organizations as activities are outsourced to specialist providers or shared through collaborative arrangements (Fig. 1.1).

When placed within a complex of organizing *processes* (rather than structures) and inter-organizational *relations* (rather than markets), there is a rational economic logic in concentrating resources in areas of activity where the organization has distinctive skills and/or a basis of competitive edge, and to outsource remaining activities to other organizations—now identified as members of a strategic network—that have developed distinctive capabilities in those specialist fields. But this logic holds only insofar as the political conditions enable it to be realized. Actors participating in market and hierarchical relationships routinely enact and encounter political pressures to explore and incorporate ways of organizing that depart from established models and protocols. In times of considerable fluidity, disruption, and uncertainty, the idea of the 'network' as an alternative form of organization serves to promote as well as legitimize such experimentation and innovation as well as account in an anodyne manner for its manifestations. By focusing on both inter- and intra-organizational relations we have a framework through which the impact of the uneven nature of power relations—between organizations and between management and labour—can be readily introduced into the analysis (see Chapter 2).

For us, the 'network' is a logic of organizing that is being diffused within established market and hierarchical governance structures—as Powell's (1990) reference to 'mixed forms' tacitly concedes. Without rejecting the concept of 'network' it is more plausible to regard 'market', 'hierarchy', and 'network' as concepts that have proven valuable in differentiating elements or dimensions of organizing practices within and between organizations, rather than as alternative designs of economic organization. Networks may be viewed as a constituent element of 'hierarchal structures' and 'market transactions', rather than a form of organization that is clearly differentiated from them (see, also, Imai 1986). As DiMaggio (2001: 23) reminds us: 'It is easy to forget that the notion of "network" is less a description of any particular form of association than it is an analytic convenience, a means of describing systems as consisting of a set of actors (units, nodes, objects) connected by a set of relations or flows.'

Even when the status of 'network' and related terms are remembered as 'analytic conveniences', the literature on network forms of organization routinely excludes consideration of the implications for workers and employment relationships. This is exemplified in Fenton and Pettigrew's (2000) overview of the literature on new and changing organizational forms. They refer to the importance of 'history, culture and politics of each firm' but offer little insight into their significance for staff. Pettigrew and Fenton (2000) make a passing observation that some staff may experience innovation as 'positive exhilaration of tackling a just cause' while for others 'the change may mean a bruising encounter with the devil' (ibid.: 291). But it is invariably 'organizations', and not their members, who are 'resting uneasily on a cusp between order and disorder' (ibid.: 291). And it is 'organizations', not employees, that face the dualities, such as 'building hierarchies and networks; seeking greater performance accountability upward and greater horizontal integration sideways' (ibid.: 296). Yet, these developments and tensions have implications for work and employment relations that are recursive—in the sense that managing such dualities is undertaken by, and contingent upon, employees who are charged with building networks whilst simultaneously occupying the cusp between order and disorder.

The main theoretical argument of our book advocates an expanded and more complex matrix of inter-organizational relations that re-inserts the employment relationship into the study of organizations (see Fig. 1.2). The absence of attention to work and employment among contemporary organizational researchers is as regrettable as it is surprising, especially given the history of scholarly contributions—from Weber's and Marx's concern with industrialization to the twentieth century analyses of bureaucratic organizations—that illustrate so well the interdependent dynamic tension between work and organizing. As Barley and Kunda (2001) document, since around the late 1960s, theorists of organizations have turned away from these broader issues to focus upon narrower more abstract questions, such as the organization's relationship with its environment, and have specialized in issues of organizational performance, strategy, and structure. Meanwhile, the study of work split off into industrial relations and industrial sociology, gradually losing influence on organizational theory (ibid.: 80–82). The problem is that isolated developments

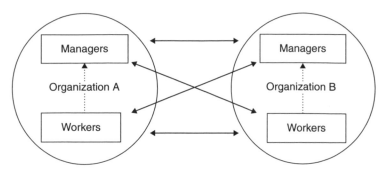

Fig. 1.2. Inter-organizational relations: crossing borders and disordering hierarchies

in each field of study makes the solving of new theoretical puzzles more difficult and weakens our understanding of new empirical phenomena.

Re-inserting the issue of work extends and enriches analyses of inter-
organizational relations in a number of ways. The extent to which trust
enhances contractual relations, for example, depends critically on the degree
of cooperation and trust forged between managers and workers, both within
and across organizations. When organizations enter into new contracting
arrangements, this is likely to generate significant shifts in the nature and organization of work: it may involve the outsourcing of workers to a new employer
providing a range of business services, or a new emphasis on working to a
specified performance contract—monitored by both the employer and the
contracting organization. As such, it is feasible that comparatively high trust
contractual relations may be established between the upper tiers of two organizations, but at the cost of new tensions and conflicts between managers and
workers, and indeed between workers employed at these different organizations. Connecting the literature on organizations to that of employment and
work is thus an essential first step towards an analysis of fragmentation that is
both more embedded in social processes and critical of the notion that changing organizational forms provides a dependable source of efficiency gains.

The employment flexibility debate

The employment flexibility debate is rooted in analysis of the changing nature
of the employment relationship. The standard, internalized type is conceptualized as involving a bounded relationship between a single employer and an
employee. However, just as the changing organizational forms debate has
ignored employment, much of the literature on employment flexibility has
focused on change on the employee side of the contract and the diversification
of employment statuses, and not on the role of changing organizational forms
in reshaping the employment contract.

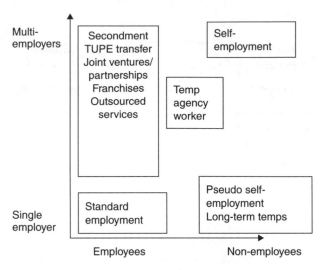

Fig. 1.3.　The twin dimensions of employment flexibility

The significance of organizational form for the employment relationship is presented diagrammatically in Fig. 1.3. The x-axis depicts variations in the internalization or standardization of the employment contract and the y-axis the extent to which the employment contract is under the influence of a single employing organization or subject to control or influence by multiple employers. The internalized, standard employment relationship is thus represented at the origin in the bottom left-hand corner. In the top right-hand corner is self-employment: the opposite of internalized employment, where there is no contract of employment and where the self-employed individual sells his or her skills to a range of organizations and is, therefore, not dependent on a particular organization for income.

Much work on changing employment relationships has, to date, focused on the contemporary diversification of employment contracts that is represented in the diagram as a movement along the x-axis from employees to non-employees. Typically, this has focused on the shift away from internalized full-time employees to a diversification of contracts including part-time, casual, temporary, and self-employed workers. Because changes in contracts occur along a number of dimensions, it is not possible to locate them neatly along a spectrum, such as from internalized to externalized. Part-time work might be considered to be close to the standard contract as there is nothing in principle stopping part-time work being organized on the same basis as internalized, full-time work with the same social rights and same regularity of employment.[1] However, the use of part-time contracts may be considered to compromise the guarantees of regular employment and income security associated with the standard contract (see Supiot 2001) particularly where part-timers are used to increase the variability of work scheduling (Neathey and Hurstfield 1995). There are even more obvious divisions between internalized labour and those on either temporary or casual contracts where the guarantees of employment and income are at best short term. At the far extreme are the so-called pseudo self-employed workers: that is, people who often work at a distance from the employer—such as homeworkers and freelancers—but who may be highly dependent upon one employer, even if there is no formal contractual guarantee of continuous employment or minimum income. In practice, the extent of differentiation between these categories of employment status depends substantially on the degree of security associated with the permanent or open-ended contract, which varies considerably between countries and within the United Kingdom between sectors and types of firms.

Variations in employment relationships that can be depicted along the y-axis have been much less widely debated. One exception is that of temporary agency workers; they are normally self-employed workers, but the agency is regarded as the legal employer even though it is the client who exercises control. The employing organization, which acts as host to the temporary agency workers, directs their work activities side-by-side with those of direct employees on similar tasks. This employment relationship is thus depicted on Fig. 1.3 as a move away from the origin on both the x- and the y-axis, involving both deviations from the status of direct employees, and control from more than one employing organization (Box 1.7 illustrates the ambiguities in the legal position of temporary agency workers).

The top left-hand side of Fig. 1.3 covers an area where employment is internalized but where there is more than one employing organization that can be considered party to the relationship. Comparatively little research has been undertaken in this area, and it is this type of employment relationship that provides the focus for our empirical work in this project. The basis for intervention by agents other than the legal employer—including clients, partners, or franchisers (Felstead 1991)—may be the need for continuing collaboration in the production process and issues of brand image and reputation. Such concerns can lead to direct interventions in the legal employer's system of work and employment organization—akin to 'corporate colonization' of part of the labour process according to Scarbrough (2000: 5); or it may be more indirect, imposed through strict contract terms that impinge on the organization of work without direct personal involvement by managers from the non-employing organizations. The form and nature of interventions vary with the degree of coordination and control across organizational borders that clients or other non-employers seek, as well as on the relative power of the contracting organizations. Employment relations may be shaped in quite different ways. Supply chains can be used to diffuse good practice in human resource policies (Beaumont et al. 1996; Scarbrough 2000), or alternatively they may be forged to shift risk to suppliers (Rainnie 1991; Turnbull et al. 1993). Throughout the remainder of this book, we seek to remedy the failure to analyse situations where there is a direct employment relationship but where other employers—acting as clients or suppliers—may be involved in shaping the employment experience, and even in controlling

Box 1.7. Who is the employer? The case of temporary agency workers

The following cases demonstrate the legal confusion surrounding how to assign the responsibilities of the employer between a temporary work agency and the host (or client) organization. In the first, the host organization is accorded employer status, while in the second the agency is deemed the employer.

- *Motorola Ltd* v. (1) *Davidson* (2) *Melville Craig Group Ltd* [2001]

In this case, an agency worker employed at Motorola for two years claimed unfair dismissal against the agency and the client firm (Motorola), having been suspended following alleged misconduct. Motorola appealed against Mr Davidson's successful claim of unfair dismissal by arguing that the legal power to control was the key issue in determining who was the employer, and that this resided with the agency, not Motorola. This appeal was unsuccessful as the Employment Appeal Tribunal was persuaded that Motorola's practical, as opposed to legal, power to control agency workers constituted it as the employer. Hence, the 'non-legal' employer, Motorola, was held to be responsible for unfair dismissal compensation.

- *Hewlett Packard Ltd* v. *O' Murphy* [2002]

This case considered whether HP or the temporary work agency, ought to be considered as the employer of Mr O'Murphy, an agency worker at HP. It considered evidence of practical contact between HP and Mr O'Murphy, including that his contract with the agency required him to be under the control of HP, that he had signed a confidentiality agreement with HP, that the contract between the agency and HP required HP to exercise 'the same duty of care towards [Mr O'Murphy] as is applicable in law between an employer and employee' and, finally, that Mr O'Murphy reported to a HP line manager and even arranged his holidays through this manager, not the agency. But the Employment Appeal Tribunal argued that the practical power of HP to control the agency worker was outweighed by the absence of a contract between Mr O'Murphy and HP. It thus identified the agency, rather than HP, as Mr O'Murphy's employer. If this ruling is followed, then companies using agencies will be able to reap the benefits of a worker's services as if he or she were an employee without incurring the obligations and potential liabilities associated with this status.

the employment relationship. Given the current fascination with how organizations pare back to their core competencies, there is a danger that, paradoxically, we forget to analyse the inter-organizational dimensions of the resulting non-integrated production and employment systems and continue to focus on organizations solely as sovereign entities rather than as embedded institutions.

1.4 The research

This book is based upon a three-year research project, which sought to analyse how more complex and potentially permeable organizational forms influence work and employment, and how shifting tensions in the employment relationship can affect the performance of 'new' organizational forms. Our research design differs from much of the contemporary literature in several ways. First, as we noted in Section 1.1, a major objective was to move beyond a focus upon the high tech or blue chip companies that provide the material for the celebratory literature on changing organizational forms.[2]

A second objective has been to place work and employment relationships at centre stage, an approach that we have contrasted with analysis that represents 'innovation', for example, as disembodied processes, structures, and boundaries abstracted from employment relations (Table 1.2). We challenge the seemingly widespread belief that innovation is the exclusive preserve of companies in the private sector, or that it is independent of political processes designed to change the relationship between the private and the public sector. Our research explicitly recognizes the dynamic tensions present at the workplace— between managers and workers in the same organization, between workers in the same and different organizations, between permanent and temporary staff, and between managers working for different organizations. If it is accepted that bounded organizations are not adequately characterized as cooperative and harmonious, tensions and contradictions are likely to increase greatly as multi-agency workplaces and inter-organizational relations add further complexity to webs of interpersonal relations.

Much research on 'new' and 'network' organizational forms focuses on the lead, contracting organization and draws inferences for the performance of the

Table 1.2. Comparison of studies of Pettigrew et al. (2003) and Marchington et al. (2004)

	Pettigrew et al.	Marchington et al.
Organizations conceived as	Elements of standardization and innovation	Emergent, contradictory practices
Focus of investigation	Types of innovation	Inter-organizational relationships, with a focus upon market-mediated provision of goods and services
Orientation of analysis	Organization strategy	Organization—employment
Attention to employee experience of innovation and change	Very limited—the emphasis is upon abstracting the construction of innovative forms of organizing from the responses of senior managers	In *most* cases interviews were conducted with a range of workers directly involved in providing goods and services
Consideration of Institutional Context	High level macro to meso	Institutions shape employer strategies of employment relations

Source: Adapted from Pettigrew et al. (2003).

'network' (the supply chain, or partnership) as a whole, despite lacking the views and information from the suppliers, subcontractors, and other partners to the exchange. More attention must be given to the broad institutional embeddedness of the practices that comprise organization/employment—from the national context to the local operation of custom and tradition. We also argue that the standard single organization-focused research design must be overhauled if we are to appreciate the implications of inter-organizational relations for work and employment. It is for this reason that the eight 'cases' presented in this book include networks of different organizations in a complex, and often messy, web of inter-organizational contracting arrangements. Given that we interviewed people from several different organizations in each network, it was possible to analyse views from a range of perspectives. Box 1.8 and Fig. 1.4 provide an overview of each case and further details are provided in an appendix to this chapter.

Our choice of 'cases' presents an opportunity to compare and contrast the operation of particular organizational forms. For example, three cases involve temporary work agencies in providing workers for the organizations involved; and there are three examples of public–private partnerships and TUPE transfers (Table 1.3). Similarly, three cases include multi-employer sites—the most

Table 1.3. Comparing organizational forms across the eight case studies

Characteristics of organizational forms	Case studies
Agencies	Post Office
	Customer Service (north-west and London)
	Teacher Supply
Franchising	Post Office
	Teacher Supply
Outsourcing	Ceramics
	Chemicals
	Customer Service (north-west)
Public–private partnerships	Information Technology
	PFI
	Customer Service (London)
Multi-client sites	Airport
	Customer Service (north-west)
Supply chain partnerships	Ceramics
	Chemicals
Multi-employer sites	Airport
	PFI
	Customer Service (north-west)
TUPE	Information Technology
	PFI
	Customer Service (London)

Box 1.8. Overview of the eight case-study networks

Brief details of the organizations mentioned in the book are provided in an appendix to this chapter. Here, we provide a general introduction to the eight case study networks, accompanied by diagrams of each organizational network.

(a) The *Customer Service network* comprises several of the contracting arrangements between a relatively new firm specializing in customer relationship management activities (TCS) and a number of the organizations with which it deals. This includes both the private and the public sectors. Two locations were investigated in depth for this project. At the multi-client call centre, employment policies vary significantly due to the influence of the client and the nature of the business contract; relations between TCS and five clients are analysed here as well as the links with an employment agency (Beststaff). At the other site, a long-term partnership deal operates between a local authority (Council X) and TCS for administering housing benefits, with employment policies for transferred workers reflecting local government traditions. At both sites, it is clear there are multiple influences on employment relations, both from the clients and the customers, as well as from government regulations in the public–private partnership.

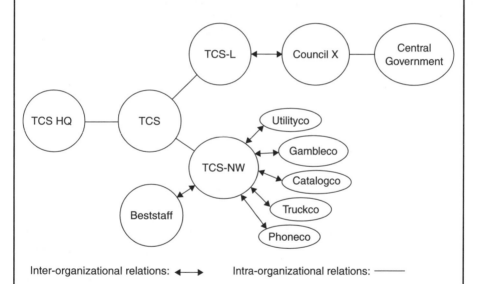

Inter-organizational relations: ◄───► Intra-organizational relations: ───

Fig. 1.4.(a) Customer Services

(b) At the *Airport*, a large number of organizations collaborate with each other to deal with the airlines' customers, providing check-in services, baggage handling, and cleaning among other things. Very close coordination is required between the different organizations to ensure that, so far as reasonably practicable, planes take off on time. Prior to the government's anti-monopoly legislation, many of these tasks were undertaken by different sections of the airport's staff, but complex processes of contracting and recontracting now operate across organizational boundaries in order to meet customer requirements in the context of a highly secure and safe operating environment. Staff and tasks are now routinely subcontracted, raising problems for worker loyalty and commitment, as well as issues of how to manage and control the inter-organizational labour process to provide high levels of customer service. Much of the focus in this case is on the relationship between the baggage and full handling firms, the airlines, and the airport itself.

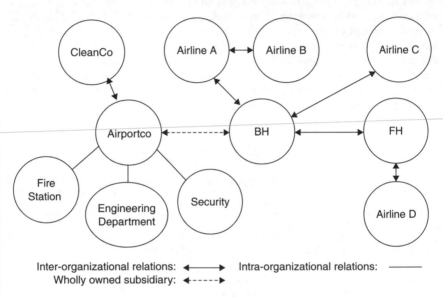

Inter-organizational relations: ←——→ Intra-organizational relations: ——
Wholly owned subsidiary: ←-----▶

Fig. 1.4.(b)   Airport

(c) Government influence was also a key trigger behind the *PFI* between a large NHS Health Trust and a consortium of three private sector firms (including hotel services, engineering maintenance, and facilities design) for the delivery of maintenance, cleaning, and catering services as well as new buildings. The contract is for 35 years, and a Special Purpose Vehicle (coordinating team) has been set up to oversee the project, gain agreement on targets and organize inter-organizational meetings between the parties. Many workers have already been transferred from the public to the private sector at this site under TUPE arrangements, and there is ongoing interaction between staff working for the NHS (such as nurses) and those employed by organizations in the consortium (e.g. porters, craft workers, and catering assistants). This is the case study where tensions between the partner organizations are probably most apparent.

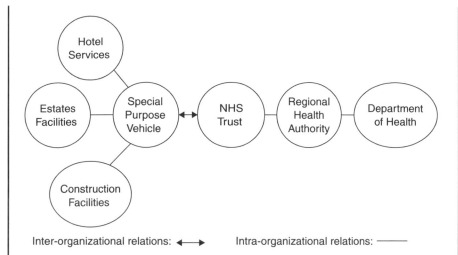

Inter-organizational relations: ⟷   Intra-organizational relations: ⸺

Fig. 1.4.(c)   PFI

(d) Another long-term contract between the public and private sectors, this time between a government department (Govco) and a large multinational IT firm (FutureTech), provides our fourth case—*Information Technology*. This is such a large contract, both in terms of money and time that it is commercially and politically very sensitive, and both parties share a common need to demonstrate that it is successful. FutureTech is required under the terms of the contract to deliver innovative business solutions, and the contract is managed through a complex process of programmes of work. Nearly 2,000 professional staff transferred from the public to the private sector under TUPE arrangements, but when these experienced staff leave they are replaced

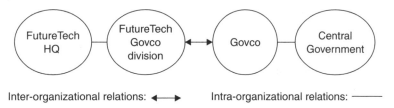

Inter-organizational relations: ⟷   Intra-organizational relations: ⸺

Fig. 1.4.(d)   IT

by workers on new contracts. A major feature of the business contract is that substantial investment of people and time is required just to oversee and manage it.

(e) *The Post Office case* analyses how employment relations and the delivery of services to customers has been affected by the break-up of POCL. Although the company still retains direct control over the 600 Crown Post Offices, over 17,000 outlets operate either as agencies (sub-post offices) or as franchises. The agencies tend to be small shops, either in urban or rural settings, which offer additional products (e.g. birthday cards) and are run as self-employed businesses. The franchises are located in larger retail stores; post office business is separate from the main activities of the store and

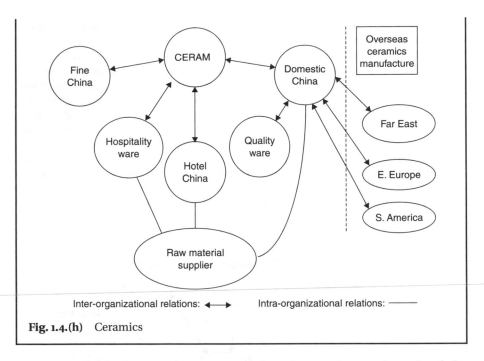

Inter-organizational relations: ◄──►   Intra-organizational relations: ────

Fig. 1.4.(h)   Ceramics

extensive of which is at the airport and at the north-west branch of the
customer services case. Only two of the eight cases comprise wholly private
sector organizations, and in both cases we focus upon supply chain relationships and outsourcing agreements. In the ceramics case, this involved local
and international outsourcing; and in the chemicals case we identified a wide
spectrum of contracts ranging from other chemicals suppliers through to road
haulage firms and a security subcontractor.

Equally important from a research angle is the fact that each 'case'
comprises two or more different organizational forms, rather than being
characterized just as a franchise, an outsourcing arrangement, or a
public–private partnership. For example, the Customer Service case at the
north-west site involved both a client–temporary work agency link and a
client–supplier outsourcing relationship. Internal employment relations at
the outsourcer's call centre were thus influenced by the presence of the
agency and by the influences of multi-clients. Similarly, the Private Finance
Initiative (PFI) case could be analysed not just in terms of the Public–Private
Partnership (PPP) and the immediate implications of the TUPE transfer, but
also in relation to the ongoing consequences of a multi-employer environment for work and employment and for inter-organizational relations. Our
research design enabled us to examine the complexity of employment relations in an environment where contracting and re-contracting are the norm,

thereby demonstrating repeatedly the limitations of analyses that are based on the notion of a straightforward relationship between a single employer and its employees.

Given our focus on the employment relationship, it was important for our choice of case studies to provide a range of different characteristics of employment. Some sites were unionized (e.g. Scotchem) while others were not (e.g. TCS-NW); in some cases, women comprised a majority of those employed at the site (e.g. the Post Office) whereas in others it was mostly men (Chemicals). In others, there was gender segregation between organizations on the same site (e.g. passenger handling and baggage handling at the airport) while others revealed more mixed workforces within organizations (e.g. TCS-L). In some cases, workers were predominantly skilled or professional (e.g. the IT case and Teacher Supply) while in others they were manual workers (e.g. Ceramics). Many of the cases comprised large sites (e.g. the PFI), but some sites were very small indeed (e.g. Post Office). The cases also varied in terms of their adherence to the traditional model of full-time, permanent employment (e.g. Scotchem was staffed primarily by full-timers while the TCS-NW site had many part-time and agency workers).

To anticipate the detailed discussion of key issues in the cases presented in Chapters 4–11, there are a number of general points of comparison across the cases, not only in terms of business contracts and inter-organizational relations, but also with respect to the character of employment policy and practice (see Table 1.4). For example, business contracts varied in their length and their specificity (e.g. a 35-year, highly specified contract at the PFI case), as well as the extent to which they were treated as formal and unwavering documents that required compliance to the letter. Levels of trust and cooperation varied within case studies, as well as between them (e.g. TeacherTemp consultants and senior teachers tended to establish close, trusting relations).

The influence of clients over the labour process in supplier firms was a common feature in the case studies (especially at TCS-NW, the airport and the POCL franchises). The complexity of these arrangements led workers to experience multiple sources of loyalty, identity, and commitment, as well as feelings of insecurity and destabilization. At quite a number of workplaces, staff from different organizations worked alongside each other, and in some cases (e.g. TCS, PFI, and IT) they were actually engaged in the same labour process. Analysis of the cases also explores how wider institutional forces, such as government bodies (e.g. the public–private contracting case studies), trade associations (e.g. chemicals) or industry research and technology organizations (e.g. ceramics), act to shape both the nature of contracting and employment practice. Trade unions also played a role in providing information to workers in several cases (especially in the TUPE transfers) and in trying to influence politicians to persuade companies to remain in an area (e.g. ceramics).

Table 1.4.   Key issues in the case studies

Case study	Key business and employment issues
Customer Service (north-west and London)	Range of contracts and differing nature of client influence on employment practice Agency workers and permanent staff work alongside each other Tensions between public and private sector cultures and approaches
Airport	Complex processes of contracting and re-contracting at workplace Influence of clients on employment practice Multiple sources for loyalty, identity, and commitment
PFI	Long-term contract as part of government drive to restructure public sector Transfer of large numbers of staff from NHS to private sector Public and private sector workers interact with each other in labour process
Information technology	Long-term contract transferring provision of IT to private sector Transfer of large numbers of civil servants to private sector Extensive contact between partners and increased teamworking
Post Office	Detailed contracts between POCL and small units set up as franchises POCL influence over employment practice and types of workers employed Insecurity for franchisees
Teacher Supply	Multiple and generally short-term contracts with schools Issues of identity and skill development for supply teachers Trust and collaboration depends on location of school and length of contract
Chemicals	Multiple contracts with firms in many sectors, often loose but long term Customer influence over employment practice especially at smaller firms Institutional forces (e.g. health and safety) shape collaboration between firms
Ceramics	Close and long-standing ties across local district enhance collaboration Growth in outsourcing beyond local district leading to tensions Restructuring of industry causing job losses and restricted careers

Further consideration of the cases is reserved for Chapters 4–11. In the next two theoretical chapters we expand on themes that have been introduced here. In Chapter 2, we explore the presence of trust, power, and employment relations within inter-organizational networks; and in Chapter 3, we address how the employment requires reconceptualization where the single employer boundary is breached by complex contracting arrangements.

Notes

1. In practice, the use of part-time work has—at least in the United Kingdom—been associated with a process of changing the nature of the employment relationship (Rubery 1998).
2. Commentators tend to describe intended goals rather than realized objectives, emergent practices rather then established customs or provisional rather than fulfilled strategies. When these are then further prescribed as appropriate for the wider population of less glamorous, public as well as private sector, organizations, it is inevitable that their relevance to the majority of workplaces is limited.

APPENDIX
GLOSSARY OF ORGANIZATIONS

1. Customer Services Case

Total Customer Solutions (TCS) was formed in the mid-1990s following the merger of two existing companies. It provides business processing services to utilities, private enterprise, and the public sector, with a primary focus on customer management outsourcing. Its services principally involve the management and operation of call centres and the provision of related information technology infrastructure. Two businesses were investigated in detail, one from north-west England and one from London.

TCS-NW is a multi-client call centre on a green-field site in north-west England. It undertakes customer-facing operations on behalf of five clients, and employs around 1,000 staff, approximately half being agency workers on temporary contracts.

Gambleco is the telephone betting division of a large pools and bookmaking company. TCS-NW provides a full national telephone operation on behalf of this client.

Utilityco is a utility company that had recently taken over *Energyco* and continued Energyco's TCS-NW contract. TCS-NW provides customer services for its quarterly billed commercial and domestic customers. This includes enquiry handling, energy registrations, billing query resolution, and debt collection.

Catalogco is a mail order home shopping company. TCS-NW deals with a proportion of both inbound and outbound sales calls on its behalf and incorporates 'order-build' activities into each call.

Truckco, part of a large motor group, is a vehicle rental company. TCS provides a 24-hour customer service operation to deal with rental requests and general enquiries. TCS-NW provides the service from 6 a.m. till 10 p.m., the remainder being covered at another TCS site.

Phoneco is a mobile phone service provider. TCS-NW provides an inbound call centre operation on its behalf, dealing with new phone registrations, PIN unlocks, balance enquiries, and credit card recharges.

Beststaff is a nation-wide recruitment agency which recruits temporary customer service representatives on behalf of TCS-NW. It has its own office with five staff on the site.

TCS-L was the first local authority contract for the company, incorporating a seven-year deal with Council X to administer and deliver housing benefits. The contract involved the transfer of approximately 100 Council X employees, alongside the considerable new investment in property, IT systems, and training. Fifty thousand benefits cases are dealt with each year and £100 million is paid out in housing benefits.

Council X is a local authority serving a London Borough of nearly 300,000. It contracted out housing benefits administration after being identified as one of the worst performing councils in London. A core of staff is retained by Council X to oversee the contract and make payments to claimants.

2. Airport Case

Airportco is a large regional airport that provides a range of services to airlines and their passengers, often through contracts with other organizations. Three departments were examined: *Security* which is responsible for aircraft, cargo and passengers, both landside and airside. Its scope includes access points around the airport, screening of items going into the hold of aircraft, and patrol of airside operations; *Engineering* which is responsible for making sure that airport facilities (buildings, utility supply, and any fixed equipment) are operating normally to ensure the free flow of aircraft and passengers; and the *Fire Station* whose job is to ensure the runways and surrounding areas are safe.

BH is a baggage handling firm that was previously a department within Airportco, but following antimonopoly regulations it was set up around 10 years ago as a wholly owned subsidiary to enable it to tender competitively for baggage handling. Where contracts also involve passenger handling, these are usually subcontracted to FH. It employs about 750 staff.

FH is one of the largest handling firms in the United Kingdom and has been operating at the airport for over 40 years. It employs 1,200 people on four major services: ramp, aircraft cleaning, operation dispatch, and passenger handling. However, it also subcontracts baggage-handling work to BH.

Airline A is a large British airline, which provides its own passenger handling and aircraft dispatch functions and that of some other airlines (e.g. Airline B) but subcontracts out the ramp handling services to BH.

Airline B is an international airline, operating in the quality market. It has a small station office at the airport but all services are outsourced, with Airline A as the main contractor.

Airline C is a key division of a leading British holiday company. Its technical centre is based at the airport, with fifteen airline representatives employed to coordinate aircraft turnrounds on a daily basis. Passenger handling and dispatch are outsourced to BH.

Airline D operates scheduled flights to and from Asia, and it has a small station office at the airport. The Manager and two assistant managers are from the home country while the twelve traffic assistants are employees of FH seconded to Airline D. Passenger handling and dispatch are outsourced to FH.

CleanCo is part of a nation-wide group specializing in airport cleaning services. It has been the main ground-cleaning contractor at the airport since the mid-1990s and has over 300 employees on site.

3. PFI Case

NHS Trust is a large acute Trust based in north-west England. It was established in the late 1990s through the consolidation of one large and one medium-sized hospital situated about 4 miles from each other. The Trust employs more than 4,000 staff and has an income of about £200 million each year. The PFI contract is for 35 years, requiring a consortium of three private sector firms to construct new buildings and provide estates maintenance, cleaning and catering services. Seven hundred ancillary staff were transferred from the NHS Trust.

Estates Facilities specializes in planning, engineering services, architecture, and project management, with growing involvement in PFI/PPP projects. It has responsibility for maintenance services in the existing hospital facilities and for the complete estates function in the new building.

Construction Facilities is a large UK-based organization specializing in civil engineering and construction projects. It was responsible for building the new hospital facilities and worked in alliance with Estates Facilities on other PFI projects.

Table 1A.1. Details of the interviews and the organizations involved at each case study

Case study name	Characteristics of organizational form	Range of inter-organizational relationships	Institutional, sectoral, and societal framework	No. of organizations in each case study	No. of interviews	No. of interviewees
Customer Service (north-west and London)	Agencies outsourcing Public–private partnership Multi-client site Multi-employer site TUPE	TCS training service north-west Billing Centre TCS north-west (5 clients) Temporary employment agency Council X	Improvement and Development Agency (IdeA) Association of London Government (ALG) Local Government Association (LGA) UNISON Central Government Documentation Policy documentation	7	60	60
Airport	Multi-employer site Multi-client site	Four airlines, engineering department, airport security, baggage handling, full handling, cleaning company, fire service	Transport and General Workers Union (TGWU) AEEU (Now Amicus) GMB City Council Aviation Authority Department of Transport	8	88	88
PFI	Public–private partnership Multi-employer site TUPE	Hotel Services Company Facilities Design Company Special Purpose Vehicle NHS Trust Monitoring Team	Health authority Public sector unions Central Government Documentation Policy documentation	3	67	57

Sector	Restructuring type	Organizational units	Stakeholders / Documentation			
Information Technology	Public–private partnership TUPE	FutureTech (Head Office) FutureTech's Govco Division Govco Govco Business Service Division Central Government	Public and Commercial Services Union (PCS) Central Government Documentation Policy documentation	2	45	49
Post office	Agencies Franchising	1 Crown Office 4 Sub-post offices 3 Combination Stores	Communications Workers Union (CWU) National Federation of Sub-postmasters	7	34	37
Teacher Supply	Agencies Franchising	TeacherTemp Head Office TempworkCo 2 north-west Offices 14 Local authority Secondary schools	Local education authority Public sector unions Central Government Documentation Policy documentation	18	63	66
Chemicals	Outsourcing Supply chain Partnerships	Scotchem 2 Suppliers 2 Transportation specialists 2 Business service contractors	Chemical Industries Association GMB, TGWU, AEEU and MSF (Now Amicus)	8	47	42
Ceramics	Outsourcing Supply chain Partnerships	5 Ceramics manufacturers	CERAM Research Ceramics and Allied Trade Union (CATU) British Ceramics Confederation (BCC)	6	38	36

embeddedness of their relations within a complex of legal, economic, social, and political relations. If inter-organizational relationships are at least partially *constituted*, and not simply surrounded, by these relations, and if relations are embedded in different ways for each organization, sector, and country, it is difficult to conceive how there might be a straightforward mapping between organizational form and economic performance. To put this another way, accounting for the emergence of these 'new' organizational forms in terms of their greater efficiency should itself be seen as an articulation of the legal, economic, social, and political relations in which they are embedded. While their development may be promoted by acclaiming their greater efficiency, such claims must be viewed as an expression of institutional embeddedness and not as a reflection of economic reality.

If it is accepted that firms are embedded in different relations of a legal, economic, social, and political character, then a first step towards a more nuanced analysis of network forms is to discard the widely held, but rarely acknowledged, assumption of same status between organizations. Dropping this assumption permits the recognition that organizations occupy different positions—of relative power and dependence—upon the terrain of political economy. These differences are significant in shaping the kind of trusting relations established. A focus on differences in bargaining power among network members, for example, raises new questions concerning how performance gains (if any) are distributed within the network. Large organizations may displace risk to smaller network members; a powerful hub of private sector organizations may lock the state into complex outsourcing deals with escalating costs; or a public sector organization may wield power by negotiating complex contracts with less experienced private sector service providers (Rainnie 1991; Harrison 1994; Smith 2000). Establishing and/or exerting control over a network can enable more powerful organizations to counter forces of fragmentation and disorder by, for example, being central to the process of setting standards that are imposed upon less powerful organizations within the network.

A second step is to bring work back in to the analysis. This matters for an understanding of the changing position of workers in the economy (Harrison 1994; Barley and Kunda 2001). It enables us to introduce such questions as: does the network form represent a new concentration of power among employers better able to avoid or oppose the collective demands of labour? Do networks promote new divisions and new inequalities among workers? Bringing work back in to the analysis also matters because the employment relationship is at the heart of all organizational forms. Any analysis of organizing that expels the topic of employment is restrictive and limited as it excludes consideration of a key feature of the dynamic of productive activity. As organizations change, new tensions and contradictions in managing employees arise, which, in turn, may act as a brake on organizational change or a pressure for further transformation and diffusion.

This chapter begins with a critical review of how the network form is characterized in the literature. The second section questions whether evidence of alliances, partnerships, and outsourcing can be attributed to their capacity to improve organizational performance. We show how consideration of the employment relationship is critical for understanding the development and operation of network forms. More specifically, we demonstrate how an appreciation of the employment relationship complicates conventional assessments of performance gains. The third section argues that inter-organizational relations vary according to forms of collaboration and competition among public and private sector organizations, as evidenced by differences in relations of trust and power. Policy interest in public–private partnerships is in part fuelled by claims that new organizational forms will improve the traditional public sector ethos among public sector workers, fostering a high performance nexus between a network form and employee commitment to high quality services delivery. Our discussion casts additional light on the nature of power imbalances, in a manner that adds to our understanding of the so-called 'core-ring' private–private network linkages. We also raise issues concerning the prospects for work. In particular, we note how different inter-organizational contracting arrangements may, in some cases, displace risk to one or more workforces but, in others, provide for greater solidarity among workers across organizations.

2.2 What characterizes the network form?

The rise of the network form is closely associated with the widely held belief that the 'Fordist' form of organizing production, built on the large, vertically integrated corporation, has had its day. The focus of the network form is the interface between organizations. Systems of production are no longer conceived as divided between activities managed within the firm and those bought on the market. The quality and extensiveness of relationships between organizations is now identified as a key to performance gains. Noting the growth and importance of partnerships, joint ventures, strategic alliances, and outsourcing contracts, it has been argued that a fundamental shift is occurring in the form of capitalist competition culminating in the 'network society' (Castells 1996), 'dynamic networks' (Miles and Snow 1986) and 'boundaryless organizations' (Ashkenas et al. 1995). The claims are strong ones, as we see from the following accounts of change:

Networks are the fundamental stuff of which new organizations are and will be made. (Castells 1996: 168)

Future [organizational] forms will all feature some of the properties of the dynamic network form. . . . We anticipate, ultimately, that key business units . . . will be autonomous building blocks to be assembled, reassembled, and redeployed within and across organizational and national boundaries as product or service life cycles demand. (Miles and Snow 1986: 73)

A change in modern institutional structure has accompanied short-term, contract, or episodic labor. Corporations have sought to remove layers of bureaucracy, to become

flatter and more flexible organizations. In place of organizations as pyramids, management wants now to think of organizations as networks. (Sennett 1998: 23)

The term 'network' is invoked to describe a wide spectrum of inter-
organizational linkages and their associated benefits. Castells claims that networks of small firms have contributed to the export successes of Hong Kong
and Thailand (Castells 1996: 160–161); they are also identified as an important
component of the more well-known industrial districts of northern Italy
(Brusco 1982, 1986). The networks at the centre of Japanese lean production, the
keiretsu, which comprise both large and small firms—with the former involving
cross-holdings of equity—are said to be a source of institutional stability
(Lincoln et al. 1992, cited in Harrison 1994: 159). Benetton is identified as an
example of a large firm–small firm subcontracting network in which a core firm
controls both the distribution of the product across a network of commercial
franchises and the manufacture of the product within homes and small firms
in and around Italy (Harrison 1994). Strategic alliances, often involving joint
ventures, are yet another example of an arrangement characterized as a network (Borys et al. 1989). Such networks involve cooperation between firms in
specific markets and processes, often with the aim of jointly developing new
products or new technologies (Buckley and Casson 1996).

This brief overview indicates a disparate image of network organizations,[1]
each presented as an alternative model to both the Fordist, bureaucratic organizational form and the competitive firm reliant on arm's length market relationships. The multiplicity of arrangements to which the term 'network' is
attributed makes theoretical specification problematic.[2] Even those networks
with a similar composition of members (e.g. all small firms, alliances between
large firms, or large firm–small firm networks) may be constituted by very different types or blends of contracting arrangements. The classic study by Sako
(1992) differentiates between 'arms-length contractual relations' and 'obligational contractual relations'.[3] Where members of a network trade on the basis
of arm's length contractual relations, there is a low degree of interdependence:
Either the buyer or seller can exit the relationship without penalty. By contrast,
'obligational contracting' is marked by strong interdependence. It is underpinned by 'goodwill trust' where both parties to the contract have a 'moral
commitment' to maintaining the relationship—and a loose principle of reciprocity over the long term (Sako 1992: 9–13). Hence, while some networks may
be characterized by specific targets and controls characteristic of formal contracts, other networks may be founded on trust and reputation (Adler 2001).

Other studies suggest, however, that neat analytical distinctions between
types of contracting are very difficult to apply (see Chapter 6). For example,
while there is a strong current of research, which views formal contracting and
relational contracting as substitutes (e.g. Uzzi 1997; Dyer and Singh 1998), there is
also evidence that they may be complementary (e.g. Deakin et al. 1997; Poppo and
Zenger 2002). In other words, many contracting modes lie along the spectrum

between ideal forms of discrete transactions and strong relational contracting. Indeed, as Blois (2002) argues, if each exchange between two members of a network is said to consist of several attributes (such as the price, form of payment, commitment to the contracting party, and attention to personal service), then some attributes may be arm's length in nature, while others relational. The overall characteristics of the exchange between two organizations are thus a blend of all the interrelated attributes.

Second, it is possible that an individual organization enters into different kinds of relationships with each client, partner, and supplier (Blois 2002; Marchington and Vincent 2004; see Chapter 6). A firm may have a long-term, high trust purchasing arrangement with one supplier and yet make one-off purchases with several 'second tier' suppliers. A third observation follows from this—that is, the characterization of an exchange between two organizations does not exist independently of the assessments made by the buyer or the seller (Blois 2002). Most studies tend to characterize the contracting relationship from the perspective of the client (purchaser) organization, but what is deemed a strong relational contractual arrangement for the client may be regarded differently from the perspective of the supplier (provider) organization. Empirical analysis, therefore, ought to draw on evidence from both sides to the exchange in its characterization of the contractual arrangement. This is an important point since, unlike the conventional approaches (such as transaction cost analysis or the resource-based view), the focus of analysis shifts from an abstracted and impersonal calculus about economic costs and benefits to an appreciation of their assessment within the participating organizations. This then allows consideration of how the risks and costs between parties to the exchange are evaluated and distributed (ibid.: 529; see Chapters 4 and 5).

All types of exchange (and their composite attributes) among members to a network are likely to change over time, reflecting a range of factors including changes in norms and understandings, changes in the network composition and external pressures on reputation, costs and performance. This point is illustrated by studies that focus on the role of interpersonal relationships in mobilizing the contracting process (see Chapter 6). Located within the broader schools of social network analysis and social-psychological literature, each economic exchange is considered to be embedded in social relations (Granovetter 1985), where face-to-face relations still matter in making networks work (Nohria and Eccles 1992a, b) and where the identity and the capacity for 'sense making' among actors shapes psychological contracts among parties (Argyris 1960; Kotter 1973). The formal and informal actions and interactions of parties, as they negotiate and make (and break) commitments over time, are said to contribute to the long-term survival of cooperative inter-organizational relationships by maintaining a balance between trust and working to contract. In particular, the willingness of parties to rely on trust to deal with uncertainty; the presence of organizational norms for conflict resolution; and individuals' desire to preserve a reputation for fair dealing all contribute to the way interactive processes cast a positive or negative tone to the relationship (Ring and Van de Ven 1994; Lorenz 2003). In this context, changes of personnel are also significant. Turnover of staff occupying the roles of 'boundary-spanners' may lead to greater resort to the formal terms of a contract where flexible, cooperative practices are not passed on to new managers (Ring and Van de Ven 1994), or it may lead to new informal terms of engagement where the new personnel have no expertise in the detailed legal jargon of the contract (Blois 2002: 531; see Chapter 5).

Given the spectrum of inter-organizational relationships, the complexity in defining attributes of any one exchange and the capacity for evolution driven by social, economic, and psychological factors, it seems neither credible nor desirable to construct a generic set of principles that distinguish the 'network form'. Does this imply, then, that attention to what is identified as the network form—in its various guises—has been a worthless endeavour? We interpret the popular attention to the network form as symptomatic of a concern to explore the nature and significance of economic activity in ways that go beyond formulations that rely implicitly, or explicitly, upon notions of market and hierarchy. The potential contribution of 'network' theory resides in its consideration of previously unexplored dynamics of competition and collaboration among organizations. Our own interest in the putative shift towards network organizations is guided by a concern to better appreciate how *employment* relationships within and between organizations (to which we attribute significant network properties) dynamically interact with the changing form of the British capitalist production system. As such, the characteristics attributed to networks provide a device with which to explore the development of changing inter-organizational relations between both private sector and public sector organizations, in relationship to employment. Our starting position is thus quite different from most studies where, as we explore in the next section, the network form is evaluated and/or advocated solely by reference to its alleged superiority in delivering production efficiencies.

2.3   Do efficiency improvements explain the evolution of the network form?

For most analysts of economic life, the significance of alternative forms of organization is assessed in relation to some universal beneficiary of efficiency or, alternatively, to the 'principal' or owner. The transaction cost approach (Coase 1937; Williamson 1985) states that organizations adapt their boundaries in such a way as to minimize transaction costs—which refer to the costs of planning, adapting, and monitoring the tasks involved in the production of goods or provision of services. A strong current of thinking in strategic management (particularly some of the US-based contributions to the 'competence' perspective and the resource-based view) claims that managers make strategic choices based on an assessment of their organization's capabilities; new organizational forms evolve as they are found to provide a more efficient 'fit' between the form of organization that most effectively applies and nurtures these capabilities and the new competitive conditions (Miles and Snow 1984, 1986; Prahalad and Hamel 1990).

These perspectives, which claim a rational, economic basis for the retention of established forms or the shift towards a network form are placed in question by the literature on technological change, which involves many detailed studies of the links between the innovation process and organizational structure (Saxenian 1994; Foray and Lundvall 1996; Hagedoorn and Duysters 2002; see Grimshaw et al. 2002b). These studies begin to disclose the diverse motivations and outcomes associated with the formation and reproduction of network forms. This literature suggests that network forms provide few measurable benefits (such as increased profitability, for example) but they are understood to deliver numerous intangible benefits, such as preferential financing, information exchange, high trust relations, trademarks, and the broadening of knowledge and experience through job rotation among subcontractors (Malecki 1997: 145). New network forms may also improve the capability of organizations to exploit new forms of knowledge—again, a potential benefit that is both difficult to measure and contingent upon the type of knowledge. With the ability to process higher volumes (bandwidth) of knowledge at faster speeds, the multiple nodes and communication paths within network forms seem to have opened up more profitable opportunities for coordinating and monitoring economic activity than is possible using 'codified' types of knowledge (as available in printed form, for use in documents, patents, e-mails, or on the web). The fact that much organizational knowledge is 'tacit' (private know-how, which flows primarily through informal networks), however, means that the sharing and coordinating of network-based technological developments may be very costly since it requires iterative consultation and travel to promote learning by doing and learning by using (Von Hippel 1987).

The issue of intangible benefits is precisely the focus of the related literature on organizational learning where it is shown how organizations collaborate as an effective part of their learning process through accessing technical capability, tacit knowledge, and shared understanding of rapidly changing markets (Teece 1986; Kogut 2000)—again, factors that are difficult to define and measure. Saxenian's well-known comparison of Route 128 and Silicon Valley is typical of such an approach:

Silicon Valley continues to reinvent itself as its specialized producers learn collectively and adjust to one another's needs through shifting patterns of competition and collaboration. The separate and self-sufficient organizational structures of Route 128, in contrast, hinder adaptation by isolating the process of technological change within corporate boundaries. (1994: 163)

A closer reading of network forms thus demonstrates that many ostensibly proven (or prescribed) benefits are plausible but intangible, and therefore difficult to objectify and measure (Buckley and Chapman 1997). Of greater importance for our analysis, these studies suggest that the extent to which intangible benefits (such as learning, or access to technical knowledge) can be achieved depends on the way in which networks of organizations manage a particular commodity—one that has all the peculiar attributes of intangibility and uncertainty—that is, labour.

High performing networks and the employment relationship

The argument that the employment relationship is integral to the formation and development of inter-organizational relations and thereby conditions performance outcomes tends to be obscured, if not ignored, in studies of network forms. Studies in the field of organizational (and management) strategy tend to make claims regarding the efficiency-improving potential of network forms with no (or very limited) regard for their interrelationship with employment.

Where employment is considered, the argument tends to be rather stylized. For example, as Priem and Butler (2001) critically observe, the resource-based view of the firm claims that individual organizations secure competitive advantage by mobilizing internal human resources, in part, by building up and exploiting the capabilities of employees. Human resource specialists have claimed that high trust employment policies contribute to strong psychological contracts (Guest 1998) and social capital formation, thereby reducing the need for direct employer–employee authority relations (Leana and Van Buren III 1999) and generating mutual gains to employers and workers (Marsden 1999: 3). Network forms may fit with this resource-based view, provided that (*a*) managers distinguish between different types of externalization and (*b*) the benefits of the high trust internal employment relationship is extended, where appropriate, to external relationships.

Where employees who act as boundary spanners between organizations are required to use discretion and judgement in their actions, the expectation is that a 'relational' form of contracting will be adopted (Fig. 2.1*a*). Where the externalized activity is not 'core' to an organization's competences, then a 'transactional' form is the instrumentally rational preference. The allocation of activities to each type is assumed to depend on the nature of human capital involved, thus following in the tradition of the flexible firm model (Atkinson 1984), where it is assumed that there is a clear divide between jobs where cooperation and commitment matter and those where they do not. The relational form is supposed to 'solve' the employment problem by extending the internalized social capital to interactions and exchanges with the network partner; and the transactional form 'solves' the problem by externalizing it to the market. Thus, partnership relationships are said to be founded on social capital within the network itself (Dyer and Singh 1998; Dess and Shaw 2001)

(a) Relational contracting for core activities

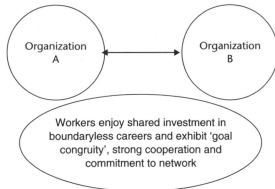

(b) Transactional contracting for non-core activities

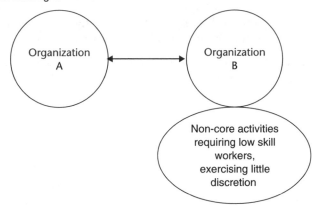

Fig. 2.1. The stylized 'fit' between employment and contracting forms: the resource-based view

and the notion of inter-organizational 'goal congruity' incorporates workers' common orientation towards another organization (Jeffries and Reed 1999).

In principle, relational network forms provide organizations with a basis for shared investment in human capital. These forms are accompanied by opportunities for 'boundaryless careers' within networks that attract employees ('free workers') with high capacities for learning and inter-organizational job mobility, and provide employers with a continuously renewed source for creativity and innovation. The replacement of large vertically organized bureaucracies with a more democratic, flattened organizational form is said to enable smaller groupings of employers and employees to negotiate more just working arrangements in which they are empowered to become more productive and customer-focused (Saxenian 1994; Arthur and Rousseau 1996). In the light of these kinds of assessments, Miles and Snow, among others, anticipate that the network form will be rapidly diffused as its superior capacity to accommodate complexity results in it supplanting other, less flexible alternatives:

The dynamic network is a far more flexible structure than any of the previous forms, it can accommodate a vast amount of complexity while maximizing specialized competence, and it provides much more effective use of human resources that otherwise have to be accumulated, allocated and maintained by a single organization. The practice of leasing entire workforces, already in use in construction, hotel management, and retail sales, is a network characteristic that will become even more prevalent in the future. (1996: 437)

Other commentators are much less sanguine about the viability as well as the morality of such network forms. 'Leasing entire workforces', for example, raises questions about the commitment of such staff to the client organization and the capacity of the client to control their contribution. Concerns have been raised over the extent and pace of destructive transformation of long-standing pillars of work organization and labour market conditions associated with the bureaucratic organizational form, with perilous consequences for employees' sense of identity and for their employment rights. Victor and Stephens point to some of the 'darker' characteristics of network forms:

Instead of a role anchored by the organization and codified in a job description, the new forms are offering a role defined by the task of the moment and location of the worker. . . . Traditional indicators of status are becoming blurred as a result of obligations that are networked and diffused, and rights that are increasingly ephemeral in this new world of ours. (1994: 480–481)

And Sennett argues that rather than providing new freedoms to make more flexible career moves, network forms make workers' decisions more risky:

As pyramidal hierarchies are replaced by looser networks, people who change jobs experience more often what sociologists have called 'ambiguously lateral moves'. . . . [and] 'retrospective losses'. Since people who risk making moves in flexible organizations often have very little hard information about what a new position will entail, they realize only in retrospect they've made bad decisions. (1998: 85)

The reason for the opposition in findings relates, in large part, to the difficulties in assuming a 'fit' between employment relations and organizational form, as claimed in studies that adopt the resource-based view of the firm. Human resources are not infinitely malleable and often will not simply comply with, or enact, whatever ostensibly instrumentally rational strategy or organizational design is formulated. Or, to be more precise, their malleability is associated with positioning within relations of power and, thus, with their capacity to resist employer demands. For analysts who disregard the significance of the employment relationship, expressions of conflict, resistance, or non-cooperation, are viewed as irrational or pathological, and the obvious solution is to replace the managers who have failed to remove the pathology, or to replace the employees who are believed to spread it. Even within the terms of orthodox thinking there are shortcomings in the analysis.

First, there are good reasons to believe that conventional measures of human capital (skill, or pay) do not offer a good or reliable proxy for determining whether the orientations of workers and the coordination of their activities are of strategic significance for the organization. There is simplistic thinking about the extent to which the rarity or cost of human capital per se makes some staff less substitutable than others, and the strategic importance they have in day-to-day operational activities. Studies show that low skilled workers have opportunities to engage in job crafting (Wrzesniewski and Dutton 2001), which affects not only individual productivity, but also the integration of operational activities. Unsuccessful attempts by organizations to separate out strategic and non-strategic posts by filling the latter with in-house and temporary agency workers, respectively, also suggest that these boundaries are not well defined (Ward et al. 2001). The value and significance placed upon 'skill' is a social and political process, and not a technical matter of objective measurement (Sturdy et al. 1992). Certain jobs may be (politically) defined as requiring low level, readily substitutable skills. Yet, this may take little or no account of the 'social capital'—in the form of tacit knowledge and long-established working relationships—residing in employees with such skills. Likewise, imbalances in inter- and intra-organizational power, which render certain groups more vulnerable to substitution, may provide employers with an overwhelming rationale for externalization in order to lower basic costs. Figure 2.2 traces the way alternative contractual arrangements may be associated with differences in the way rent (the cost savings, or improved profit margins) from networking arrangements is distributed. The diagrams differ according to differences in the balance of power both between contracting organizations and between managers and workers within and across organizations. The four alternative modes represent additional possibilities to those traditionally conceived, as presented in Fig. 2.1.

First where there is a strategic concern for long-term relational contracting around core activities, coupled with a strong concern to build inter-organizational identification, organizations may nonetheless be inclined to enter into contractual arrangements in a way that is not consistent with even rent distribution with one or more workforces (Fig. 2.2(a)). A gloss of relational contracting may thus be maintained among managers in the networked organizations A and B, with the risks and costs of the contract for activities passed down the line to the external workforce in organization B. Secondly the positioning of certain member organizations within a network may enable them to enjoy greater market power than others, resulting in the potential for a skewing of rents as one or more of the network partners is forced to accept lower profits, despite commitment to a strong trusting contracting relationship in the provision of non-core activities (Fig. 2.2(b)). As a likely consequence, their workforce is also disadvantaged by reduced wages, erosion of conditions, and/or increased work intensification. Thus while relational contracting may, in some cases, be consistent with a win–win scenario, with rent shared among managers

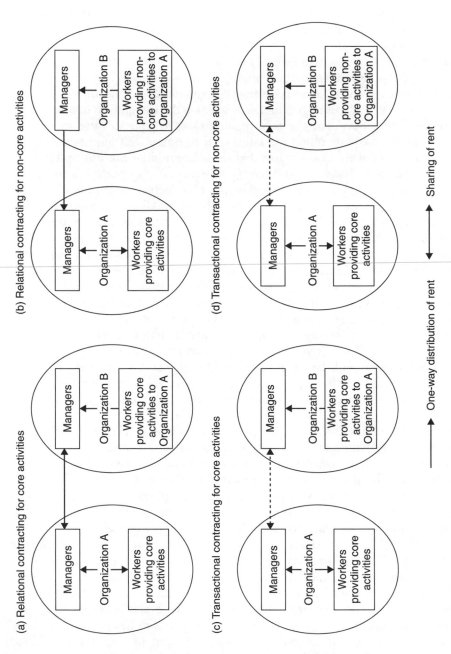

(a) Relational contracting for core activities

(b) Relational contracting for non-core activities

(c) Transactional contracting for core activities

(d) Transactional contracting for non-core activities

One-way distribution of rent

Sharing of rent

Fig. 2.2. Network forms and the distribution of rent

and workforces of networked organization (as shown in Figure 2.1), there is also the possibility of either a sharing of rent among managers at the expense of exploiting the workforce of organization B, or appropriation of rent by organization A at the expense of organization B and its workforce.

Diagrams (c) and (d) in Fig. 2.2 present alternative scenarios for contracting. Importantly, relational contracting may not be established, even where activities are of mutual strategic importance to the organizations, if organizations are unwilling to negotiate long-term, or secure contracts (Fig. 2.2(c); see also Purcell and Purcell 1999; Scarbrough 2000). Moreover, despite the fact that both organizations provide 'core' business activities to organization A, the rent may be distributed unevenly so that organization B's workforce—at the 'wrong end' of the network form—are low paid. (See also Guy 2000; Rubery and Grimshaw 2001). The final example of contracting for 'non core' business activities present a distribution of rent which benefits the contracting organization A at the expense of organization B and its workforce (Fig. 2.2(d)).

As such, interlinkages between type of inter-organizational relations and the employment relationship are overdetermined. The formation and development of inter-organizational 'networks' does not simply proceed on the basis of a logic of efficiency. Rather, their formation is conditional upon balances of power, including those within employment relationships—both within and between 'networked' organizations. Operationalizing different types of contracting relationship may be reliant upon attracting or developing employees who are willing to tolerate, or facilitate, their development. The efficiency and effectiveness of network forms is dependent upon the actions of people who work under employment contracts, and, as such, the contradictions and resistances found within the standard contract between a single employer and employee persist, albeit within a complexified set of relationships. The development of inter-organizational relations provides new opportunities for cooperation and division, which are additional to, and interact with, the opportunities for conflict and for mutual benefit generated by the internal employment relationship (see Chapter 3).

In the next section, we build on this critique to consider alternative analyses of the formation and functioning of network organizational forms. We consider the possibility that alliances, partnerships, and subcontracting relations may be established and maintained primarily as a means of consolidating power and displacing risk—either to the network partner organization or to its workforce. Hence, network forms may enable some organizations to improve their performance while, for others, at the 'wrong end' of the network, pressures to form or preserve networks may, in fact, constrain their ability to improve performance, or, in the extreme, worsen efficiencies in addition to degrading the terms and conditions of many employees. A focus on relations of trust, power, and risk demonstrates how efficiency is a second-order issue in terms of understanding the dynamism underpinning changing organizational forms.

2.4   Network forms as institutionally embedded relations

A central problem with much of the literature on the network organizational form is the (largely implicit) notion that it represents a new and important move, or even a 'solution', in addressing the twin pressures faced by all organizations—public and private sector—both to compete and to collaborate. Notably, it is claimed that networked organizations secure a competitive advantage by carving out some activities for inter-organizational collaboration (e.g. through outsourcing the functions of accounting and human resource management) while reserving others for competition (such as project design, or research and development), as the latter are retained 'in-house'. In this formulation, all network members are understood to benefit since transaction costs are minimized and a best fit between organizations is achieved:

> In order to understand all of its ramifications, the dynamic network must be viewed simultaneously from the perspective of its individual components and from the network as a whole. For the individual firm (or component) the primary benefit of participation in the network is the opportunity to pursue its particular distinctive competence. . . . Each network component can be seen as complementing rather than competing with the other components. Complementarity permits the creation of elaborate networks designed to handle complex situations . . . It also permits rapid adjustment to changing competitive conditions. (Miles and Snow 1986: 65)

There is, however, a great deal of empirical evidence which suggests that inter-organizational relations in network forms are not necessarily characterized by a complementary sharing of benefits or by an evenly distributed pattern of capital accumulation. Establishing strong ties of collaboration between organizations that are able to resist or police asymmetrical power relations *may* lead to a consolidation of mutual interests. But, more frequently, the presence of asymmetries operates to promote pressures for less collaborative, more contractual, forms of behaviour both within and between networks.

More adequately resourced and/or connected organizations are better positioned to establish strong network ties that operate, more or less intentionally, to displace risk to less advantaged organizations with repercussions for their workforce, leading to a consolidation and concentration of power at particular points in the circuit of capital accumulation, rather than a more balanced spread of accumulation and risk among suppliers, assemblers, and distributors. Where the state is involved, both as a supplier and as a purchaser of a wide range of goods and services, networks renew questions regarding the (contradictory) relationship between state and capital (O'Connor 1973)—as illustrated by the popular concern over the use of public–private partnerships, where privately owned assets are leased to the state. Advocates of such partnerships claim that the disciplines of the private sector can secure the most efficient provision of public goods and services. Opponents argue that private sector providers fall into two, sometimes overlapping, categories: well-established suppliers who negotiate highly lucrative contracts with governments desperate to demonstrate the fruits of their policies, albeit at the longer-term expense of the taxpayer; and smaller, marginal operators who fail to provide the promised level of service. In each case, opponents argue that profits are extracted from contracts not so much by deploying resources more effectively but by cutting labour costs by intensifying work and/or eroding pay and conditions for new hires, if not for transferred employees. In subsequent empirical chapters, our case study evidence demonstrates how changing forms of competition and collaboration among private sector organizations (Chapter 4) and among private and public sector organizations (Chapter 5) interact dynamically with the employment relationship, adding a further dimension to patterns of segmentation and inequalities in power.

We now further explore these issues in an effort to illuminate the way notions of trust, power, and risk are central to an analysis of both private–private and public–private inter-organizational relations. We consider arguments and evidence around three themes: the limits to strong collaboration between organizations; unequal power relations between organizations; and public–private contracting.

The limits to collaboration

There is strong evidence that some networks may be established in order to promote collaboration between capitalist enterprises, and that such collaboration may become reinforced over time. However, despite clear statements in some of these studies regarding the context-specific, or sample-specific nature of the findings, too many descriptions of the network economy make generalized claims regarding the benefits of cooperative agreements, drawing only on those pieces of evidence that fit with the scenario of inter-organizational relations based on trust, cooperation, and harmony. The following excerpts illustrate this problem:

The network is economically feasible because the specialization of each supplier makes the final total cost lower. It can be sustained because long-term bonds, which generate trust, lower transaction costs. A 'fairness' in the sharing of the value added is achieved through the mechanism of trust and through valuing the relationship in itself, which makes it easier to solve specific problems. (Jarillo 1988: 39)

The nature of the new business relationship will result in stronger and more enduring ties based on a mutual destiny, one shared by groups of both suppliers and customers. (Davidow and Malone 1992, cited in Smith 2000: 102)

Such claims ignore a number of problems arising from the possibility that high trust networks encourage consolidation of capital interests. Developments in, and uses of, information technologies to coordinate activities, for example, may not incorporate the concerns of employees, especially where flows of information are controlled by strongly interconnected business interests in ways that escape employee awareness and public accountability. As Smith argues:

Where in the lean production networks is information regarding workers' health and safety transmitted? Where are the hiring and promotion practices of the various divisions of a firm and its subcontractors tracked? What corporate networks share information on discrimination on the basis of gender, race, ethnic identity, or sexual preference? Which intercapital networks in the 'new economy' have opened their computers to local environmental groups attempting to monitor pollution resulting from the activities of firms within the networks? (Smith 2000: 113)

A second problem concerns the issue of relative bargaining power between labour and capital. Greater collaboration among holders of capital, built on strong, high trust relations, may or may not improve workers' terms and conditions, and any deterioration in employment conditions may generate negative feedback effects in shaping business performance (Grimshaw and Rubery 2003). On the one hand, a consolidation or strengthening of the position occupied by employing organizations may be forged through institutionalizing high level managerial meetings among network members concurrent with a fragmentation and dispersal of mid-level management groups and workforce groups across the various networked workplaces. On the other hand, high trust relations may be forged through a solidaristic process of networking across all levels, engaging representatives from all groups in realigning strategic collective interests (see Chapter 6).

A third problem is that across the economy as a whole, it is quite possible to imagine a strengthening of strategic interests among organizations within any one network in the midst of increasing competition between networks (Young et al. 1996; Smith 2000). While there is clearly a strong tendency for some commentators to emphasize collaboration over competition within networks, which in itself is problematic, little attention is paid to the way changes in internetwork competition may shape conditions within networks and among firms in the economy more generally. For example, the dynamics of district-based networks may be fundamentally transformed by the withdrawal of one member organization, which enters instead into a global network of production (Chapter 4). In fact, studies from the field of organization studies argue that the new paradigm of networking may be better described as one of 'hypercompetition' (D'Aveni 1994; Ilinitch et al. 1996). In such circumstances, collaboration with selected competitors becomes a frantic or expedient means of avoiding the marginality of perfect efficiency.

For these reasons, it is important to acknowledge the presence of power differentials among network members (and their external stakeholders) in enabling certain organizations to impose performance goals on other network members, subject to their ability to resist and their capacity to renegotiate terms (Sydow and Windeler 1998). Indeed, a number of studies have illuminated the power differentials present within networks, although attention has generally focused on those forms usually described as 'core-ring', or 'strategic'. The argument that such forms lead to a concentration of power within networks is considered in the following section.

Unequal power relations

A number of studies take issue with the way network forms provide a basis for the redistribution, or consolidation, of power among organizations and the displacement of risk resulting in security gains for its more powerful members, and greater vulnerabilities for the comparatively powerless (Mytelka 1991; Semlinger 1991*b*; Rainnie 1992; Harrison 1994). Organizations routinely exploit situations where less powerful partners, or suppliers, pay lower wages and offer less generous non-wage costs (such as pensions and holiday and sickness entitlements). Where the purchaser organization enjoys a strong position of market power in the industry, cost reductions may be achieved by forcing subcontractors to accept a squeeze on their profits by pushing down prices. In this way, networks represent a mechanism by which powerful firms displace risk to those with less power.

These examples are illustrative of a *segmentation* of organizations within networks, typically between the small and the large, where managers of more powerful organizations exploit differences among dependent network members by playing one off against the other. Harrison (1994) describes a 'core-ring' network arrangement where new flexible production systems have been decentralized alongside an entrenching of unequal economic power in favour of large organizations—what he calls 'concentration without centralization'. That said, identifying power imbalances within networks is not simply an issue of relative organizational size. As we show in both Chapters 4 and 5, differences in market structure on the purchaser and provider side do matter. Where the contracting organization enjoys a strong market position, for example, it is more likely that subcontractors have a strongly dependent relationship and are therefore liable to assume a disproportionate share of the risk. Power is exercised by lead network firms as they orchestrate market competition between members and non-members of the network to put pressure on suppliers, subcontractors, or weaker partners. Crucially, the unequal exercise of power means that performance improvements enjoyed by the lead firm may not correlate with reduced production (and transaction) costs across the network:

The efficiency of outsourcing as a strategic game is not dependent on its economizing effect on production and transaction costs. . . . An outsourcing company can profit from lower prices of subcontracted supply which are not derived from higher productivity. Furthermore, increased flexibility . . . can also originate from the enforced higher pliability of the subcontractor. Finally, in order to reduce risk, the outsourcing company need not share it, if it can succeed in shifting some of its risks in sales, manufacturing, control and R&D to the exchange partners. (Semlinger 1991*a*: 106)

An appreciation of the complex dynamics of inter-organizational relations suggests that trust, power, and risk are relevant concepts for examining the processes and relations that comprise network forms. The prospect of establishing different kinds of trusting relationships within networks, for example, is enabled or hindered by the wider institutional structures (Lane and Bachmann 1998) and informal social norms (Arrighetti et al. 1997), as well as the technological and economic context (Sako 1992: 241–243). Differences in societal institutions (involving trade associations, employer associations, trade unions, and government legislation) shape the extent to which the potential risks of strong trusting relations may be minimized, or prevented altogether. Burchell and Wilkinson's (1997) three-country survey of firm networks suggests that, as a generalization, trust relations flourish in Italy on the basis of a social convention that one's word is one's bond. In Germany, long-term trusting relations depend on statutory support given to the weaker party in the contract. But in Britain the absence of both conditions means that trusting relations depend much more strongly on specific informal personal contacts. In general, the risks and rigidities of long-term contractual relations appear to be minimized where *inter alia* societal norms and institutions allow for convergent expectations of trading partners and there is a shared sense of fairness concerning the conduct of the stronger partner towards the weaker partner. The importance of the broader institutional environment, therefore, begs the question as to whether a network form in Britain based solely on strong interpersonal relations of trust is a sufficient condition for improved performance, given the relative absence of supporting societal norms and institutional arrangements.

As we explore in Chapter 6, relations of trust can undoubtedly be important in forging and lubricating inter-organizational relationships as they provide a less mechanical, formalized means of addressing complexity and uncertainty. However, the exercise of power, in the form of threats and sanctions, offers an alternative mechanism for coordinating expectations and controlling relationships (Luhmann 1979). Sydow and Windeler (1998), for example, have suggested that 'network effectiveness' depends not only on the power of a hub firm 'in creating and organizing networks in such a way that the network action and income–outcome relation are improved upon', but also on its capacity to appropriate a greater portion of the generated surplus from the network (ibid.: 275–276). Again, as with trust, the way in which power operates within networks depends on the form of institutional embeddedness. Supportive institutional structures and social norms may lessen the risk of forging trusting relations, and thereby reduce the need to exercise power for controlling network relationships. Thus, in countries with 'thin' institutional arrangements (like the United Kingdom), the coercive exercise of power (and the associated costs of conflict) may be preferable to the high costs and risks of securing contracts on the basis of trust alone, as parties 'often find it easier to bear the risk of open conflict than the risk of misplaced trust. Power may generally be the second best choice but it is a good choice if trust seems not affordable' (Bachmann 2001: 351).

Yet, it is not necessarily the case that 'power' is 'the second best choice', or even that it is a 'choice' in any purposive, intentional sense. It is entirely possible, and even probable, that many organizations do not consider trust as a primary or even a supplementary basis for inter-organizational coordination. Instead there is a habitual, institutionalized reliance upon one-sided, coercive contracts—in the sense that suppliers are obliged to accept the terms dictated by a purchaser or be punished by losing the business. Where networks involve 'contracting between unequals' (Dore 1996), and where there is a relative absence of norms and institutions supportive of long-term trusting relations, attempts to match business goals, or to reconcile cultures, are likely to prove frustrating. 'Matching' is likely to take the form of conceding; and 'reconciling' is more likely to involve cloning. This applies as much to organizations on the perimeters of the 'core-ring' network form as to organizations engaged in partnerships, joint ventures, or strategic alliances. In the case of public–private partnerships, as we discuss in the following section and explore through case-study evidence in Chapter 5, private sector partner managers are institutionally empowered by their greater experience of market-based contracting, which puts them, in certain important respects, in a stronger bargaining position when negotiating and working together with the public sector partner.

Public–private contracting

In extending our focus to networks that involve public sector and private sector organizations, we note that public–private partnerships (PPPs) are commended for their potential to improve performance through sharing private sector techniques and transforming the traditional bureaucratic organizational model. The United Kingdom is at the forefront of change in the way public services are delivered. Contracting out to the private sector and PPPs have challenged and transformed traditional notions of the government's role as employer and service provider (Deakin and Walsh 1996; Corby and White 1999; IPPR 2001; Grimshaw et al. 2002a; Sachdev 2001). The development of a 'network' approach to public services delivery reflects, on the one hand, a belief that government lacks the ability to solve economic and organizational problems, requiring instead the supposed incentives associated with private ownership and market organization (Cutler and Waine 1994). On the other hand, it involves an embrace of the apparent benefits of network organizational forms, which are said to present new flexible practices, in place of the supposed inefficiencies and rigidities associated with the bureaucratic, hierarchical organizational structure (Huxham 1996; Kickert et al. 1997). The general case is made that network organizations (such as PPPs) strengthen opportunities for innovation, reduce costs through mutual achievement of business objectives, and improve career prospects for workers through establishing 'boundaryless' job ladders (Ashkenas et al. 1995; Arthur and Rousseau 1996).

Research on previous 'network' forms (such as Compulsory Competitive Tendering) and more recent assessments of PPPs have, however, questioned the cost and performance efficiencies associated with delivery through public–private contracting. First, immediate cost savings accompanying the market tender for services may be offset by other less readily quantifiable costs, such as reduced services quality, or an erosion of workers' public sector ethos (Mailly 1986; Corby and White 1999; Hebson et al. 2003). In the case of Private Finance Initiatives (a PPP involving private sector investment in capital infrastructure) and large IT outsourcing contracts, costs over the lifetime of the contract have a tendency to escalate beyond the baseline agreement (Robinson et al. 2000; Miozzo et al. 2003).

Shared services provision with the private sector typically involves the transfer of workers to a new private sector employer, leading to further concerns that workers become fragmented around two (or more) tiers of terms and conditions. Legal protection is patchy and is no defence against subsequent changes to terms and conditions following the tendering process, or against the setting of worse conditions for new recruits (see Chapter 3). Also, while benchmarking of service activities is said to be necessary to generate a measure of relative efficiency (Cm 4310 1999: 35–41; OECD 1997), in practice it is difficult to construct reliable benchmarks (Boyne 1998). Reasons for this include problems of accessing information that is commercially sensitive, difficulties in reaching a subjective evaluation of factors that are not easily measurable (Deakin and Walsh 1996)—such as organizational learning or degree of political responsibility—and the impossibility of evaluating the extent to which a change in organizational form has generated improvements without being able to hold all other factors constant (ibid. 1996).

A more fundamental and far-reaching critique of the appropriateness of encouraging public–private contracting questions the basis for judging their performance solely (if at all) on private sector measures of competition, efficiency, and entrepreneurialism. This is because public sector employees are obliged to demonstrate a sensitivity and attentiveness to a range of other considerations:

responsiveness to parliamentary and public opinion, sensitivity to the complexity of the public interest, honesty in the formulation of advice, and so on . . . a system of representative government does require officials to act as the custodians of the procedural values it embodies. The contemporary concern with efficient management, with performance, and with securing results, should not be allowed to obscure this fact. (Johnson 1983: 193–194, cited in Du Gay 1996)

This argument clashes with the ostensibly non-ideological principles underpinning public sector reform (under the Blair government), which hold that the controversy over whether the public or private sector ought to control public services delivery is of secondary importance to the quality of services delivered—'what matters is what works'. The policy emphasis on a new network model of public services, founded on the principles of market incentives and private sector managerial expertise, undervalues and marginalizes the contribution that a set of distinctive principles can make to the quality of public services, including the dedication of those delivering these services to their clients. Such dedication is difficult to foster when the primary object of the service provider is to extract profit from the work undertaken by its employees. As the managers of private sector providers are acutely aware, they are not in business as charitable organizations. They are obliged to extract a profit from their operations, and this frequently requires them to erode pay and conditions and/or to intensify work processes. As we explore in Chapter 5, at risk are the traditional characteristics of a public sector ethos, such as fairness, reliability, and antipathy to corruption. An alternative prognosis suggests that reform may valuably build on a public sector ethos as a central component. Moreover, an element of such a model might be exported to those private sector partners and subcontractors keen to improve services provision and employment conditions.

Our earlier discussion of the limits to collaboration and power relations alerts us to the uneven way contracts for services are negotiated, implemented, and adapted over the life of a services agreement. As long as market-based principles underpin the direction of public sector reform, it is likely that differences in expertise in operating in a market-based environment (however imperfect) enable private sector organizations to enjoy the upper hand in negotiating and managing contractual relationships with the public sector (especially concerning the design of flexible price contracts and risk sharing agreements). This is a first dimension to the power imbalance between public and private sector organizations. A second possible dimension is sensitivity to reputation. If performance standards deteriorate, the greater visibility of the public sector network partner (a government department, a local authority or the NHS, for example) means that it will be at the receiving end of customers' complaints, despite the fact that it is only responsible for monitoring services delivery, not services provision. The greater capacity of the private sector partner to operate in a more anonymized market context (it can always win contracts in the less transparent private sector markets) means that challenges to its reputation can be deflected by seeking revenues elsewhere; an option not available to the public sector partner.[4] In the most extreme case, private sector suppliers may intentionally run down the quality of their service to ensure that a satisfactory return on capital is made prior to its failure and winding up. Subsequently, a new entity may be created to avoid negative reputational effects—something that is rarely possible for the public sector partner whose reputation may be damaged by the selection and effects of a failing partner.

The implication of this dynamic is that forms of public–private contracting can hinder the ability of the state to implement policy in the public interest. It may be difficult for national governments to regulate the activities of capitalist enterprises in a way that coheres with government policy (Reich 1991; Smith 2000). Public sector managers may, over time, be better equipped to monitor contractual agreements with private sector partners and to negotiate new terms for additional work. As we explore in Chapter 5, however, the problem is that the boundaries within which negotiations take place are predominantly set by the (relatively non-transparent) needs of the private sector enterprise (in response to shareholder demands for certain returns to capital investment, or to changing strategic policy from headquarters). In this context, the danger is that shifting expenditure demands made by the private sector partner may well be met by the individual public sector partner organization—thus satisfying both partners, and potentially reinforcing a high trust relationship—but the real cost adjustments fall outside the network, whether through a redistribution of spending from other areas of public services or by mortgaging into the future.

2.5 Conclusion: why the employment relationship is central to understanding network forms

Inter-organizational relations are of central importance to a contemporary understanding of organizational performance, distribution of rents from economic activity (among organizations and workforce groups), and important questions concerning the better regulation and design of the employment relationship. The problem, however, is that the literature on the various types of network organizational forms rarely connects to these issues. Consideration of the employment relationship is superficial and/or marginal to such analysis.

This chapter has argued for the need to reconsider the dynamics of contracting arrangements in network forms. First, instead of a focus on efficiency, as the driver for new organizational forms, we have argued for attention to the interrelated notions of trust, power, and risk and the way these underpin different kinds of inter-organizational (private–private and public–private) relationships. Second, we have argued that the dynamics of contracting in network organizational forms cannot be fully understood without appreciating the complexities of the employment relationship. It is important to introduce labour into an assessment of networks of inter-organizational relations. This is not simply because labour comprises a distinctive set of interests to be considered in understanding the distributive processes associated with network forms. Its inclusion is necessary also because it represents a fundamental dynamic—between organizational structure and the contradictory capitalist employment relationship—whereby employers seek to mobilize its capacities by pursuing relations of cooperation, on the one hand, but also by engendering relations of tension and conflict, on the other.

This contradictory dynamic is already multifaceted within the single organizational form, but additional levels of complexity arise within the network form. So, for example, whether a network form provides a means for performance improvements may, in some circumstances, depend on the organizations' *joint* capability in coordinating the labour process, in extending notions of shared organizational goals among workers, and in developing positive opportunities for skill development and careers. In other circumstances, as we discussed above, a network-type arrangement may be favoured primarily because it offers the possibility to displace costs and risks to the workforce of a partner organization, thereby reducing in-house conflicts and disputes between employer and employee. This dimension of performance is left unexamined in most analyses of network forms. They are inattentive to the potential for new patterns of conflict and cooperation within and between networked organizations, and to how organization boundaries are continually being redrawn in ways that reflect relative labour costs, industrial relations conditions, and the pliability of internal and external workforces. In the next chapter, we examine these and other issues in much more detail, with a particular focus on the need to reconsider the assumption of a single employer boundary—an assumption which has, until now, limited our understanding of the employment relationship.

Notes

1. The picture is further enriched or confused by using the term network to describe the *internal* restructuring of (typically multinational) corporations into what Castells refers to as the 'horizontal corporation'—'a dynamic and strategically planned network of self-programmed, self-directed units based on decentralization, participation and coordination' (1996: 164–166). In the horizontal corporation, autonomous business units compete with each other on certain defined areas of business performance as if they were independently established organizations. Staff departments, such as HR, may be required to generate revenues by servicing clients outside of the host organization, thereby transforming themselves from cost into profit centres.
2. It is not surprising that Williamson, for example, who is credited with formalizing the theoretical principles of 'market' and 'hierarchy', only offers a very loose characterization of 'hybrids' as all other forms 'of long-term contracting, reciprocal trading, regulation, franchising and the like' (1991, cited in Blois 2002: 524).
3. Sako's empirical research developed Macneil's (1974) critique of legal contract theory (which, in turn, built on the work of Macaulay 1963), which identifies a spectrum of contractual relations running from the discrete transaction to relational contracting.
4. In conventional transaction cost analysis, reputation effects are often claimed to limit the possibility of one partner acting opportunistically. However, Williamson (1985) does acknowledge that this process is imperfect. As he puts it, 'Some managers may shrug them off if the immediate gains are large enough and if they cannot be required to disgorge their ill-gotten gains. (Swiss bank accounts have attractive features in that respect)' (ibid.: 138).

3

Blurring the Boundaries to the Employment Relationship: From Single to Multi-Employer Relationships

JILL RUBERY, JILL EARNSHAW, AND MICK MARCHINGTON

3.1 Introduction

Debates about the changing nature of work and the prospects for the retention of the so-called standard employment relationship have become more widespread recently (Handy 1985; Rifkin 1995; Cappelli et al. 1997; Supiot 2001). This literature has focused to large extent on the fragmentation of work and increasing insecurity, often associated with the proliferation of 'non standard' forms of employment (Atkinson 1984; Felstead and Jewson 1999). Growing numbers of pseudo self-employed workers, agency temps, zero hours contractors, and home-based teleworkers have all attracted attention to the issue of whether these forms of work fall within our understanding of the standard employment relationship; a bounded and long-term relationship between a single employer and an employee. These concerns within the literature are mirrored in the practice of employment law where increasing numbers of cases apply to situations where the definition of employee status is in some sense ambiguous, and employment regulations have increasingly been extended to include within their scope workers who fail the full test of employee status (Earnshaw et al. 2002).

So far, however, attention in both social science and employment law has focused mostly on the appropriateness of a narrow definition for the employee side of the employment relationship. This chapter argues there is a parallel need to question the *employer* side of this conceptual box. Employment change needs to be understood through the changing nature of organizations and inter-organizational relations. The need to focus more on the employer side of the employment relationship applies not only in relation to its legal regulation, but also to the management of human resources, the analysis of changing employment opportunities, and the collective regulation of employment/industrial relations. The *legal framework* can be considered to be both a force that shapes the formation of organizational and employment relationships and a phenomenon that is shaped by such developments. This two-way relationship is evident in the increasing numbers of cases, as we document below, that call into question the uniqueness of the definition of the employer that is central to the current legal framework governing the employment contract. These have implications for how an employing organization interprets its responsibilities, both towards its own employees when working under the influence or control of clients and towards employees of other organizations when they are working on its premises or under its direct or indirect control. The legal framework in this area is thus evolving through case law, even though no systematic review has yet been undertaken of how the law needs to be reformed to guarantee employee rights in the context of permeable organizations. Regulation does, however, impact on the formation of inter-organizational relations. For example, the TUPE regulations provide for the terms and conditions of employment set by one employer to be carried over to another employer following merger or some forms of contracting out. Such regulations, as we discuss further below, affect not only the impact of contracting on employment conditions but also the incentives to engage in contracting. Other employment regulations, such as minimum legal standards to be observed by all employers, may also reduce incentives to use contracting in order to reduce employment costs.

The development of inter-organizational relationships also has significance for the *management of human resources*. Where employees of one organization work in environments open to pressure and influence from other employers, the relevance of key notions of HRM such as corporate culture, organizational commitment, loyalty, and identity are called into question. The presence of multi-agencies raises doubts about where the locus of control and authority lies and where an employee's duties of loyalty and commitment should be directed. The possibility of designing or maintaining a coherent and consistent set of human resource policies and practices across inter-organizational relationships is complicated because of potentially competing employer goals.

The reshaping of organizations and the move away from the integrated and bureaucratic organizational form also has implications for both *employment opportunities and employment relations*. Some accounts see these developments as increasing worker autonomy, discretion and skill, while others are concerned that responsibilities for training and skill development may become more diffuse, reinforcing a tendency towards a low skill economy. For some commentators (Kanter 1977), fragmentation of organizations may open up opportunities to change, for example, the gender division of labour within the organization, by challenging the restrictive norms and principles embedded in the bureaucratic form and by removing unnecessary and artificial layers of hierarchy and control. However, it also exposes groups and individuals to more intense and more complex forms of competition, requiring constant attention to both internal and external rules. Fragmentation poses particular challenges for the collective regulation of employment. Where organizations are embedded in a set of inter-organizational relations, the power in a particular employment relationship may not lie with the legal employer but with the employer's clients. The growth of inter-organizational relations increases the need to consider the employment relationship beyond the specific workplace or enterprise. However, just as HR practitioners and analysts have stressed employee commitment to a single organization as the means to achieve employee cooperation and productivity, so their industrial relations counterparts have focused attention on the single employer through the medium of partnership agreements.

The development of inter-organizational relations, therefore, has implications for how the employment relationship is conceptualized, regulated, and managed within the fields of employment law, human resource management, labour market analysis, and employment relations. We now turn to a more detailed consideration of these issues.

3.2 Broadening the legal definition of the employer–employee relationship: from single employer to multi-employer?

The legal framework surrounding the employment relationship has traditionally been conceived as involving a single employer and a single employee, and it has been tacitly assumed that legal rights and duties could be delineated primarily within the boundaries of a single organization. Common law rights and duties—such as the duty of confidentiality and good faith—arise by virtue of the contract of employment and of necessity, therefore, concern only the parties to that contract. Similarly, the statutory employment protection rights which have increasingly overlaid this common law foundation since the 1960s, are largely predicated upon the notion of an 'employee', as legally defined, working for a single employer. The focus on a single employer has, in fact, contributed to the determination of employment status itself. This is because in deciding whether an individual should be regarded as an employee or self-employed under a contract for services, a number of factors are considered, some of which relate to the exercise of 'employer' functions such as the right of control and the power to discipline and dismiss. The fact that in more complex organizational forms these 'employer' functions might be exercised by a non-legal employer would not be considered by employment tribunals when adjudicating on employment status (Table 3.1).

The point is most clearly demonstrated by considering the lack of clarity surrounding the position of agency workers in law. Regardless of how such workers are managed on a day-to-day basis by the client organization, the agency rather than the client has traditionally been regarded as their legal employer. However, the agency is not in a position to undertake some of the key tasks associated with an employer's role in relation to a directly employed

Table 3.1. Employer–employee rights and duties in a multi-employer/agency environment

	Non-employer influences on the employment relationship	Current position with respect to legal responsibilities
Control of work	Client has effective responsibility for control of agency work, seconded workers etc.	Control of work one of the legal tests for employer status—cases that have deemed there to be an employment contract with client have been overturned at appeal
Supply of work	Agency workers, freelance worker may work exclusively for one client	Long-term relationship between parties maybe 'capable of generating an implied contractual relationship' but case by case decision
Equal pay	Differences in pay for same or equal work may be found at same workplace among workers with different employers	Comparison only permitted in same employment or between associated employers
Transferred workers	Transferred staff retain terms and conditions of previous employer	Transferred staff not able to make comparison with ex-colleagues even if in same workplace if their terms remain frozen/rise less quickly after transfer

Sex and race discrimination	(a) Client may offer bonuses to supplier employees (b) Sex and racial harassment may occur when employees working in multi-employer environment (c) The principal or client may discriminate by sex or race with respect to supply of agency workers	(a) No remedy under sex discrimination if bonuses vary by gender as employer not liable for action of client (b) Decision that an employer had the responsibility to protect their workforce from unlawful behaviour of non-employees overturned as had not addressed question of whether employer had discriminated against the particular employees. (c) Sex and Race Discrimination Acts outlaw discrimination by a principal but comparison only allowed with other agency staff not principal's own staff
Discipline and grievance	Business to business contracts may give clients a right of veto over staff. May be dismissed at behest of a third party including a client	Client request to dismiss (or not to deploy) can be considered an 'other substantial reason' for dismissal and thereby to be a fair dismissal. If sex or race discrimination at base, cases can only be brought by respective enforcement agencies not by individuals
Health and safety	Health and safety of workforce on a multi-site is dependent on actions of non-employers or employees of other employers	Law provides for legal responsibility by main contractor for health and safety but applies to criminal law; individual employee can only make civil claim against own employer
Duty of good faith	Duty to work honestly/faithfully for own employer and not to reveal confidential information—difficult to apply when working cooperatively with non-employers or under direction of non-employer	Implied term in employment contract but difficult to interpret in multi-employer settings

workforce—such as controlling the work process or being in a position to establish and verify the circumstances which may lead to disciplinary sanctions. The inability of agencies to exercise such 'employer' functions, as well as the fact that there is no obligation on agencies to provide individuals with work on a continuing basis and nor for individuals obliged to accept assignments offered ('mutuality of obligation'), has typically resulted in courts and tribunals concluding that the relationship between the agency and the worker cannot be regarded as a contract of employment; hence, the individual is deemed to be self-employed rather than an employee. For example, in the case of *Montgomery* v. *Johnson Underwood Ltd* [2001] IRLR 269, the applicant had been placed within a client company for over two years before her assignment was terminated by the agency at the behest of the client. An employment tribunal hearing her claim of unfair dismissal against both the agency and the client concluded that, on balance, the factors pointing to the existence of an employment contract with the agency outweighed those against. However, included in the list of factors against a contract of employment was a finding that there was 'little or no control, direction or supervision'. On appeal, the Court of Appeal held that the tribunal's finding of a lack of control was fatal to its decision that the applicant was an employee of the agency: 'A contractual relationship concerning work to be carried out in which the one party has no control over the other could not sensibly be called a contract of employment (ibid. 2001: 271).'

Accordingly, the applicant could not claim unfair dismissal against the client—because the agency was regarded as the employer—or against the agency—because she was found not to be its employee. The Court of Appeal's ruling thereby ignores the whole rationale behind the weighing of various factors, which is to differentiate the autonomous self-employed from those in a position of economic dependency. However, at around the same time the Employment Appeal Tribunal in the case of *Motorola* v. *(1) Davidson* and *(2) Melville Craig Group Ltd* [2001] IRLR 4 took an arguably more enlightened approach by deciding that the applicant, who had been placed with Motorola for over two years, should be regarded as an employee of Motorola (see Box 1.1). Although recognizing that the legal power of control was vested in the agency, they refused to ignore the day-to-day practical control exercised by Motorola over the applicant. Unfortunately, in the subsequent case of *Hewlett Packard Ltd* v. *O'Murphy* [2002] IRLR 4, the Employment Appeal Tribunal reverted to a strict contractual approach. In essence, it concluded that despite working for a client firm for six years, an agency worker could not be its employee since there was simply no contract of any kind between them. However, a more recent decision by the Court of Appeal (in the case of *Franks* v. *Reuters Ltd and anor* [2003] EWCA Civ 417) highlights an interesting development in the law. While accepting there was no express contract between Franks (an agency worker) and Reuters Ltd, for whom he had worked for five years, it considered that a contract between them could be *implied* from the circumstances of his work and from what was said and done both at the time he started work and subsequently.

The Court stated that 'dealings between parties over a period of years, as distinct from the weeks or months typical of temporary or casual work, are *capable* of generating an implied contractual relationship'. This case frees tribunals from some of the previous inflexibility in adjudicating on employment status, but does not produce any certainty of outcome because each case is determined on its own merits.

The inability of the legal tests to recognize the economic dependency of many individuals who fail to qualify for employee status has been recognized partially in that some employment protection rights have been extended to 'workers'. By virtue of section 230 of the Employment Rights Act 1996, workers are defined as 'those who undertake to do or perform any work or services for another party to the contract whose status is not, by virtue of the contract that of a client or customer of any profession or business undertaking carried on by the individual'.

This brings within the ambit of statutory employment protection those who work under a contract for services but who are not in reality running their own self-employed business, such as agency workers, some casual workers, and labour-only subcontractors. However, no such recognition of the mismatch between the legal framework and the reality of modern day working appears to have occurred in relation to the issue of multiple employers. As Becker (1996: 1527) has put it:

Contemporary labour law is marked by a disjunction between theories of rights and duties based on privity of contract between employer and employee and new forms of work relations that disrupt this model of employment by increasingly interposing intermediate employers between the entities of labour and capital.

Similarly, UK equal pay laws were also formulated with a single employer in mind. The Equal Pay Act 1970 specifically requires that comparators must be 'in the same employment' (section 1(6)) and this normally limits claims to the same employer. Exceptionally, employees are regarded as being in the same employment where they are employed by 'associated' employers—meaning that one is a company controlled (i.e. voting control) by the other or that both are controlled by a third company. Even within the same organization the legal provisions are limited in their ability to rectify inequalities in pay because a comparator must be of the opposite sex. Once distinct legal employers are involved, the Act becomes powerless to intervene, even if employees of different organizations work together on a daily basis.

This limitation is particularly apparent where contracting-out has taken place under the provisions of the TUPE Regulations. These state that employees who are assigned to the section of the undertaking transferred are, in effect, part of that undertaking, and hence at the point of transfer they cease to be employed by the transferor and become employees of the transferee. However, their pre-transfer terms and conditions are preserved and, especially where the transfer involves the contracting out of public services to the private sector or arises out of a private finance initiative, the staff transferred may be working alongside their old colleagues who did not transfer. They may even have their work checked by those members of staff. Nevertheless, despite this, the two groups of employees are no longer 'in the same employment', so transferred staff would not be able to use their former colleagues in the public sector as comparators in an equal pay claim if, for example, their own terms and conditions remained frozen after the transfer whereas the public sector staff continued to receive pay rises. In a similar way, inequalities in pay between agency workers and those they work alongside cannot be rectified by the Equal Pay Act.

These strict constraints are not apparent to the same extent in EU law. Article 141 of the Treaty of Rome extends the permitted comparison to those employed 'in the same establishment or service' and this has enabled successful claims to be made across Regional Councils (see *Scullard* v. *Knowles and Southern Regional Council for Education and Training* [1996] IRLR 344) and local education authorities (see *South Ayrshire Council* v. *Morton* [2002] IRLR 257). However, the European Court of Justice in the case of *Lawrence* v. *Regent Office Care* ([2000] IRLR 608) ruled that a local authority and the private contractor to whom the cleaning service was contracted out could not be regarded as being 'in the same establishment or service'. Their reasoning was that the discrepancy in pay could not be traced to a single source, such as a national pay scale or a common collective agreement. A further case awaiting consideration by the European Court of Justice on the same issue (*Allonby* v. *Accrington & Rossendale College* [2001] IRLR 364) concerns an FE college which dismissed all its part-timers in anticipation of legislation which would outlaw their being discriminated against *vis-à-vis* their full-time colleagues, and re-employed them through an agency. Had the EU Draft Directive on Temporary (Agency) Workers been enacted, this would have provided for pay equality between agency staff and employees of the client on similar work after a specified period, but at the time of writing, it has yet to reach final agreement.

A further limitation of the Equal Pay Act is that it targets only *contractual* disparities in remuneration packages and not, for example, discretionary bonuses, which would necessitate claims under the Sex Discrimination Act 1975. Here again, however, the legislation contemplates claims only against the legal employer; moreover that employer is vicariously liable for the unlawful actions of its own employees (by virtue of section 41 of the Act) but not for those of another employer even if the two employers are involved in a joint enterprise or activity. Thus, for example, if a male employee was offered a bonus by the manager of one of his employer's clients and such a bonus was not offered to a female employee, even though she was engaged in the same or similar work, the female employee would be without a remedy under the Act. She could not claim unlawful discrimination against her own employer because it would not be liable for the manager's actions and although the client firm would be liable, it would not be her employer.

Only in cases of sexual or racial harassment has there been any attempt to overcome this limitation—not by making the legal employer vicariously liable for the actions of non-employees, but by holding that an employer subjects its employees to the detriment of such harassment if it is in a position to control whether it happens (see *Burton & Rhule* v. *De Vere Hotels* [1996] IRLR 596). However, this ruling has now been disapproved by the House of Lords in the joined cases of *Macdonald* v. *Advocate General for Scotland* and *Pearce* v. *Governing Body of Mayfield Secondary School* [2003] IRLR 512 on the basis that the fundamental question of whether the employer had *discriminated* against the particular employees by treating them less favourably on grounds of sex or race had not been addressed. Interestingly, agency workers have a right of action against the client firm in which they are placed because both the Sex Discrimination Act (in section 9) and the Race Relations Act 1976 (in section 7) specifically outlaw discrimination by a 'principal'—defined as a person who makes work available to be carried out by individuals employed by another person and supplied to the principal to do the work. In the case of *Harrods Ltd* v. *Remick* [1997] IRLR 583 a woman employed at an outlet within Harrods was able to bring a claim of race discrimination against Harrods even though it was not her employer. However, the statutory provisions do not appear to allow contract workers to compare their treatment with that of the principal's own staff but only with other contract workers of the opposite sex or of a different racial group.

The behaviour of non-employees raises the matter of discipline and grievance more generally. Grievance procedures envisage complaints by an employee about the actions of an individual employed by the same employer, yet in a multi-employer setting this may obviously not be the case. In a similar vein, employers have, in theory, no right to discipline agency staff working 'for' them or on their premises but who are not directly employed by them. In reality, however, agency staff may well be dealt with by the client firm, rather than asking the agency to remove them, especially where misconduct has involved both agency staff and the client's own employees. More generally, it is not uncommon for a client to have the right of veto over its contractor's staff, and this can lead to the dismissal of an employee at the behest of a third party. The dismissed employee is permitted to claim unfair dismissal only against the legal employer, who can justify such a dismissal for 'some other substantial reason' (see Section 98 of the Employment Rights Act 1996) even where the employer has no particular wish to lose the services of the individual concerned but is constrained by a provision in the contract between the two organizations (see, for example, *Dobie* v. *Burns International Security Services* [1983] IRLR 278). Of course, if the non-legal employer had expressly required a dismissal due to discriminatory motives, then that employer could be guilty of unlawfully 'instructing' the legal employer to discriminate. However, only the Equal Opportunities Commission (EOC) or the Commission for Racial Equality (CRE) can bring proceedings in respect of such matters. The influence exercised by a non-legal employer may also be apparent when considering a franchised outlet. In law, staff working at a franchised outlet are employed by the franchisee rather than the franchisor but the franchisor may still exert considerable control over the franchisee's operations, including specifying through the contract a detailed work process or providing a framework for discipline and grievance for the franchisee to use for its employees (Felstead 1991, 1993).

Health and safety is one area where an employer is able to exert influence beyond its own organizational boundaries. For example, under the Health and Safety at Work Act 1974 the main contractor has responsibility for health and safety not only of its own workers, but also to employees of subcontractors and to non-employees who may be affected by its operation (including the public). This would encompass not only duties to subcontractors, but also the reverse—in other words a subcontractor could be prosecuted for failing to ensure the health and safety of employees of the contractor—see, for example, R versus Mara ([1987] IRLR 154). Equally the duty to non-employees would apply even when there was no contractual relationship between the employers, as would be the case, for instance, on a multi-employer site. Nevertheless, even though the Health and Safety at Work Act reaches beyond the boundaries of a single organization, it leads only to criminal sanctions against the wrongdoer and cannot be used by an injured employee to obtain compensation via a civil claim. In this respect, the legal framework is more limited because an employer's civil duty of care arises by virtue of the employment relationship and therefore applies only to its own employees. Legally this is unproblematic where employees are working for their own employer on the employer's premises alongside other employees of the same employer. However, matters become more complex where employees are working in cross-organizational teams, or are injured whilst carrying out work for another employer or working on that employer's premises.

Since a personal injury claim in the United Kingdom proceeds by way of an allegation of negligence, an injured employee would have to show that his or her employer had failed in the duty of care. While it is clear that an employer's duty does not cease merely because the employee concerned is working on the premises of another employer (see, for example, General Cleaning Contractors Ltd v. Christmas (1953) AC 1880), it is less easy to prove breach of the duty. Moreover, the injured employee's employer cannot normally be held vicariously liable for an accident that has been caused by the negligence of someone employed by another employer. Such difficulties in attributing liability are also apparent in deciding who bears ultimate responsibility when public service delivery is fragmented through chains of subcontractors.

The duty of good faith arises because it is an implied term in the contract of employment; this requires employees to work honestly and faithfully for their employer's interests, as well as not reveal their employer's trade secrets and other confidential information. However, as argued in Chapter 8, the ambiguous nature of the employer–employee relationship in more complex organizational forms means that employees may find difficulty in identifying with the culture of their legal employer, but instead feel some commitment to another employer. This may come about because relationships between organizations are difficult to sustain merely by virtue of tightly drawn contractual provisions or key performance indicators: to be successful they may require cooperative working between individuals and teams. Nevertheless, from a legal perspective, it is clear that an employer who wished, for example, to protect confidential information which might be accessible to those employed by another employer, would be obliged to do so by means of express contractual provisions.

So far, we have considered the framework of employment law relating to individual employer–employee rights and duties, but trade union law also operates largely within the boundaries of organizations. One of the most important aspects of collective employment law bounded by the concept of the legal employer is the right to participate in industrial action. The changes to the legislation in this field brought about by Conservative governments during the 1980s progressively narrowed permitted action to a single employer and a single workplace. Thus, workers are now permitted only to picket their own place of work, a 'trade dispute' in respect of which lawful industrial action may be taken is confined to a dispute between workers and *their* own employer (thereby outlawing sympathy strikes and other 'secondary' action), and action to persuade an employer to stipulate in a commercial contract that the other party should recognize a union or that the contract should be performed only by union labour, would not be lawful. Statutory recognition procedures are also predicated on a single employer, yet this does not take into account the difficulties which multi-employer situations may present for the meaningful definition of bargaining units. For example, unions will not be able to include agency staff within the definition of a bargaining unit as they belong to another employer, and the linkage of bargaining units to the legal employer could result in the recognition of unions for some workers in a workplace but not others. Moreover, employees may belong to a particular bargaining unit for the purpose of negotiating terms and conditions but its relevance for issues such as discipline and grievance or hours of work may be reduced because they are located in workplaces where the rules of the client organization tend to dominate.

This scrutiny of the legal framework surrounding the employment relationship and of relevant case law demonstrates that the traditional focus on regulation within the confines of a single organization remains largely untouched. Apart from isolated statutory provisions, for example those relating to discrimination against contract workers and aspects of health and safety, on the whole employment protection legislation contemplates claims by employees only against their own employer. This model has become increasingly inappropriate because, with the rise of organizational networks, many employees find themselves effectively working for more than one employer. In consequence, they may in reality be subject to the influence of a non-legal employer in indirect, or sometimes even direct, ways. Yet, such influences, even where they result in detrimental consequences to the employee, are rarely amenable to legal challenge. In short, the law is simply out of step with the reality of working patterns in a growing number of organizations.

3.3 The management of human resources in the permeable organization

The management of human resources is increasingly identified as an issue of strategic importance for employing organizations, a perspective particularly associated with the resource-based view of the firm (Barney 1991) that sees organizations as following distinctive paths of development based on the nurturing of internal resources that are relatively rare and inimitable. Accordingly, employers need to match their HR strategies to external market contingencies but also foster the development of internal human resources to achieve a distinctive comparative advantage. This approach emphasizes the importance of congruence between human resource policies and organizational objectives, rather than, for example, with more general professional or occupational orientations that spread across organizational boundaries. Recent research has focused on the links between human resource management and performance (e.g. Pfeffer 1998; West et al. 2002; Guest et al. 2003), whereby implicit assumptions are made that all workers (including temporary or agency staff) are expected to identify with goals set by the employing organization.

An emphasis on each organization pursuing an integrated set of business objectives and HR practices sits rather uneasily with two sets of recent developments. First, it is at odds with the move away from bureaucratic, and in principle internally consistent and transparent, regulations towards more flexible internal structures, associated with the policies of delayering and decentring of responsibilities. Decentring is likely to exacerbate problems in establishing and communicating a consistent message, in line with business strategy. There has been an active debate within the literature over the compatibility between these twin requirements—for an integrated and consistent HR strategy and the need for alignment with business needs (Legge 1995; Boxall and Purcell 2002). This dilemma has focused around the issue of whether all organizations should pursue a high commitment (best practice) bundle or adopt a more flexible approach, allowing business units to aim for best fit with the external environment. One solution has been to emphasize corporate culture as the glue to keep the decentred organization orientated towards the same overall goals, but it is not clear how far a common culture is compatible with differences in substantive policies. Purcell (1999) has tried to move beyond this debate by rejecting the universal best practice solution as inapplicable to different business situations, and the best fit concept as incompatible with a dynamic and strategic approach. Purcell's formulation provides a more dynamic interactive framework for analysing the tensions between internally and externally orientated HR strategies, but it has focused on the voluntary strategies of companies and not on the impact of interventions from clients over internal management actions. However, Swart and Kinnie's (2003) recent research on knowledge intensive firms (KIFs) shows how clients are seeking to influence the HR practices of their suppliers in both direct and indirect ways, as well as attempting to shape the identities of the people working for these organizations. These authors suggest that the balance of power between suppliers and clients has a major impact on the development of HR practices and organizational identity in firms; we develop this further in subsequent chapters when data is presented from our research in organizations representing a range of sectors, not just KIFs.

The second development is the trend towards outsourcing and inter-organizational contracting. This might seem paradoxical in a context where the nurturing of specific internal resources is seen as key to competitive success but the HRM literature assumes this allows employers to develop their core resources within the bounds of the organization while externalising those activities that lack strategic importance (Lepak and Snell 1999). Organizations are enjoined to be selective in their application of HR policies, particularly high commitment systems, and either adopt differential HR practices within the organization (as in the flexible firm, Atkinson 1984) or outsource non-strategic activities.

This simple distinction between internal strategic and external non-strategic activities is altogether too neat because it focuses on only one aspect of the business to business contracting process, the decision to outsource. Yet, every time one organization chooses to outsource, another organization accepts a new client, and is placed under some pressure to meet that client's demand for particular levels of service or product, often with specific requirements relating to how human resources are to be managed. In the HRM literature, there is focus on the remaining core activities and not on how non-core activities are provided, an approach that is both incomplete and misleading. Not only are supplier firms excluded from the focus, but also an organization that is a client in one case may be a provider or supplier in another. Moreover, analyses of sub-contracting may be misleading if they assume that externalization is used primarily to protect the core workforce. Authors such as Cappelli et al. (1997) and Ackroyd and Procter (1998) (in the United Kingdom and the United States of America respectively) have argued instead that outsourcing is used to place pressure on the remaining core and submit all activities to the test of externalization. Therefore, far from insulating the core, the process of externalization exposes these workers to heightened competitive pressures. Location within networks of complex inter-organizational relationships may limit the independence of the organization's business and human resource policies, as pressure through the supply chain can be used either to diffuse improvements in HRM (Beaumont 1996; Hunter 1996; Scarbrough 2000) or to shift risk to supplier organizations, thereby restricting the suppliers' scope to develop strong internal human resource policies (Rainnie 1992). In a multi-client environment there are multiple sources of external pressure leading to potential areas of inconsistency and conflict, particularly where there are strong imbalances in power relationships between the organizations involved. While an organization may be relatively powerful in some relationships, it can be relatively weak in others (Marchington and Vincent 2004), and indeed relations between clients and suppliers may change over time due to the locking-in effect of contracting or other external changes.

The extent of client interventions in a supplier organization depends upon both their ability and their keenness to exert influence. *Keenness* depends on the importance of the outsourced activity to the client's own business strategy and reputation. Under these conditions, after-the-event remedies for poor performance, through enforcement of the contract, may provide delayed and insufficient forms of control. Relational contracting in principle provides a solution but this involves foregoing the price and control advantages of transactional contracting based around repeat competitive tendering. In the UK, few firms appear willing to provide guarantees of contract renewal (Purcell and Purcell 1999) even those claiming to work in partnerships. Moreover, many companies, when deciding to outsource, may underestimate the strategic importance of day-to-day operational activities (Boxall 1998). Furthermore, even if efforts are made to forge high trust relations between key boundary spanning agents, it does not ensure trust extends to those workers engaged in forging and maintaining the partnership on a daily basis. The unitarist perspective that is implicit in the notion of organizational trust and relational contracting serves to obscure the continued contested nature of the employment relationship (Ezzamel et al. 2001). If we accept unified orientations are a fiction, clients may be strongly motivated to try and exert direct influence on the labour process in order to ensure conformity with their own objectives.

However, the actual ways in which clients influence the labour process also depends on their *ability* to intervene, which in turn is shaped by the balance of power between organizations and the nature of outsourcing. Factors that increase ability to intervene include geographical proximity (and indeed geographical overlap of the client and the supplier workforces at multi-employer sites), regulations that require client involvement in checking and monitoring work and client involvement in training the supplier workforce. The latter may be at the discretion of the supplier or imposed by the client. At the other extreme, a supplier may be dominant enough to pursue its own independent policy and resist all attempts by clients to influence the service provided. Where this power is based on monopolistic access to resources or on long-term contracts to provide services to the public sector, insulation from client requests can exacerbate mismatches between the suppliers' arrangements and the needs of the service. For example, one outcome could be continued deficiencies in the supply of trained and motivated labour (see Chapters 5 and 9).

The notion that the internal operations of an organization may be subject to influence by external clients needs to be incorporated into mainstream HRM analysis. So far there has been relatively little empirical work on the implications of interventions by non-employers on the internal labour process and, by implication, the employment relationship with the exception of studies of temporary agency workers, the work by Felstead (1991, 1993) on franchising, and a few studies of supply chains. Even within this limited empirical material, most of the focus has been on the dual influence of the legal and the non-legal employer; apart from Scarbrough (2000) and Swart and Kinnie (2003), studies fail to focus on multi-clients or multi-employers.

Our own case studies provide more extensive empirical evidence on the influence of multi-employers on HRM. In Chapter 7 we explore the implications of the development of permeable organizations for internal hierarchies. Advocates of 'flexible' human resource policies increasingly stress the need to escape from bureaucratic internal hierarchies and rules so as to reward and motivate staff according to their current performance, market value and the business needs of the organization (see White 2000 for critical discussion). However, even HRM textbooks from the United States of America, where institutional pressures for consistency are perhaps even weaker than in the United Kingdom, recognize the limits to diversity. Beliefs in the fairness of managerial practices underpin the psychological contract and it is felt this is best promoted through the development and application of consistent HR policies, particularly for workers who have to cooperate at work to achieve common objectives (Baron and Kreps 1999: 51–54). Employers may try to follow the flexible firm prescription and seek to have 'the best of both worlds' by providing high commitment policies for the core and more market-mediated arrangements for the periphery. However, a contracting out 'solution' inevitably results in a larger number of organizations acting as suppliers for a range of clients, and in this context interventions by clients may further disturb internal hierarchies and systems of employment. Management does not, of course, always seek to retain the integrity of the internal system but may use externalization to put pressure on the internal system; for example, recourse to temporary work agencies or outsourcing may be designed to establish a new lower floor to the internal pay hierarchy. Consequently, decisions to outsource, and even threats to explore outsourcing possibilities, can alter the balance of power within employment relations.

In Chapter 8 we analyse the implications of multi-employer environments for the concept of organizational commitment, and associated notions of corporate culture and the psychological contract. These have perhaps been seen too simplistically as handy tools to overcome the problems of organizational coherence and strategy in the context of fragmentation and decentring. Organizational identity is regarded as a key issue in shaping worker commitment (Guest 1998b: 42), but this generates major questions about whether an organizational entity can make a psychological contract with an employee. An organization is neither a person nor a social entity (as opposed to a legal entity as party to the legal employment contract) and should not be anthropomorphized or indeed reified as a coherent, unified agent. These conundrums have also led to discussions about whether psychological contracts should be—or indeed are—forged at the company, establishment, or work group level (Guest 1998a: 652).

Employment relationships have been seen traditionally as nested within the boundaries of the organization—within the work group, the department or the company as a whole but inter-organizational relationships introduce a nesting that involves a principal that is not part of the company (McClean Parks et al. 1998: 718, citing March and Simon 1958). McClean Parks et al. (1998: 698) have suggested extending theories of the psychological contract built around full-time permanent employment so as to incorporate the experience of contingent workers. This requires adding the concept of multi-agency; temporary agency workers attempt, through the same single act of labour, to satisfy their obligations simultaneously to two employers—the agency and the client. This simultaneity raises questions about organizational commitment and loyalty, and presents conflicts and contradictions with respect to lines of authority and workload. This approach can be generalized to include anyone who is under direct or indirect pressure to work in the interests—or under the control—of a client organization while simultaneously being required to follow instructions from their own employer. 'Volition' is also an important dimension, as agency workers are more constrained in their choice about which type of employment to accept, but commitment within the psychological contract is assumed to be based in volition. Clearly, lack of volition applies to agency workers but it could be extended to any employee who is expected to show loyalty and commitment to non-employers and where the conditions set in contracts by clients impinge negatively on their working conditions. Employees typically have little or no influence over the bidding process between organizations (Colling 2000: 78) but this can have major consequences for their employment experience (Cooke et al. 2004).

Work on the psychological contract complements other literature focusing on potential conflicts of loyalty experienced by temporary agency staff, and on spillover effects on the attitudes and orientations of permanent staff (Geary 1992; Pearce 1993; Gasteen and Sewell 1994; Gottfried 1994; Rogers 1995; Saxenian 1996; Matusik and Hill 1998; Ward et al. 2001). There has also been analysis of whether public sector workers continue to identify with public service after they (and their work) have been outsourced to the private sector (Pratchett and Wingfield 1995; Hebson et al. 2003). Problems of organizational commitment and identity due to the presence of multi-employers extend beyond these examples, as the cases reviewed in Chapter 8 reveal. Non-employers may try to foster the commitment and loyalty of supplier employees through the use of monetary and non-monetary incentives or by offering training in client culture and orientations. In some cases the client may seek to encourage employees to act in ways that are not in the direct and immediate interests of their own employer. Clients may also be keen to present the appearance of a seamless organization to customers, for example, by requiring non-employees to wear client uniforms. The outcome of these efforts is influenced by the relative status and attractiveness of the legal employer or the client to employees. Furthermore, the importance of organizational commitment as a device to motivate staff may have been exaggerated because cooperation and collaboration across organizations may depend as much on other forms of solidarity and identity; for example, commitment to public service, to doing a good job or to notions of solidarity with other employees/trade union members in similar positions to themselves employed by other organizations. There may be particular dangers in overemphasizing organizational identity in the management of inter-organizational relations, where such notions compete with, or undermine, employees' commitment to a public sector or customer service ethos (see Chapter 5). Introducing the issue of multi-employers into the debate on organizational commitment and identity, therefore, not only adds an additional layer of complexity but also calls into question the extent to which employees' feelings of commitment and identity can be readily manipulated by HR policies.

3.4 Fragmentation: consequences for employment opportunities and employment relations

Little regard is paid to the consequences of fragmentation for the quality of employment opportunities and employment relations. Optimists claim fragmentation offers opportunities for new ways of working, based around cooperative and less hierarchical relations that provide workers with opportunities for self-development through experience gained with a wider range of employers (Arthur and Rousseau 1996). To the extent that these new forms of working involve reward systems based on shares in companies, some would argue that there is a move to a post-capitalist system of employment relations (Hodgson 1999). However, most literature in this area focuses on new forms of working in particular sectors or for particular groups—primarily for so-called knowledge workers. Pessimists, in contrast, argue that fragmentation exposes workers to greater risks (Cappelli et al. 1997), shifts responsibilities for skill development onto them and provides new opportunities for segmentation along race and gender lines. This diversity of views mirrors the contradictory interpretations of the internalization of employment within large, integrated bureaucratic organizations; for some, such as Marsden (1999: 3) it provides 'firms and workers with a very flexible method of coordination and a platform for investing in skills'. For others, such as Marglin (1974), it offers capital a means to establish control over the labour process. Moreover, it is argued that bureaucracies have internalized within their values and procedures the power relations and social norms at the time of their formation, thus presenting an obstacle to the achievement of gender equality (Kanter 1977).

Our argument is that the impact of changing organizational forms has to be understood and interpreted within its specific context, including the power relations that shape both capital–capital and capital–labour relations. Drawing on our case studies, these controversies are explored in Chapters 9–11. Chapter 9 focuses on the impact of organizational change on skills, both in terms of job design—skill in the job—and the provision of training for individual workers. In a context of permeable organizations, however, the potential influence of the network on the development of skills and the acquisition of knowledge also needs to be considered. One argument in support of the transition from internalized employment systems to reliance on a wider network is that labour mobility between companies (Finegold 1999)—and through strategic alliances and partnerships between companies—offers greater opportunities to learn from other organizations.

In the first place, there is a need to take into account the changes in the quantity and nature of tasks that arise simply as a result of the process of contracting. In particular, there is likely to be an increase in auditing and relational work, particularly for the key boundary spanners (see also Chapter 6). These developments also influence the number of layers of supervision and whether work outcomes are monitored by direct or indirect methods. The differing interests of clients and suppliers can also impact on work systems, taking a variety of forms. For example, clients may promote higher quality work through the supply chain with implications for HR policies. Alternatively, they may have a primarily short-term interest in work organization within the supplier company and as a consequence constrain the development of a longer-term approach designed to upskill the system of work organization and the training of employees. However, even where clients support a policy of skill development in principle, there may be conflict between clients' production requirements and their willingness to engage in relational contracting to enable the supplier to invest in skill development. There is a danger that fragmentation of the supply chain may result in an institutional failure to allocate responsibility for either the development of a skilled workforce or of new and more productive ways of working. Employers, even within integrated organizations, are reluctant to engage in training because of the asymmetry in costs and returns (Cappelli et al. 1997; Crouch 1997). The former are immediate and certain, the latter longer-term and uncertain, dependent not only on the stability and cooperation of trained staff but also on the continuation of the business contract for which the skills are relevant. When multiple organizations or agencies are involved, opportunities to pass the buck increase. Employers may be even more tempted to rely on the skills produced by other firms in the network without considering how these skills will be reproduced in the future. Relatively powerful employees may demand training to enhance their employability, but there is an immediate dilemma for management in that this can increase staff turnover among groups of workers they are keen to retain. These problems may be exacerbated in inter-organizational networks as individual employees can sample external opportunities as well as demonstrate their skills to alternative employers. Not only is there a danger that specific skills will be in short supply in the future, but also organizations may lose the internal capacity to produce those skills, even if they should later consider returning to in-house provision (Cooke 2003). In short, networks may encourage the pursuit of short-term solutions to skill development, if only because permeable boundaries make the protection of internal investments even more risky. Moreover, while there may be a need for greater specialization, and potentially for more flexible organizational forms suited to the particular work processes of highly skilled 'knowledge' workers, this optimistic analysis pays little attention to the issue of where knowledge is developed, nor by whom it is funded or controlled. The notion of sharing knowledge does not fit easily into the resource-based view of the firm where comparative advantage depends upon developing unique forms of knowledge and skill. Whether network arrangements lead to sharing of knowledge or learning is thus an empirical issue, dependent upon power relations and the nature of activities involved in specific inter-organizational relationships.

The potential impact of fragmentation on gender equalities and gender relations at work is also similarly contingent and variable, as we see in Chapter 10. While there is validity in the argument that the bureaucratic form was based on the male model of continuous career full-time workers and that the organizational cultures that developed around the bureaucratic form were reflections of male power and masculine values, it does not follow that their replacement with new, more flexible, or open systems will necessarily *promote* gender equality. Fracturing the system opens up possibilities for change and creates new employment opportunities for groups that have been excluded historically, but now show themselves to be both committed and able to work at a high level. In that sense, restructuring is likely to provide new opportunities for women that might remain closed in a slowly changing system. Furthermore, there are opportunities for more flexible arrangements, capable of adapting to a wide range of lifestyles and participation patterns and more opportunities for the use of 'feminine skills'—such as communication skills—due to an increase in relational work. Against these arguments, however, one must recognize some limitations and dangers. It is possible that as women move into new employment areas, these jobs become feminized and thereby downgraded (see Reskin and Roos 1990; and Crompton and Sanderson 1990 for examples from the United States and the United Kingdom). Moreover, more flexible arrangements do not prevent these divergences from the standard employment relationship being used as a means of differentiation and marginalization. Finally, progress at the workplace towards gender equality has come, in part, through the development of equal opportunities policies integrated within a wider HR framework. The fragmentation of organizations and devolution of responsibility for HRM to line managers and to supplier companies can put these policies in jeopardy. This problem has been recognized in particular in relation to the gains in equal pay through new job evaluation schemes in the public sector, and trade unions have included in their campaign against the two-tier work-force in the public sector the right for equal value job grading to be retained when work is transferred to the private sector.

We examine the implications of inter-organizational contracting for worker voice and representation in Chapter 11. The trade union campaign in 2002/3 about the two-tier workforce might suggest that trade unions are now begin-ning to focus on the need to intervene in the shaping of inter-organizational relations if they wish to influence the employment relationship and protect condition. The historical role of trade unions and collective bargaining in the United Kingdom has been restricted primarily to the regulation and protection of workers' economic interests, narrowly defined at the sectoral, company, or workplace level, with limited opportunities to engage in policy debates at the societal and national level (Crouch 2003a). This traditional orientation has left these institutions exposed to the impact of economic restructuring, as their only legitimate voice has been within organizations that have voluntarily entered into recognition agreements. Where these have disappeared or been restructured away from organized establishments, union influence has declined. Moreover, it is only through membership of the European Union that the United Kingdom is moving towards a comprehensive set of minimum labour standards. The voluntary tradition in the United Kingdom has meant that collective bargaining agreements have not been generalized to cover whole sectors, and until the 1980s trade unions remained highly sceptical of using the legal system to provide minimum rights because they saw this as a potential challenge rather than as a complement to collective bargaining—at least in areas such as minimum wage policy. Furthermore, the lack of legitimacy at the national level excludes unions from debates about the restructuring of the economic and social system, in contrast to the experience in many other EU member states where, as one half of the social partners, unions are formally involved in wider policy issues.

The emphasis on company-level bargaining has been at the expense of industry or sector level negotiations that would have provided a labour market level of protection. Although the unions themselves were initially keen on company-level bargaining, this later became the preferred policy of Conserv-ative governments. Through the dismantling of sector level agreements and the focus on voluntary agreement at the most 'relevant' local level, the UK labour market system was ideally structured to favour devolution, outsourcing, and contracting so as to secure reductions in wage costs. This was the explicit objective of the compulsory competitive tendering policy in the public sector in the early 1980s, introduced at the same time as the rescinding of the fair wages resolution that removed the need for public sector contractors to pay fair—that is, collectively agreed—wages. It was only pressure on the UK gov-ernment to apply the TUPE Regulations to public as well as private sector work-ers that prevented privatization being used as a device to cut the wages of transferred staff. Nevertheless, the lack of a comprehensive collective bargaining system left many transferred workers, together with new recruits of private sector contractors in public services, facing worse conditions than under public sector employment. Overall, therefore, the decision by trade unions to focus attention on their strong points—well-organized companies and workplaces—ultimately left UK workers exposed to a contracting culture, where employers could reap significant benefits because there was limited employment protection. Furthermore, hostility towards trade unions in the 1980s and 1990s virtually guaranteed that most new companies were likely to develop outside the ambit of trade union influence.

Against this negative assessment, there is a counter argument that focusing on economic issues and concentrating activity at the workplace and company level can be a source of strength in an era when there is little legitimacy for broader social movements, involving alliances between trade unions and socialist movements. Moreover, since it is the organizational level where employers are trying to reshape employment relations, UK trade unions may be better placed to influence these developments than those union movements that are oriented primarily towards sectoral or national bargaining and whose legitimacy is now being challenged by the business community as a cause of inflexibility. It is in this vein that the trade unions in the United Kingdom have focused on a modernization agenda, and in particular on the development of the partnership and organizing approaches (Heery 2002; Waddington 2003).

The partnership approach rests on the assumption that the best way for trade unions to protect and enhance their members' interests is to cooperate with employers in order to achieve mutual gains. It is argued that employers are more prepared to offer good wages and conditions, employment security, and training if workers agree to operate flexibly, contribute to improved decision-making through involvement and participation, and show commitment to organizational goals. The pay-off for trade unions under this scenario is that they are offered recognition, allowed access to new recruits and given time for meetings during working time, as well as being provided with information and guaranteed access to senior managers. As with high commitment HRM, partnership rests on the win–win assumption of mutual gains. The TUC has lent support for this approach through its Partnership Institute and its collaboration with the Involvement and Participation Association (IPA) (Coupar and Stevens 1998). Even proponents of partnership (e.g. Guest and Peccei 2001) acknowledge the balance of advantage lies with management more than it does with workers and trade unions. Most of the quoted studies are drawn from simple organizational forms, often in a single industry or a single workplace. In these circumstances it is relatively easy to visualize the benefits that might flow from having an agreement covering the entire workforce that can identify with the employer to try and beat off the competition.

The ability of partnerships to secure advantages for unions in a multi-agency context is much more doubtful given the presence of potentially conflicting objectives both between workers and between organizations. Tensions are always likely across a network because competing firms have different interests and requirements from the business contract. This can also spill over into relations between workers on different contracts, either through pressures on terms and conditions of employment or through the allocation of blame for failure to other actors in the network. This can be exacerbated if penalties are invoked for poor performance or there is a strong likelihood that business contracts will be cancelled. If suppliers work for a large number of clients on contracts of varying lengths and complexity, they are unlikely to want to be tied into a partnership agreement across the board for fear that this will remove any flexibility. Moreover, if these business contracts are for quite different types of service and require workers with specific technical skills, there are few opportunities for transferring workers from one contract to another. In this situation, therefore, employers will see little advantage in being tied into a long-term partnership deal, which promises employment security for all workers. Although some employers may actively use agency workers who perform well as a source of future recruitment, most are likely to view them as a cost rather than as a resource and there is little prospect of them receiving any of the potential advantages that flow from partnership. Indeed, a strong partnership deal between unions and management at a particular organization may actually worsen the position of contingent workers as the core organization seeks to cut costs elsewhere, especially if a major reason for subcontracting has been to shift risk to a third party. 'Permanent' staff might also have negative views about agency workers, partly because they are seen as a threat to their own continued employment, but also because some agency workers in areas of skill shortage are able to earn premium rates without necessarily having equivalent skills. In short, there are immense difficulties in making partnerships work effectively across organizational boundaries.

For the partnership strategy to be influential, it presupposes the orientations of large companies are geared towards effective performance in the real economy. This assumption can be challenged by evidence that UK organizations are primarily interested in financial returns (Froud et al. 2000), and by association, growth through acquisition rather than success in developing and consolidating their share of specific markets. Without a production orientation, the case for social partnership at the level of the organization, from the perspective of the employer, becomes much weaker. Furthermore, there have to be further commitments to internalize most production activities or extend partnership arrangements to include subcontractors and business partners. Neither of these commitments appears on the agenda in current debates about partnership.

The organizing approach puts a primacy on recruiting new members rather than servicing existing ones, and in attempting to develop workers (and worker representatives) so that they can deal directly with their own problems rather than having to rely on full-time officials. This works on the principle that grass roots activism is the best way to mobilize and sustain union renewal because it is embedded within the workplace. As with partnership, the organizing model has been supported by the TUC through the Organizing Academy (Heery and Abbot 2000). Similar conceptual problems arise in relation to the organizing model when it is applied across organizational boundaries, especially if networks do not have the benefit of long-standing and well-developed union agreements. Attempts to organize across business contracts would not only be difficult but would not provide leverage for new recognition or bargaining agreements as union recognition procedures are based on the presumption of single employer workplaces. The difficulty of mobilizing workers in a non-union environment, either through a partnership or an organizing approach, is well documented (Terry 2003), especially if management takes a negative stance towards unions. This is yet more difficult if work is fragmented and undertaken by workers who have little opportunity to compare notes about their employment conditions. Moreover, it requires remarkable resilience for agency staff openly to declare themselves as willing to be a union representative in an environment where it is known that unions are not welcomed. The possibility is that they will not have completed their training, let alone started to mobilize other workers, before the contract comes to an end. Furthermore, unions are unlikely to reap immediate benefits trying to organize groups of workers in small workplaces, especially if they are on short-term contracts or do agency work.

Rather than trying to create closer relations with other staff working for the same organization but employed at different workplaces, an alternative approach might be to secure pacts or develop relations with similar workers employed by different organizations at the same workplace. Potentially, this could be a source of strength in PPPs where workers have been transferred from the public sector under TUPE arrangements and retain their union membership and connections with other members of the same union branch. However, at a minimum, this depends on the new employer continuing to allow time off for meetings and on a core of transferred workers remaining committed to union activity.

Much of the analytical problem is that industrial relations—like human resource management and employment law—is predicated on assumptions of a hierarchical and bounded relationship between an individual employer and its employees. Most UK definitions of the subject focus on the single employer–employee relationship, with a strong emphasis on the contested nature of workplace activity. Even though they may have disagreed on most issues, even Clegg (1970) and Hyman (1975) both conceived of industrial relations in terms of the employment relationship ('institutions of job regulation' and 'control of work processes', respectively). The current leading industrial relations text (Edwards 2003: 9) takes a similar line in locating the employer–employee relationship at the centre of the system, not explicitly recognizing that workers at one site may be employed by other organizations. Similarly, analysis of trade union renewal focuses on the recruitment of traditionally under-represented groups such as part-time workers, women, ethnic minorities and young people (Terry 2003; Waddington 2003), and new initiatives are typically examined within the confines of de facto enterprise unionism, both within the organizing and the partnership models (Heery 2002). There is no systematic consideration of whether or how agency workers might be represented at the workplace or how trade unions might seek to organize and mobilize workers in a multi-client workplace subject to competing demands from different clients.

Other literature also tends to suffer from this limited perspective. For example, Taylor (2002) focuses on how bargaining agendas have shrunk dramatically *within* organizations and that a 'representation gap' has emerged due to declining levels of union membership. The key question for unions, therefore, according to this analysis, is how to repair problems within organizations to prevent further declines in membership. A further problem is that many scholars treat forces beyond the level of the organization—such as product market pressures or supply chain links—as if they were important merely in terms of setting the context within which employment is regulated, and therefore not open to influence by actors within the organization. The notion that customers might seek to actively influence and control employment relations within the firm is rarely addressed explicitly and generally the employer–employer relationship is seen as totally separate from the employer–client relationship. Similar assumptions are also evident in studies of public sector employment relations, and even if there is explicit reference to privatization or contracting out of services to the private sector (Mathieson and Corby 1999), these are seen as contextual influences rather than a key part of the process of setting terms and conditions. There is no analysis of how the dynamics of interaction between organizations in the two sectors might shape and influence patterns of employment relations.

3.5   Conclusions

From each of the perspectives examined in this chapter, there is a clear need to escape the limitations of analysing the employment relationship within the box that is bounded by the single employing organization. The reality is altogether more complex. The definition of the individual employment relationship as between one legal entity—the employing organization—and an individual employee is incongruent with the situation where individuals are contracted by organizations who are engaged in complex inter-organizational relations. Other agents act instead of, or in addition to, the 'legal' employer to control employment relations and shape terms and conditions of employment. Furthermore, protection of the individual employment contract provided by the legal framework at times of merger or takeover, results in another employing organization being required to contract under the same terms and conditions as the previous employer.

The problems that arise in the management of employment in a context of inter-organizational relations are not, however, only related to issues of mismatch between the regulatory form and the social context. The situating of employing organizations in a web of inter-organizational relations provides a framework through which we can understand the development of employment relations in the context of the restructuring of capital–capital relations. The twin tensions between cooperation and conflict underpin both capital–capital and capital–labour relations. These tensions and opposing tendencies need to be considered conjointly rather than separately. Just as we need to reject simplistic notions that employment relations are formed solely by the promotion of mutual gains or by the pursuit of conflict, so we need to recognize that inter-firm relations rely on elements of cooperation, competition, and dominance. Moreover, as the employment relationship is a central aspect of organizational activities, so the management of the cooperation/competition dynamics of inter-firm relations interact with and shape the internal form of the employment relationship.

We implicitly reject the notion of a dichotomy between the internal, sheltered labour market on the one hand and market-mediated employment forms on the other. Instead the internal labour market reflects the influence of both internal objectives and the external environment in which it is located (Grimshaw and Rubery 1998; Beynon et al. 2002), including the influence of inter-organizational relations. This approach suggests that effective employment protection depends not only on collective regulation at the organization level but also on the institutionalization of the external environment in which the organization is located. In order to cope with fragmenting production systems, institutionalism needs to be rebuilt through regulatory mechanisms that apply universally across the labour market or the supply chain and provide effective countervailing power to the new configurations of capital.

4

The Strategic Management of Contracting in the Private Sector

MARILYN CARROLL, STEVEN VINCENT, JOHN HASSARD,
AND FANG LEE COOKE

4.1 Introduction

This chapter focuses on structures and outcomes in contractual relationships between private sector firms in Britain. In line with the rest of this volume, we draw on institutionalist perspectives. These encourage researchers to look beyond functionalist and managerial approaches to organizational structure and strategy in order to understand how particular outcomes are embedded within particular social structures and relations (also see Granovetter 1985; DiMaggio and Powell 1991). As argued in Chapter 2, concepts of power, risk, and trust are central to structures of inter-organizational relationships. Here, we assess this proposition against data from three cases of private–private contracting: ceramic tableware manufacturers, a chemical pigments producer and a range of its suppliers, and an airport.

This chapter is divided into five sections. In Section 4.2 we briefly review the existing literature on contractual relations. Section 4.3 introduces the three private–private contracting case studies. Section 4.4 highlights those institutional factors which strongly influence the contracting and outsourcing strategies of the case study firms. In Section 4.5 we examine more closely the reasons behind the firms' decisions to outsource or retain activities in-house, whether these have resulted in performance gains or costs, and the nature of risk, trust, and power relationships between the firms involved in the contractual arrangements. Finally, in Section 4.6 we summarize and contrast the findings from our three case studies.

4.2 Strategy and structure in British outsourcing

The literature on outsourcing throws up a variety of, sometimes contradictory, ideas about the uses of contractual relationships. Domberger (1998) suggests four rationales for strategic outsourcing that may elicit competitive advantage for the firm. First, *capacity outsourcing* is associated with the supplementation of internal processes to accommodate peaks and troughs in demand. Here, outsourcing can provide firms with greater flexibility and productivity by using subcontractors to cover fluctuating demands for labour (Cooke 2001). This 'just-in-time' deployment of human resources also brings savings that are both direct (e.g. reducing headcount and overtime working) and indirect (e.g. cutting administration and backup costs, saving recruitment and training costs, cutting down time, and reducing industrial relations problems). Second, *specialized outsourcing* is associated with niche economies where a firm may profit from the rising comparative advantage of specialized service providers. These firms may be able to 'achieve economies of scale, exert monopsony buying power, achieve greater workforce flexibility, pay lower wages, etc.' (NEDO 1986: 54), and therefore accomplish tasks at a cost lower than in-house provision.

Third, and in potential contradiction to the previous rationale, companies may enter into outsourcing arrangements due to the *market discipline* provided by organizations competing to win business. Here, the more specialized the business activity, the lower the degree of competition, thus limiting the extent of market discipline. Finally, Domberger highlights *cost reduction* as a prominent reason for outsourcing often linked to the previous rationales. Costs may be reduced in a variety of ways, for example, by transferring staff to another organization to divide trade union coverage. In general, outsourcing may create various opportunities for firms to shift the burden of risk and uncertainty associated with the business (Williamson 1985).

Coombs and Battaglia (1998) make another useful distinction. They note that the term 'outsourcing' was originally used to refer to firms externalizing activities previously undertaken internally. The definition was then expanded to include the use of other organizations to extend and acquire capabilities. The boundary between the two types of contracting is somewhat blurred as in reality organizations often attempt both to externalize activities previously undertaken in-house and to improve on issues such as quality, diversity, and performance (ibid.).

The strategic management literature also encourages consideration of the relationship between what firms do and what they contract for. Here, the distinction between 'core' and 'peripheral' outsourcing has provided a useful heuristic. Core outsourcing is associated with the firm's main domain(s) of expertise. Peripheral outsourcing, on the other hand, relates to activities that do not affect this core activity. The boundary between the two concepts is vague and open to interpretation, and writers are in conflict over the degree to which it is possible or desirable to contract in supposedly 'core' areas. On the positive side, under the right conditions contracting relationships can create partnerships between contractors and clients that may facilitate learning and cross-fertilization between the two firms (Powell et al. 1996; Child and Faulkner 1998). This is seen to be particularly appropriate where the benefits of knowledge acquisition outweigh the risks associated with the loss of firm-specific knowledge to the wider market (Matusik and Hill 1998).

Other writers contradict this view and present evidence that outsourcing can lead to serious problems in maintaining continuity in skill supply (MacKenzie 2000; Marchington et al. 2003; Vincent and Grugulis 2004). In many cases firms seek to outsource skilled work to save associated training costs and assume that the new supplier will complete the task. In light of the widely reported UK skill shortages, outsourcing may be a cause of skill loss to manufacturing industry where the stock of craft abilities takes a long time to build up. As Prahalad and Hamel (1990: 84) so succinctly point out, '[o]utsourcing can provide a shortcut to a more competitive product, but it typically contributes little to building the people-embodied skills that are needed to sustain product leadership'. It would seem that a variety of outcomes have been observed. We suggest that in order to understand why this variation occurs a broader frame of reference is required to consider how relationships emerge from and are embedded within a particular set of social relationships (also see Sayer and Walker 1992; Ackroyd 2002).

Marsden (1999) draws on transaction cost economics to consider how outcomes are affected by the relationship between contractual specifications and the environment within which they are embedded. In entering into exchange relationships organizations have to make choices about the type of contract used. The economic advantages of a strictly specified contract (*ex-ante* specification) are related to market competition as the price of exactly specified goods can be compared to the price of the same goods elsewhere. The economic advantages of a loosely specified contract (*ex-post* specification) relate to 'uncertainty about demand and the difficulty and resultant costs of defining all the relevant information' (1999: 237; also see Williamson 1975, 1985). The more complex and/or uncertain the externalized activity, the more likely the contracting firm has to rely on a strong, trusting relationship with the contracting partner to deliver the expected level and quality.

Outcomes also depend on the way that trust and power are embedded within the socio-economic structure of the relationship. Sako (1992) makes a similar distinction to Marsden. Hers is between arm's length contractual relations (ACR), where requirements tend to be specified in advance, and obligational contractual relations (OCR) where relations are continuously negotiated and redefined over time (see Chapter 2). Laws and broader social regulations play a crucial role in determining which contractual form is chosen. For Sako, Britain's relatively weak regulatory context pushes inter-organizational relations towards the ACR type as, unlike her comparator case, Japan, there are few definite structures encouraging corporate cooperation. In a similar study of contracting in Britain and Germany, Lane and Bachmann (1997) conclude that strong forms of regulation—derived from a more legalistic orientation towards trade associations and firm governance—encourage 'systems trust' and more cooperative forms of behaviour in Germany as outcomes are more predictable. In the United Kingdom, because there are few institutionalized codes to make behaviour predictable, 'potential trustors are more likely to use their power since they find it easier to bear the risk of open conflict than the risk of misplaced trust'

(Bachmann 1999: 24). Trust, risk, and power are intertwined within organizational fields, and are thus central to the dynamics of inter-organizational contracting (see also Chapter 6).

Firm structure would also seem to be important. The resource-based view of firm strategy asserts that managers seek competitive advantage by exploiting the organization's internal strengths, or sources of economic advantage, and reacting to particular external opportunities (Barney 1991). From this perspective, the structure of resources that the organization has, the social structure of markets (where opportunities are identified) and the type of contract used are intimately tied together. Boxall and Steenveld's (1999) study of engineering consultancies argues that a critical mass of well-managed human assets or 'table stakes' is required to operate as an effective unit within this particular sector. Where an organization is unable or unwilling to meet these table stakes they will be obliged to use a consultant-engineering firm for any services needed. This is despite the fact that the knowledge these workers develop can be vital to the firm's continuing economic viability. Also, given the complex and contingent nature of engineering work, the firm receiving the service may find it difficult to specify tightly the contract at the outset. From this perspective the power relationship between the organizations is, in part, associated with the degree to which one organization is dependent on the others for human or capital resources in order to remain competitive. Indeed, commentators have observed that contractual forms of organization are rarely conducted between equals (Friedman 1977; Dore 1996; see Chapter 2), meaning that one organization is often in a position to dictate the terms of the contract to the other (also see Roper et al. 1997).

In summary we argue that while the strategy literature has done much to extend our understanding of the risks and rewards associated with different forms of private sector contracting, it has done less to inform its audience about where particular risks or rewards will occur. In order to understand outcomes, we suggest a broader ranging analysis is required that considers the relationship between the form of contracting taken, the embedding of the contract within a particular set of institutionalized practices, and the distribution of power and dependencies between the parties to the contract. The use of power to extract value from the deal is likely to stop short of compromising the viability of the economic relationship as a whole (Krepps 1990; Dore 1996). However, who bears the risks, how trust is formed between the organizations, and how social practices are affected are subject to wide variation depending on how transactions are embedded within a particular social space.

4.3   Introducing the case studies

This chapter focuses on three case studies that involve contracting arrangements between private sector organizations (Table 4.1). Our first case study is that of ceramics manufacturing in North Staffordshire. This has been described

Table 4.1. Contracting arrangements in the three case studies

	Client firm	Provider firm	Types of contracting
Ceramics	Domestic China and other ceramics manufacturers	Ceramics producers overseas	Overseas outsourcing (cost reduction and/or product diversification)
		Other local ceramics manufacturers	Local district outsourcing (capacity and specialist products)
Chemicals	Scotchem	Transport, cleaning, and raw materials suppliers	High trust, non-contractual, and collaborative relations
	Scotchem	Securiforce	Low trust, increasingly contractual, and non-cooperative relations
Airport	Airportco	Ancillary service providers such as cleaning	High trust, non-contractual and collaborative relations
	Airlines (e.g. Airlines A, B, and C)	Other airlines, baggage and passenger handlers, aircraft cleaning, and catering firms	Single and multi-tier contracting relations, varying strategies, and levels of cooperation
	Handling firms (e.g. BH, FH)	Other baggage and passenger handling firms	Single and multi-tier contracting relations, varying strategies, and levels of cooperation

as 'the last industrial district' of its kind in the United Kingdom (Day et al. 2000) with a concentration of manufacturers and suppliers within a 7-mile radius of Stoke-on-Trent. As we see, despite institutional forces encouraging common forms of behaviour, the competitive context conspires to create considerable variety in contracting arrangements, with some retaining local suppliers and others sourcing products overseas. Given the shrinkage of the industry as a whole, overseas outsourcing brings into question the long-term viability of the district (Carroll et al. 2002).

Like firms in the ceramics industry, Scotchem operates in an increasingly competitive environment, with considerable pressure from Asia where cheap products are made. It has maintained a leading position within the sector, but feels increasingly under pressure to innovate—to experiment with new technologies, products, and organizational practices in order both to reduce costs and differentiate itself from its rivals. Scotchem's contracting has been affected by this more competitive context. In particular, Scotchem has sought to innovate and save money through various relationships with suppliers, ancillary services, and haulage firms. As we see, the distribution of risks and rewards in each of these areas is affected by the structure of the industry and the regulations that exist within the chemicals sector (Marchington and Vincent 2004).

Increasing levels of competition are a feature of all the case studies. However, while in the ceramics and chemicals cases this comes from other organizations competing in the sector, in the Airport case, additional competitive pressure comes from the anti-monopoly regulations. Here, baggage handling was opened to competition precisely because it had been a lucrative monopoly for Airportco. Airportco has retained three functions deemed to be essential for running the airport safely, namely engineering, security, and the fire service. It contracts out all other services. The customer airlines regard aviation as their main business and usually outsource everything else including passenger and baggage handling. In turn, the handling firms may subcontract work between each other, for example, where a firm specializes in either passenger or baggage handling and then re-subcontracts the non-specialist part of the operation to another handling firm. All this creates a complex web of contracting and subcontracting arrangements at the airport (Rubery et al. 2003).

4.4 Institutions of social practice in contractual relations

The nature of inter-organizational relations is mutually influenced by social practices at the levels of the sector, the organization, and the individual (Marchington and Vincent 2004). This multi-levelled approach to analysis helps to distinguish between different forms of social practice and how these relate to outcomes. Here, we consider the organization and sector level practices in terms of how these affect contracting decisions (individual level practices are considered in Chapter 6). When managers in our cases were asked about the factors that affected contractual relations they mentioned variously the local community, employees (and how these were controlled), trade unions and trade associations, the legal requirements of the government, competitors, customers, suppliers, and the wider labour market, as well as the nature of the capital resources available. Moreover, managers placed different emphases on these factors in each of our cases.

Significant community based socio-economic forces at the level of the sector and organization have long shaped and framed industrial behaviour in the Potteries. Commercial potting has taken place in the area since the fifteenth century and until fairly recently owner-management was typical. Even in some of the larger firms family involvement remains strong. These family ties have helped to preserve links between firms through social networks and institutions (such as the Potters' [dining] Club where managers meet and discuss issues of common concern). Collaboration in manufacturing improvement and joint problem solving is also facilitated by CERAM, the Research and Technology organization for the industry, and the fact that some leading firms jointly own one of the major raw materials processing plants. Close proximity to suppliers of raw materials and manufacturing equipment is seen as a distinct advantage by firms in the area—relationships can be preserved and problems resolved quickly and less formally. Although the firms compete for market share, these close relationships and shared interests also mean that there is a great deal of cooperation, as demonstrated by a number of collaborative outsourcing arrangements between ceramics manufacturers in the local area.

Scotchem's parent company, Multichem, was created recently following the merger of two large pharmaceutical companies, and the 'spin off' of their industrial chemicals facilities to form a new company. Since then there have been various changes at the organizational level in an attempt to reduce fixed costs and increase the competitiveness of the business. The company now holds 'strategic stock' and its unionized employees are required to work with increased flexibility, transferring between one batch-run and another more quickly than before. Multichem's strategy is to present a coherent and strong brand image associated with quality and reliability in a variety of related industrial chemicals. It uses a global web of regional selling organizations that sell the full range of products, cross-selling wherever appropriate. Scotchem is relatively protected from the worst vagaries of the market by Multichem's advantageous position as one of the leading firms in the global market for quality industrial chemicals. There are significant opportunities associated with its subsidiary status, and the particular value-added strategy that Multichem operates.

A large organization such as an airport makes a strong impact on the local community, and Airportco is keen to be perceived as an ethical organization by using a range of strategies involving local authorities, the community, and the labour force. The business objective of Airportco is to promote economic growth and development in the area and, in turn, enhance air travel. This strategy also sits well with Airportco's prevailing local authority culture and ethos, which includes avoiding redundancies and keeping essential activities such as security in-house. As a senior manager of BH, a baggage handling firm and subsidiary of Airportco observed:

Sometimes a director has different responsibilities and accountabilities to that of a shareholder, and sometimes that does affect the way in which things are done . . . the shareholders obviously want the airport to be successful and do not want to be associated with an airport that is having difficulties, industrial disputes or any form of disruption that may impact upon the perception the community would have. (BH, Managing Director, male)

In all these cases, therefore, contractual forms are dependent on the pre-existing market structures and nature of social regulation within particular sectors, as well as the way that particular firms are embedded therein. Subcontracting manufacturing to other producers, both local and overseas, remained a viable possibility within the Potteries, not least due to the weaker regulations and independence of the management. However, at Scotchem this possibility is closed off due to the strategic opportunities and constraints imposed by Multichem, the paucity of viable contractors in the wider market, and the nature of regulation within the chemicals sector generally. Airportco has roots in the public sector and its decisions are influenced by objectives promoting economic growth and development in the region and being seen as a responsible employer by the local community. It has defined three services as central to its operation that involve significant health and safety risks and carries these out in-house. These include security, an activity that many organizations regard as 'peripheral' and contract out. This calls into question an assumed distinctiveness of core and peripheral activities and suggests a strong relationship between what is defined as 'core' or 'periphery' and the interaction observed between the organization and the context within which it operates. In the following section we shed further light on the subject by looking at the reasons for outsourcing and considering how risks and rewards are, to a certain extent, determined by how particular relationships are socially embedded.

4.5   Socially embedding risk and reward in contractual relations

Rationale—how and where to contract?

Before considering in detail contractual relations in the ceramics case it is worth noting that the nature of outsourcing within the industry has been constantly changing and continues to do so. Even the term 'outsourcing' itself is used in different ways in this context. Traditionally, 'local outsourcing'—that is, subcontracting among firms within the local district—both of material supplies and finished, or part-finished products has been a feature of the industry. As one manager pointed out:

We used to make our own clay, glaze, colours, grind our own gold . . . but that's now been pushed out to specialist suppliers, so we're all assemblers, that's what we are. We are designers and assemblers. So we have been outsourcing for thirty or forty years in terms of material supplies. (Fine China, Manager 1, Male)

Outsourcing of ceramics production tends to happen when a company runs into problems with manufacturing capacity or where there is a small run that needs to be produced. The advantage is that control can be maintained over production and capacity can be freed up so that other more lucrative work can be completed in-house. Both the Employers' Confederation and Trade Union regard outsourcing locally as quite traditional behaviour. As a Director at the Employers' Confederation noted, 'they've always been in each other's pockets in that sense' (British Ceramics Confederation 1, male).

Domestic China has subcontracting arrangements to produce tableware for other local manufacturers, including Qualityware. Although there are sometimes issues about quality, industry managers trust local producers who they know are perfectly capable of producing the product to the required standard and the product can still display the 'Made in England' back-stamp. As a director of Qualityware confirmed:

We source some stuff through Domestic China at the moment, because they are better at making that particular component than we are. And we will do that in specific areas where it is absolutely what the market needs, because when you buy Qualityware you expect it to be made in England. (Qualityware, Manager 1, male)

Ceramics manufacturers also outsource non-standard products to specialist firms within the area. For example, Hotel China outsources a range of cookware to a local specialist, and Fine China outsources ceramic door furniture and non-ceramic, branded items such as tablemats, napkins, and enamel boxes.

In another type of arrangement indicating the close ties between local companies, in the processing of raw materials Domestic China has entered into a joint venture with Hotel China, Hospitalityware, and another manufacturer to purchase their own body preparation mill,[1] described as 'a comfortable arrangement':

We carve up the profits and, depending on turnover, you get the biggest slice. And we get the biggest slice because we take the biggest amount of volume out of that . . . The MD and his team at that factory, the only confidentiality there is that they do not divulge the recipe of the body to any other member of the consortium, simple as that! (Domestic China, Manager 2, male)

Outsourcing overseas is a recent and more controversial development. There is little doubt that this can be cheaper than continuing to source all orders in-house, as wage levels are often far lower abroad. The lower priced end of the ceramic tableware market has been particularly hard hit by international competition and firms that do not occupy a favourable position as a strong 'aspirational' or niche brand producer are more frequently choosing to exploit low cost overseas labour markets, where 'rare' skills are more widely available. Even well-known 'upmarket' producers such as Qualityware have chosen to have some of their lower priced ranges produced overseas. This is done either by opening plants abroad which, as Carroll et al. (2002) note, is often still referred to as 'outsourcing' within the industry, or by subcontracting manufacture to companies in developing countries. Where competition is fiercest, the powers of traditional institutional forces appear to have been undermined as leading firms explore these opportunities.

Domestic China, for example, is an export-oriented company that has out-sourced production extensively to overseas companies in recent years. At the 'top' end of the market it is difficult for the company to compete because it does not have a strong brand image or well-known name. At the lower 'cut-throat' end of the market retailers are constantly exerting pressure to drive prices down. Combined with cheap overseas imports, this has forced a number of competitors out of business. Outsourcing at Domestic China started with bone china goods supplied from an Indian factory followed by hand painted goods from China. Domestic China now buys in products from several Asian countries, as well as Eastern Europe and South America—'all the low wage countries around the world, basically' (Domestic China, Manager 5, male).

Although the overall decision to outsource overseas was based on cheaper costs, according to Domestic China's General Manager (Sourced Products), the choice of supplier depends less on price than the relationship with the supplier and the potential risks associated with quality issues. Managing this relation-ship became crucial following the outsourcing of bone chinaware to India, which replaced Domestic China's competencies in hand decorating (hand banding and lithography, for example) and led to some loss of local skills. The company now sees its two main competencies as under-glaze print and auto-mated mechanized multicolour printing on flatware, and will not risk informa-tion about these processes falling into the hands of its contractors. Transfer of knowledge in the form of manufacturing expertise takes place only so that the overseas company is able to manufacture to the required standards. The General Manager of the unit concerned said: 'We will give them a little tit-bit and bring them through as we develop further and further the more sophist-icated stuff' (Domestic China, Manager 2, male).

The Ceramics and Allied Trades Union (CATU) has mixed views on the effects of overseas outsourcing on the local economy. On the one hand, it is felt that this can devalue the product and exploit workers in countries with low pay and poor terms and conditions. On the other hand, it has enabled some firms to stay in business and continue to employ local people: 'Is it better to lose a few to look after the many? Or do you say, "we're not going to accept this at any cost and we'll fight to keep production here?" It's a difficult dilemma' (CATU 2, male).

The view of the Employers' Confederation is that manufacturing in Stoke-on-Trent brings a significant amount of 'value-added' to the product, as well as to the local 'heritage' industry (which the City Council is currently trying to pro-mote). However, they believe that this can coexist with a certain amount of overseas outsourcing. As an example Qualityware has a variety of its products manufactured abroad, but continues to invest heavily in its Stoke-on-Trent site and is a major tourist attraction.

Due to the potentially hazardous nature of the chemicals sector it is rela-tively highly regulated. Some regulations, such as those related to health and safety in handling hazardous materials, are statutory. Others are imposed voluntarily through the Chemicals Industries Association (CIA), reflecting the UK government's traditional abstention from industrial regulation. The role of the CIA has been to obviate the requirement for legal regulation through the establishment of strong voluntary codes within the industry. Here, the need to maintain a good image as a responsible member of the chemicals industry business community may be used as a lever to ensure that organizations adhere to a particular code of behaviour. 'Responsible Care', a Code of Conduct that is a precondition of membership of the CIA, has significant guidelines on inter-organizational relations (as well as intra-organizational relations). The Code specifies, for example, that procedures are needed to ensure that the potential risks associated with a particular contract are assessed and that contractors have a good health and safety track record.

Where possible, Scotchem uses its purchasing power both to lower prices and to drive though CIA regulations. For example, Scotchem has a list of pre-ferred haulage suppliers, with haulage firms concentrating on a particular route or a type of business. While one operator specializes in business with Switzerland and the Netherlands, another specializes in smaller loads of mixed goods and these firms may be played off against one another to secure price reductions. Also, as part of the Responsible Care agenda, Scotchem has pushed through a formal code of conduct for hauliers. This has regulated the behaviour of the haulage firms and individual drivers, who have had to incur additional costs in order to meet its requirements or simply not get any new work from Scotchem. The number of preferred suppliers reduced from about fifty-five to thirty as a result of implementing the Code of Conduct, suggesting that not all hauliers could operate with the costs of the more regulated context. However, those that remain are willing to accept the arrangement, and many of the larger firms appear content as they already operate with similar codes. (Indeed they thought the new Code of Conduct would remove 'cowboys' from the books, sta-bilizing the relations for those that remained and increasing their portion of the business.)

This more regulated context has affected Scotchem's outsourcing strategy as well as its expectations of those organizations that supply it. In marked contrast to Domestic China, this restricted the areas within which the organization might gain from outsourcing to 'low risk' ancillary services. Only cleaning and security services have been outsourced since Scotchem was created. These contracts all saved on labour costs as in-house staff were made redundant or offered early retirement and were replaced by cheaper staff employed by contractors.

The nature of contractual relations is also affected by the structure of the industry, which is dominated by a handful of companies in the 'value added' end of trading. Scotchem is reluctant to do business with these, as they are typ-ically direct competitors. However, the 'value-added' strategy of Multichem did lead to a very limited amount of outsourcing with competitor firms, particularly where Scotchem could not produce a pigment to a high standard. Multichem's sales organizations, which are formally separate from Scotchem, would purchase small quantities of some pigments so that they might offer customers the fullest possible range of high quality products. It is also common for Scotchem's competitors to purchase pigments from them for similar reasons. As with the ceramics industry, the bottom end of the market is more competitive; it is typically based in lower wage countries and provides fewer guarantees in relation to quality and reliability. Given its production strategy, Scotchem is also reluctant to cooperate closely with these firms. Where a suitable, non-competitor customer or supplier is found, long-term knowledge-sharing partnerships are likely to become established as both organizations are likely to have a vested interest in the other's survival (see also Chapter 6).

Airportco identified its three main activities as engineering maintenance, security, and the airport fire service, and all other services have been outsourced. Managers agreed that successful management of these three activities is vital to maintaining the airport's image as a conscientious local employer. As at Scotchem, the desire to protect the reputation of Airportco in the face of potential social regulation is important when considering the risks taken in these areas. The engineering department does outsource some activities, such as lift maintenance, on the basis of cost. However, the majority of the work is kept in-house with its own trusted staff. The engineering department has its own contract with the airlines and handling firms, stipulating that the airport's facilities—its buildings, utility supply, fixed equipment, and automatic walkways—must have an availability rate of at least 95 per cent. Meeting this obligation is seen as vital to the success of the airport.

The airlines normally contract for back-up services such as ground handling, aircraft cleaning, and catering. The main priority is that these services should be coordinated so flights can depart on time. As already noted, an intricate web of contracting and subcontracting arrangements exists, particularly between the airlines and the handling firms. Most handling contracts last for two or three years with a 60- or 90-day notice of change. Larger airlines sometimes offer longer (commonly five-year) contracts. Airline A, for example, a large UK carrier, contracts out 50 per cent of its functions. It operates its own passenger handling and aircraft despatch functions, but contracts out baggage handling services to BH. Another scheduled airline, a national carrier based outside the United Kingdom (Airline B) subcontracts its ground handling services to Airline A, which carries out passenger handling for Airline B but re-sub-contracts other services; baggage handling, for example, is subcontracted to BH. Airline A has won the handling contract with Airline B three times and, according to the Station Manager of Airline B, this was partly because of the positive public perception of Airline A and partly because 40 per cent of Airline B's managers used to work at Airline A.

There are many other examples of equally complex relationships. Airline C, a holiday charter airline, also contracts out all ground-handling services. Its main handling contract (passenger and baggage) is with BH—a subsidiary of

Airportco—and BH, in turn, subcontracts passenger handling, boarding and despatch to FH, an independent company that offers full handling services. There used to be a tacit arrangement between BH and FH that BH would only compete for contracts at Terminal 1 and FH at Terminal 2, to prevent wasteful duplication of handling equipment at each terminal. Each company would then subcontract its secondary business to the other, that is, BH would sub-contract the passenger handling to FH and FH would subcontract the baggage handling to BH. However, the relationship soured when BH took over the full handling contract with Airline C at Terminal 2 from FH. FH considers BH is encroaching on its territory. Although the Operations Director of Airline C said they had not been under any pressure by Airportco to change to BH, the General Manager of FH complained that deals had been done 'behind the scenes'.

These three very different cases illustrate the changing nature and complexity of contracting relationships and the difficulty of assuming a neat divide between the types of activities that are appropriate to outsource or retain in-house. In the following sections we consider the performance implications, and the nature of risk, trust, and power relationships between client and provider firms.

Performance gains or costs?

Despite the advantages of local subcontracting, the company performance of Domestic China improved dramatically following the decision to outsource some of its production overseas. In line with the industry's traditions, the controlling family was initially reluctant to take this route. However, during the 1990s the strength of the pound badly affected Domestic China's export market and in 1999, despite the success of the hotelware side of the business, the company made an overall loss for the first time in its history. The company responded by reducing the number of its UK sites and sourcing a proportion of its products overseas, thereby becoming profitable again within two years. The company had £200,000 worth of outsourced turnover in 1999, £3m in 2000, and approaching £7m in 2001. The expectation is that this trend will continue.

According to Domestic China managers, outsourcing abroad has brought many advantages. First, the cheaper cost of overseas production allows Domestic China to compete at the lower end of the market. Second, it can access skills—such as hand skills—that are in short supply in the United Kingdom, while continuing to develop in-house processes, such as automated multicolour printing, 'areas which we want to protect as core' (Domestic China, Manager 5, male). Third, it has been able to expand its product range into specialist areas, such as stoneware, which it does not manufacture in the United Kingdom. Although the product is made elsewhere, according to this same manager Domestic China's customers are still dealing with a name they know and trust. Fourth, Domestic China can design products employing techniques that it does not have. Fifth, buying in frees up manufacturing capacity in Stoke-on-Trent for use by other parts of the business, such as the successful hotelware side. Furthermore although the 'Made in England' back-stamp is not so import-ant at the cheaper end of the market, it is at the higher end, particularly for the export market, so Domestic China concentrates its UK manufacture on this type of product. Finally, Domestic China also offers advantages to its overseas manufacturers in terms of expertise in design, marketing, and distribution.

In contrast to the apparent evidence of performance gains in ceramics, con-tracting for the security function at Scotchem, which was strongly affected by the health and safety culture of the chemicals sector, led to additional costs associated with the management of risk. At the time of our research Scotchem was not successful in forcing the outsourcing firm, Securiforce, to accept these additional costs, and relations between the two were described as strained. Securiforce operates the gatehouse, which has responsibilities for managing goods and people on and off the site, some telephony duties, and special duties, in emergency situations. While the in-house service had traditionally transferred 'old hands' to the gatehouse from production facilities when they were nearing retirement, Securiforce employed workers on an agency basis. These workers had little local knowledge of the site personnel and industry standards and practices. This resulted in unforeseen costs associated with the need to change practices to suit this new social group. For example, whereas previously the gatehouse was flexible in communicating with the warehouse (e.g. to allow lorries on to the site as they arrived), Securiforce workers enforced a strict schedule that led to additional costs for lorries that arrived too early. Also, whereas previously the security guards knew the location and respons-ibilities of specific staff, and could direct visitors accordingly, other Scotchem employees now had to ensure that visitors were directed to the right place.

Securiforce did little to 'manage' these additional costs; the contract it held with Scotchem was not important to the overall success of its business. The Securiforce manager with responsibility for the Scotchem site was rarely pre-sent and there was no on-site supervisor with responsibility for coordinating local changes with Scotchem. For example, Securiforce was instructed to con-duct health and safety training for emergency procedures, but this had not been completed. There appeared little that Scotchem could do to change the situation other than not to renew the Securiforce contract, something that they had threatened to do previously but with little effect. One Manager said:

We've told them that we have put it out to tender, alright, to see what the other compan-ies are going to offer. We really feel as though this is trying to give them a kick up the backside. . . . The support coming from Securiforce could be far, far better. (Scotchem, Manager 8, male)

At the airport a positive example of a high performing subcontractor is CleanCo, which won the cleaning contract in the 1980s, and has since continued to tender successfully for the work, expanding into new areas of the site. There is no service level agreement—Airportco monitors the performance of CleanCo using three measures: cleaning quality measured by technical equipment, sickness absence, and turnover of cleaning staff. Managers on both sides work together, holding regular meetings, and they described the nature of the relationship between the two organizations as a partnership rather than contractual. According to CleanCo's Regional Manager, mutual learning between the organizations is about 'understanding each other's needs and about how CleanCo people learn to deal with Airportco people in order to keep the relationship smooth' (CleanCo, Manager 1, female).

Good contractual performance at the airport was certainly contingent on a willingness to monitor the contractor. Airline B placed great emphasis on quality and has a very 'hands on' approach. It has a station office at the airport that constantly monitors the performance of its subcontractors. As the Station Manager remarked:

Airline B will not accept poor quality of service from the handling firms, while other airlines will accept what they are given. Airline B built its reputation on quality and we have to maintain that image. (Airline B, Station Manager, male)

As mentioned previously, Airline B subcontracts ground handling to Airline A which carries out passenger handling but, in turn, subcontracts the baggage handling to BH. Airline B monitors the performance of BH although this should really be Airline A's responsibility. According to Airline B's Station Manager, Airline A does not have the resources to monitor performance and is 'very passive' about what happens. If Airline B is not happy with the service workers from the sub-subcontractor firms provide, it will approach them directly, even though it is not, strictly speaking, entitled to do so.

To summarize, the international market for ceramics manufacturing enabled ceramics firms such as Domestic China to take advantage of reduced costs of overseas outsourcing. Other ceramics firms, such as Fine China and Hotel China, did not outsource overseas but were happy to subcontract to other local firms whose performance standards were deemed acceptable. In the case of Scotchem, outsourcing of the security function reduced costs initially, but resulted in unanticipated costs as the service deteriorated and Scotchem managers had little success in trying to force improvements from Securiforce. At the airport there was no single, uniform strategy for managing the quality and performance of subcontractors. In the case of multi-tier outsourcing the question of who was responsible for monitoring performance standards of 'sub-subcontractors' (the client or the subcontractor) varied between contracts. Again these results question not only the notion of a clear distinction between core and peripheral activities, but also the assumption that it is the peripheral activities that more easily lend themselves to outsourcing. As we have seen, overseas outsourcing of 'core' products by Domestic

China had been (relatively) problem-free and resulted in a vast improvement in overall company performance, whereas outsourcing of a 'peripheral' activity (security) at Scotchem had resulted in serious performance issues.

Risk, trust, and power relations

The relationship between what the firm contracts for and how risks and rewards are embedded within a particular structure is well illustrated by the ceramics industry where there is a marked contrast between the types of organization that outsource overseas and those that do not. Although Domestic China's experience of outsourcing to foreign manufacturers has been characterized as positive, other manufacturers were unwilling to take on what they saw as too great a risk. In order to survive and succeed, 'upper end' ceramics firms chose to rationalize their product range and concentrate on niche markets, such as 'aspirational' tableware or hotelware. Despite the attraction of lower production costs, these firms had major anxieties about the quality and reliability of overseas sources. For example, managers at Hotel China stressed the importance of 'hands-on control'. Their experiences, on visits to countries such as Mexico, had been of poor manufacturing conditions and low quality standards. Managers at Fine China mentioned the difficulty of control 'at arm's length', the importance of retaining the 'Made in England' back-stamp and, crucially, the view that overseas outsourcing would mean compromising on quality, which would be hugely detrimental to the brand image.

Domestic China's managers took a different view. They identified two sorts of risk: the risk of problems when outsourcing to overseas suppliers, and the risk of currency fluctuations affecting the export market. Increasing currency risk acted as a pressure on Domestic China to consider outsourcing overseas. The level of supplier risk, on the other hand, depended on the type of product:

The supplier risk in ceramics isn't big unless you are into niches, so bone china and that type of stoneware. There is a little bit of risk there because there are not many people out there who can do it. If it is porcelain with a decal [printed transfer design] on it there are over three thousand manufacturers in China alone who can do that, so you can just chop and change. So the supply risk isn't huge. (Domestic China, Manager 5, male)

However, outsourcing overseas generated new risks for workers and firms in the Stoke-on-Trent area. Although redundancies had been a common occurrence in the ceramics industry Domestic China's managers stressed that they had tried to keep these to a minimum through natural wastage and redeployment. The shop floor workers seemed sympathetic to the pressures facing their employer, although many were evidently concerned for their long-term prospects:

They do try to keep the redundancies . . . as low as they can and keep us all in work. I know we've seen bad times, but they've always shuffled along . . . They are actually for the workers, I've got to admit that. (Domestic China, Production Worker 1, female)

At the moment there isn't anyone that can do the flatware as good as Domestic China can . . . but how many years before someone else is able to catch up?

Q. And the worry is that overseas will catch up?

Oh yes, definitely. Because they come round with the cameras and watch you. They're clicking. They come round from different countries and they bring their videos and their cameras (Domestic China, Production Worker 2, female).

Managers at Domestic China were fully aware that their actions could create risks for other manufacturers in North Staffordshire as overseas manufacturers caught up on the technical competencies of the region. This made the long-term employment prospects in the local industry look 'bleak'. As one senior manager predicted:

You are going to have one or two manufacturers left. Sad. I am caught up in the middle of it, and causing it at the same time as having to do it, because the margin we make on sourced product is big and fat and healthy, and it supports Domestic China's UK manu-facturing. (Domestic China, Manager 5, male)

As we saw in the previous section, Scotchem used its purchasing power in an attempt to spread the cost of risk management to its contractors. There were many other examples of the organization using its internal competences and purchasing power to spread risk. For example, Scotchem used its dominant position to defer risks associated with purchasing and managing raw materials. Many raw materials are required in order to produce pigments. These have varying degrees of importance, complexity, and rarity in the market. There were a few 'special' relationships with suppliers of the key ingredients that were the source of much collaborative work. In these special relationships Scotchem used its internal competencies to identify opportunities to diversify products and save costs, thus spreading risk (see Chapter 6). Typically, however, small independent agents were provided with a range of raw materials that they source for Scotchem. The agents are responsible for ensuring that the mater-ials are supplied in the right quality and quantity. As such, they act as a buffer between Scotchem and the raw materials suppliers, ensuring adjustments in demand and absorbing risks. As one agency manager confided:

We had one experience a couple of years ago where we bought a new product which was rejected. We have got two hundred thousand dollars worth of material we cannot get rid of and they wouldn't take it back, we had no strength with them at all so we had our fin-gers well and truly burnt. (Chemsupply, Manager 1, male)

Like Domestic China, Scotchem used a range of contractual relationships in a way that cut costs to ensure continued production on the site but in so doing it reduced overall employment levels. In this case, the relatively dominant mar-ket position of Scotchem and its institutionalization within Multichem and the chemicals sector generated better long-term prospects for those employees that remained. It was Scotchem's more peripheral services providers and materials suppliers that complained variously of tight margins, difficulties in recruiting enough quality workers, and generally having to do what Scotchem dictated.

In the Airport case, both airlines and handling firms agreed that the airlines held a great deal of power in the subcontracting arrangements. On some occasions, airlines used their purchasing power to secure contracts at a low cost and then to insist on certain performance standards after the contract had been signed. On other occasions, airlines might decide to switch their handling contractor if they believed that the handling firm was acquiring too much bargaining power. For example, Airline C decided to replace FH with BH as their handing firm in part because FH was trying to tie Airline C down with a wholesale handling contract across airports in the country and in part because Airline C felt that awarding the handling contract to BH, a subsidiary of Airportco, would enhance the airline's relationship with Airportco. According to Airline C's Operations Director

FH had forgotten who was the supplier and who was the customer and they felt that they were dominant and that they could do things the way they wanted to do them. My view is very different. We are the customer, we are paying the money and they should adapt to do things the way we want them to do it, but they would not. (Airline C, Manager 2, male)

Within (and perhaps because of) this unequal power relationship the quality of various interpersonal relationships was identified by ground staff as important. According to one shift controller from FH, the airlines sometimes made 'ridiculous' demands which the handling agents had no choice but to accommodate. A good working relationship with the airline's gate representative, however, could enable the shift controller to smooth over the consequences of, for example, a short delay in take-off. But the ability of handling firms to respond to airlines' demands was constrained by the complex multi-tier subcontracting arrangements. For some time, BH had provided handling services for Airline C but relied on a sub-subcontractor, FH, to deliver passenger handling, boarding and despatch. BH struggled to manage the performance of FH:

The only power that BH has got is not to pay, and that does not happen easily. If the sub-subcontractors don't deliver the service there is very little you can do . . . I was told to back down from chasing my subcontractors for not delivering their services . . . I feel that I am letting my customer airline down and I could have given them a better service if the senior management had backed me up. (BH, Manager 3, male)

Interpersonal relations were made more complex by subcontractors bypassing master contract holders to manage relations directly with the airlines, just as the airlines (e.g. Airline B mentioned earlier) bypassed the main contractor and intervened directly with the contractor's subcontractor. Reasons for airlines and subcontractors' direct involvement with non-contractual parties in the service delivery included the perceived lack of resources of the main contractor, the need for quality control, or simply as a 'right' (see also Chapter 7).

An example of how the awarding of contracts can affect informal working practices occurred when another charter airline switched the handling contract from BH to FH. BH staff will not now assist FH staff if help is needed loading and unloading for that airline because they see it as a contract that has been lost. The situation was reversed when the Airline C contract was taken over by BH: 'The day that we operated that contract we were told by FH staff and management that we could ask for assistance on any flight except for Airline C so you have to look at it from the human aspect there. It is very emotive and we'd rather not get drawn into those positions' (BH, Managing Director, male).

4.6 Summary and conclusions

In this chapter, we have assessed corporate decision-making in a way that is sensitive to the actions of the firm within its particular business sector. We have attempted to describe the process behind decisions regarding contractual relations, or the lack of them, and the specific structural context that informs these. Overall our analysis has illustrated how strategic decisions, and the redistribution of risks that these affect, are formulated within a wider context defined by social practices and institutions. Thus, while we find evidence of the reactive and opportunistic formulation of strategy provided by the resource-based view of the firm, more work needs to be done to tease out how outcomes are determined by particular firm-in-sector relations, and the way in which opportunities are unevenly distributed.

Here, we have illustrated how in each of the three case studies there are different orientations to contacting that reflect—among other things—local culture, social norms, and institutional codes. As such, our findings challenge conventional conceptions about 'core' and 'non-core' activities. For example, despite literature that suggests that core contracting can be used to extend internal capabilities (see Matusik and Hill 1998) in the ceramic tableware industry an alternative conclusion appears more compelling. Competitive pressures have forced some firms to source production overseas, generally without suffering quality problems and without loss of 'core' expertise and knowledge. Others have chosen to specialize in 'aspirational' or other niche markets. In both examples, competition has induced firms to concentrate on high quality production within the United Kingdom, thus narrowing traditional 'core' capabilities. It would seem that in the case of strong international price competition, the risks associated with either maintaining production or failing to outsource formerly 'core' products can become greater than the risk of losing proprietary knowledge.

In the chemicals case, due to the structure of the market and the forms of regulation that existed therein, opportunities for using contractual relationships to extend internal capabilities were limited to a few key suppliers and customers. More complete accounts of these cooperative relationships are provided in Chapter 6. In this chapter we concentrated on ancillary services contracts and illustrated how, despite their supposedly peripheral status, regulations at sector level can have an impact upon both how they are managed and how costs and benefits are distributed. Scotchem attempted to offset risks and costs associated with the industry by using its purchasing power to shape its suppliers' behaviour (with varying degrees of success). As the case of Securiforce demonstrates, when a supplier is, for whatever reason, not willing to invest resources in managing its relationship the ability to offset costs and risks is significantly reduced.

And finally, Airportco's decision to retain three activities in-house (engineering, security, and fire) and to outsource others (e.g. cleaning) was, to a considerable degree, contingent on its emergence from a public sector context. At the airport there is a very complex mix of contracting arrangements, notably between airlines and sourcing of baggage and passenger handling, with some evidence of multi-tiered contracting arrangements (e.g. some airlines also manage contracts for other airlines) and differences in the role of the end-client organization in monitoring the performance of 'sub-subcontractors'. Rather than notions of 'core' and 'periphery', organizational level factors such as the strategic positioning of the airline and access to local knowledge about the operations of other firms were important in determining how to contract.

Given that British managers have often been accused of adopting a reactive orientation it might be argued that it is entirely appropriate to consider how particular structural locations lead to particular strategic ends. Our research tentatively suggests that some firms are more likely to risk contracting for goods and services than others due to the particular sector within which they operate, as well as their product market position within that sector. This point came through particularly strongly in the ceramics case, where it was those firms that competed at the lower end of the tableware industry that saw most benefit in outsourcing abroad. In contrast, we found evidence that companies at the 'aspirational' end of the market wished to maintain the traditional base of institutionalized social practices in the Stoke-on-Trent region, and saw their long-term competitive advantage as emerging largely from this. Equally, however, smaller haulage firms found it more difficult to manage Scotchem's new code of conduct and 'high class' airlines considered reputation in their choice of handling services suppliers.

The research also demonstrates that decisions about contracting have ramifications that go well beyond the boundaries of the firm. While outsourcing was apparently beneficial in terms of Domestic China's bottom line profits it had a wider socio-economic cost for the region. Rather than investing in the dwindling skill base of the local labour market, skills were purchased from developing countries. Beyond those who constitute the local labour market, this would have knock on effects for other firms in the region, trade union membership, suppliers, customers, and the reputation of the industrial district as a whole. Thus, in qualification to those that have only considered the costs and benefits that accrue to firms within particular relationships, it would seem that ignoring the context within which firms operate leads to an under-socialized view of how the costs and benefits of outsourcing are distributed in practice.

Finally, the type of social regulation also matters. Stronger forms of social regulation, such as those imposed by the CIA at Scotchem or the Civil Aviation Authority at the airport, have effects running across sectors and regions and encourage standardized forms of behaviour (also see Sako 1992; Lane and Bachmann 1998). Weaker regulations, such as those community-based ties associated with the maintenance of the industrial district around Stoke-on-Trent, only affect sectional interests. Despite significant local actors campaigning against outsourcing beyond the boundaries of the industrial district, Domestic China was able to contract overseas with few difficulties. They could specify in great detail exactly what their contractual partners did for them without adhering to any externally imposed codes. By contrast, in the chemicals case, industry regulations affected the contracts Scotchem held with almost all suppliers, peripheral or otherwise, and these led to particular types of contractual relationship. If it were not for the fact that the CIA imposed regulations as a condition of membership, relationships with haulage firms and the security company may have been relatively simple and cheap to administer. However, an unregulated context may have equally made fewer demands of the staff involved and led to a less informed workforce. It is also unlikely that relationships with key raw materials suppliers would have been as close and productive in terms of the development of proprietary knowledge if it were not for the common set of rules within which the businesses operated (also see Chapter 6).

Note

1. A plant which processes the clay and other ingredients to produce the 'body' from which the blank ceramic items are made.

Public–Private Contracting: Performance, Power, and Change at Work

DAMIAN GRIMSHAW AND GAIL HEBSON

5.1 Introduction

Questions of organizational boundaries are at the forefront of UK policy efforts to reform delivery of public services. These involve increasing use of partnership arrangements between public and private sector organizations, as well as the more traditional policies of outsourcing activities to private sector subcontractors. Public–private partnerships (PPPs) have provoked a great deal of attention in the popular media. On the one hand, PPPs are seen to represent privatization by stealth, a drain on government expenditures, and a threat to the high standards of both services provision and terms and conditions of employment among public sector workers. On the other hand, PPPs are seen as a key element of public services reform since they embrace private sector expertise, diffuse the risks of new capital investment, and provide new flexible career trajectories for public sector workers. Arguments and evidence have been presented on both sides of this wide-ranging controversy, including the report by the IPPR's Commission on Public Private Partnerships (IPPR 2001), as well as more critical reports funded by the major public services trade union UNISON (Sachdev 2001; UNISON 2001; see, also, Pollock et al. 2001).

Policy debate concerning PPPs is, in part, rooted in divisions found within academic study of public administration and strategic management. There is a fast-growing literature on the way decisions regarding organizational boundaries are taken against a given set of complementary resources in networked organizations (see Chapter 2). Extension of these ideas to a public sector model, where outsourcing and partnership are said to represent the practical steps towards refocusing on 'core' competencies, includes the development of a strategic management framework and the application of a transaction costs model (Domberger 1998). By contrast, other studies emphasize the embeddedness and peculiarities of public services provision associated with long-standing processes of decision-making, bureaucratic rules, and the fiduciary responsibility of the state (Stiglitz 1989; O'Toole 1993; Du Gay 2000). Such studies argue that public sector reform ought not to be reduced to a question of identifying core competencies or exploiting opportunities for new sources of added value, but rather ought to involve a strengthening of citizenship (Crouch 2003a, b).

To date, very little case-study research has analysed the implications of public–private contracting in terms of both performance (including the quality of services and the distribution of risks) and the nature of the employment relationship. In this chapter, we raise two questions largely absent from other studies (Chapter 2), namely how performance gains (and losses) are distributed between unequal partners and how changing organizational boundaries shape the employment relationship. These questions are illuminated by analysing four different forms of public–private contracting arrangements. Section one provides a brief overview of evidence to date concerning public–private contracting arrangements and their implications for performance and employment. Section 5.2 introduces the four case studies. Sections 5.3, 5.4, and 5.5 analyse the data by exploring issues of performance, power, and change at work, respectively.

5.2   'Blairing' the public–private divide

Under the leadership of Tony Blair, the Labour government has made PPPs 'a cornerstone of the government's modernization programme for Britain' (Milburn 1999, cited in IPPR 2001: 33). PPPs are described as an 'innovative hybrid approach' to public management (IPPR 2001: 38) and are said to replace outmoded alternative models, including the traditional rules-based, hierarchical approach and the 'new public management' approach.[1] They are said to be distinctive because they are constituted by 'a risk sharing relationship between the public and private sectors based upon a shared aspiration to bring about a desired public policy outcome' (IPPR 2001: 40). But, in practice, partnerships appear to have become a catch-all phrase, covering any arrangement where a public service is delivered in cooperation with the private sector (PSPRU 1998; Grimshaw et al. 2002). As such, it is not clear that PPPs present a distinctive, alternative approach that transcends previous approaches to public services management.

Use of the term 'partnership' is symbolic of New Labour's chosen ideology underpinning reform, through which there is an explicit effort to eschew any notion that ownership is better either under the public or the private sector:

Nobody argues that the private sector offers a panacea to transform our public services. There are indeed significant ways in which the private sector can learn from the public sector . . . What matters is what works: that the public can choose the services they need, that they provide good value for money, and that they deliver higher standards. (OPSR 2002: 26)

Nevertheless, despite the apparently neutral language and ideology, the years since 1997 have witnessed a remarkable increase in the role of the private sector across all areas of government activity. Perhaps the best known (and most controversial) is the Private Finance Initiative (PFI), where a private sector consortium designs, builds, finances, and operates an asset-based service, typically involving the construction of new buildings and provision of ancillary services (estates, maintenance, cleaning, and security) for an agreed charge.[2] Other examples include long-term service provision contracts (such as for IT systems), joint ventures (involving a joint equity stake), wider markets (where the private sector partner exploits public sector assets commercially) and strategic partnerships (where partners are directly involved in policy formation and implementation) (IPPR 2001).

Implications for risk, cost savings, and staff transfer

Proliferation of PPPs has occurred amidst growing controversy and debate. First, it is not clear that the risk is balanced between private and public sector partners. One difficulty involves agreeing which elements ought to be covered by a risk assessment. In particular, the definition of risk does not incorporate risk to the users, or to other public sector agencies other than the commissioning body. Also, even where it is possible to list risks *ex ante*, in many projects (mainly IT outsourcing deals) the public sector partner has been unable to enforce penalties. Finally, private sector contractors are able to reduce risk substantially through refinancing loans at lower interest rates once the contract has been signed (IPPR 2001; Pollock et al. 2001). Overall, there is a polarization of evidence, with claims that risk transfer (mainly involving the risks of construction) has enabled the public sector to achieve value-for-money (Arthur Andersen 2000) and counterevidence that asymmetry of risk allocation in fact benefits the private sector (Pollock et al. 2001).

A second issue involves debates over whether PPPs deliver cost savings. The 'discipline' of the market is assumed to drive down costs, both through competitive bidding among a range of providers for the contract and through regular 'benchmarking' of prices for activities throughout the contract (Domberger 1998). However, competition at the point of tender for the contract may be limited by the large costs of bidding (Broadbent et al. 2000; Grimshaw et al. 2002). Regular benchmarking may also be problematic, especially where it is difficult to obtain information from competitor firms. Nevertheless, PPPs offer an additional route to potential cost savings since services provision is managed through formally specified contracts, which offer potential scope for control and monitoring (including penalties for poor performance). Also, periodic renewal of the contract may act as a competitive incentive to induce higher motivation among workers and management (Domberger 1998). However, significant resources may be required for the specification, monitoring and measurement of contracted services (Marchington et al. 2003). Also, the flexible price structure of many PPP deals raises the risk of cost escalation, presenting problems of managing an essentially unknowable cost trajectory.[3]

A third issue of contention centres on the role of staff transfer in many PPPs and the implications for terms and conditions of employment for public services workers. TUPE Regulations provide only limited protection (see Chapter 3). In particular, TUPE does not protect new employees recruited by the private sector firm, leading to the widely publicized problem of a 'two-tier workforce' where different groups of workers carry out similar work for different sets of terms and conditions (Willis 2001; UNISON 2002; Toynbee 2003). Since 2000, government policy has shifted—under pressure from public sector strikes and a high profile 'living wage' campaign in East London (Grimshaw, 2004)—resulting, ultimately, in statutory provisions issued in 2003 which require contractors to provide recruits with terms and conditions which are 'no less favourable' than those of workers transferred from local government.

But questions remain concerning the prospects for the traditional notion of a public sector ethos. On the one hand, the new emphasis on outcome and away from process is said to reflect the reorientation towards 'consumer' needs and to foster a mutual sense of commitment and purpose among workers employed by the public and private sector partners (Brereton and Temple 1999). On the other hand, the market-based principles underpinning PPPs are expected to lead to an emphasis on private gain over public service, personal accountability over collegial process, and discretionary individual remuneration instead of uniform pay and promotions systems (O'Toole 1993, 2000; Du Gay 2000; Hebson et al. 2003).

5.3 The case studies

Four cases of public–private contracting are analysed in this chapter (Table 5.1). They represent a mix of private sector involvement across different areas of public sector activity: central government (the IT case); health (the PFI case); education (Teacher Supply); and local government (Customer Services). In addition, the value and duration of contracts varies considerably from more than £1 billion over 10 years for the IT case to the daily rates paid by schools for supply teachers provided by TeacherTemp.

The pressures that led to contracting differed for each case. In the IT case, the pressure on Govco stemmed from the 1991 government White Paper ('Competing for Quality', HMSO 1991), which established the policy that, wherever possible, government work should be market tested with the work going to the provider of best value for the taxpayer. At the time, this was the largest government outsourcing contract and, for FutureTech, was important in reinforcing their visibility in the market for government services provision. The PFI case began in 1998 – after a rather protracted process dating back to 1993–4 of

Table 5.1. Four cases of public–private contracting arrangements

Case	Public sector partner	Private sector partner	Nature of contract		Number of staff transferred
			Approximate initial value	Length (start date)	
IT	Govco	FutureTech	More than £1 billion[a]	10 years (1994)	2,300
PFI	NHS Trust	Consortium (cleaning firm, construction firm, estates firm and a design consultancy)	£66 million	35 years (1998)	500
Teacher Supply	Individual schools	TeacherTemp	Varies	From just 1 day to 2 or more school terms	n/a
Customer Services	Council X	TCS	£18 million	7 years (1998)	Approx. 100

Note:
[a] An approximate figure is presented to preserve anonymity.

approving the building scheme, tendering, and selecting a consortium—as one of the first wave of PFI hospital deals encouraged by government ministers in the health sector. Initially, the four private sector partners each held a 25 per cent stake in a 'Special Purpose Vehicle', charged with coordinating services provision in line with the needs of the purchasing partner, the NHS Trust. In education, the introduction of Local Management of Schools in 1988 gave head teachers control of 80 per cent their school budgets, leading simultaneously to an erosion of the power and influence of Local Education Authorities (LEAs) (especially in personnel and financial management—Ironside and Seifert 1995) and to a withdrawal from LEAs as the main provider of temporary cover in favour of private sector agencies. Our case focuses on the provision of supply teachers from a large agency, TeacherTemp, to schools in the North West region. In our fourth case, local authorities faced increasing pressure during the 1990s to ensure efficiency and effectiveness in services provision, in a context where PPPs were encouraged by government (Marchington et al. 2003). Coupled with a crisis in housing benefits administration in London (our case was singled out as one of twelve which were 'named and shamed'), Council X was keen to exploit private sector investment in IT. For TCS, the selected partner, this was their first local government contract.

5.4   Performance gains from public–private contracting?

The shift from internal, bureaucratic provision of public services to an arrangement involving private sector firms has the potential to reduce costs and improve the quality of service delivery for reasons relating to market discipline, contract performance, and private sector expertise. Considering each issue, we find mixed evidence of the relative costs and benefits across the four cases (Table 5.2).

Market discipline

It is difficult to make a quantitative assessment of the costs and benefits of organizing services provision through private sector providers, in part because of the intangibility, or unmeasurability, of many of the outcomes. As such, our

Table 5.2.   The gains and losses of public–private contracting

	Market discipline	Contract performance	Private sector expertise
IT	FutureTech agreed 50% reduction in unit (baseline) costs—but difficulties in benchmarking make it difficult to control other prices	Profit share and options to impose penalties—but costly problems arising from mis-specification	Potential for more rapid innovation in IT—but new developments restricted by tight contract
PFI	Consortium passed 'value for money' test—but high costs of bidding reduces competition at bidding stage	Flexible tariff to match performance level—but costly problems arising from mis-specification and disagreement over monitoring process	Potential for innovation in services delivery and HRM—but adversarial approach threatens cooperative IR tradition
Teacher Supply	No evidence of cost reductions—but some head teachers happy to pay more for a better service, despite national concern over 'soaring' costs	Generic contract to match all needs—but gaps in contract cause conflict with what is expected of supply teachers and some failure of monitoring performance	Agencies save head teacher's time—some problems of distinguishing good from bad agencies
Customer Services	Access to technical and organizational expertise more important than price	Bonuses and penalties in line with KPI—but problems of formalizing channels of communication and disagreement over monitoring process	Potential for more rapid innovation in IT—but operational 'isolation' of TCS contract hinders improvements; expertise derives from ex-public sector staff

aim is largely to highlight some of the anticipated and unanticipated consequences in each case. In two of the cases, public and private sector managers agreed that because the market-based process of tendering for services forced firms to compete prices downwards, the public sector enjoyed a reduction in costs compared to that estimated for in-house provision. FutureTech agreed to a 50 per cent reduction in unit costs over the 10-year contract and the PFI consortium was officially selected on the basis of it meeting 'value for money'.

In the other two cases, price was not the driving condition in the tendering process. In the Customer Services case, TCS did not submit the cheapest bid (TCS-L, union rep. 2, male). Instead, TCS won the contract because it promised considerable investment in IT systems, training, and property, and continuous improvement of key performance indicators (KPIs). In the Teacher Supply case, schools faced higher costs when using private sector agencies in favour of LEAs (which traditionally controlled all temporary cover) for the provision of supply teachers. Nevertheless, some school head teachers were happy to pay higher fees because this saved their time spent searching for cover and made it more likely that they would meet their goal of having a teacher in the classroom.[4] A senior official with the Association of Teachers and Lecturers supported this view:

Political principle is one thing, but do I really want angry parents? [Agencies] ring in the evening and you have a supply teacher there for 8.30 am. The agencies make it very simple. There is no technical reason why the LEA could not do that, but they did not think of it. (ATL, Union rep. 2, female)

Importantly, unlike the long duration of contracts in the other three cases, schools and agencies continuously agree contracts, often on a day-to-day basis. As such, head teachers are less likely to become locked in to an expensive arrangement. However, satisfaction at the level of the school with the trade-off between costs and the efficient supply of teachers ought not to obscure evidence of concern at a national level. During 2001, parliamentary questions were raised regarding 'whether excess profits are being made in this privatised sector' (Willis 2001, cited in Barlin and Hallgarten 2001: 5) and several reports in the media identified problems of increasing costs (Grimshaw et al. 2003).

Nevertheless, the market for teacher supply does involve a large number of firms competing to provide services to schools; as yet, there is no evidence of price collusion among the large players, nor of a trend towards monopoly provision. By contrast, the market for PFI contracts is widely recognized as being dominated by a handful of powerful firms and consortia, thereby diminishing the downward cost pressures of market competition. One of the reasons for this, as we found in our PFI case, is that it is expensive to bid for a contract. Proposals must include highly detailed design plans, financial accounts, and legal arrangements, which incur high costs to designers, lawyers, and consultants.

A final consideration regarding the potential benefits of market discipline is how to establish benchmarking of costs throughout the duration of a long contract. In the IT and PFI cases, given the length of contracts, there was a concern from the outset to try to build in to the contract some mechanism for matching costs against market rates. Govco required FutureTech to conduct regular benchmarking of costs and performance levels against competitor organizations and the NHS Trust required the Consortium to benchmark prices after the first seven years of its 35-year contract. However, evidence for the IT case suggests that it is extraordinarily difficult to exploit the cost pressures of market competition through benchmarking, due both to the difficulties of obtaining cost and quality information from competitor IT firms and the non-comparability of some areas of IT provision. Indeed, Govco only expected to be able to benchmark around half of all outsourced activities because of these problems.

The PPPs also involve a radical change in the way services are coordinated. In particular, the purchase of activities through a formally specified contract, rather than through a traditional open-ended employment contract, is associated with potential opportunities for new forms of control and monitoring of the level and quality of services provision. Indeed, public sector managers in the IT, PFI, and Customer Services cases argued that a key benefit was the opportunity to build quality considerations and changing budget pressures into the contract: the contract between the NHS Trust and the Consortium had a flexible monthly payment that could be adjusted to match performance standards; Govco's contract with FutureTech built in financial penalties where performance was below standard and profit sharing where it exceeded a stipulated minimum level; and Council X built in bonuses and penalties in line with measures of KPI.

In practice, however, our evidence suggests that it is very difficult for the public and private sector partners to agree penalties—largely because of the difficulties in specifying tasks in the contract, in identifying the performance standards and in agreeing the design of monitoring and evaluation methods. Specification and pricing of tasks is complicated. IT services outsourced to FutureTech were subdivided into thirty types—each priced separately—based on productivity and volume characteristics of work done. If a job task changed then Govco and FutureTech negotiated what this meant for the unit price. The PFI contract included hundreds of pages of details covering the different ancillary job tasks. For example, there were ten pages on cleaning tasks (barrier cleaning, operating the Washtech 300, theatres, laboratories, etc.) and ten pages on food hygiene (refrigeration, transportation, microwaves, etc.). Each area of activity was matched with an output specification, which defined what was required of the private sector partner—ranging from eight pages of detail for switchboard services to thirty pages for estates maintenance[5] and job tasks were costed following a time and motion model. The Customer Services contract did not specify job tasks, as such, but key performance indicators, which set out what was expected in terms of administration costs and response times. Reflecting these complex processes of specification, our interviews uncovered a great deal of dissatisfaction, from both public and private sector managers, regarding the difficulties of 'managing to contract'. Even trivial problems of mis-specification could consume a great deal of managerial time:

We suddenly realized there is nobody who hangs curtains. Someone has got it in the Concession Agreement [the PFI contract] to take them down, but there is nothing to say who will put them up.

Q. Can the person who took them down put them up?
No. I know it sounds silly

Q. Wouldn't you just follow custom and practice?
No, because that is why we have a Concession Agreement. (NHS Trust, Manager 5, female)

Managing to contract not only challenges customary norms defining job boundaries, but also may weaken channels of communication between managers and workers across the different organizations. Council X workers who transferred to TCS-L were often unwilling to retain long-standing social bonds with their ex-colleagues (working in the same building) due to a belief that the latter were policing the performance indicators too stringently (TCS-L, Supervisor 2, female) (see below). Also, Council X staff were instructed to communicate with their ex-colleagues through the newly established TCS call centre, which sometimes meant waiting 30 minutes to be connected (Council X, Manager 3, male). At TeacherTemp, we were told by one of the agents that some school head teachers choose to communicate with the agencies, rather than directly with supply teachers in their school:

We send a teacher into the school and they will ring and say, 'Fred Smith is in school today, could you just ask him if he will come in tomorrow, or will he do his marking for tomorrow?' . . . No respect for the teacher, or the company who is offering the teacher, and it's very sad really. We have had supply teachers go in where no-one has spoken to them. (TeacherTemp, Manager 2, female)

The Teacher Supply case was distinctive from the other three by the absence of mechanisms between contracting parties to adapt continuously towards a common understanding of what was specified in the contract. In the IT case, we found that mis-specification of one part of the contract for IT services resulted in Govco agreeing to pay an additional £0.9 million to FutureTech— since Govco was found at fault for its 'very sketchy' initial outline of business requirements (Govco document). But at the Teacher Supply case, contracts were characterized by unresolved grey areas in terms of what supply teachers were expected to do, causing innumerable problems. TeacherTemp managers suggested they had certain expectations of their supply teacher—to be on time, to fit in with the school, to do playground duty, and to mark work before leaving for the day—but recognized it was impossible to specify these in a contract. Conflict between head teachers and supply teachers was inevitable:

[Additional tasks are] kind of expected, but they [supply teachers] don't have to. Because you can't contract for the things teachers have to do. (TeacherTemp, consultant 1, female)

While *ex-ante* specification and pricing of job tasks presents one set of problems, a more significant difficulty in our four cases concerns the need for contracting parties to agree systems for monitoring and evaluation. In the PFI case, private sector managers (many of whom had transferred from the NHS Trust) were dissatisfied that the performance system introduced in the late 1970s—which the Trust did not apply rigorously—was now used as the basis for evaluating levels of services delivery. Consequently, managers of the estates firm were happy to encourage workers to manipulate the system to their advantage (Estates Company, Manager 3, male). However, Trust managers were equally dissatisfied the consortium was not abiding by its duty to self-monitor services delivery as specified in the contract. It therefore carried out independent monitoring, but the results were challenged by the private sector partner:

They are saying at the moment that our independent results to support any bits and pieces that we've done are a complete waste of time and don't stand up. Now the Trust's legal advisors have advised us to say they can't say that—that our results stand. (NHS Trust, Manager 6, female)

At TCS, there was a strong feeling among managers that Council X's system of monitoring was too stringent. In keeping with new legislation (enforced soon after the contract was signed), Council staff have retained control in making the final decision on housing benefit claims (Marchington et al. 2003). This made it difficult to assign responsibility to one party or the other regarding the time taken to process claims—one of the KPIs. In addition, Council X checked all claims, rather than a sample. The wider local government view was that it ensured accurate decisions were made and guarded against errors made by rising numbers of temporary staff employed by TCS-L. But TCS staff complained of delays:

The fact that you have to have the local authority make the final determination on a claim I think is wrong. . . . If they checked 50 per cent of the cases, they would still get a feeling of whether what we are doing is right or wrong, but the customer would get their payments quicker. (TCS-L, supervisor 2, female)

Monitoring of supply teachers is particularly difficult because the agency, as the legal employer, can only rely on indirect information provided by the school head teacher, or the supply teacher; a reluctance to carry out site visits means that agencies typically do not engage in direct monitoring. But head teachers were concerned that even when they provided information to the agencies, there was little they could do to ensure this information was being acted upon:

We have had some abysmal teachers in as well, absolutely abysmal. And yet sometimes there is very little you can do until they have actually been in school and you have had them and you can phone them [the agency] and say, 'I do not want to have that person again'. . . . When you ring they say, 'Don't worry, you are not the first school to have complained'. And my question is, 'How many others?' (School B, senior teacher 2, male)

Private sector expertise

PPPs offer the potential for public sector organizations to exploit private sector expertise. The evidence from our four cases suggests that such claims ought to be interpreted with some caution. In the Customer Services and IT cases, the decision to outsource was strongly influenced by the expectation among public sector managers (and trade union officers) that the private sector would have better access to, and be in a stronger position to exploit, new information technologies. For Council X, this also included the expertise of TCS in setting up a call centre. However, these expectations were marred by problems. One Council X manager argued that TCS 'didn't bring much technology with them' and pointed to problems in meeting response times in the new call centre (Council X, Manager 3, male). In the IT case, an ex-Govco systems engineer who had transferred to FutureTech believed that the contractual focus on costs constrained opportunities to experiment with new technology:

Technically, we were very good in the old Govco IT Office, probably because we didn't have funding barriers. . . . We worked closely with ICL on a lot of leading edge development. . . . It was because we didn't need to be risk averse. . . . When FutureTech took over we became technically constrained . . . We became commercially aware but not commercially competent. (FutureTech, Manager 38, male)

In the Customer Services case, any technological expertise which TCS may have brought to the arrangement seems to have been drowned out by a number of negative factors. TCS suffered problems of down time of their revamped operating system, unfilled staff vacancies and frequent changes in housing benefit regulations. Moreover, since this was TCS's first (and only) housing benefit contract it was unable to draw on a wider pool of specific knowledge and experience within TCS. It was also geographically isolated from other TCS sites. In fact, much of its expertise derived from staff who transferred over from the public sector. One Council X manager argued that this fact exploded the 'myth' of private sector expertise (Council X, Manager 3, male). Notably, while the first TCS-L general manager in charge of the contract was from the private sector, as the problems mounted the company recruited a manager from local government who had experience of managing housing benefits (Marchington et al. 2003). Similarly, at the PFI case, the multinational hotel services company relied largely on the knowledge of transferred staff; it had not redeployed staff from elsewhere in the corporation with specialist know-how (NHS Trust, Manager 6, female). In these three cases, there is little evidence of private sector expertise. Indeed, the process of inter-organizational learning is decidedly one-way—from the public sector to the private sector.

The Teacher Supply case provides a positive example of the expertise offered by private sector agencies. There was general consensus among all head teachers and other senior school staff that, compared to the role played by the LEAs, private sector agencies were more efficient:

The problem with the LEA system was that you would have a long list of teachers to start ringing. . . . The advantage of the agency is that it is one telephone call and they do all the ringing. (School B, senior teacher 2, male)

Overall, the four cases demonstrate mixed evidence of gains and losses that arise from the outsourcing of activities to private sector firms. The possibility of costly, and often unintended or unanticipated, problems raises the question as to who bears the burden of these costs. The next section considers how the relative costs and benefits are distributed between parties to the contract.

5.5   Risk sharing or an imbalance of power?

While many studies of inter-organizational relations implicitly assume homogeneity of contracting organizations, there is a need to question the distribution of risk and the ability of one of the contracting organizations to act opportunistically (Chapter 2). Here, we investigate the proposition that differences in 'power' (loosely defined) shed light on the distribution of gains and losses from partnership. Such differences might mean that one of the contracting parties is able to secure a larger slice of the benefits accruing from performance improvements, or, conversely, shoulders a disproportionate share of the risk where problems arise. In addition, where parties to the contract do not share common performance goals, the organization in the stronger position may attempt to steer new policies and practices in a direction that conflicts with the espoused strategic goals of the contracting partner. Such a scenario may be especially applicable to PPPs where there are good reasons to believe that public and private sector organizations do not share common goals. We heard this kind of view from many public sector managers and union officials who were concerned about the stress placed by private sector managers on profit maximization at a cost to the delivery of quality services:

The overall standard of services has decreased, because at the end of the day they are only here to make a profit . . . They say they are making a loss, but everything is cut to the bone far more than it ever was. (NHS Trust, Manager 6, female)

The agencies are not untruthful, but it is a business and they just need enough people out there getting them income. They are becoming less and less discriminatory. (School N, senior teacher 16, female)

Differences in organizational goals mean that public and private sector partners may be pulling in different directions. The challenge for partnership is thus to forge a set of shared interests around which trusting relations can be developed. Chapter 6 analyses these trusting relations in more detail, with particular attention to the role of 'boundary spanners'. Here, we question the extent to which each partner enters the trusting relationship from a position of equal bargaining strength.

Table 5.3.   Factors contributing to 'power imbalance' in PPPs

	Expertise in outsourced activity	Expertise in negotiating and working to contract	Shelter from reputation effects	External support
IT				
Govco	Medium–high, declining	Low–medium	Low	Medium
FutureTech	Medium, rising	High	Medium–high	High
PFI				
NHS Trust	Medium–high, declining	Low, rising	Low	Low
Consortium	Medium, rising	High	Medium–high	Medium
Teacher Supply				
Schools	High	Low–medium	Low	Low
TeacherTemp	Medium	High	High	Medium
Customer Services				
Council X	High	Medium, rising	Low	Medium
TCS	Low, rising	Medium	Low–medium	Low

Four factors contribute to the relative balance of power in PPPs (Table 5.3). The first concerns the relative level of expertise in the outsourced activity. On the one hand, outsourcing requires the client to surrender a significant level of expertise in order to exploit the assumed benefits from greater specialization. On the other hand, without expertise in the externalized activity it is difficult for the client to effectively manage the monitoring of services delivery and specification of new work. The four cases differ in the extent to which expertise was retained in-house. At Govco, a core of staff with specialist IT and contract management skills was retained in-house to evaluate services provision. Managers argued this was critical to maintaining bargaining leverage:

We retained expertise, loosely under the heading 'Intelligent Customer'. . . . These people came with experience from within Govco and were in a strong position to provide some sort of reality check on any ideas that were coming from FutureTech. (Govco, Manager 19, male)

Over time, however, this source of bargaining strength was expected to diminish as FutureTech developed new IT systems in areas where retained Govco staff had little experience. Moreover, Govco managers recognized that many of their highly skilled IT staff had better prospects elsewhere in the IT industry and that it would be difficult to fill vacant posts in the specialized area of contract management. In the Customer Services case, Council X retained expertise due to its control of the final processing of housing benefit claims. Its advantage was reinforced by the fact that TCS faced a steep learning curve in the business of administering housing benefit claims. Also, given its subsequent decision not to pursue other housing benefit contracts, TCS did not make sufficient investment in developing the required expertise.

Second, a shift to market-based contracting arrangements may be expected to deliver a comparative advantage to private sector organizations, relative to the public sector, since they have greater experience in managing services delivery to meet contractual requirements. This is best illustrated by the PFI case. From the early stages of negotiating the contract, while the Consortium had a large bid team and could draw on past experience of negotiating contracts, the NHS Trust employed a group of just three staff—and all three quit soon after signing the contract. Moreover, while the Consortium financed a 'special purpose vehicle' (SPV) with two full-time senior managers to manage the contract, the NHS Trust relied upon existing management staff who had to fit in their new role alongside other responsibilities. Lack of expertise and resources within the Trust gave the Consortium a relatively free hand in setting and interpreting details of the contract. This was clarified in conversations with the General Manager of the SPV:

[NHS management staff] are completely overwhelmed by the work they have to do. . . . We could screw them every day of the week if we wanted to. We educate them about the contract because the Trust bid team has moved on. . . . The senior manager found that the Trust managing team didn't understand the Concession Agreement. . . . We train them to see things how we see them. (SPV, Manager 1, female)

NHS managers admitted their lack of expertise hindered their capacity to win a good deal for the Trust. We were told that training in legal matters did not start until 18 months after the contract was signed, that the Trust did not hire new staff with experience of signing public–private contracts and that NHS managers were forced to rely on the SPV for guidance:

The SPV was streets ahead of us, and the balance of power shifted from day one when the services were transferred. . . . So when you are trying to monitor and audit from the Trust point of view to make sure you are getting value for money we were on the back foot . . . And they knew we wouldn't know anything and they used it to their advantage . . . Because there was no input from the Trust, we learned initially from SPV manager. . . . It was extremely superficial and it's only now with [legal firm] that we know what we learned was a load of rubbish. (NHS Trust, Manager 6, female)

Evidence of apparent opportunistic behaviour, therefore, appears to be consistent with a strongly uneven balance of expertise in negotiating and working to contract. In the IT and Teacher Supply cases, the private sector partner also enjoyed an advantage, albeit not as extreme as in the PFI case (column 2, Table 5.3). In the IT case, evidence of Govco's weaker expertise in managing contracts is supported by the fact that FutureTech had managed the flexible price nature of the 10-year contract to its advantage. While the baseline IT services were on target to meet the 50 per cent reduction in costs, FutureTech more than offset this by charging Govco for additional services. After 6 years, the total value of the contract had more than doubled. Our interviews with Govco managers suggest that the reasons lie partly with the complicated and time-consuming process of assessing submissions for additional work. Divergent interests between the two partners means that not all submissions necessarily meet Govco's organizational goals. While recognizing this fact, Govco managers told us that their ability to carry out a comprehensive cost-benefit analysis of each submission, in a way that would satisfy FutureTech managers, was constrained by limited resources (Govco, Manager 36, male).

The Customer Services case provides an exception to this general pattern. Three years into the contract, Council X managers became more successful than TCS in renegotiating the contract to meet its terms (Marchington et al. 2003). Moreover, many suspected that the true volume of the work in the original tender had been underestimated. Some TCS managers argued that at the bidding stage the aim was to win the contract as 'a loss leader', in order to build a reputation and expertise as a basis for future local government contracts. Ultimately, however, the complex nature of the back office work, the strong focus on meeting the needs of (often desperate) claimants and the limited opportunity for 'growing' the size of the contract meant that TCS could not improve its bargaining position. During the early stages of the contract, TCS focused efforts upon those KPIs that provided more lucrative returns, rather than the whole bundle of KPIs. However, Council X responded quickly by restructuring the payments to ensure this could not be done:

It was possible with the original KPIs to cherry pick. If they were particularly good at something, or it was easier, it was possible to specialize in that and pick up the profit . . . The way it is now structured is that unless all of the indicators are returned to a minimum standard you get nothing even in relation to the areas where they do particular well. (Council X, Manager 2, male)

The third factor which shapes the degree of power balance between partners is sensitivity to reputation.[6] Again, our evidence shows that there may be an imbalance between public and private partners (column 3, Table 5.3). In all four cases, the private sector partners have operations across a variety of sectors (and countries, with the exception of TCS-L) and the ability to win future contracts depends less on their reputation in a narrow area of services delivery. There is also evidence of a lack of diffusion of reputation effects. In the IT case, despite publicized evidence of FutureTech's poor performance in other PPPs, we were told that Govco did not investigate such claims. This suggests either that the partnership had become over-sheltered, or that there was simply no other realistic alternative IT supplier (due to the high costs of entry or the specificity of technical know-how). In addition, in all cases, problems of poor standards of services provision were typically interpreted by the public (through the media, or the end-users—patients, housing benefit claimants, etc.)

as the fault of the public sector partner, largely because it is more visible. While this may have the indirect effect of pressuring the public sector partner to switch suppliers, it does not have the effect of diffusing the reputation of particular private sector suppliers into the public arena.

Fourth, each partner may benefit from external support, such as from regulatory bodies or from other divisions within the organization (column 4, Table 5.3). In the IT and Customer Services cases, the public sector partner benefited from external support. One of the duties of the government's Public Sector Accounts Committee is to monitor the provision of IT services and, given the size and significance of Govco's contract with FutureTech, the Committee made regular public statements which arguably provided a check against unscrupulous claims. Council X managers met regularly with other managers from neighbouring local authorities and were able to compare notes on the management of outsourced operations. Council X also benefited from the internal publication of a report on services provision carried out by a management consultancy. The report identified problems of 'low and inconsistent productivity' and insufficient reporting of performance and output levels. It also recommended 'an escalation of pressure to a higher level on both sides' to raise the profile of the contract:

[As a result of the Report] the Chief Executive and senior managers [from Council X] have become very involved, put an extra political dimension on it . . . saying this has got to happen. . . . The balance of power . . . probably has shifted a bit back to us. (Council X, Manager 1, male)

These two cases diverge, however, in the external resources available to the private sector partners. FutureTech benefited considerably from the expertise and knowledge diffused from other divisions of the multinational organization. Indeed, many of the managers we interviewed were transplanted from divisions in the United States to the United Kingdom in order to transfer their expertise in running similar contracts. By contrast, TCS managers complained of a lack of wider expertise. Finally, it is notable that NHS Trust managers benefited very little from external governmental support. It appears that the government's policy efforts during the 1990s focused too narrowly on the question of how to win private sector support for PFI hospitals and neglected the issue of how to deliver sufficient expertise and support to the individual NHS Trusts charged with negotiating and managing contracts.

5.6   Changes at work

In this section we focus on workers who transferred from the public sector to the private sector and assess evidence of increased job insecurity, disillusion with performance targets and changes in traditional public sector values. Further evidence concerning the fragmentation of terms and conditions (such as pay, for example) is provided in Chapter 7. Importantly, a straightforward comparison of workers' relationship with their past and present employers is not possible. This is because workers have moved from a relationship with a single public sector employer to a triangular relationship, involving a private sector employer and a public sector contracting organization. Change is a result of both the switch to a private sector employer and the new role of the ex-employer—the public sector partner—in policing the contract, whether from a weak or a strong bargaining position.

Job insecurity and work intensification

In three of the four cases (Teacher Supply is the exception), the outsourcing of services was accompanied by transfer of staff from the public sector to the private sector organization (see Table 5.1). In the PFI and Customer Services cases, the transfer of staff was very quickly followed by job cuts, implemented by the private sector organization, but agreed (contractually) with the public sector partner.[7] At the PFI case, the post-transfer job cuts were in large part a result of the simultaneous closure of one of the Trust's hospitals (four miles away) and rationalization of services on the main site. The contract estimated that the 1998 full-time equivalent workforce figures of ninety estates staff and 519 hotel services staff would be reduced to fifty and 353, respectively, by 2001.[8] These cuts had a major impact on workers' perceptions of security. Also, they seemed to go beyond what was needed for the rationalization of the two hospital sites:

They are running us ragged. They've only got half the amount of porters [compared to pre-PFI], but patients are sat there waiting for two hours while they try and get a porter. (Hotel Services Company, porter 6, male)

The impact of the job cuts was aggravated, and complicated, by the way it was managed. The NHS Trust was keen for the private sector firms to follow the Trust's HR procedures, requiring all staff to re-apply for their jobs through formal competitive interviews. However, as it was not the employer, the Trust could only request this; its role specified in the formal contract was to finance the redundancy payments. In practice, however, the private firms did follow the Trust's procedure. Workers were denied the opportunity to apply for voluntary redundancy or early retirement and had to apply for a job interview. The Trust HR manager argued that the job interview process was the best way to ensure good staff did not leave. But after the job cuts had been decided, some of the managers from the private firms expressed reservations, perhaps reflecting their closer involvement with the process (Estates Company, Manager 3, male). Also, several workers blamed the redundancies on Trust managers, since they were perceived to control the process and because they made the redundancy payments; the private sector partner's role in recommending the total number of job cuts in the PFI contract received little attention.

Agency work is by its nature insecure. In the Teacher Supply case, stability varies directly with length of contract, with some teachers dependent on day-to-day contracts and others working continuously for more than one term at the same school. But perceptions of security also depended on whether the person had signed on with the agency because they could not find a permanent contract (such as many of the newly qualified teachers), or because it was believed to represent a positive trade-off between insecurity and increased flexibility (Grimshaw et al. 2003). Moreover, some were paid a guaranteed weekly income by the agency (provided they did not sign with another agency), which enhanced security and encouraged some not to seek permanent work.

Perhaps more striking was evidence concerning work intensification as a result of increased pressures to work to performance targets. This was particularly marked in the PFI and Customer Services cases where, despite significant differences in the ability and expertise of the public sector partner to monitor services provision (see above), workers complained about pressures to work to contract. In these cases the nature of the contractual relationship, and in particular how the performance of the private sector partner was measured, was central to how workers understood their work. The emphasis upon performance statistics, and the resulting work intensification, caused disillusionment among some workers:

There is more pressure. . . . They are keen on keeping our times. The design company get paid on results so they want us to get as much work out as possible. (Estates Company, maintenance worker 7, male)

The atmosphere—everyone's got their heads down. You've got to tick this and that and then they come over and see how much you have done. It's becoming very much like a factory production line. We are under stress to reach targets. (TCS-L, caseworker 3, female)

At FutureTech, the pressures of the contractual arrangements were borne by individual workers who found themselves working longer hours to meet contractual deadlines while ensuring quality was not compromised (see Chapter 10). Again, the Teacher Supply case is an exception. Working with an agency enables teachers to avoid many of the pressures faced by school teachers. However, in a form of vicious circle, increasing use of supply teachers within schools further increases work pressures on schoolteachers since they often have to cover for the additional duties not carried out by supply teachers. A key difference between this case and the other three is the absence of contractual monitoring of service delivery. The problems of monitoring and evaluating performance of supply teachers (see above) generate an almost complete absence of contract performance pressures on supply teachers, with schoolteachers and pupils potentially paying the price where performance is inadequate.

Overall, therefore, evidence of change at work is not solely the result of a shift to a new private sector employer, but also involves the particular form of the contractual arrangement between public and private sector partners. Indeed, it is impossible to compare the public sector employment relationship with the private sector form because the public sector partner influences the private sector employment relationship through its role in policing the contract for services. This feature was present in many workers' accounts of change:

The client side have revelled in our failure. . . . They love that the nature of their work is to catch us out. (TCS-L, Manager 3, male)

I've got no time for the Trust, people in the Trust are just rubbish as far as I am concerned. We used to work for the Trust and a certain person is now a monitor for the Trust who was in charge of us. And he's pulling us up on different things that before when we worked for the Trust it was 'leave it, don't bother with that'. (Estates Company, maintenance worker 7, male)

The private sector partner may actively shape such perceptions. For example, a private sector manager might tell workers that increased work intensification is due to contractual targets stringently enforced by the public sector partner, when in fact it reflects their own difficulties in managing staffing, or a policy of reducing labour costs. The employer can thus exploit the contractual arrangement to displace workers' discontent over working conditions, laying the blame at the hands of the 'non-employer'. Such practices appear likely in the PFI case, where, although the Trust was in a relatively weak position to impose stringent performance targets, many workers blamed Trust managers for work intensification. Conversely, in the Customer Services case, the visibility of the monitoring procedure suggests that TCS-L managers had no need to exploit workers' discontent with Council X. These contrasting cases demonstrate that it is difficult to draw a straightforward relationship between the shape of power imbalance between parties to the contractual arrangement and change at work. In both cases, workers experienced increased insecurity and work intensification despite the fact that the public sector was in the driving seat in the TCS case, yet in a position of weak bargaining strength in the PFI case. In the IT case, where power relations were relatively balanced between FutureTech and Govco, we found less evidence of job insecurity or work intensification as a result of the contractual arrangement.

Public sector values

The combination of disenfranchisement with their old public sector employer and the pressures of working to strict performance targets presents challenges to the degree to which workers are able and willing to retain the kind of values that sustain a traditional notion of public sector ethos. While we do not claim that an ideal form of ethos ever existed in these public sector organizations, it is nevertheless of interest to note the direction of trends (Table 5.4).[9]

In all cases, to varying extents, employees were expected to focus upon their own performance and to take on more risk and responsibility for their own careers. This individualistic culture presents a challenge to traditional norms of collegiality. In the IT case, ex-Govco workers had to accept responsibility for

Table 5.4.   Pressures on traditional public sector values

	Individualistic culture	Profit motive	Working to contract
IT	Workers responsible for career development	No evidence	Resilience of informal relations with ex-colleagues at Govco and difficulty of specifying IT work enables some workers to escape strict contractual performance monitoring
PFI	Job re-application requires individual sense of flexibility	Some ancillary staff perceive profit motive hinders ability to provide quality service	Collegiate relations with NHS staff and desire to deliver quality public service ensures working beyond contract
Teacher Supply	Supply teachers learn to bargain for individual terms and conditions with schools and agencies	Some reservations about agencies' need to sell placements to teachers and teachers to schools	Narrow contract of supply teachers conflicts with broad ethos of teaching profession
Customer Services	Accepted by team leaders but rejected by caseworkers	Some caseworkers perceive profit motive conflicts with needs of end-users	Limits ability of caseworkers to communicate fully with claimants.

their individual career development. As one team leader put it, 'The onus is always on the individual, it's your career, unless you do it, it won't happen'. In the Customer Services case the HR manager called for employees to 'own their performance'. Caseworkers at TCS were very critical of the new individual performance culture. However, workers in team leader and specialist IT roles were more likely to embrace this new brand of individualism:

One of the good things to happen is that . . . positive contributions to the organization, to work, . . . [are] acknowledged and recognized frequently, and formally and informally as well. So high performance is rewarded. Within the local authority structure . . . you could-n't ever distinguish between one member of staff and another. (TCS-L, Manager 3, male)

In the Teacher Supply case many supply teachers felt they could not rely on the agency or the school to nurture their careers. This fuelled an individualistic bargaining culture whereby teachers negotiated additional payments for duties such as marking and parents evenings—duties that are ordinarily considered to constitute the professional work of a schoolteacher. But this behaviour was perceived as opportunistic by the permanent teachers we spoke with.

A second source of pressure on workers' values was the new private sector employer's emphasis on profit. Workers at the Customer Services and PFI cases had close contact with the public and felt an especially strong sense of unease. In both cases, many workers had joined the public sector because of an altruistic motive and this conflicted with the new goal of making profit:

If I wanted to work for a private company I would have applied for a job in the private sector. . . . I am not driven by profit or bonuses. . . . When it is about making money out of this type of business we all cringe because to me the two don't go hand in hand. (TCS-L, caseworker 3, female)

You see, the Hotel Services Company is a business like every other business. They are out to make their pennies and the feelings of people are not paramount—they can't be because they have to make their money. (Hotel Services Company, Domestic 6, female)

Rejection of the profit motive suggests that at this early stage of PPPs employees' commitment to more deeply rooted values of altruistic motivation is ongoing—a finding supported by the emphasis workers attached to the need to deliver a 'public service', another key tenet of a traditional public sector ethos. Sustained commitment to the 'public service' also provided workers with a legitimate means of resisting pressures from managers to work to contract, a third pressure on the public sector ethos. Many workers we interviewed argued that the strict contractual monitoring of their work restricted the time available to do favours for colleagues or to provide a rounded service to end-users:

If I go on a job and if they [nurses] ask can you do this and do that I will. But we've had to stop that now because . . . all our times are monitored. We do sneak them in because we beat the times on the docket nine times out of ten. Sometimes you can't. (Estates Company, maintenance worker 5, male)

In the past you had your stint on the counter and dealt with someone's queries, and then you go away and do it and they come back and they say thank you very much. We would get thank you cards. . . . You don't get as much of it now. In the backlog it is really hard to get involved with them because you are on a clock now. (TCS-L, caseworker 5, female)

At FutureTech, many transferred IT staff were still proud to be delivering IT services in a public sector setting. Some still identified more with Govco than FutureTech even eight years after transfer:

I've been with FutureTech now eight years. You still sometimes . . . talk about them rather than us. It's strange. I think a lot of it is because FutureTech, as a company, seems so far away. . . . I've always worked on Govco accounts whether it was in the Civil Service or now, and nothing has sort of changed in that essence. You still feel very much towards them [Govco]. (FutureTech, Programmer 1, male)

Thus, across the different cases, many ex-public sector employees still view their job primarily as delivering a public service, rather than serving the goals of a private sector company. These findings alert us to the importance of understanding the way workers actively make sense of the employment relationship. While changes in work intensification and job insecurity were imposed upon workers, they were more able, it seems, to resist pressures which challenged their general approach to work—especially those pressures which demand they work to contract in the name of profit maximization.

5.7 Conclusion

This chapter has analysed four very different cases of public–private contracting and assessed the implications for performance, power, and change at work. In terms of performance, none of the cases achieved the anticipated improvements in all three areas of market discipline, contract performance and private sector expertise. For example, while the private sector agencies providing supply teachers were relatively successful in filling vacancies in schools, contractual difficulties in monitoring performance led to problems. Also, while the mega-contract agreed between Govco and FutureTech was able to institutionalize contractual mechanisms for managing performance, Govco did not fully benefit from the supposed downward cost pressures of the market. In the Customer Services case, there was dissatisfaction among public sector managers regarding TCS's expertise in delivering new information and communication technologies. And in the PFI case, there was a great deal of friction regarding contract specification and the process of monitoring performance.

But the question of whether public–private contracting generates performance improvements has to be accompanied by the question of whether potential gains (and losses) are evenly distributed. Our analysis investigated the balance of power between public and private sector organizations, as well as the extent of change experienced by workers. As we argued in Chapter 2, once we introduce notions of power and risk, it is very difficult to postulate a clear set of relationships between the type of contracting arrangement and the form of employment conditions. In particular, there is no reason why a balance or imbalance of power between contracting organizations should be directly associated with a particular form of employment conditions. Also, there is no reason to suppose that if the employer (the private sector in the case of transferred workers) enjoys a position of bargaining power in administering the contract with the purchasing partner (the public sector organization) then its workforce will necessarily be sheltered from cost cutting.

The four cases illustrate these complexities. The PFI case is illustrative of a contracting arrangement that was highly one-sided in favour of the private sector partner. Nevertheless, we found no evidence that the private sector, as the employer of some 400 transferred workers, passed on cost savings to its workforce. There was increased work intensification, job insecurity and pressures to work to contract. The Customer Services case provides a contrasting example where power relations were relatively balanced between partners. Again, we found evidence of job insecurity and work intensification, but in this case it was more strongly related to the public sector organization's role in monitoring performance than to evidence of opportunistic behaviour by the private sector employer. In the IT case, FutureTech was in the driving seat, reflecting its greater expertise in managing the contract, although Govco did benefit from external regulatory support. But in this case power relations in the contracting arrangement had relatively little influence on change at work, with the exception of the insecurity generated at times of contract renewal. This reflects the relatively intangible nature of IT services provision, which lessens the day-to-day monitoring and evaluation of work. Finally, in the Teacher Supply case, the balance of power depended on the type of school entering into a contract with the agency; schools in deprived areas had a relatively weak bargaining position. Also, there was high variation of employment experience among supply teachers with some able to bargain for relatively stable conditions while others experienced insecurity. However, while some supply teachers may have learned to shelter themselves from the vagaries of contracting, the costs were displaced to permanent schoolteachers (and pupils) who faced pressures to cover duties not written into the supply teachers' contracts.

Our analysis of the contracting arrangements, as presented in this and the previous chapter, demonstrates considerable scope for tension, problems, and conflict between partner organizations. Until now, we have focused upon the causes and consequences of these tensions. In the next chapter we turn our attention to the way managers actively seek to contain or resolve these conflicts. These 'boundary-spanning agents' shape the strength of trusting relations between organizations. The important issue is whether trust can act as a counterweight to the kinds of conflict and power imbalances identified so far.

Notes

1. For reviews of the traditional approach and 'new public management', see Fry (1989) and Lane (2000), respectively.
2. Prior to 1992, government borrowing was used by the public sector to employ private companies to construct new infrastructure. The change to PFI in 1992 represents a shift to a form of leasing, rather than the purchase of assets, since the private sector funds and builds the asset and charges the public sector for the flow of services from the asset (Grout 1997). PFI is, thus, defined as a contract for services over a specified period of time, which is quite different to the previous practice where public bodies would contract for the construction of pre-specified building requirements.
3. Insufficient knowledge regarding future payments is, at the aggregate, a significant problem for government. During the early to mid-1990s there was concern within the Treasury that it did not have accurate knowledge of future payment commitments to private sector partners, a problem it referred to as a 'fiscal time bomb' (Private Finance quarterly 1996, cited in Kerr 1998).

4. Importantly, compared to the costs of employing teachers on permanent contracts, supply teachers are cheaper. Some head teachers may therefore seek to reduce costs by buying in supply teachers on daily rates (with no holiday pay, pension contributions, etc.) instead of replacing permanent posts.

5. For example, the twelve pages for domestic services include details of standards to be achieved for each area/item cleaned (e.g. polished hard floor surfaces must have 'soilage and debris arising out of the day's activities removed. Spots, soil build up, black marks from shoes, wheels etc. removed', PFI Concession Agreement), maximum response times for *ad hoc* cleaning (from 'within 10 minutes' to 'by agreement') and performance indicators.

6. In conventional transactions cost analyses, reputation is often claimed to limit the possibility of one partner acting opportunistically, subject to certain conditions including that 'defections' from cooperative behaviour are made public knowledge and that contrived, as opposed to real, claims of defection can be verified (Williamson 1985: 395–396). The four case studies demonstrate that these conditions are by no means easily achievable.

7. TUPE regulations only protect staff at the point of transfer. While there is some evidence of partner organizations adhering to a customary practice of protecting jobs and terms and conditions for 12 months after the date of transfer, there is no time limit specified in the legislation.

8. In terms of headcount figures, there were more than 200 planned job cuts.

9. For a more general account of pressures on the public sector ethos see Hebson et al. (2003), where we develop the framework suggested by Pratchett and Wingfield (1996).

6

The Role of Boundary-Spanning Agents in Inter-Organizational Contracting

MICK MARCHINGTON, STEVEN VINCENT, AND FANG LEE COOKE

6.1 Introduction

Previous chapters in this book have examined the nature of inter-organizational relations both in the context of private–private and public–private contracting. For the most part, these have focused on relations between organizations and on the consequences of inter-organizational contracting for the employment relationship. This chapter is concerned with the role that boundary-spanning agents play in the creation and maintenance of inter-organizational relations. Boundary-spanning agents are the people who are formally and informally responsible for maintaining the contract over time, and who interact with their opposite numbers in the client or supplier organization. Obviously, their actions are shaped and influenced both by the nature of the contracts and any imbalance of power between the organizations, and may be determined to a greater or lesser extent by the degree of formality contained in these contracts. Moreover, as we have argued elsewhere, the institutional frameworks within which inter-organizational relations take place are also highly significant in setting the parameters for day-to-day exchanges (Marchington and Vincent 2004). At the same time, however, boundary-spanning agents operate to some extent independently of the formal contract, and they create and develop relationships with their counterparts in other organizations. Their own personal characteristics and previous work experience influence the way in which contracts are managed over the short-term, as does the extent to which trusting relationships are forged with those responsible for undertaking similar tasks in the organizations with which they collaborate.

In essence, the role of boundary-spanners is potentially contradictory. On the one hand, it requires the development of close, open, and trusting relations in order to achieve positive results for their own organization, while on the other the maintenance of distance and formality helps to protect their own organization from the risks associated with breakdowns in inter-organizational relations. These are often presented as alternatives, but some (Poppo and Zenger 2002) would argue that they may just as easily work in a complementary fashion and that formal contracts can aid the process of achieving close inter-organizational relations.

The remainder of this chapter is organized as follows. In Section 6.2 we review briefly the nature and meaning of trust in the context of the work of boundary-spanners before introducing—in Section 6.3—the case studies that form the basis of this chapter as well as providing data on the types of people who fill the roles of boundary-spanning agents. The following two sections contain the bulk of the empirical data, and analyse the way in which boundary-spanners see (*a*) the development of close trusting relations with their counterparts in other organizations as critical for contracting to be effective (for their own organization), and (*b*) the maintenance of formality and distance as important to ensure that their own organization limits the risks and maximizes the advantages to be achieved from inter-organizational relations. It is acknowledged at the outset that this is not a simple question of either achieving trust or maintaining distance, but that both elements are contained to greater or lesser degrees in any contract. Moreover, this mix may vary between individuals and issues, as well as over time. Finally, we discuss the implications of these findings for further research on the role of boundary-spanning agents. We also need to make it clear at the outset that we do not naively believe that trust is an end in itself, but one means by which organizations can maximize their own—and maybe other organizations'—advantage from collaborative relations.

6.2   The role of trust in the work of boundary-spanning agents

For most writers on inter-organizational relations, there is little or no mention of boundary-spanning agents, and it is assumed that the formal contracts between organizations are able to specify and determine relations sufficiently well that there is no need to consider the role played by individual actors (see, for example, Coombs and Ketchen 1999; Kaufman et al. 2000; Takeishi 2001; Fryxell et al. 2002). Even studies that do explicitly deal with the work of boundary-spanners (e.g. Ring and Van de Ven 1994) refer to it as 'backstage interpersonal dynamics'—in other words, it does not count as mainstream activity. To some extent, this is due to the methodologies employed in such studies whereby data is collected via surveys of a single respondent in each organization. It also means that there is limited recognition of either wider institutional or industry/sector norms or the activities of boundary-spanners in leveraging inter-organizational relations (Bartel 2001), fine-tuning broad contractual arrangements, or resolving—or perhaps creating—problems at the workplace (Lorenzoni and Lipparini 1999). The most developed framework for analysing the role of boundary-spanning agents is by Williams (2002) from his research on a range of public sector organizations. He argues that four sets of activities are undertaken by boundary-spanners in order to make contracts operate more smoothly. These are

Building sustainable relationships. This requires the ability to 'visualise reality from the perspective of others' (ibid.: 115), and the skills that are required to undertake this effectively are communication and listening, understanding, and empathy. Trust is a key feature underpinning this activity.

Managing through influence and negotiation. Since boundary-spanners typically lack hierarchical authority over the people with whom they deal, they need to be able to persuade others both in the formal and the informal arena (ibid.: 118).

Managing complexity and interdependencies. This comprises a mix of technical ability, experience of different cultures, and creative and entrepreneurial capabilities.

Managing roles, accountabilities, and motivations. Since this takes places in an area where tensions and contradictions are to the fore, delicate judgement is required for this to be effective and 'good' partners are expected to be flexible in their approach.

A number of key features emerge from this list of activities. It is recognized that the work of boundary-spanning agents is complex and potentially contradictory because they operate at the edge of organizations, often trying to persuade other people over whom they have not any real authority. On the one hand, this means that they need to be continually aware of their own organization's needs, able to move between a reliance on strict contractual requirements, and a willingness to take advantage of deals that are likely to benefit their own organization. On the other hand, they must be able to empathize with the needs and priorities of those working for collaborating organizations and appreciate the effect their actions may have on longer-term and wider inter-organizational relations. Issues of trust, risk, and power are intertwined in all of these considerations, but trust—however defined and conceptualized—is probably the most important factor.

There are multiple definitions of trust, but all revolve around the willingness of one actor to put themselves in a position whereby another actor could take advantage, but feel reassured this will not happen and their vulnerabilities will not be exploited (Barney and Hansen 1994; Sako 1992). Similarly, there is an assumption that both parties should be prepared to ignore the short-term gains that can be made when the other party is in a weaker position in exchange for longer-term benefits that may accrue through mutual cooperation (Lorenz 1988; Dore 1996). Macaulay (1963: 64) regards trust as an alternative to elaborate and strict legal contracts, and he suggests that the latter can prevent the emergence of good exchange relationships. An elaborate contract 'indicates a lack of trust and blunts the demands of friendship, turning a cooperative venture into an antagonistic horse-trade'. Poppo and Zenger (2002: 721), on the other hand, view strict (transactional) contracts not as an alternative to trust and relational contracting, but as complementary (see Chapter 2). They argue that 'managers tend to employ greater levels of relational norms as their contracts become increasingly customised and to employ greater contractual complexity as they develop greater levels of relational governance'.

Others regard trust in inter-organizational relations as flowing from a code of social interaction that is reinforced or shaped by wider institutional norms and traditions. In this view, Luhmann (1988: 97) states that, 'if you choose one action in preference to others in spite of the possibility of being disappointed by the action of others, you define the situation as one of trust'. Lane and Bachmann (1997: 229) see trust as a risky investment in that 'the trustor can never completely rule out that the trustee sees it as advantageous to cheat and does not comply with the assumptions that the trustee has made in regard of his behaviour'. Risk is reduced if each partner can be assured the other will not try to cheat, something that is facilitated by shared background beliefs and tacit assumptions binding the partners together. Bachmann (1999: 15) is clear that these are 'much more important in determining social actors' behaviour than explicit calculations over potential gains and losses associated with specific decisions'. Trade associations and other institutional forces (such as the law) are seen as critical in helping to create an environment that is conducive to trust formation between different organizations. For example, Lane and Bachmann (1997: 239) show how 'trade associations may create a common stock of rules which, by promoting transparency and predictability, achieve a degree of synchronization of members' expectations. These provide the basis on which trust in business relations can develop'. Conversely, where the institutional order is patchy or unreliable, 'potential trustors are more likely to use power since they find it easier to bear the risk of open conflict than the risk of misplaced trust' (Bachmann 1999: 24). This helps to explain why levels of trust may vary between case studies.

Low-trust inter-organizational relations typically exist on the basis of limited personal contact between partners and are restricted to occasional meetings between senior managers. By contrast, those established on the basis of close relations are likely to be characterized by multiple and frequent contacts at a range of levels, by devolved decision-making, by joint teams and by extensive social engagements (Hunter et al. 1996: 251). The importance of face-to-face contact has been noted repeatedly in studies of close inter-organizational relations, as too has the lubricating effect of geographical proximity between partners (Lorenz 1988; Bachmann 2001). Gulati (1995) argues that familiarity brought about through prior contact between organizations can help to reinforce inter-organizational trust, largely because boundary-spanners (to use our terminology) learn how potential partners operate, and are prepared to drop their guard and commit to close relations in subsequent deals. Of course, this implies it is in everyone's interests to seek close inter-organizational relations for mutual gains, and this is not necessarily the case (Marchington and Vincent 2004).

Table 6.1. The role of boundary-spanning agents in inter-organizational relations

The role of boundary-spanning agents	
In developing and maintaining close, trusting inter-organizational relations	In maintaining distance and formality in inter-organizational relations
Accepting the principle that open and transparent communications between parties can achieve mutual benefits	Recognizing the exchange is rooted in the selling process and that the other party needs to maximize its gains
Engaging in regular problem-solving meetings and social events across organizational boundaries	Collaboration predicated on acceptance that power underpins trust and inter-organizational relations
Working beyond or without a contract to ensure that goods or services are provided to meet others' needs	Formal monitoring of the contract and focus on whether other organization has met key targets

Table 6.1 outlines the key issues relating to the work of boundary-spanning agents and this forms the basis of the subsequent empirical analysis.

6.3   Inter-organizational contracting and the role of boundary-spanning agents

The role of boundary-spanning agents in four case studies are analysed in this chapter, including three public–private contracts—the Private Finance Initiative (PFI), housing benefits administration, and teacher supply—and the chemicals case. Each displays features that provide different insights into our analysis of the work of boundary-spanning agents. Table 6.2 reminds readers of the key features of the contracts, as well as providing further information about the types of people involved in boundary-spanning activities at the client and supplier organizations, and a summary of the most interesting features of each case.

It can be seen from Table 6.2 that the contracts varied in terms of formality and length, with the public–private partnerships (PPPs) typically for longer time periods as well as detailing performance indicators and provisions for penalty charges. In the PFI case, the entire ancillary services operation (including catering and building maintenance) had been outsourced and the major responsibility of the public sector client was to ensure this was undertaken in line with the contract. The contract between the local council and TCS for housing benefits administration was more straightforward, but it incorporated an agreement that included sets of key performance indicators (KPI) with penalty charges should these not be achieved. A considerable amount of time and effort went into managing the contract, over and above that devoted to administering housing benefit cases. In contrast, the contracts for teacher supply were short-term, often no more than one day at a time, and in many cases

Table 6.2. The role of boundary-spanning agents in context

Case study	Nature of contract	Boundary spanning agents		Mechanisms for managing contract	Key issues in case
		Client organization	Supplier organization		
PFI	Public–private partnership 35-year contract Outsourcing of all ancillary services and use of private capital to construct new buildings	Hospital Trust Senior managers liaise with SPV First line managers deal with daily issues	Private consortium firms including: Facilities Construction Hotel services Estates facilities Business manager, line managers SPV	Formal contract including service level agreements and penalty clauses SPV Monthly and weekly liaison meetings Informal discussions	Implications of PFI for inter-organizational relationships Role of SPV in monitoring performance Transfer of some managers from NHS to private sector
Customer Services (London)	PPP 7-year contract Outsourcing of most areas of housing benefits administration	Local authority Senior manager oversees contract Managers and office staff deal with TCS daily	TCS General manager responsible for delivery of contract Managers and office staff deal with council daily	Formal contracts including performance indicators and penalty clauses Quality monitoring team Monthly and weekly liaison meetings Informal discussions	Implications of PPP for inter-organizational relationships Tensions in administering housing benefit Transfer of some staff from local authority to TCS

Teacher Supply	Short-term agreements between agency and each school Use of temporary supply teachers to cover absent staff/unfilled vacancies	Schools: Head, deputy, or senior Teacher responsible for all activities TeacherTemp: Senior manager responsible for initial contact Consultants responsible for each placement	Routine visits to schools by consultants Daily telephone contact between schools and agency representatives	Quality of supply teachers depends on type of school School faces major problem if teachers unavailable or lack skills
Chemicals	Broad framework agreements Outsourcing of security, transport, and cleaning	Scotchem: depends upon supplier Managers: Purchasing director, Transport manager, Administration manager Junior staff: Purchasing office, Transport office, Administration office	Transport firms: senior managers typically managing director or regional manager Security: Senior manager, Regional manager Catering: Regional manager	Regularity of meetings varies between cases Regularity of telephone contact varies between cases	Range of suppliers dealt with differently by Scotchem Influence of forces beyond the organization on boundary-spanners' work

subject to very short periods of advance notice. Often, a school would not become aware of the need for cover until late in the day, and based on previous experience they tended to contact their preferred agencies first. The implications of inter-organizational relationships in this case are, therefore, very different from those in the long-term PPPs.

The nature of contracts in the chemical firm network was typically much less formal, perhaps aided by the fact that many had operated for several years and public money was not involved. Moreover, since many contracts were with other large firms also represented by the Chemical Industries Association (CIA) (the industry body), and because both suppliers and clients knew the market well, there were sizeable pressures to comply to avoid getting a poor reputation. The contracts for cleaning and security operations were awarded for shorter and specific periods, but even here, despite the fact that it would have been possible to write a contract that stipulated particular duties, a relatively loose framework was used. The transport firms had rather less security, relying on Scotchem's prior record to expect work to be forthcoming, but typically the firms only received confirmation of work a day or two in advance.

The numbers and types of people involved in boundary-spanning activities also varied considerably between and within the cases. At Scotchem, not many people were heavily involved in inter-organizational relations, and most were senior managers, such as the Purchasing Director and the Transport and Administration Managers. Within the supplier organizations, typically very few people were involved, which was hardly surprising in the case of small road haulage firms or in the security firm where operations were decentralized. Contracts in the teacher supply case were maintained by a small number of consultants at the agency and one or two senior staff at the schools. The agency operated with a relatively flat organizational structure, with specialist consultants in area offices working with and visiting a specific set of local schools. The TCS-Council X case effectively operated at two tiers with the senior managers meeting weekly and monthly at performance review sessions. These varied in formality and tension over the course of the contract, depending on performance and personalities, and the original targets were changed. Basically, one person from the client and one from the supplier were responsible for the overall contract, and other managers and housing benefits staff had day-to-day contact—which was relatively easy as they were co-located and their work processes were intertwined. In the PFI case, a similar distribution of activities between more senior and more junior managers was also apparent, although in this case there was the added presence of the Special Purpose Vehicle (SPV). There were at least ten senior and middle managers from both the NHS Trust and different companies from the consortium involved in meetings organized by the SPV. Although there was no fixed rule about regularity, they were held at least monthly 'to iron things out' and 'to share good practice', as the SPV General Manager put it. Junior managers from the Trust and staff from the private sector firms interacted with each other on a daily basis.

In the PFI and customer service cases, there had been transfers of staff from clients to suppliers. In both cases, the new supplier needed specialist expertise, both in terms of subject knowledge and in terms of personal contacts. TCS had no experience of administering housing benefits and therefore sought expertise that would complement and add value to their customer relationship management and systems knowledge. Some managers were also brought in from other local authorities to work alongside existing TCS staff. Similarly, while the private sector consortia of firms in the PFI had experience of running catering operations or providing maintenance support for other organizations, their knowledge of the health sector was relatively limited. In the teacher case, many of the agency staff had previously worked as teachers themselves, and felt their previous experience helped them understand the problems faced by schools.

Of course, transfers of boundary-spanning staff did not happen in all the cases. This was most noticeable at Scotchem where managers either worked their way up the hierarchy in a particular specialist field (e.g. transport) or moved around between different jobs and functions. At TCS, apart from the General Manager, several boundary-spanning agents had transferred into the housing benefits operation from other posts in the firm, especially those connected with call centre activities. Interestingly, there was no evidence of boundary-spanners transferring from suppliers to clients.

Having briefly reviewed how the contracts varied between the cases and identified the boundary-spanning agents, we now move on to examine their activities in more detail. This will be done in terms of two potentially contradictory sets of pressures—the attempt to establish trust and informality, and the maintenance of arm's length relations and formality.

6.4   The role of trust and informality in inter-organizational relations

Three sets of mutually reinforcing activities played a key role in building high trust relations between the contractual parties. These were, developing open and transparent communications, engaging in regular problem-solving meetings across organizational boundaries, working beyond or without contractual specification of tasks or confirmation of requirements. In most cases, boundary-spanning agents made deliberate efforts to achieve close and trusting relations with their counterparts in other organizations.

Open and transparent communications

Boundary-spanning agents on both the client and supplier sides of the contract repeatedly stressed that trust and informality were essential components in building relationships with colleagues at other organizations. In the chemicals

case, the principal senior managers involved in the inter-organizational relationship between Scotchem and Acidchem, for the supply of a key raw material, both spoke warmly about the importance of close personal relations. For
example, Scotchem's Purchasing Director was very positive about the value of
open and transparent communications in setting the tone for the relationship
between the two companies:

We don't actually negotiate with each other. We talk about our needs five years from now
and work out how these can be supplied. Things tend not to be written down, there are
no contracts. It all depends on trust. Trust is very important and we honour our commitments. (Scotchem, Director 3, male)

The deputy managing director at Acidchem was less effusive but also convinced about the value of this close relationship. He said:

With some customers, it's just a sell, the classic sell. It is only with key customers [such
as Scotchem] that we have this wider relationship, in terms of closeness and degree of
integration. (Acidchem, Director 1, male)

This view was echoed in the teacher supply case. Several senior staff with
responsibility for liaising with the agencies pointed to the importance of being
able to trust the agency to supply good quality teachers. This meant that
schools tried to strengthen links with a small number of agencies rather than
spread their net more widely. As one of them commented:

We've got this relationship whereby what we are building up is trust, and when they send
me someone I am fairly trusting in the fact that I know what I am getting. It's another reason for not expanding the agencies (with which I deal). I work with two at the moment
simply because we have built up relationships and I think that is very important. (School E,
Senior Teacher 6, male)

Open and transparent communications, in which both sides of the contract
would speak candidly about work-related issues, seemed to be the bedrock of
trusting inter-organizational relations, while the absence of effective methods of
communication was synonymous with distrust and suspicion. The boundary-
spanning agents at TeacherTemp worked principally in local offices, and it was
this group of staff who had the most frequent contact with schools. Consultants
at some of the offices felt it was better to tell a school there were no suitable
teachers available that day rather than send someone they knew was inappropriate. One of the managers explained that the test of a good relationship was a
willingness to discuss problems rather than look for alternative agencies:

We've built up great relationships with them [the schools] and they trust us a lot and
we've always said 'if there's anything wrong you must tell us and we will put it right'. And
I think that's building relationships when the Head will say 'your teacher wasn't very good
today'. Some schools wouldn't tell you, they'd just go somewhere else. (TeacherTemp,
Manager 2, female)

Similar attempts at relationship building were also apparent in the housing
benefits case, especially on the part of the supplier, TCS. The General Manager's

style was charismatic and he stressed repeatedly that the development of close, open, and trusting relationships with his counterparts in the local authority was essential for the contract to work:

And what we are doing is building trust . . . It's about being honest and not trying to hide anything in terms of the services delivered. So we put our hands up and say if service delivery is weak. I think it's a true partnership now. We work very, very well together. (TCS-L, General Manager, male)

The senior manager from the council also agreed that trust was essential if the contract was to work effectively. To some extent, greater amounts of informal contact and more open relations had been facilitated through learning how to work in partnership during early years of the contract. It was acknowledged that neither side really knew what to expect from the outsourcing arrangement. There remained constraints on how far trust could develop, most importantly from his point of view due to performance levels still being less than required. He noted:

There is certainly a greater level of trust now than there was in the early days of the contract, and I think the commitment is there on behalf of TCS to deliver the service. The only problem remains their ability to do so. (Council X, Manager 1, male)

One tactic used by a number of the private sector suppliers, following the transfer of services, was to recruit managers either from the client or from other parts of the public sector on the assumption this would improve understanding and empathy, as well as help to develop close links. This was very apparent in the PFI and housing benefits cases, and indeed in the latter, the General Manager had come from another local authority where he had been actively involved in trying to keep housing benefits in-house. In the PFI case, ex-Trust managers were regarded as a particular asset to the private sector consortium because of

their site knowledge and general experience in dealing with the Trust. They know how to mobilize key personnel to get things done and to by-pass problems. (Hotel Services Company, Manager 2, female)

Trusting relations, therefore, appeared to depend upon the provision of reliable service from firms with a good reputation, and there appeared to be an implicit link between trust and the quality of communications between the parties. In effect, by developing open and transparent communications boundary-spanners were able to exchange information in order to demonstrate that the other organization was reliable at satisfying customer needs. Furthermore, by doing this the supplier also helped the customer realize its wider objectives. For example, when there were changes in Scotchem's requirements or when Acidchem predicted a potential break in supply, both organizations attempted to communicate these eventualities far enough in advance for contingency plans to be arranged. In effect, reputation and reliability were founded on clear and transparent communications that were facilitated by regular formal and informal meetings.

Regular problem-solving meetings and social events

All the inter-organizational relations discussed in this chapter had an administrative system that involved both formal and informal cross-boundary meetings—in line with Sako's description of OCR-type relations (see Chapter 2). These meetings were typically about business needs, and they were often fixed at regular intervals, but they also provided an opportunity for discussions about other issues as well as a chance to cement relationships. The General Manager at TCS-L believed that their high trust relationship with the council was achieved by maintaining close personal (informal) contact with the Client Manager responsible for monitoring the contract and regular (formal) meetings between the two parties. He felt the former were rather more important in setting the tone for the relationship and in ensuring performance targets were achieved so that his 'clients' (the officers and the councillors) and claimants were adequately served.

One of the TeacherTemp staff who had previously been a teacher stressed how visiting the schools on a regular basis and talking with senior staff face-to-face made it much easier to develop a relationship:

We build relationships with headteachers by calling regularly and seeing how the teacher has got on. If it's a new teacher we do it at the end of the day so we can see how they have got on in their first placement. (TeacherTemp, Consultant 4, female)

On some occasions, most notably in the chemicals network, contact also spilled over into joint social events. The links between Scotchem and Acidchem were particularly close, and probably stronger than most because of their mutual dependence on each other for continued business. Meetings were held at the Scotchem site on a routine basis, social events were organized and there was also evidence of joint collaboration on specific technical problems—for example, providing raw material in granular form and different packaging systems. Not all relationships were as strong as this, however. For example, Cargoline was one of the smaller road haulage companies that worked with Scotchem for many years and its Managing Director saw that regular meetings and close links with Scotchem's Transport Manager were important for future business. These were maintained through a series of contracts, but he was also very aware of the dangers of becoming too reliant on just one person to continue the business. He told us:

We've been doing Scotchem for five or six years and the Transport Manager has been our contact all the time. As he has progressed within the company our contacts have altered. You always worry because we might lose the business. I think he keeps us sorted, as a rule. We have a chat about football and that seems to sort it all out. (Cargoline, Owner, male)

The inter-organizational relationships between Scotchem and the firms supplying security and cleaning services were also dependent on opportunities to meet people from the other organization to discuss work-related issues.

In the case of Faciliclean this seemed to work well, according to both parties, because a supervisor was available on site each afternoon and she always visited the Scotchem Administration Manager to 'see if there is anything special, if there are any problems or anything'. By contrast, although the initial contract between Scotchem and Securiforce had not been specific about requirements, meetings had not occurred and the breakdown of interpersonal relations made the management of this contract tense and problematic. The Administration Manager complained:

They have a supervisor, but I don't know the last time he was on site. He should be here about once every fortnight. I'd be lucky if he was on site three times this year. The Securiforce manager called me from the gatehouse a few weeks ago, but he had not made an appointment so I refused to see him. (Scotchem, Manager 8, male)

This case is particularly useful because it shows how the client placed considerable emphasis on regular and close interpersonal contact in order to make the contract work effectively, and how, in the absence of this, problems were difficult to resolve. In this, as in other cases, effective management of the relationships also required boundary-spanning agents to work beyond or without contracts in order to deliver the required performance levels.

Working beyond/without contract

Inter-organizational relations at Scotchem provide several examples where the formal contract was ignored, bypassed, and even absent from the ongoing exchange relationship. Apart from the Securiforce case, Scotchem and several contractors worked beyond or without contracts in order to further the interests of one or both parties. For example, as part of the business process, transport firms were issued with a time to arrive at the Scotchem site to pick up deliveries. However, haulage firms often requested earlier or later pick-up times to ensure that they were able to meet ferry time-tables or because of delays on the motorway. While Scotchem gained little from changing the arrangements, as payments did not vary, they were willing to accommodate the wishes of their suppliers in the interest of good business practice. Similarly, through interpersonal exchange between Scotchem and Acidchem, many areas of mutual interest beyond the provision of raw material have been identified. For example, managers from the two organizations met to discuss transportation strategy, human resource issues, and outsourcing arrangements. While these activities were unrelated to business contracts between the firms, they did help to save costs, so contributing to the long-term stability of both organizations and promoting positive perceptions of each other.

The PFI offered some of the most interesting insights into the roles played by boundary-spanning agents because the SPV monitored the contract. Its objective was to provide a conduit through which all services provided by the private

sector consortium were delivered to the NHS Trust in accordance with specifications. The General Manager of the SPV felt that a key aspect of her role was
to overcome contractual problems through an informal approach, thereby
shifting the focus of the relationship away from the more specific details within
the contracts themselves. She felt these were too unwieldy and did not allow for
variations that would occur during any task within the contract. The SPV
General Manager believed there was sufficient trust in the system to accept the
agreement in principle. Furthermore she also felt it was 'in nobody's interests
to see the PFI fail, and that close communication and contact, close working
relationships (were needed) just to get to know each other better'. In other
words, as with most of the cases reviewed above, there was a belief from senior
managers—in this instance from the SPV—that trust and the development of
close interpersonal relations facilitated better performance. Unfortunately,
interviews with a range of boundary-spanning agents working for the Trust and
for the private sector firms did not appear to support this optimistic stance.
Indeed, both parties expressed major concerns about the behaviour of the
other, as we see in Section 6.5. In these circumstances trust did not develop and
there was a tendency to use power to reinforce contractual requirements.

6.5   Trust and formality in the context of economic exchange and service provision

In the previous section, we illustrated how boundary-spanners, especially
those at more senior levels, stressed the need to develop trust in order to generate mutually beneficial outcomes. However, it was also clear that boundary-
spanning agents recognized their relationships were essentially rooted in
economic exchanges, in conceptions of profit and loss where there may not
always be a win–win scenario. Clients were aware of the need to get value for
money in their dealings with suppliers and in most cases of the availability of
alternative suppliers should they not perform at a satisfactory level. Equally,
suppliers were aware of their need to 'sell' services to clients, especially at the
time of contract formation and renewal, but also on an ongoing basis for those
contracts that were short-term in nature—such as at the schools or between
Scotchem and the haulage firms. Ironically, despite the fact that these activities
can create tensions between the parties, the ability to save money through an
exchange or sell more products and services to a client is often predicated on
having previously established trust at an organizational level.

In this section, we examine data from the four cases to illustrate how economic
imperatives underpinning these contracts influenced the work of boundary-
spanning agents, especially in relation to their own organization's objectives.
We do so by exploring three distinct features that are intertwined in the process
of managing the business relationship: the sales process and organizational
advantage; power relations and trust; formal monitoring of the contract.

The sales process and the balance of organizational advantage

We have already argued that reputation and reliable service were regarded as essential to the establishment of trust, but this has to be contextualized within business relationships based on the profit motive and the need to sell services. The effects of recurrent contracting were most apparent in the relations in the teacher supply case, and particularly in both sides' awareness that selling took place every time a supply teacher was placed at a school. The senior manager at one of TeacherTemp's local offices had previous experience in the area of commercial recruitment, marketing, and sales, and she felt this helped her considerably in her current role:

I wouldn't say I was a hard-headed sales person but I like to win. I always believe in what I do, and I like to win nicely. (TeacherTemp, Manager 2, female)

She was not the only manager to describe her work as sales, however, not only in relation to the schools but also in persuading individual teachers on their books to go to specific schools, especially those that were known to be difficult. This was a major issue for the agencies since it was in their interests to ensure as many teachers as possible received placements and that as many schools as possible received supply teachers. One consultant stated:

My job is to sell to the school, and also sell the schools to the teachers, so we don't generally have many teachers saying 'I won't go'. (TeacherTemp, Consultant 1, female)

Given differences in the quality of teachers and the attractiveness of schools, this raised a problem, but the need for profit meant that teachers and schools were often provided with less than full information. Interviews with supply teachers themselves indicated this happened frequently (Grimshaw et al. 2003). Several boundary-spanners at the schools also suggested that profit motive was what drove the agencies and consultants were not really concerned about the quality of teachers or the needs of the schools. On some occasions, staff in the schools felt the agencies went too far in trying to get new business or place a teacher. One head teacher (School G, Senior Teacher 8, male) referred to some agencies as acting like 'double-glazing salesmen', pestering the schools without need. Another was even more bitter:

They just cold-call the school, touting the inadequates they have on their books. They phone too much, they are a nuisance. If I wanted them I would ring them. (School C, Senior Teacher 4, male)

In this case, the different parties to the relationship had contrasting views about the sales process, with the agencies regarding it as legitimate while those in the schools were much more circumspect, and in some cases felt it was actually counterproductive. Similar points arose in other cases. For example, equally dissimilar perceptions arose in the housing benefits case with the TCS-L General Manager describing relations as very open while his counterparts at the council remained cautious and even resentful of the contribution made by the private sector. One was particularly scathing about the lack of private sector expertise:

We thought the private companies had all the expertise and had a lot to offer to the public sector. But all they did was to recruit people from the public sector to run the business for them. We learn nothing from them and the public sector ends up losing all the good people. (Council X, Manager 3, male)

Boundary-spanning agents are in a highly precarious position if they are keen on a traditional career within organizational boundaries because their work is visible and, literally, at the 'very edge of the organization'. First, their career prospects appeared to depend on the success of the contractual relationship and their ability to manage under the scrutiny of both parties. They were expected to bridge the differences—often with personal charisma and interpersonal skills rather than official authority—between the two parties, especially when contractual difficulties arose. Parties could pull out of the contract before the due date if it proved difficult to maintain, and in this situation, boundary-spanning agents were likely to be affected more adversely than ordinary workers. Moreover, even if business relations were well managed at the operational level, senior management may still decide to alter contractual agreements for wider strategic objectives. The Administration Manager at Scotchem was highly aware that his role was precarious because, at the time, his employer was debating whether to outsource more contracts to an external facilities management specialist:

If Faciliclean get the rest, excluding the catering side, they will want to put a site manager on the contract here. At the end of the day, if Faciliclean has a site manager and Scotchem is paying me to be a facilities manager, then one of us goes. (Scotchem, Manager 8, male)

Similar points were highlighted in the PFI case, when an estates manager from the service provider was removed rather than managers from the client. One summarized it this way:

Middle managers are often the scapegoats and get sacrificed by the senior managers when things go wrong. In fact, senior managers can be the scapegoats as well. (Estates Company, Manager 1, male)

Power relations and trust

The use of power in shaping relationships and outcomes came across strongly in the private–private contracts between Scotchem and its supplier firms (see Chapter 4), despite recurrent reference to 'trust' and 'relationship building' themes during interviews with senior managers both at Scotchem and its suppliers. For example, the Scotchem Transport Manager spoke in terms of the friendly nature of relations between his company and the road haulage firms, but he also made it abundantly clear where his own interests ultimately lay:

There's always been a social element, it's a close knit fraternity on the haulage side. (However,) I use the buying power that I have to benefit my company. That's what I'm employed for. The threat of pulling our business is very scary to some people and I've used this to our advantage. (Scotchem, Manager 7, male)

Boundary-spanning agents from the transport firms recognized that trust was established in the context of a very unequal relationship, and if Scotchem wanted something there was little doubt they were expected to comply in order to maintain future contracts. This was not presented as an overbearing approach by the individuals there, but accepted as an economic inevitability of the client–supplier relationship. If, for example, they arrived late for a slot at the site, they acknowledged the drivers might have to wait several hours until a new slot was found. Similarly, if a load had to be on the ferry at a certain time, the transport firm accepted the obligation to allow sufficient extra time to get there in case of hold-ups or breakdowns. Cargoline's owner said:

We have a good working relationship with Scotchem and that's the main thing. But that's our core business and you tend to bend over backwards or jump when they say jump . . . You have these core companies and you have got to retain those. (Cargoline, Owner, male)

Unlike the previous example, the PFI case was relatively new and relationships appeared slow to develop. Boundary-spanning agents from the NHS Trust were extremely critical of how their inter-organizational relationship was working, and they had major doubts about the objectives and actions of the private sector firms (see Chapter 5). They were concerned the private sector companies had no interest in patients or generating improvements in health care generally but were there purely to make a profit. For example, the Estates Manager told us that 'the only reason the PFI consortium does it [this contract] is to make money, but there is no true value added in what they do'. One of the managers responsible for monitoring the contract on behalf of the Trust totally dismissed the notion the private sector firms were engaged in a partnership. Her view was:

They [the private firms] are good at sending you off down the wrong track, they are experts in splitting one person off against another in the Trust. Nothing you ever say is forgotten, and all of us have had to learn that you do not trust any of them as far as you can throw them. (NHS Trust, Manager 6, female)

Despite the highly positive rhetoric about trust and openness displayed by the TCS-L General Manager, his counterpart in the council was much less convinced that open and trusting relationships were a necessary and sufficient condition for contracts to work effectively. He was also acutely aware that it was potentially dangerous for the council to get too close to TCS, as he was the guardian of public money and probity. He provided a slightly different view from TCS of what partnership and trust actually meant to the council:

It is in the spirit of partnership but the contract always comes to the fore when we start talking about penalties. We have got an open relationship, it's got to be, but if it is going to work we need distance, it's more informal than it should be. (Council X, Manager 1, male)

His view was shared by more junior managers on the client side who felt that TCS was rather better at saying what it intended to do than what it had actually achieved, or talking themselves out of a difficult situation and then not delivering satisfactory performance subsequently. For instance, the Housing Services Manager for the council observed:

One of the things TCS tends to do is tell you things are more advanced than they really are, things are up and running when they are barely off the ground. I've had to put things on the council's agenda because we need co-operative ways of working to get priority cases dealt with. It's got very little to do with nurturing a relationship with TCS. (Council X, Manager 3, male)

This suggests that where the parties do not have similar objectives, do not share an understanding of what has been agreed in the contract and are not influenced by wider institutional norms, it is hard for trust to develop through informal means. Moreover, as we saw in Section 6.4, it is extremely difficult to establish shared trust if one party fails to meet (implicit or explicit) contractual requirements. Under these circumstances it is highly likely that formal monitoring processes will be used to ensure that objectives are reached, as this ensures services are delivered as well as providing a benchmark against which any future trust can be gauged.

Formal monitoring of the contract

Boundary-spanners operate within spaces allowed by business contracts, and they are the people who have to find ways to put formal agreements into effect. Their influence depends on how much room there is for interpretation in the formal contract, as this is unlikely to specify everything in detail. Even if there is room for informal arrangements, in order for this to work some degree of trust needs to exist between the parties. In the PFI case, major concerns were expressed by managers and supervisors working for the private firms, many of whom had been transferred from the local NHS Trust. These managers were dismayed to find that new performance criteria had driven informality out of the system, reducing greatly the opportunity to do extra jobs as 'specials'. At the same time, however, managers were conscious of the need for the private consortium to increase revenue by charging the Trust for additional work done. This led to tensions according to one of the operations managers:

The Trust will look hard not to pay and [the private sector firm] will try to look hard to get paid. There is no real love between us, but we still scratch each other's backs and try to get the best out of each other. (Estates Company, Manager 3, male)

The nature of the contract also meant that jobs could not be undertaken until the correct paperwork had been supplied and approval had been given by both parties to go ahead. This inevitably led to time delays and frustration on the part of departments that wanted work to be done, and typically it was the boundary-spanners who bore the brunt of complaints. In the past, it was argued, jobs would be completed and the paperwork would follow later as part of a transaction within the boundaries of the NHS. The fact that 'everything now needed to be in black and white' was a major source of frustration.

For boundary-spanning agents at TCS-L, the daily realities of dealing with their counterparts on the council, most of whom they used to work alongside, were equally problematic. They highlighted the complexities and problems that arose in determining how much benefit claimants were due to receive. The language used by this group of people was much more cautious and even hostile. For example, one noted:

With 100 percent determination [the validation process] we are always arguing with them upstairs, it's always going backwards and forwards. When we don't get anywhere near we have to get managers [from the council side] involved. They are the referees. (TCS-L, caseworker 4, female)

Clients regularly complained about the amount of time taken monitoring and overseeing the contract and the fact that performance gains appeared illusory (Marchington et al. 2003). The Council's Client Manager reflected that monitoring was much greater and more detailed than they had ever envisaged, in terms of meetings with TCS, monitoring performance, and interfacing with politicians. The philosophy underpinning their work was fundamentally different from that which operated under the council. This quote sums up the conflicting perspectives well and highlights the importance of the formal contract:

It's a difficulty for TCS because they are driven by commercial considerations and therefore any change that exposes them to a commercial risk has to be covered. Whereas the Council's perspective in the past was 'let's deliver the service and we'll worry about the resource implications afterwards'. (Council X, Manager 1, male)

In the absence of high trust inter-organizational relations the client relied on the formal contract to ensure the supplier did not act in a profiteering manner. This was particularly critical where the contract was signed only recently and was long-term in nature. In these examples it was expected that trust would deepen over the life of the contract if suppliers met KPIs, and it meant that the boundary-spanning agents responsible for the contact on a daily basis had to demonstrate conformance to requirements.

6.6 Conclusions

It is often assumed that inter-organizational networks operate smoothly and with high-trust relations, thus facilitating improvements in overall performance. In this chapter, we have shown that while the achievement of close, trusting relations between boundary-spanning agents is a key factor in inter-organizational relations, it is not the only objective. Indeed, the need to protect one's own organization, typically through the maintenance of distance and formality and the use of power, is an equally critical aspect of these relationships and is apparent in the data presented in this chapter. The precise balance between these two potentially contradictory goals depends on the nature of inter-organizational contracts, as well as on the level at which the boundary-spanning agents operate and whether they work for the client or the supplier organization. There is little doubt that their roles are influenced, often implicitly rather than overtly, by power relations in the network. Moreover, the work of boundary-spanning agents, as well as the contracts on which they work, is also shaped by institutional pressures—such as through membership of the same trade association or legal obligations.

The work of boundary-spanning agents clearly depends on the nature of contracts. For example, the length of contracts in the PFI and housing benefits cases removed the need for daily negotiations about price, but instead led to a focus on performance indicators and daily work problems—such as how to deal with a particular benefit claim or a maintenance job on a hospital ward. The staff involved in servicing these contracts worked closely with similar staff in the other organization, and unless there was a major problem contact was maintained and the parties had to learn to cope with one another—for better or for worse (Cooke et al. 2004). By contrast, there were frequent contacts between TeacherTemp and the schools, and because supply teachers rarely had long-term placements, new sets of working relations had to be forged each day or week. Similarly, the consultants and the staff responsible for getting supply teachers had to set up new contracts on a regular basis rather than relying on the continuation of existing contracts. The situation in the chemicals case was mixed, with some continuity (e.g. between the chemical firms) and some fragmentation, such as when different drivers were deployed on Scotchem deliveries.

Although some boundary-spanning agents from the client side had responsibility to monitor the contract rather than work alongside staff from the supplier (e.g. in the PFI and chemicals cases), in others—such as the teacher supply case—they were actually engaged in similar work. In the housing benefits case, TCS workers responsible for calculating payments had to present their case to a council employee who judged whether it was correct. If not, that meant further investigations or another attempt to write the letter to claimants, all of which led to delays in payments. This annoyed the TCS workers, not least because they often continued to disagree with the council verdict, especially when it was made by someone with whom they used to work and for whom they had little respect. This ensured that the process of agreeing claims was fraught with difficulties and often flamed by interpersonal hostilities. In this context, boundary-spanning agents working for the supplier felt relations were dominated by distrust rather than by consent and cooperation.

The use of words such as 'trust' was more likely the higher the boundary-spanning agents were up the organizational hierarchy. In the chemicals case, this was particularly prevalent on the client side, while in others—such as the housing benefits case—suppliers were more likely to use the rhetoric of trust in their descriptions of how the contract should be managed at an interpersonal level. While the Client Manager from Council X believed trust was essential, he was also highly aware of his public obligations, and therefore suspicious of allowing relationships to become too close. In both these cases, boundary-spanners lower in the hierarchy were much less positive when describing relations with other organizations. In the case of supply teachers, the word 'trust' was used by people on both sides of the contract, but especially by TeacherTemp consultants. In this case much depends on the type of school with which the agency was dealing, and its ability to attract 'better' quality supply teachers. Boundary-spanning agents working at schools from deprived areas or with discipline problems found it more difficult to persuade their agency contacts to send them good teachers, and not surprisingly they were less positive about the quality of interpersonal relations. In the PFI case, apart from some references by the SPV General Manager to trust, most boundary-spanning agents felt relations were tense, one-sided, and lacking any real foundation.

Perceptions of trust also depended on the balance of power. In the chemicals network, while people on both sides used the word, it was clear the client typically dominated the relationship—with the possible exception of the inter-organizational relationship with Acidchem where a high degree of mutual dependence between the companies, as well as institutional similarities, had led to higher levels of trust and collaboration. In other cases, however, there were few institutional norms binding the parties together. Boundary-spanners at the haulage firms, for example, while keen to maintain close relations with their Scotchem contact, recognized that their desire for 'trust' was seen in the context of economic muscle. In the two PPPs trust was a term used mostly by more senior managers working for the SPV (in the case of the PFI) or for the supplier (in the case of housing benefits). In the former case, boundary-spanners from the client side felt the suppliers were only really interested in making profits and using 'spin' about patient care to give their arguments credence. Given that NHS managers felt they had no choice about whether to sub-contract work due to government edicts, it is hardly surprising interpersonal relations were adversely affected. In the housing benefits case, more junior boundary-spanning agents working for TCS-L felt relationships were predicated on distrust. In both cases, therefore, trust was hard to sustain in the context of differences in style and orientation (e.g. profits versus patient support) as well as in their day-to-day experiences of dealing with the other side. In the teacher case, both parties recognized selling was taking place, but they felt the development of close and trusting relations might help to achieve better outcomes; short-circuiting formal processes might help the school get better teachers and the agencies place staff without having to use the rituals that might be needed with a new or more distant contact. However, schools from deprived areas were less able to take advantage of this because they lacked power.

In the public–private contracts, a number of boundary-spanning agents moved from the public sector into posts with the private firms. This provided suppliers with readymade expertise, and at the same time potentially weakened the public sector client. This was particularly apparent in the PFI case where it was felt the NHS had lost out significantly, and it was clear that TeacherTemp has been able to strengthen its legitimacy by employing ex-teachers as consultants. In housing benefits, TCS was less able to reap advantages because the council continued to maintain control through the determination process. Interestingly, however, transferred staff had little desire to return to the public sector as, for some, the move had opened up new career possibilities and different skills. Of course, this was not universal and other staff found their traditional skills—especially technical skills—were no longer valued.

In summary, it is clear that the work of boundary-spanning agents comprises elements of trust formation and formal distance, the precise balance depending on circumstances. We would argue it is easier for trust to develop if there is strong institutional support for open and transparent communications, as was the case between the two chemical firms. Moreover, broad equality of economic dependence also helps to create the conditions under which mutual trust is more likely to be formed and sustained. This is much harder to establish in an institutional vacuum where there is no common, agreed code of conduct to guide behaviour, and boundary-spanners need to ensure their own objectives are met at all costs. We are not suggesting it is impossible for trust to emerge in situations of economic imbalance but in these situations, it is less risky to maintain distance from the other party and instead rely on power to protect one's own organization.

7

Employment Policy and Practice: Crossing Borders and Disordering Hierarchies

JILL RUBERY AND JILL EARNSHAW

7.1 Introduction

The model of a single employing organization with well-defined boundaries and considerable control over its internal policies has traditionally provided the starting point for analysing the employment relationship. This model certainly underpins the current system of employment law and individual employment rights and is still pervasive in debates on human resource management and occupational psychology (for a review see Colling 2000; Rubery et al. 2002; and Chapter 3). Developments in each of these fields do suggest increasing awareness of the complexity of employment relations and the 'decentring' of organizations (see Chapter 3). The flexible firm model (Atkinson 1984) describes how, in principle at least, different employment strategies may be used for different groups of workers. Similarly, in human resource management, debates on 'best fit' have identified a need for internal flexibility to align employment practices with business and productivity objectives that may vary across internal units, even if it is still not clear how such internal flexibility can be combined with the consistent policy approach needed to underpin a high commitment human resource strategy (Legge 1985, 1989; Purcell 1989; Purcell and Ahlstrand 1994; Boxall 1998; Kinnie et al. 2000). These discussions have not, however, addressed the influence of multi-employers and clients in the shaping of the employment relationship.

Despite the interest in more 'flexible' internal human resource arrangements, most policy development in the employment area—whether found in employment legislation, codes of practice, or trade union demands—is predicated on internal coherence. Even when the basis for differentiation between workers has been changing—from skill to competence and from job grade to performance criteria—there is still an expectation, at the workplace level and in society, that internal employment policies are based on some consistent principles and rules. The UK trade union campaigns against a two-tier or multi-tier workforce in the public sector (UNISON 2002), as a consequence of public–private partnerships, have clearly resonated with public perceptions of the appropriate and fair way to organize employment—that is, to aim at internal coherence and consistency (Baron and Kreps 1999). This notion of consistency and coherence can be interpreted as involving at least three elements; first, the provision of similar terms and conditions to those who are employed at the same workplace on similar tasks; second, the legitimation of differences in treatment between groups or individuals by reference to some principles that underpin the HR policies—for example, by reference to skill, effort, experience, performance, seniority, etc.; third, that the constituent elements of human resource policies are supportive and not contradictory. The need for internal consistency within each of the elements of the human resource package is a prior condition for the overall package to provide a strong and consistent message (Boxall and Purcell 2003: 56).

In this chapter we explore to what extent within our cases—drawing particularly on the airport, customer service, IT, PFI, and Post Office cases—we find evidence of employment policy and practice being subject to competing and potentially conflicting influences from 'multi-employers' or 'multi-agencies'. In taking this approach we do not assume that inter-organizational relations are the only factors preventing organizations aiming for or achieving internal coherence and consistency; the problems of viewing organizations as unified entities or of assuming that policy objectives are fully implemented and without perverse effects are well-documented in the literature (Morgan 1990). The contribution here is to extend and thereby reinforce critiques of representations of organizations as monolithic coherent entities with abilities to act as if directed by single agents with a single coherent vision and objective. If organizations are analysed instead as a set of relationships with a multiplicity of actors, the focus on the inter-organizational relations and their influences on employment serves to extend and add complexity to this critique of conventional organizational analysis (see Chapter 1 and DiMaggio 2001).

There are parallels to be made between the argument we are seeking to develop and a debate that has dominated the literature over recent years, that is, employers' search for flexibility. The tension for employers in seeking more flexible employment arrangements can be characterized as a tension between internal order and hierarchy versus external opportunism (Cappelli et al. 1997a, b). The flexible firm facilitated the adoption of different strategies for different groups of employees, thereby breaking the internal hierarchy and the constraints associated with the standard employment contract while, in principle, retaining a coherent, fair, and logical progression system for the core employees. The core/periphery strategy is supposed to yield not only numerical, but also financial flexibility—that is, opportunities to reject a unified coherent pay structure across the core and periphery boundaries and provide greater discretion to management in its reward strategies. Tensions between the internal and the external can be expected, however, to increase in a context of permeable organizations. This is because employing organizations are not only seeking to exploit new external opportunities without creating internal chaos, but are also having to adjust their internal systems to fit with the demands, needs, and requirements of external organizations that are clients, collaborators, or suppliers. These ideas have been developed in the context of supply chains (see Scarbrough 2000 and Chapter 3) but the main focus of the flexibility debate has been on contracting out and not on the influence of clients.

7.2 Pressures towards and against ordered hierarchies and consistency in employment policy and practice

Table 7.1 sets out these potential pressures for internal consistency on the one hand and for flexible response to external opportunities and influences on the other. It does so under three headings—managerial motivations, employee and trade union motivations, and the regulatory conditions that shape the costs and benefits of fragmentation versus integration. The first section focuses on pressures towards internal consistency, the second on the contexts in which management and workers/trade unions may seek to make opportunistic use of the external environment and where regulations encourage such activities, and the third on the influences on internal organization emanating from inter-organizational relationships and external regulatory and other conditions. This distinction between agents using the external environment to pursue their own interests and responding to external pressure to meet other agents' demand or requests is useful but not watertight. For example, internal agents may use external inter-organizational relations as a form of leverage to bring about the restructuring of internal hierarchies.

As section one of Table 7.1 outlines, the benefits for management from internal consistency and hierarchy derive from three main factors—reduction in transaction costs, the facilitation of coordination of activities (including redeployment of workers between contracts and sites) and the establishment of a coherent, integrated, and transparent set of employment rewards as a basis for seeking commitment of the workforce. Such commitment is expected to be more easily obtained where there is a perception of fairness and due process in the employment relationship. Managers are also more likely to favour consistent and organization-wide policies in a context where employment law and quasi-law (such as codes of practice) assume that systems will be applied fairly and systematically between groups, or if not, that the differences between the groups will be clearly defined and not subject to random change. Trade unions and employees, taken as a group, are likely to favour consistency not simply because this accords with some notion of fairness, but because by establishing rules and procedures that apply to groups or to all staff, the impact is to limit managerial discretion and favouritism (Marsden 1999: 3). The presence of

Table 7.1. Internal and external influences on human resource policies

Managerial	Regulatory	Employees/trade unions
1. Internal consistency		
Facilitates coordination of activities and redeployment. Basis for psychological contract. Coherent/consistent rules legitimize managerial norms/authority relations. Contributes to perceptions of fairness.	Presumption of coherence/consistency across workplace/ organization in, for example, Equal Pay Act, unfair dismissal legislation. Codes of practice expected to be adopted for organization/ workplace as a whole.	Notions of fairness based on rules/custom not absolute justice. Rules/consistency principles used to limit managerial discretion. Opposition to multi-tiered workforce as breaches principles of fairness/creates potential competitive threat to primary conditions.
2. Use of the external market to evade internal constraints and/or costs		
Differentiated strategies— core/periphery—to achieve cost reductions/tailor employment conditions to suit different groups/ product market conditions. Less transparent systems provide managers with more discretion/more power. Use of external contracting may put pressure on internal wage levels	Opportunities to evade regulations/comparisons through contracting out (e.g. pension provision not covered by TUPE, new recruits not covered by TUPE, agency staff available on different terms and conditions).	Differential bargaining power reflected in either separate pay and grading structures or in differentiated treatment-for example bonuses/PRP/ overtime opportunities, additional payments, etc.
3. Pressures from external organizations		
Internal management may need to respond to client demands/requirements, to share employment functions with client or to manage direct interventions by non-employers/clients in employment functions.	Client may have regulatory responsibilities for checking/auditing work. TUPE requires the maintenance of terms and conditions of transferred staff, not harmonization with new organization.	Transferred staff retain same employment conditions/same union as previous employer. Comparisons of 'fairness' made across employing organizations. Career opportunities seen across employing organizations.

trade unions and collective bargaining is, therefore, likely to provide a check on the extent of arbitrariness in the employment practices and to increase the degree of transparency.

Against these incentives for consistency, there are countervailing pressures towards inconsistency or disordered hierarchies. For managers the main incentives are to evade the constraints of the internal hierarchy (including pro-visions relating to pay rates, flexibility, working time, etc.) by taking advantage of labour on the external labour market available to work under different norms or rules. Where there are pressures for internal consistency and fairness, managers may use the external market, either to solve a recruitment or reten-tion problem by providing more favourable terms than would be possible under an internal contract or to reduce labour costs below the internal levels. This use of the external market will be in part dependent on the incentives within the regulatory system. The TUPE Regulations reduce such incentives, at least for transferred staff, except for the incentive to reduce the costs of pension provision which is not covered. However, even in a TUPE transfer, new recruits are not covered by the protection. Trade unions and employees are likely to favour consistency, but individual groups or indeed individuals may also be keen to exert their own individual or group-related bargaining power, particu-larly where this derives from specific external factors.

Pressures toward disordered hierarchies may increase when organizations are embedded in a set of inter-organizational relations. Internal managers may be under pressure—by contractual specification or as a result of non-contractual interventions by clients from whom they seek repeat business—to pay attention to the demands of the client in shaping their own internal practices. This shaping could include the wage structure (if clients' contracts provide for different wage rates or incentive systems), the system of work organization, the working time operation, the quality of the work required, and the monitoring and disciplining of staff. Such client interventions are likely to be stronger the more that clients have direct regulatory roles in checking and supervising work. Where the inter-organizational relationship has involved the transfer of staff, disordered hierarchies may be almost inevitable as the TUPE regulations do not allow for harmonization of terms and conditions with the employees of the new employer[1] (see Cooke et al. 2004). Moreover, employees who have been transferred across or who work closely with clients and non-employers may not confine their comparison of fairness to the employees of their own employer. Working in a multi-employer setting may, therefore, change even employees' and trade unions' commitment to internal consistency as the only or main basis for fairness.

7.3   Disordering hierarchies within the case studies

With this framework, we need therefore to turn to our case studies to see how inter-organizational relations cut across and interact with internal practices based on principles of hierarchy and consistency. We take up these issues across three broad dimensions of human resource management practice: pay and other elements of the reward system; employment security; and work organization, control and discipline.[2]

Pay structures

While pay structures imply the creation of some form of social order (White 2000: 27), the internal pay structure has always reflected dynamic tension between 'the needs of the internal market for equity and fairness and the differential price at which labour can be purchased in the external market' (White 2000: 27). This dynamic tension between the internal and the external can take different forms. Recently 'new pay' theorists have played down the importance of internal consistency and urged management to relate pay more to business needs and to the external market value or power of the individual (Lawler 1990, 1995). Much has been made of tensions between individual and overall business performance within this new approach to pay, but there is a further problem that the value attached to particular activities is both difficult to measure and may be unstable and short term. The transitory and inconsistent nature of business contracts—some profitable, some less profitable—may make it difficult to align pay with business performance in circumstances where organizations wish to foster longer-term employment relationships. Rapid variations in pay unrelated to individual skill or effort may not be good strategies for recruitment and retention. As Purcell (1999) argues, the task for human resource policy is not necessarily to align with current business interests as this may make subsequent readjustment to changing conditions more difficult. The internal problems of aligning pay with the current profitability of business activities may outweigh the benefits even from management's perspective.

Inter-organizational relations and contracts represent another but often neglected dimension to this internal/external tension. Such influence operates in three main ways: through clients requesting variations in internal pay structures; through management using external contracting organizations as a means of changing their cost structures and in some cases to place pressure on the shape and level of the internal pay structure; through the regulatory framework that, for example, in the case of TUPE leads to firms offering terms and conditions that diverge from their own internal systems if they take on transferred staff. Examples of all three influences can be identified within our case studies.

Client influences on pay structures. At TCS, the customer services organization, the business consists of a whole complex of different contractual arrangements with external clients to provide customer services. However, there is no consistency in the value of these contracts—and their implicit wages and conditions. The terms of the contract vary according to the ability to pay of the client and the willingness of the client to pay for quality, as a senior union official for UNISON, responsible for establishing a partnership agreement between TCS and the union in another TCS call centre site, makes clear:

That is where the problem comes is that you have done a deal with Company X based on call handling times of X based on the rates and then you work it back into what the rates of pay are. Therefore the different contracts are worth different amounts of money to

TCS which means they have to adjust their salary levels accordingly. That will cause a problem if people switch from product to product. If they are dedicated to a certain contract then that is not a problem. (TCS, union official 1, male)

To a large extent TCS manages these variations through operating its sites on different terms and conditions. Not all these variations are related to the value of client contracts; indeed some reflect the history of the company, with pay rates higher at sites inherited from TCS's period as a public utilities company than at TCS's greenfield sites or sites taken over from other companies and where TUPE regulations often apply. At TCS-NW, we were able to observe the tensions between internal considerations and client specifications, without the complicating influence of TUPE transfers (see Rubery et al. 2004). Even here, however, there was added complexity arising from the use of temporary agency staff alongside TCS staff. The main pay policy of TCS-NW can be described as that of paying a flat rate of pay to staff on TCS contracts with only limited scope for enhancement (up to £500 per year) for experience or multi-skilling. The main on-site variations in pay were therefore between TCS and agency staff, with agency staff lower paid than TCS staff even when more experienced or multi-skilled.

This flat pay hierarchy, however, hides major differences in work intensity, skills, and job security. In practice there were significant differences between the five TCS client contracts in their implications for both work intensity and skill but the differences were not reflected in pay differentials. These contracts were held with companies drawn from the energy sector (Utilityco), the betting industry (Gambleco), truck and vehicle hire (Truckco), mail order clothes (Catalogco), and mobile telephones (Phoneco). There were major differences in skill levels required (as reflected in training times that varied from two days to three weeks), in work intensity (with Phoneco requiring a fixed number of logged in hours, while other contracts required specified call answering rates, waiting times etc.) and in job security (with Phoneco insisting on 80 per cent of the staff being on permanent contracts, while the proportions were often reversed on other contracts). The insistence from Phoneco that quality should come above work intensity and cost reduction in practice upset the internal hierarchy in that those employed on the Phoneco contract had the most chance of a permanent contract, the most straightforward task and the lowest work intensity. Yet, they received the same pay as those on other contracts where both work intensity and stress levels were much higher—particularly in collecting bad debts on the energy contract. TCS management, in fact, rejected a request from Utilityco to pay a higher rate to reflect the additional skill and stress associated with this particular contract in order to retain the hierarchy between temporary agency and TCS staff and to facilitate redeployment of staff across contracts. However, client specifications had led to the payment of bonuses on some contracts (Catalogco) and had undermined the internal policy of creating a hierarchy of skill and pay between agency and permanent staff. According to TCS policy all staff were to be hired on agency contracts but offered a TCS contract after six months satisfactory performance. However, Phoneco staff had to be offered TCS contracts earlier and other agency staff were having to wait more than six months for TCS contracts; in the meantime they were often deployed on the more skilled work or trained to work across more than one contract. This breakdown in the internal order was beginning to cause resentment, as a permanent Customer Service Representative on the Gambleco contract commented:

what they call multi-skilled, a multi-skilled person who works for TCS is on more money than a multi-skilled person in Beststaff, so this is an on-going issue at the moment as well in the Employee Forum. (TCS-NW Gambleco, CSR, female)

The airport provides another example where the presence of multi-clients impacted upon the reward system for passenger handling company staff. This passenger handling company, FH, provided services for up to forty-eight airlines; for the most part staff were assigned to specialized teams as each airline had different computer systems and procedures (although staff might still work for more than one airline). Passenger handling was a strategic issue for airlines, even if contracted out, and most were concerned to provide specific incentives for the passenger handling staff to identify with the airline; this normally took the form of a range of 'perks' or incentives, ranging from free flights to bonuses for charging for excess baggage. The FH staff were paid according to a common grading system but seemed to accept that variations in the valuation of the perks offered by the airlines was the luck of the draw:

It doesn't bother us because at the end of the day, these people are checking the flights in. They deserve to get what they can get from the flight . . . Each team has different perks. You miss out from one team and you get it from another. (FH, worker 5, male)

However, some staff were seconded to airlines where they were paid at higher wage levels, according to the client's specifications. More serious problems were then encountered in reintegrating staff back into the FH normal operations because staff would face consequential pay decreases. Indeed, according to seconded staff we interviewed, they would see a return to normal working at FH as representing failure in their career aspirations.

From these two examples we can see how clients' requirements may infiltrate right inside the skin of the supplier organization. Next we consider where organizations may seek in turn to reach out to the external market to avoid internal constraints or to pit the internal against the external.

External contracting and pay structures. At both TCS and the airport, considerable use was made of temporary agency staff to fulfil a range of functions, such as facilitating rapid recruitment, reducing risk and overheads, assisting in identifying productive or reliable workers for permanent contracts, as well as a means of lowering wage costs. As all permanent staff were recruited from agency workers, the effect was also to provide a form of pay career ladder. A major incentive for temporary agency staff at both sites was the chance to move on to a permanent contract that was better paid and more secure. Thus, in resorting to external labour supply both TCS-NW and a number of airport organizations could be said to be re-establishing a pay hierarchy but with the first grade or starting point based on externally employed staff on low wages. However, at both sites the idea of a consistent internal pay hierarchy between experienced staff with permanent contracts and temporary staff with lower pay and less experience and responsibility was never fully achieved. At TCS-NW the hierarchy, as explained above, was disturbed by the specific requirements of clients. At the airport temporary agency staff were found across all skill levels as a consequence of the highly seasonal nature of the business, but temporary agency staff were still employed at relatively low wages even when asked to perform a skilled and responsible job. For example, new-season recruits into the role of dispatcher—the person responsible for coordinating the dispatch of the aircraft—were often on temporary contracts, paying as little as £5.50 per hour. This dissonance between responsibility and pay was said to be facilitated by expectations that dispatcher jobs could provide a step towards a career in the airline industry, possibly even towards training as a pilot.

Externalization can also place pressure on the rates of pay established within the internal hierarchy. Such a process appears to have occurred in the Post Office case. Over recent years the Post Office has become increasingly involved with external organizations, particularly retailers, as it seeks to integrate post services with other retail services, to reduce loss making in stand alone crown offices. In addition to the standard sub-postmaster arrangements, the Post Office has developed a range of franchise agreements. These offer opportunities to extend postal services to new retail outlets, but can also be used to release capital and land values from central post offices that have been given over to franchise operations. Moreover, the franchisees can operate their businesses on the lower pay levels prevailing in retail. To remain attractive to potential franchisees, the Post Office has opted not to transfer staff to new franchises to avoid the need for staff transferred under TUPE to be paid at the relatively high Post Office rates. This would be unattractive to franchisees. However, this policy is not necessarily sustainable as the restructuring of the Post Office is reducing the density of outlets in the same geographical area, thereby increasing the problems of redeploying staff from branches that have been turned into franchises. As a short-term measure, a new policy was introduced allowing in some cases the franchisee only to provide the premises and the capital, with the Post Office continuing to employ the staff, but with new hires taken on by the franchisee at lower wage rates. Possibly in anticipation of continuing problems with the franchising policy, but also spurred on by general lack of profitability, the Post Office has begun to adjust its own internal pay structure to move more in line with the rates prevailing in retail and customer service operations. A new pay grade was brought in without any new job evaluation and was widely regarded as simply a lower rate of pay for the same type of job:

One set of changes was introduced last September. This involved the creation of the Customer Service Advisor position for new-starters which was effectively reduced terms and conditions compared to those hired before its introduction. The pay level of new recruits is £4.80 ph. compared with £8.20 for someone with experience on the old terms and conditions. This is despite the fact that they are doing the same work. (Post Office Retail Network, Manager 2, male)

A similar process is observable at the airport. Here, pressures to enter competitive tenders for external providers drew attention to the relatively high rates of pay offered by the integrated airport authority, Airportco. To allow it to compete, Airportco adopted a number of tactics, including setting up separate spin-off companies based around lower terms and conditions (with staff redeployed rather than transferred to the new companies). Later it built on this policy by introducing 'market rates' for all new hires, thereby cutting wage levels by significant amounts even in the remaining integrated activities. However, there are continuing tensions between the new recruits (some of whom have now been in post for several years) and the staff on the protected old terms and conditions) (see Chapter 11). This adjustment of internal hierarchies to counter potential competitive bids from the private sector has also been found in studies of the impact of Compulsory Competitive Tendering in the 1980s where staff that were in direct competition with private sector providers were subject to changes in their pay and working arrangements (Cutler and Waine 1994).

TUPE regulations and pay structures. Three of our case studies—the housing benefits, PFI, and IT cases—were operating with staff transferred under TUPE regulations. In all three cases, a whole set of different terms and conditions were payable across the organization to staff doing roughly comparable work, dependent upon the terms and conditions under which they were transferred. This diversity of conditions was beginning to cause concern at both TCS and FutureTech:

now TCS has grown so big, we have so many different sets of terms and conditions across the whole company we have got to look to harmonize some of those. It is going to become unmanageable so we are going to have to have some sort of template that says what we offer our employees across the board in general terms. (TCS-L, Manager 6, male)

What we're currently working with, FutureTech and PCS, is a programme called harmonization. This was initiated a couple of years ago and the idea is that to benefit both organizations we'll harmonize the conditions of employment across all the different contracts that we have, so that PCS only negotiates with us once a year, or whatever. That's the vision. We're a long way from there. (FutureTech, Manager 27, female)

Some of these problems of diversity arose between sites and business divisions but even at the workplace level, TUPE was causing problems for the management of staff within the workplace due to the added complexity and variability in the terms and conditions under which staff were employed. At the PFI, working time premia and arrangements were known to depend not on commonly established terms and conditions but also, as one of the porters commented, on

when they started. The trouble is there are a few different contracts. You've got weekly that started with the Trust, monthly that started with the Trust like myself. Then you've got monthly, two or three different contracts. So you've got the ones who started with Hotel Services Company, and they're completely different again with a different pay scale. (Hotel Services Company, porter 4, male)

The frustration for the managers of TUPE transferred staff appeared to lie not so much in the differences in costs associated with the transferred staff, but in the problems the differentiation created for developing a common system for managing performance and reward. At both FutureTech and TCS-L the management had been unable to include the TUPE transferred staff in their performance appraisal and bonus schemes because the TUPE staff were paid on a different set of terms and conditions and could not be offered bonuses unless they transferred to new contracts. This was a minor matter of frustration for management at TCS:

And in a way for him (HR manager) it is quite difficult because he knows when he lays the package out that all things being equal they are better staying on the TUPE-ed conditions. Unless you are really able to perform out of your socks we cannot always guarantee benefits. (TCS-L, Manager 7, female)

At FutureTech the situation was more complex because staff on FutureTech terms and conditions were entitled to bonuses but those on protected TUPE terms were not. In practice the TUPE staff were usually offered some bonus, but the differences in payouts were still significant:

The compensation issue for ... employees ... who are still on their old contract style, is that they are not managed, their salary is something that is sorted out through collective bargaining ... So unlike a standard package person we may say you contributed magnificently here, have all this. You can't actually do this ... I spend a huge amount of my time talking to leaders, helping them to balance in their minds that they're giving somebody a ... £1,000 bonus ... whereas they're giving this guy over here a £2,000 bonus, explaining to them that that is actually fair and equitable because the guy over here has other benefits, for example hours. (FutureTech, Manager 27, female)

Moreover, although the TUPE staff terms and conditions offered particular benefits with respect to redundancy pay, pensions, and working time, in practice it was those who transferred to the new contracts who moved more quickly up the promotion ladder as they were deployed on contracts outside the transferred area of work. Promotion had become more geared to general computer competence than to specific business knowledge.

None of the organizations in our study took the option of using the TUPE transfer terms and conditions as the basis for an integrated pay system. Instead new recruits were all employed on different terms and conditions. Staff who chose to transfer to the new employers' contracts not only had to accept new substantive conditions but also faced major culture change, associated with different principles for reward and performance. An IT specialist at TCS-L found much greater difficulty in claiming for any overtime worked under the new TCS contracts, even though in principle they were entitled to payment:

When I've tried to claim I have been paid it but . . . I'm made to understand what a negative impact it has on budgets. . . . They'd allow you to work those hours if it didn't have a big negative financial impact for them. (TCS-L, Manager 3, male)

At FutureTech those who transferred to the new conditions were expected to work flexibly without specific rewards or time off and not to discuss their pay. This contrasts with the much more transparent system that had operated at Govco and continued to apply to the staff who remained on mirror image conditions:

Basically we either bank hours or the bosses authorize overtime, which is paid overtime. As far as [names colleague on FutureTech terms and conditions] is concerned he would be expected to work whatever hours are necessary to get the job done with some tenuous promise that he might get a bonus out of it at the end. (FutureTech, programmer 1, male)

I can't say how much I get paid, because it's supposed to be individual confidential pay for performance so obviously there are still pay scales but we don't know what they are. (FutureTech, programmer 2, male)

These more subtle differences in the operation of the pay systems make it clear why trade unions have been concerned that the codes of practice being negotiated for public–private contracting should require contractors to provide terms and conditions for new staff that are not just 'broadly similar' but in fact 'no less favourable' than those in the public sector.

This exploration of how inter-organizational relations are interacting with pay and conditions has revealed a range of management problems that arise out of the differences in terms and conditions across the participating organizations. Some of these differences are used strategically by organizations to change internal pay rates, through either a process of coercive comparisons or the creation of a pay progression ladder from external temporary worker to internal employee. However, these strategies can create problems of inflexibility and prevent the development of effective partnerships as the two pay cultures and systems continue to operate side by side. The development of inter-organizational relations is reducing the consistency and transparency of pay structures because of the differences in pay principles between participating organizations and, indeed, because private sector organizations are more likely than public sector organizations to require staff to keep compensation issues confidential.

Security of employment

Security of employment is a potentially important element in an organization's human resource strategy. The flexible firm model suggested that differences in employment security could provide the pivotal difference between two approaches to human resource management. Job security is offered at the discretion of management as an inducement to particular groups or individuals instead of being organized under universal rules such as 'last in first out' that operate to limit managerial control. However, not only is this neat distinction between core and periphery workers difficult to uphold in practice, it has also become evident that the flexible firm does not necessarily operate to improve security for the core. On the contrary, contracting out may be designed in part to bring external competition within the boundaries of the organization, to increase competitive pressure on the internal wage–effort bargain (Cappelli et al. 1997a, b; Ackroyd and Proctor 1998).

External contracting may, thus, both enhance and undermine the job security of the remaining internalized workforce. Inter-organizational relations, in general, can be expected to have both positive and negative influences on employment security. These influences include the stability of contract relations and the specifications of the contract. These may impact on the security enjoyed by groups or individuals within the supplier organization in ways that are not related to their attributes as productive employees but to the nature of the client–supplier relationships. We have already cited the example of Phoneco, at TCS-NW, where permanent contracts were offered to relatively new recruits on to this contract while other agency staff were left waiting for longer than the specified 6 months before being offered contracts. This direct impact of client interventions on the internal offer of job security has been a neglected issue but applies particularly within multi-client supplier companies (see Scarbrough 2000 for another case).

The extent to which employment security is a tool of human resource policy will be influenced by employment law. For example, the TUPE regulations require staff to be either transferred or, if redundancies are declared, these have to be shown to be unconnected with the transfer but arise from other grounds of economic necessity or technological change (and not because the transferred workers are too expensive). These regulations can provide reassurance to staff during the process of transfer:

Jobs I think was the main thing. . . . FutureTech was a big company . . . they'd obviously got thousands and thousands of trained programmers, what was going to stop them bringing their own people here? And just saying sorry we don't need you anymore, goodbye . . . As it happens we were reassured to a large extent by the fact that it became apparent the TUPE recommendations were going to apply to the transition and that if FutureTech had got any plans that they knew of to make any changes they had to be made known up front. (FutureTech, programmer 1, male)

While this protection is designed for the benefit of employees, it may have indirect benefits for management by reducing the probability that experienced staff will seek to leave once a potential transfer is mooted. Retaining the specialized business expertise embedded in the transferred Govco staff was important for the Govco/FutureTech transfer. However, in practice the protection offered is limited as it is difficult to separate out the impact of the TUPE transfer from other factors. The PFI coincided with the rationalization of two hospitals which meant that redundancies carried on alongside the PFI and were the responsibility of the Trust, not the new contractors. Moreover, security does not just involve continuation of the employment contract, but also security in the important dimensions and characteristics of that employment (Burchell et al. 2001). One of those characteristics is the nature of the employer or the business by whom one is employed. At the PFI the transfer of staff from the Trust to a large Estates facilities company had introduced considerable feelings of insecurity, even though there was no immediate threat to continuing employment. This insecurity related to the change in the nature of the employer. The transferred staff were concerned that their new employer had no specific interest in health services and might lose interest and sell their stake in the PFI to yet another employer:

It is like a cloud hanging over your head. The Estates Facilities Company can't be interested in the little business of the maintenance department. This department makes a heavy loss every year, so [it] will not stay here. They can't turn the department round just like that to make a profit. We are not here to make a profit but to provide a service. (Estates Company, maintenance worker 2, male)

There was also concern that they would lose their particular job and career that they saw as defined in health, not as a generic job skill to be applied in other sectors:

The Estates Facilities Company is a big company, they have contracts going on everywhere, the lads are worried here. . . . Are they going to come in one morning and say right we would like you to go another site today. How do you say, not me, I work for the hospital—we *don't* work for the hospital. I think a lot of people are under the impression that we have got that cover, that this is our place of work. I've got my doubts to be honest with you. The [Company] is investing a lot of money in us, we are getting trained. (Estates Company, maintenance worker 6, male)

Although TUPE preserves and protects some aspects of the employment relationship, in the form of terms and conditions of employment, the transfer to a new employer provides opportunities, both permitted within the legal framework and otherwise, to make changes on a range of fronts which may significantly alter the employment context. Again at the PFI there was concern that the new management planned to cut overtime earnings opportunities which were considered essential to turn low paid jobs into a living wage:

The Hotel Services Company will look into cutting the overtime, then many people will leave. We need the overtime to top up the wage, if that is gone, then there is no point staying. They should pay a higher basic wage so we don't have to work long hours of overtime. . . . I prefer to go if the redundancy pay is good. (Hotel Services Company, Chef 1, male)

The TUPE provisions guarantee only basic pay and contractual overtime, but this example again illustrates the insecurity introduced by change of employer because of the lack of protections for non-contractual aspects of the employment relationship. Personal feelings of job security also relate to how staff are managed and monitored. One of the big changes at both the housing benefits and PFI cases was in the way in which the new employers implemented the sick-pay scheme; in principle, the scheme followed that of the previous employer but there were major differences in implementation, leading to enhanced feelings of insecurity. At the PFI long-term sick cases were to be investigated through counselling (e.g. home visits) to determine whether the employee was well enough to get back to work or to take ill health retirement. This practice invoked much resentment from the workforce:

They should trust us enough. If we are sick, we are sick. They don't need to check. . . . They are just trying to catch us out. (Estates Company, maintenance worker 3, male)

Inter-organizational relations thus complicate the notions of employment security in three main ways. First of all, the possibilities of externalizing employment can provide greater security to those within the organization but may also be used to increase coercive comparisons between internal conditions and those of external contractors. Second, the influence of business to business contracting on employment security is not just felt through variations in volume of demand but also through variations in the specifications of client contracts. Third, the regulation of inter-organizational relations—particularly TUPE—introduces a whole set of ambiguities and complexities into what is meant by job security. TUPE restricts the extent to which workers faced with contracting out are liable to termination of an employment contract but how far job security can actually be maintained in the context of a change of employer is open to question.

Control: supervision, authority, and discipline

One of the main legal tests as to the existence of an employment relationship is whether the employer exercises control over the work of the employee. Such control is central to the benefits that an internalized employment relationship is supposed to confer on employers who can use authority rather than recontracting to direct and monitor the activity of employees. Furthermore, employer control of the work process may be a precondition for an employer to be able to deal fairly and knowledgeably with the discipline and dismissal of staff (see Chapter 3 and Earnshaw et al. 2002).

However, the notion of control and authority is complicated by the presence of multi-agencies or employers who may attempt to exercise control over the work of non-employees. The development of the network form has been associated in the literature with notions of empowerment, but these analyses concentrate on primarily 'knowledge workers' (Saxenian 1996) and fail to address how fragmentation of organizations complicates processes of control and authority. At the very least, fragmentation is likely to lead to the multiplication of layers of control, as there needs to be internal supervision of employees plus external verification of and control of work related to contracts and service level agreements (see Chapters 2 and 5). Moreover, the presence of multi-agencies, almost by definition, means that lines of authority will not be embedded in consistent internal hierarchies; instead lines of supervision and control are likely to cross organizational borders. Low status or low qualified staff may even exercise authority over other staff, reflective of the relative power of their organization in the contracting relationship rather than their own position within an organizational hierarchy. Moreover, where someone in one organization is responsible for an operation involving participation of multiple agencies, there may be problems for that staff member in being able to exercise appropriate levels of control over the external organization.

The multiplication of layers of control is particularly likely to apply where regulatory conditions provide non-employers with direct responsibility for the work undertaken by non-employees. This situation applied in a number of our case studies. In the customer services case, Council X was responsible for housing benefits; this led to experienced staff transferred to TCS being subject to checks and controls by ex-colleagues in the council when previously they had been trusted to authorize the decisions themselves. That these distinctions are considered seriously by council auditors was made evident in the experience of one of the agency staff we interviewed there. He recalled that when he had been working at another council in a team manager position the auditors at the council had refused to validate all his decisions, as he was not a council employee but an agency worker. The Post Office retained regulatory responsibility for all the post office activities where undertaken in sub-post offices or franchises where they had no direct role in employment issues. This responsibility involves real risks for the Post Office—for example, it is the Post Office that incurs responsibility for errors made by non-employees with respect to the Giro bank.

Even when there are no extra regulatory issues, the process of fragmentation adds new layers of control that in practice involve supervision by non-employers: At the PFI, ward sisters are responsible for checking work dockets of maintenance staff employed by a partner organization; at TCS-NW clients listen in to the phone calls made by staff and in some cases feed back comments directly to the staff concerned; at the airport, airlines use their own representatives to oversee the departure of aircraft, a task which cuts across the role of the dispatcher, whose job already involves unclear lines of authority:

The airline representatives are there in a supervisory role. They give instructions to the staff from the handling agents. They are there to ensure that things are done to the airline standard, to how we like it. They are very active. . . . They interact with every service there is. (Airline C, Manager 1, female)

These airline representatives tend to take on more than they are really trained and competent to do, buoyed on by the power that being representatives of the airline confers:

some of the reps are taking a bit too much control on turn-rounds and so the dispatcher sits back. It should have been the other way round. He should have told the rep what the situation was. . . . when you're calling for a tug, we call for one, not knowing that the rep called five minutes ago. And it's not really their place to call for a tug, unless it's special circumstances. . . . they occasionally do things that are going beyond their job. (FH, worker 9, male)

These interventions by the airlines extend beyond specific action to ensure on time departure to more general monitoring of behaviour and apparent motivation of handling staff. These interventions can be both direct and indirect:

If I see the handling agents not performing as they should, I will not speak to them in person but speak to their supervisor . . . (Airline C, worker 3, female)

or

If we see the passenger handling agents looking untidy and unmotivated or doing things which I think they shouldn't be doing in the public area, I always go and speak to them even though I am not their manager. . . . (Airline C, Manager 1, female)

Interventions by clients can compromise fairness and consistency in the management of staff. Such problems were encountered by contractors to the Post Office, particularly where a national chain was attempting to establish a coherent human resource policy for the whole business but had to negotiate and deal with Post Office representatives from a range of relatively autonomous regional offices. Where employees have been transferred from one employer to another, as in the case of TCS-L, there may be problems because the supervisory system is seen by the transferred staff to lack legitimacy, largely because the supervisors are not regarded as having the appropriate skills and business experience and knowledge (see also Chapter 8).

The confusion in lines of control and authority that we found in our case studies also has implications for performance appraisal and indeed more serious discipline and dismissal procedures. Such cross-organizational interventions lead not only to a form of double jeopardy for employees, but also to problems of internal consistency and fairness for management. As clients are concerned to improve the quality of the service provided, many feel it legitimate to make interventions with respect to the specific performance of individuals. One of the problems that line managers identified with these interventions was that the client often had only partial knowledge of the situation and might overpraise or overcriticize a member of staff:

The airline only has one flight a day, so they look at every detail and want perfection. . . . e.g. they complain why that agent has not smiled all day but do not know that she may have been working since 3 o'clock in the morning and that she has had a bad day. (FH, Manager 4, female) a Post Office manager will, for example, send a circular to the store manager telling them they have had wonderful sales for this period, or other items where they have exceeded expectations, . . . The fact that that manager might have controlled the staff very badly, might not have controlled the people in relation to their holidays, might have had 70 per cent of his staff off sick at any one time, might have given our area manager an absolute nightmare in terms of having to staff their office, might have had balancing inaccuracies, they only look at one aspect and that is the bit that they're concerned with. (ConvenienceCo, Manager 2, male)

In some cases the client has a very strong influence on deployment of staff: For example, at TCS-NW, it was Gambleco that made the decision as to which staff would be moved on to its premier line for high value customers. In other organizations there were more efforts to limit the clients direct control of staff deployment, particularly, when they want a member of staff removed:

Some airlines come to the FH manager to ask for another agent rather than a particular one they were given because they don't like the person's performance. But they won't get it because it is no good for the development of that individual. Instead, FH managers will talk to the agent to try to improve the situation. (FH, Manager 4, female)

Interventions by clients may be dealt with more by redeployment than by direct discipline. However, in some circumstances the intervention by the client is more decisive; where the Post Office is the client, it is the client—not the employer—that may effectively determine dismissal. A client may make it clear to the partner organization that it will withdraw the contract if a certain person is not dismissed. In one particular case we came across, the person's own employer had been inclined to be lenient as they believed there had been extenuating circumstances:

He didn't have any personal gain from it . . . POCL immediately said the guy cannot work in another post office at all. . . . we either found another job for him to do within the organization, which we couldn't do at the time, or we followed POCL's instructions/guidelines, to dismiss, but the whole thing, the whole procedure of interviewing the lad, suspending the lad, terminating the employment was dictated by Post Office Counters. (ConvenienceCo, Manager 2, male)

The client also frequently becomes directly involved with disciplining non-employees when the staff are provided by temporary work agencies. In these cases the client has more knowledge of the day-to-day activities of the worker than the employer. In our case studies it was more often the client that initiated complaints or disciplinary actions as the temping agency was not directly aware of performance issues. However, whether the action was pursued by the client directly or was taken up with the agency varied both between cases and between managers in the same organizations:

(some of the Managers) . . . . All we want them to do is to send them to us. We don't want them to get involved remotely, but they do. . . . It's just a simple case of if somebody's late it will be the fifth time that they're late before we see them and then they'll say we don't want them back. And we're like, we've never spoken to them. You're asking us to remove somebody that we've never seen, to reprimand. That's the problem. (Beststaff, Manager, female)

Further complications arise because discipline and dismissal are not appropriate terms when the person concerned is self-employed rather than an employee, as was the case in almost all the cases of temporary work agency staff we came across in our studies. One reason why client managers do initiate disciplinary proceedings when the person is not an employee is because of a desire to have an internally consistent policy with respect to discipline in the workplace. This can be particularly important where the disciplinary incident involves both agency staff and direct employees—for example, in the case of a fight involving staff from both groups as described to us at TCS-NW. Moreover, many of the agency staff accepted the legitimacy of the client taking up issues with them:

Well yes because I work for these people while I'm here in this building so I'm responsible to make sure that I do what everyone else does in this building so if I did something wrong . . . I suppose I'd be disciplined by TCS and then they pass that on to the agency. . . . it would seem strange being disciplined more by your agency, because what can they do when they're nowhere near here, they don't know what's going on. (Phoneco, CSR agency worker, male)

Thus there are ambiguities, even from the perspective of the worker, as to which organization has the right to exercise discipline and assess performance.

7.4 Conclusions

Human resource management issues have predominately been viewed from within the box of the single well-defined organization. Where outsourcing and other contacts with the external market are contemplated, these have often been seen as helping to create or reinforce divisions between the internal and the external. Some recent work has highlighted the interactions between the external and the internal environments and the role of externalization in promoting coercive comparisons and competition within the internal employment systems (Cappelli et al. 1997a, b; Ackroyd and Proctor 1998; Grimshaw and Rubery 1998). This work needs to be combined with the development of supply chain analysis to understand the influence of clients on the internal employment policies and practices of suppliers. Often the same organization is both a contractor and a supplier and it is the interactions between these roles that need to be analysed. Furthermore, the whole discussion of the interface between internal and external has not always been analysed within the context of specific institutional and regulatory frameworks. The TUPE regulations, even if not always fully understood by either management or workers, are nevertheless an important force in shaping the process and conditions for outsourcing and the experience of that process for the workforce concerned.

These interactions between internal and external organizations apply both to the provision of substantive terms and conditions of employment and to the management of the labour process. Fragmentation of organizations and the labour process has become a fashionable development, spurred on by opportunities to reduce costs in a UK labour market characterized by widely divergent pay and conditions between sectors and firms. Moreover, organizations have been urged to focus on the strategic and to leave the operational activities to the market. However, operational issues are in practice often found to have strategic value and clients who seek the cost advantages of outsourcing may still strive after the quality advantages of internal operations, leading to direct interventions in the supplier's human resource functions. This involvement cuts across the system of internal consistency and hierarchy that still remains a feature of the internalized employment relationship. In some contexts, this cross-cutting needs to be viewed as a means of restructuring the internal employment relationship and associated hierarchy of pay and conditions. In others, the outcome is simply to confuse and complicate the management of the employment relationship.

Our discussion has focused on how inter-organizational relations impinge upon and react with internal employment relations. The interventions of non-employers are missing from conventional analyses that see the employment relationship as a traded bargain—albeit unequal—between a single employer and the employee. By introducing these inter-organizational relations into the analysis, the bargain that underpins the employment relationship can be seen to be embedded in a set of inter-capitalist relations that may shift risk and responsibilities both between organizations and between employers and employees. The differences between the collaborating organizations—as measured by their power in the contracting relationship, their business strategy and their position within different value chains (see Chapter 2)—result in potentially conflicting influences on internal employment policies and practices, particularly where there are multiple non-employers involved. Thus some clients may seek to push down prices and wages while others may focus on quality, reliability, and the fostering of commitment. The outcome of the development of inter-organizational relationships is not always or simply to generate low cost, market-mediated contracting arrangements. Indeed the empirical study of the operation of these inter-organizational relationships reveals the continuing need for active cooperation of labour in the process of delivery of goods and services, even when spread across a range of organizations brought together in principle by market relations or contracts. This cooperation often operates at all levels of the associated workforces, not just at higher management level, as assumed in much of the organizational trust literature (see Chapter 2). It is this need for cooperation that in practice may paradoxically do most to limit the possibility of developing strong and consistent internal employment policies, as the external contracting or collaborating organizations may seek through contracts or direct involvement to influence the internal employment relationships in contradictory directions. The tension at the heart of the employment relationship that derives from the dual imperatives towards conflict and cooperation is thus exacerbated, and certainly not resolved, by the formation of employment relationships in a multi-agency setting.

Notes

1. Currently, there is little the transferee can do by way of harmonization because the House of Lords' ruling in the case of *Wilson* v. *St. Helens Borough Council* ([1998] ICR 1141) means that even consensual variations to employees' terms and conditions by reasons of the transfer are ineffective.
2. Issues related to organizational commitment and to skills and training are discussed in Chapters 8 and 9.

8

Commitment and Identity Across Organizational Boundaries

FANG LEE COOKE, GAIL HEBSON, AND MARILYN CARROLL

8.1 Introduction

There has been, in the last two decades, a growing managerial interest in human resource initiatives aimed at increasing employees' motivation and commitment to organizational objectives in order for firms to gain competitive advantage. So much so that, as Parry and Tranfield (1998) noted, many UK companies' current improvement programmes aim to change the organization's social system to gain commitment from the workforce. Emphasis has also been placed in the HRM literature on the development of a strong company culture, encompassing shared beliefs and values, as a means of developing employee commitment (Legge 1995; Gallie et al. 1998). As Guest (1998*a*, *b*: 42) noted, 'the concept of organizational commitment is at the heart of any analysis of HRM'. Enthusiasts of the high commitment model of HRM argue that employees should be treated as valued assets, a source of competitive advantage through their commitment, adaptability, and high quality (of skills, performance, and so on) (Guest 1987). This discussion of high commitment assumes implicitly that organizations are in charge of their internal HR policies without intervention from other organizations (Marchington and Grugulis 2000; Rubery et al. 2003).

However, the notions of organizational commitment and identity that are difficult enough concepts to define in a single organization context, become even more problematic in situations where the notion of the single employer is open to question (Rubery et al. 2002). The presence of more than one organization exercising influence within the employment relationship is particularly likely in contexts where there are multiple employing organizations on a single site and where the employees of these different organizations have to cooperate in a labour process to produce goods or services. Even where there is physical distance between the different employing organizations, issues of competing or multiple employers may still arise, for example, in situations where workers employed by a service supplier firm are expected to present themselves to external customers as members of their non-employer client firm. In these contexts it may be difficult for the employing organization to impose on the workers its organizational values and culture without simultaneously having to juggle with those of other organizations in the relationship. In some contexts, non-employer client organizations may even take a more proactive role than employer organizations in the management of workforce commitment, identity, and loyalty.

Yet, this additional complexity may be considered a continuity of that found in single employer organizations. There is, in fact, little evidence that strategies by management to foster commitment are particularly successful; at the very most they are more successful with some groups of workers than others (Gallie et al. 1998). There is a wealth of evidence that challenges the success of cultural management as workers express cynicism about management motives rather than internalizing the values of the company (Du Gay and Salmon 1992; Willmott 1993). It would seem that commitment and identity refuse to be fashioned by management strategies, whether orchestrated by employers or non-employers (Gallie et al. 1998).

Moreover, concepts of organizational commitment and identity have been found to be under pressure due to increased job insecurity and the increasing discussion of boundaryless rather than bureaucratic careers as the likely employment form of the future (Rubery et al. 2002). Some studies, primarily of more highly skilled workers, show individuals identify more with their occupation or professional group than the employing organization, the latter becoming merely a backdrop to these 'projects of the self' (Grey 1994).

The concept of multi-employers, therefore, adds further complexity to the notion of organizational commitment. However, while this suggests that the notions of commitment and identity may become even more elusive, they nevertheless remain central in theorizing changing organizational forms. As Barley and Kunda (2001: 78) argue: 'to determine whether organizational boundaries are constructed differently today requires data on where people work, with whom they work, and, most importantly, how they conceptualize their identity and the social collectivities of which they are part'.

While other chapters in this book explore how the nature of work may have changed for managers and workers in our case studies, this chapter focuses upon how workers make sense of these changes. By exploring the commitment and identities workers forge in these contexts it is possible to demonstrate why studies of the employment relationship and organizational analysis must be interlinked. Assumptions about the nature of inter-organizational trust and risk-sharing in network forms are problematized, as we find that it is lived relationships at work, and their implications for the development of identities and associated commitments that, in part, shape the nature and form, and indeed the success or failure of these changing organizational forms.

We draw our evidence from three of our case studies across four sites: the Airport, the TCS-NW call centre, the public–private partnership (PPP) of TCS-L and Council X and the Private Finance Initiative (PFI) case. These are multi-employer and/or multi-client sites where the workers carry out their tasks, often subject to the management of both their employer and the non-employer client organizations. However, the nature of the relationships between employers and non-employers in each site varies considerably, determined by the nature of the work, the power relationships between the contractual parties, and the degree of risk-sharing and inter-organizational trust. For example, although TCS-NW and TCS-L are part of the same company, the nature of the work, the way work is organized and the contracts managed give rise to two diverse sets of challenges for the TCS management in streamlining its HR strategy and eliciting commitment from the workforce.

The first part of the chapter will explore the practices used by employers and non-employers to foster commitment from workers in the context of these relationships. Some of these actions may be strategic, some may not be intended to be strategic but both types may have strategic effects. The chapter then goes on to explore the impact of these strategies and suggests that the ability of management—both in employer and non-employer organizations—to foster commitment varies from site to site and within sites, and between specific groups of workers, for example, temporary and permanent staff. Analysis of workers' attachments to organizational values, culture, and goals highlights the complexities of the process of identification with—or indeed the rejection or dis-identification with—employers and non-employers. Not only do we tease out evidence of both continuity and change in the formation of commitments and identities, but we also find that the commitments displayed go beyond the confines of organizational boundaries as commercially/managerially/legally conceived, as employees draw upon alternative sources of commitment and identification to make sense of an increasingly complex organizational world. However, this increased complexity cannot, we argue, be reduced simply to the employer/non-employer divide and crucially, if we are to grasp the realities of new organizational forms, the structuring force of employee commitment in the shaping of changing organizational boundaries must be recognized.

8.2   Employer and non-employer strategies

Existing accounts of organizational commitment, and the anticipated organizational benefits that ensue if this is successfully fostered, might lead us to expect that employers and non-employers would actively compete for the hearts and minds of employees, strategies which may bring the organizations into conflict. However, our data suggests that this assumption must be grounded in the context of specific contractor and client relationships. We found that employers respond differently to the 'potential' challenge of the non-employer, depending upon the locus of control in the relationship between them (see Table 8.1). For example, in the Airport case we found that, as clients, the power of the airlines over the handling agents meant that the handling companies did not have a deliberate strategy in place to foster employee commitment. HR policies such as the use of permanent employment contracts, promotion and allocation to work for better airlines as 'carrots' for stable and productive employees were general HR policies aimed to curb the high labour turnover rate rather than a deliberate effort to counteract the influence of the non-employers.

The handling agents' managers were not unhappy with the airlines showering their employees with HR initiatives such as bonding exercises and performance-related reward to elicit their commitment.

I don't feel unhappy at all about the airline trying to be involved in incorporating and motivating my staff as a team. I just have the problem and they have the glamour. At the end of the day airlines are our customers. (FH, Manager 5, female)

Table 8.1. Employer and non-employer's strategies for workers' commitment

Case-study organizations	Employer (E)	Non-employer (Non-E)
Airport FH (E) BH (E) Airlines (Non-E)	Permanent employment contract Career progression Assigned to work for better airlines	Airline uniforms Incentive schemes Teambuilding activities Agent of the month award Performance monitoring
Customer Service TCS-NW (E) Clients (Non-E)	Organizational culture and core values Consistent HR policies across client contracts	Involvement in training and performance monitoring Incentive bonuses Involvement in selection procedures Targets
TCS-L Council (E) Council (Non-E)	Emphasis on private sector 'customer-focused' culture Communication initiatives (newsletter and team notice board) Targets	Expectation that traditional public sector commitments would continue Performance monitoring (of contract)
PFI Private contractors (E) NHS Trust (Non-E)	Emphasis on private sector 'performance' culture Enhanced training and career opportunities Greater involvement in decision-making (managers) Targets	Expectation that traditional public sector commitments would continue Performance monitoring (of contract)

Significantly, the handling firms wanted to keep the airlines happy and therefore it was in their interests for their employees to show commitment to the clients rather than to themselves. While there were some disadvantages, particularly losing handling agent staff who left to become airline staff, this appeared to be a price worth paying to secure airline business.

Instead, it was competition between clients, all non-employers, where management strategies to foster commitment came into play. The airlines were very conscious of the risk of using a fragmented employment system (e.g. by subcontracting service provisions of certain parts of the business) on issues such as organizational image and workforce loyalty. They often used a variety of methods to amplify the visual image of, and the workers' psychological identification with their organization in order to minimize the risk.

For example, some airlines required the handling agents to wear the airline uniform instead of their employer's uniform. Several airlines (mainly the high profile ones) also devised incentive schemes and team-building activities as a management strategy to increase workers' commitment and effort. One airline offered free standard flights to Europe for good performing teams and FH's managers were invited to the airline's Europe base at least once a year on a day trip to have a party with their airline counterparts there. This airline also provided an incentive bonus for the handling agent's check-in staff for implementing the excess baggage claim to generate extra revenue. Since the incentive was introduced, the revenue has increased dramatically. Another airline has an 'agent of the month' initiative where it is the airline who decides who the agent will be. An 'agent of the year' award was also being planned. In addition, most airlines invite the agents 'for a Christmas party or for meals and things like that' (FH, worker 3, male). These initiatives all started with a few scheduled airlines but more and more airlines have adopted them. The perceived need for, and purpose of doing this is frankly admitted by a manager from Airline C:

It is a manipulation but in a nice way, through building a nice relationship with the [handling agents]. Some people are very dogmatic and say 'you will do this'. But I see it in a different way. They are not just there to serve us. They are serving 70 different companies at the same time. So we are all in the same boat . . . So that's why I think that if we can keep them on our side and treat them with respect, then when it comes to a day when we need something desperately, they will always be good to us. (Airline C, Manager 4, female)

Significantly, the aim of such strategies is to ensure effort is expended in the interests of one airline as opposed to others. Airlines' strategies to gain the commitment of workers are a means to an end rather than the end in itself. Moreover, in a multi-employer context, the non-employer's presence does not necessarily contradict employer strategies of managing staff.

In our multi-client call centre case, the call centre management played a more proactive part in asserting TCS's own role in the relationship in an attempt to secure commitment and loyalty from its staff. On the one hand, the call centre managers were aware that individual client companies needed to ensure that the customer service representatives working on their contracts were trained in aspects of their client's brand or organizational image to enable them to present themselves on the telephone as the clients' own employees. On the other hand, the effective management of the call centre operation required TCS to have a coherent strategy on employment issues. It tried to achieve this in two ways: first by adopting standardized HR practices across all the contracts, including a standardized pay structure and a site-wide performance and development system (see Chapter 7 and below), acceding to relatively few attempts by clients to introduce their own initiatives, and second by making strenuous efforts to emphasize its own overarching culture as a means of managing its staff.

Emphasis on its own culture, rather than that of its clients, is a strategy adopted by TCS both to secure employees' commitment and to provide a unifying force in the workplace. This culture revolves around five core values:

- our customers are our business
- we will respect every individual in our company
- we will adopt a performance-based approach
- we will be flexible and decisive
- quality as a way of life.

These core values were emphasized by managers as a means of creating uniformity and consistency in the management of staff in a situation where different client contracts placed widely differing demands on Customer Service Representatives (CSRs) in terms of the nature, complexity, levels, and mix of skills required. According to the managers and team leaders, they provided a coherent framework around which to base these client demands. As a manager on the Catalogco contract explained:

We have the five core values, so whether you are on Phoneco, Catalogco, or Gambleco your managers will be coming from the angle of those five core values and managing it in much the same way. (TCS-NW, Catalogco, Manager, female)

Some managers clearly believed that TCS required its clients to adopt the same values, or even that the company deliberately 'chose' clients whose values were similar, to avoid threatening the strong culture:

Phoneco has four core values as well and they are very, very similar, in empowering their people, respecting their people, and I think that was probably one of the reasons why Phoneco decided to go with TCS because it's very, very similar, and we found that when we visited them at their site as well, which is good for us. (TCS-NW, Phoneco, Manager, female)

However, clients did shape, to some extent, the way work was carried out. Customer service representatives were required to greet telephone callers in such a way as to give these customers the impression that they were speaking to an employee of the client company. Here, the clients also intervened to influence the commitment and performance of the staff working on their contracts. Some clients introduced their own bonus schemes. Catalogco staff could earn a bonus for reaching a 10 per cent 'order-build' target, and individual Truckco staff could earn shopping vouchers for passing on the most contract sales leads to the client.

However, the direct involvement of the client companies was considerably less than that in the airport case. TCS did, in fact, in some instances resist such interventions by the client companies for the reasons discussed above. For example, Truckco wanted all CSRs working on its contract to wear full Truckco uniforms. Since there was, unlike in the airport case, no face-to-face contact with customers this could only have been an attempt to reinforce the CSRs' image of themselves as Truckco employees, and to distinguish them from the CSRs on other contracts. This request was turned down by TCS although, as a compromise, the Truckco CSRs were given T-shirts with the Truckco logo on and were allowed to wear these on 'special occasions'.

The key difference between this case and the other case studies is the remoteness of the clients from the employees in this site. As the clients did not have a continuous presence on the site, when they did intervene this was tied to the need to increase the appearance of a seamless organization to customers; employees were required to display commitment to the clients via the customer rather than to client management itself. However, their remoteness made it easier for TCS to resist any strategies which were deemed to weaken possible commitment to TCS.

In the case of PPPs there was recognition by the new private sector employers that the commitment of ex-public sector workers (as opposed to managers) may not be easily moulded by human resources policies. In the TCS-L case, for example, private sector partners identified the need to tackle a 'value clash' between the public and private sector if workers were to feel they 'belonged' to the new organization. The Office Manager responsible for TCS communications in Council X was very conscious of this:

I think the learning curve is getting people to understand and appreciate the fact they now do not work for the council, they now work for a company and that little feeling of belonging is different because there is a different culture between a council group of employees and private industry . . . I think the worry certainly initially is will a private company just be trying to make money out of the business and will they really care about the community and the people that we service. (TCS-L, Manager 7, female)

A key way that TCS-L fostered commitment was by ensuring staff fitted into the TCS culture. There was a general feeling that those who did not fit into the new culture had left. It was stressed that they had not been forced to do so:

I think that we've been lucky in that the people that have left have been the ones that we wanted to go and I just think they felt the pressure of the culture change and that some of their attitudes and behaviour just don't fit in any more. They were conscious of that, so moved on. (TCS-L, Manager 4, female)

Weaning out those who did not fit into the TCS culture went alongside strategies that aimed to instil a sense of belonging to TCS. In the final stages of our case study TCS initiated a monthly newsletter alongside the establishment of 'communications champions' where one member of each team was responsible for maintaining the team notice board. The aim was directly related to making employees feel involved and that they belonged to TCS. In general, TCS appears to be more aggressive than the airport ground handlers in implementing its commitment strategy, particularly at the TCS-L site. It appears to have identified a greater need to try to instil workers' commitment to itself as their employer rather than the clients.

However, internalizing new cultures and values goes alongside a continuing need for past commitment to remain intact. In the case of TCS-L, the new employer used strategies to distinguish itself from the ex-employer, particularly with the offer of increased training and career opportunities, while also stressing continuity of the employment contract and employment experience.

In the PFI this took the form of a focus upon the customer which was used interchangeably with the more traditional focus upon the 'public interest'. Employees' concern for the public interest allowed private sector managers to implement new working practices, using the name of the 'customer' to stress continuity with the past and reduce any possible resistance. For example, the Project Director of the Estates Company brought in flexible working practices in the name of the customer:

Customer care is very important. We have to be flexible because it's customer care; the patients will suffer if we are pedantic in our attitude. (Estates Company, Manager 1, male)

The non-employer's claims on the commitment of workers in the case of PPPs becomes complex as their position as the ex-employer forms the backdrop to whether any strategic intervention would be perceived as legitimate. Workers' feelings of betrayal at being transferred (see Chapter 5) may mean the non-employer is not in a position to ask for the commitment of these workers. Indeed the public sector partner did not actively use incentives to induce commitment from employees and, perhaps more surprisingly, did not use strategies to ensure past commitment continued. Nevertheless, there was a sense that public sector managers *expected* traditional commitment to the 'public service' to continue, regardless of the breakdown of the public sector employment relationship on which traditional commitment had been based. The Client Manager for Council X took this for granted:

Most of the people actually delivering the service have for most of their working lives been working for Local Government. So I think the public service perspective is there. (Council X, Manager 1, male)

Rather, strategies of the non-employer focused upon enforcing the contract, which unintentionally allowed the new employer to instigate further a shift of commitment from transferred employees. We found that new employers in PPPs could argue that work intensification was due to meeting contract speci-fications which the public sector partner had enforced more stringently as the partnership developed. In this sense the employer used the monitoring of the contract by the public sector to displace any discontent over working conditions, laying the blame at the hands of the 'non-employer'. Here, we can see a complementarity between the strategies of the employer and the non-employer in relation to workers. The need for control that was exerted over the employees was often the outcome of the public sector partner redressing the balance of power between itself and the private sector partner. However, the employer's response was to introduce working practices premised on work intensification rather than the investment of additional resources. The non-employer's strategies to regain power were successful to a certain extent but only because they coincided with those of the employer.

Whether these strategies were successful will now be discussed as we turn to how different groups of workers across the four sites made sense of these relationships and strategies by forging specific identities and commitments. The different levels and directions of commitment and identifications can be explored through three possible routes to attachments: organizational culture/values, organizational goals, and individual identifications.

8.3 Organizational cultures and values

As we have seen, both employers and non-employers used attachment to organizational values and cultures to foster senses of belonging and commit-ment from workers. In some cases these strategies appeared to have worked. Our case study evidence shows that employees of one (supplier) organization may display more commitment to non-employer (client) organizations than to their own employers. This was particularly true at the Airport where the client organizations did not need to try too hard to enforce their organizational iden-tity or to win commitment from these workers. Passenger handling agents commented that simply wearing the uniform made them identify more with the airlines:

Wearing the airline's uniform does make you feel that you are part of the airline, and in a way it gives you more confidence, because people who are travelling with you do not see you just as the handling agent but the actual airline and they can relate to that, rather than just seeing everyone wearing the same uniform checking in different flights. They are confused because they will say 'well, what's this company [FH] checking in the flights?' So it does help wearing the same uniform [as the airline]. (FH, worker 3, male)

Some people will take this even further. For example, some of the dispatchers and other handling staff felt more committed to the airlines because they saw their current job as a stepping stone to help them get a job with the airline eventually. FH has been losing staff to airlines at a high frequency because working for an airline sounds far more glamorous than working for a handling firm, in addition to the much more appealing fringe benefits. They even actively portray themselves as the airline employees even though the handling firm is their real employer, as evidenced by the seconded staff. The airline representatives seconded from FH to Airline D wear Airline D's uniform instead of FH's uniform, but they retain their FH staff identity card for security. When they are at the gate, for example, they tend to turn their FH ID badge over to conceal their true identity from the boarding passengers, even though this is against airport security regulations.

Our commitment will be to Airline D because if they think we are not good enough, then we have to go back to FH. We would be looking to stay with Airline D for as long as possible because you get better benefits as airline staff. It is much harder working for the airline but the reward is there . . . We have to be nice to our old bosses because it might come to a situation when we have to go back to them . . . But if I have to go back to them, it would only be because I need the job. But I would feel that I am going back a step. I think I would go for another airline. (FH, worker 1, female)

Undoubtedly, the airlines' winning of the handling agents' commitment is largely facilitated by their more prestigious external image than that of the handling firm they work for. This finding supports that of Bartel's recent study (2001), which suggests that those people working across the boundaries of their own and other organizations may be more committed to their own employer if they feel that their employer enjoys high external prestige. By contrast, if their own employer's external prestige is low, then their commitment tends to be reduced.

In the multi-client call centre there are conflicting accounts of whether the TCS strategy to use organizational culture as the basis for worker attachments was successful. Significantly, the cultural management strategy can only be successful if this is confirmed in the experience of working in the call centre. Some of the CSRs' responses confirmed this view. Comparing TCS with a call centre he had worked in before, one said, 'Everything was timed, everything was monitored and you were pulled up every day about things and it doesn't happen here. You can have a period where someone won't ring you for ten minutes but you don't get pestered about that. It's just more relaxed here' (TCS-NW, Truckco, CSR agency worker, male).

However, for some CSRs, targets, call monitoring and other surveillance techniques were a prominent feature of their experience of work at TCS:

Each week our team leader records all our calls and then we will get a print-out at the end of the week telling us how our calls have averaged out. It's talk time, 'not ready' time, everything is monitored and we are given that every week to see how our performance is, and we are told if we are falling behind on anything. (TCS-NW, Catalogco, CSR agency worker, female)

Whether these differences arose because of the different nature of the contracts, inconsistencies in management style, or a combination of both is not clear. However, it does appear that the emphasis on culture and values as a unifying device has not been entirely successful here.

A crucial factor in this failure is the different status of the workers in this multi-client site, in particular the presence of large numbers of agency workers, (approximately 50 per cent of the CSRs) employed neither by TCS nor the clients, but recruited and paid by the temporary employment agency, Beststaff. Teams contained a mixture of agency and permanent CSRs on the same work, and the attempt to promote a common, company-based culture was extended in principle to all staff at the workplace, including Beststaff workers. Indeed, agency workers were encouraged to see themselves as TCS employees in an attempt by managers to foster loyalty and commitment and to reduce staff turnover. TCS managers stressed that there was no difference in the way agency and permanent staff were managed on a day-to-day basis. They were, in theory, subject to the same Performance and Development process involving monthly 'one to one meetings' with their team manager. This common approach was, in principle, reinforced by the offer of a permanent TCS contract after six months' satisfactory service. However, as we saw in Chapter 7 (see also Rubery et al. 2004), this site-wide management system did not operate in practice as it was designed in principle. Agency staff were less likely to be included in the Performance and Development process and TCS-NW did not fully honour its promises of permanent contracts, according to seniority. Instead, what mattered most was which client contract agency staff were employed on. Some agency workers were not given a satisfactory explanation as to why they had not been offered a permanent contract after six months and at this point, according to a Beststaff manager, many decided to leave.

The triangular relationship between the client, the call centre operator and the agency affected the development of a strong organizational identity at TCS. Staff were required to present themselves on the telephone as an employee of the client, were managed on a day-to-day basis by TCS and, in the case of temporary staff, received their wages from Beststaff. This, in fact, meant that these temporary staff gained little comprehensive knowledge and experience of any specific organizational cultures, either the employer or non-employer's, and therefore it is unsurprising that, although the relationship between these three organizations was carefully explained to new staff during their induction period, widely varying opinions were expressed by CSRs, both agency and permanent, when asked whom they saw as their employer. Some agency workers identified with the client firm: 'I'd say [I work for] Gambleco. But that's what I've been used to because I was only on Utilityco for a few weeks. But we're always told that we work for TCS or Beststaff' (TCS-NW, Gambleco, CSR agency worker, female).

Another worker, although well aware of her role within the relationship between the client, TCS and the agency, still identified with the client:

I always say I work for Catalogco. So I always say Catalogco, but it's TCS. I also know that I'm only employed casually by Beststaff. (TCS-NW, Catalogco, CSR agency worker, female)

Some of the permanent staff also mentioned a feeling of loyalty to the client, especially where there was regular telephone contact with the client's own staff, as in the case of the Truckco contract. Some agency workers did, however, identify with TCS while others clearly identified with Beststaff and would approach them, rather than TCS managers, if any problems arose.

Identification with the client by the call centre workers, as in the airline case, may simply reflect the CSRs' desire to tell people they worked for a more prestigious or well-known organization than TCS or the agency. However, the inconsistency in their perceptions as to who was their actual 'employer' tellingly reveals the difficulties faced by TCS in trying to foster a common identity for its staff. While the CSRs faced demands from customers, clients, line managers, TCS and Beststaff, interestingly, none of our CSR interviewees mentioned the TCS culture and core values as a means of coping with these, sometimes conflicting, pressures. This suggests that these ideas, strongly emphasized as a unifying force by managers, had not had a significant impact on staff below junior managerial level.

In PPPs, as we have seen, a contradictory situation emerged as employers emphasized a new culture for workers while also requiring a certain amount of conformity to traditional public sector values. Different groups of workers were required to straddle this divide to different extents. In relation to managers, we found that the employer strategies of generating commitment were generally successful. Managers who had transferred to the private sector felt empowered by their new roles and for some this had led to a direct transfer of commitment, not only from one employer to another, but from one sector to another:

I would find it difficult to go back to Council X, working for a local authority. I have developed a lot more under TCS. The management skills I have developed under TCS could transfer easily to another private company. (TCS-L, supervisor 2, female)

Some caseworkers at TCS and maintenance workers at the PFI Trust made positive identifications with the new employer because of increased training and career opportunities. In the PFI case, supervisors were given training in staff development and 'change management' and maintenance workers were trained in key aspects of health and safety. This strategy appears to have been successful as some maintenance workers were impressed by the training they had received under the new employer and compared it favourably with the poor performance of the Trust in this regard:

We are getting training. Under the hospital we never got any training, we were just left behind, we didn't carry on with modern trends, we didn't get any upgrading training, the facilities company are very on the ball. We've been on a Gas course, we are registered gas installers now, Health and Safety courses. All sorts. (Estates Company, maintenance worker 6, male)

However, in general, strategies developed to gain the commitment of workers in PPPs were not so straightforward and the experience of past cultures, values, and relationships in the public sector could not be easily erased. In particular, the influence of fellow workers upon identification was found to override the influence of management policies. In TCS-L, for example, the effectiveness of colleagues rather than TCS culture in shaping loyalties was recognized by the HR manager. He described how newly recruited staff were being socialized into an ethos associated with local government, and therefore their loyalties were to this culture rather than that of TCS:

You wonder who are the real influences on them, picking it up on the shop floor, and if the influence is a very strong local government ethos. (TCS-L, Manager 6, male)

A direct response to this was the initiation of the TCS-L newsletter and the 'communications champions' discussed earlier but in the interviews with case-workers these were not mentioned.

Indeed, there was evidence that for many workers, although not managers, there was a direct rejection of the strategies that had been developed to gener-ate commitment, either because they conflicted with existing values or were seen as control devices. For example, the new opportunities for progression that were the main 'carrot' of TCS-L were rejected by many of the caseworkers, as these were formed upon a new management structure based upon 'people management' skills rather than expertise in housing benefit. TCS team leaders and managers no longer enjoyed the trust and commitment of caseworkers and were compared unfavourably to managers in the Council who had worked their way up from caseworker level:

Line managers under the Council could help us with the more difficult cases. They've [the new managers] lost that skill. They don't assess cases now; they've got nothing to do with the assessment of cases now. All they do is management. . . . We don't have respect for them. (TCS-L, caseworker 4, female)

This contradicted the emphasis upon teamworking that the TCS culture wished to instil, again pointing to the importance of organizational culture matching organizational practice if it is to be a source of attachment for workers.

8.4   Organizational commitment beyond organizational goals

The above discussion suggests strong commitment to either the employer or non-employer cannot be assumed to arise from the management strategies of either. However, we found evidence that workers met organizational goals and carried out their work in ways that ensured relationships between contractors and clients ran more smoothly than the contractual arrangements should in theory allow.

There was, of course, some evidence of the 'forced commitment' found by Burchell et al. (2002) where workers simply meet organizational goals because of job insecurity. In the Airport case, for example, one reason that many inter-viewees from the handling firms gave to explain why direct control from the airline was acceptable was that the airline was seen as their job provider, and therefore efforts should be made to keep the airlines happy. 'They have a lot of say and power. At the end of the day, if they are not here, there will be no jobs for us' was the resonant expression from the handling shop floor. Elements of this could also be found in the multi-client call centre of TCS. Some agency staff were clearly aware of their 'inferior' status, and mentioned that they felt under pressure to work extra hours or to accept inconvenient shifts. As one CSR remarked:

They used to say, 'if you don't like it you know where the door is.' That was the attitude— we were only temporary. But really, the bulk of the workforce is temporary. (TCS-NW, Catalogco, CSR, female)

However, more positive ways were needed of securing worker commitment to organizational goals in a context of an increasing importance of 'relational work' (Barley and Kunda 2001) in the achievement of organizational goals. In these changing organizational forms the relationships workers need to establish to carry out their job become ever more important, providing an increasing role for worker agency. But the factors influencing the exercise of this agency is more complex than models of organizational commitment would suggest.

For example, in the Airport, commitment to non-employer airlines among handling staff is achieved through the generally perceived need to work to a 'common goal'. This is to get the aircraft off the ground on time. Although our interviewees work for different firms and some of them are competitors at the airport, they all seemed to recognize a responsibility to work towards the common goal of aircraft on-time performance based on the highest quality and safety possible. Some staff from the airlines are so aware of this commitment to the 'shared goal' that they see no conflict of interest between the airlines and the handling agents, a confidence based on the dominance of the airline's business objective:

Although we all work for a different company, the end goal is the same. We all want the flight to go on time and without complications. So it doesn't matter who is giving the orders. (Airline C, Manager 4, female)

The internalization of the on-time performance targets also provides a main source of cooperation and coordination on the ground which enables employees of airlines and contractors to facilitate each other's work beyond the usual call of contractual obligations. On the apron, the baggage handlers help each other out informally to deliver the service, for example, lending or borrowing equipment between each other:

The lad who is at the other end of the phone [asking for help] is the same as me. I will just say, 'Yes, you are alright, just take it and put it back where you got it from at the end of the day.' It's a give and take. We help them and they help us to make life easier. (BH, Supervisor 2, male)

Inside the aircraft, a similar scenario repeats itself:

We don't really argue, but everybody is on top of each other all the time [fighting for the limited space and time]. So you get used to it . . . We do help each other out, if something needs passing or doing, we will just do it if it is easier for us to do it. Some of them will do the same, but some of them won't. (FH, worker 11, female)

On the whole, cooperation between different groups of workers on the ground largely happens on a voluntary basis depending on the personality and depending on the situation on both sides.

People tend to help each other on the apron. For instance if I was taking bags in and a couple of bags fell off straight away there's horns beeping and people are letting you know but you don't hear it. They'll pick them up and they'll follow you. Everybody's very helpful in that way . . . You work daily with them and you just see them as part of your team. It has to be, it wouldn't really work otherwise. (BH, baggage handler 7, male)

This was supported by data from the PPPs. The commitments displayed were not generated by the management strategies of either the employer or the client organizations but were based on workers' past relationships and loyalties forged with other workers in the public sector. For example, in the PFI case study, past traditional commitments made to NHS Trust colleagues and the continuing commitment to delivering quality service to the public ensured domestics and maintenance workers continued to work beyond contractual obligations. The costing and timing of work that was involved in reaching the performance criteria of the contract meant it was often difficult for workers to provide this value-added service but, as shown in Chapter 5 they continued to try and do so.

However, this was not based on a straightforward identification with the non-employing public sector. The increased control over their work was often experienced as the public sector exercising control without responsibility rather than the outcome of the public sector client reclaiming power from an opportunistic private sector partner. Furthermore, this was interpreted as the public sector putting the contract before the interests of the service users or 'customers'. The caseworker below challenges the Council's priorities:

I get frustrated because I'm not worried about the individuals upstairs [from the Council]. I'm worried about the people that are ringing me. I'm there to help them and that's where I see my role. (TCS-L, caseworker 2, male)

Commitment could not be gauged from a simple compliance to the goals of either the private or public sector organizations. Commitment does not seem to be in the control of either the employer or the non-employer and this demonstrates the importance of moving away from a 'top-down' approach to the understanding of how commitment is formed and managed. We found that employees in PPPs are not loyal to their current or their ex-employer, but to the 'service'; including those who work within it and those who receive the service. In the PFI case study, when workers were asked who they felt they worked for, many replied that they worked for something bigger than the private company or the Trust; they worked for the hospital:

I would add something else. I work for the community. We all do in our own way, that's the way I see it. And I do work for the Trust. We have a very good relationship with the staff, we're all friendly, the nurses, the doctors, the auxiliaries, whoever we have contact with. If we're really short we can just say, we're short, we need help. Say we haven't got a patient there quick enough. The friendship and the rapport you build up over time, they come and help you. So the company, the Trust, the patient, its a big circle. (Hotel Services Company, porter 3, male)

Working towards a common goal of public service was an important means by which workers juggled the interests of past and present employers. Furthermore, it became apparent that for these workers the external image of the hospital or council was prestigious for these workers, supporting the findings of the airline case study, where the power of external image helped to generate commitment.

It is obvious that this willingness to engage in mutual support often comes, not from individual workers' commitment to their employer or non-employer organizations, but from the desire to help other people who are in the same situation, to reciprocate favours received, and to do a good job. Nonetheless, these informal working practices, or what may be called 'community spirit', have important implications for the nature of the inter-firm relationship under which tasks are carried out by employees from different employers. Indeed, it would appear that these new organizational forms both introduce new intensive working practices while also opening up spaces for new forms of commitment and identity beyond the control of management.

8.5   Processes of identifications and 'dis-identifications'

Recent work on organizational identity has recognized that workers display multiple identities and these shift over time and in specific contexts (Gallie et al. 1998; Bartel 2001). Indeed, rather than focusing upon the concept of 'identity', which has connotations of *being* one thing rather than another, there is an emphasis upon identifications, which captures the processes of identifying *with* something. This sits more easily with notions of fluidity and multiplicity that are central to contemporary theorizing.

Indeed, workers in some of the cases reflect upon these issues as they recognize the need to portray a dual identity of both their employer and the airline and make effort to balance the act:

When the passengers come to check in, we portray both the image of . . . FH and the airline, because at the end of the day you are checking in for the airline, but if the passenger has a problem, you've got to send them down to them [the airline]. So you've got to portray both, you've got to be well-managed and everything, because you are representing both. (FH, worker 3, male)

Significantly, this worker does not portray this as contradictory; it is simply a feature of organizational life. We also found that individuals' career aspirations and attachments to specific values were a key motivating force for identifying with either an employer or non-employer. For example, as discussed earlier, the importance of new opportunities for career advancement were the key to why workers identified with one employer or non-employer rather than the others. Crucially, when these were not available there could be a dis-identification with all parties. For example, one permanent CSR working on the Gambleco contract even failed to identify with TCS-NW as an employer: 'I don't tend to think of TCS as an employer. I just come in and do my job and go home' (TCS-NW, Gambleco, CSR, female).

In relation to public sector workers, the need to recognize multiple commitments is not confined to studies of PPPs; public sector workers have always to some extent operated within a complex and often contradictory set of loyalties, including loyalty to the department, the organization, the profession, the institution, and the community (Pratchett and Wingfield 1996). However, we were interested in whether public sector workers faced contradictory pulls on commitment distinctive from those in the past, specifically because of the potential value conflicts that emerge as the injection of the profit motive enters the delivery of public services (see Chapter 5).

In the PPP case an ambiguous status was not a result of confusion but a negotiation of the change and continuities in the employment relationship as workers straddled diverse loyalties and held on to the aspects of public sector identity they valued. Although there was a rejection of the profit motive (see Chapter 5), a focus upon the 'public service' helps workers make sense of change and resolve the dual pulls of public and private sector organizations. However, when workers feel this is challenged and the profit motive is overriding the aim of public service delivery a dis-identification with the new private sector employer can occur, as a caseworker reveals:

I just come into work, go home and get paid. I would have preferred to stay at Council X because under Council X our priorities were set. Even though TCS say they are committed to the customer, they are in a business, whereas Council X wasn't in a business and we see that difference. It's always targets and timescales and statistics, whereas with Council X it was just get the claims done and pay the benefit. (TCS-L, caseworker 4, female)

However, there was also evidence that such conflicts can be reconciled over the course of time as can be seen from the caseworker below who described her gradual change in outlook to one that was more compatible with the TCS culture:

My brain thinks like Council X. It shouldn't do, and it has taken two years to get to where I am now, toeing this corporate line. Don't get me wrong, I'm not saying that I didn't actually believe these values before [points to poster with TCS values] but they were not at the forefront of my mind. I am surprised actually, I thought I would be one of those 'I'm a council worker' but I'm moving towards more of these things [points to TCS values poster]. I am beginning to think like my boss does in terms of statistics and how we are seen and the relationships we have with the other groups and organizations that are tied directly into us. (TCS-L, caseworker 5, female)

Significantly, the form identifications take cannot be imposed upon workers in changing organizational forms. They are not straightforwardly loyal to either the client (their ex-public sector employer) or their employer but forge new identifications based upon commitment to the service delivery and other workers. Employers and non-employers are not the motivating force behind commitment in PPPs, and this was also the case, to some extent, at the airport and TCS-NW. However, value conflicts and a rejection of work intensification can mean that in PPPs *dis-identifications* with the private sector employer are the central processes of identification, and these are not necessarily matched by a positive identification to the non-employer.

8.6   Discussion and conclusions

In this chapter we have discussed a number of issues related to organizational commitment and identity across organizational boundaries in both the private and the public sector. The aim of the chapter has been to fill the gap in our current understanding on how multi-agency factors and inter-organizational relationships influence workers' identity and organizational commitment, and what actions, if any, firms take to foster organizational identity and commitment among people employed by another organization (Rubery et al. 2003).

Our evidence suggests that the existing HRM framework of analysis of organizational commitment proves to be too narrow in an increasingly fragmented form of work organization (Rubery et al. 2002). The management of work control and organizational commitment is often actively carried out by, or certainly involves, other organizations, such as client organizations, in the business relationships. This raises the question, to what extent can organizational culture be used as a unifying force in organizational forms where organizational boundaries are blurring and the management of the operations may involve a range of people representing different organizations? We are faced with situations where strategies used by employers to forge new commitments may not be enthusiastically embraced by workers. Significantly, commitment could not be predicted on the basis of employer or non-employer status.

Our case study evidence shows the importance of recognizing the different starting points from which workers are located in terms of access to, and knowledge of, different organizational cultures. A focus upon the division between employer and non-employer fails to capture how management strategies, and their relative success, can only be gauged in the context of workers' experiences and knowledge of different organizational cultures (based on past working histories as well as the present as is the case of transferred workers), the contract status of workers and the relative physical proximity and reliance on employers and non-employers.

Perhaps the key finding of our research is the pivotal role low-skilled workers can play in the shaping of these new organizational forms. Barley and Kunda's (2001) distinction between non-relational and relational roles is particularly useful here in describing our cases as they demonstrate that changes in tasks change the nature of social interactions in work and it is these changing interactions that shape and alter organizational forms.

This puts people doing the work and the relationships and identifications they forge at the centre of the analysis of changing organizational forms and this has generally been glossed over in studies of the network form. While existing research concentrates on the theory of inter-firm trust and risk sharing, workers are getting on with the real life of working in these new organizations and being the ones who ensure organizational goals are met. They do so using other focal points for commitment than those promoted by the employer and non-employers, such as commitment to common goals and co-workers, individual career trajectories, and the satisfaction of doing a good job.

Therefore workers may *act* as if they are committed to the organization by performing their work in ways that coincide with the organization's goals. However, the reasons why they do this may have little to do with the internalization of organizational culture and values (Fleming and Spicer 2003). For example, the aim to impose a new culture in PPPs to instigate a transfer of commitment by workers appears to be unsuccessful. This is also the case in the multi-client call centre, where the CSRs did not mention the TCS culture or core values, emphasized by management as a means of coping with the demands placed upon them. Equally, workers may be more committed to their non-employer client organizations than they are to their employer organizations for a number of reasons, such as employment security and career opportunities, as was exemplified in the Airport case. This highlights the fact that commitment is a complex issue which 'transcends the managerial agenda' (Gallie et al. 1998: 234) and that 'organizational commitment is less a matter of personnel policies and more a matter of broader values' (Gallie et al. 1998: 260). This is a key area of continuity between the traditional single employer context and the more recent phenomenon of multi-employer organizations.

This puts the employment relationship, and in particular the commitment and identity of workers, at the centre of the analysis of changing organizational forms. Significantly, it is not the issues of multiple and shifting identities that threaten the relative success of employers and non-employers in eliciting the commitment of their workers; rather it is the erosion of terms and conditions and in particular feelings of employment or job insecurity that may generate problems. As we have seen in Chapter 5, our case-study evidence does show that low motivation and commitment is directly related to feelings of job insecurity, supporting other research findings (Burchell et al. 2002). Furthermore, as suggested in the TCS-L case, many workers may have already left the organization because of feelings of unease or even betrayal during the transfer process, using exit as the ultimate expression of non-commitment to the new organizational form. These negative effects may call into question the ability of PPPs to succeed where these public and private sector partnerships require employees to display a complex mix of commitment to the client and traditional public sector service delivery combined with commitment to the 'customer' and an awareness of contracts. Private sector partners may, therefore, face a difficult task as they both seek to challenge *and* draw on traditional public sector identity and commitment in a context where trust is lost.

Finally, in the multi-client call centre and the airport the fragmented nature of business contracts and (therefore) the variation in employment contracts raises the question of how successful the employers' and non-employers' strategies can be. Although TCS attempted to gain commitment by emphasizing a common culture and a consistent set of HR strategies and, in some cases, resisted interventions by the clients, two factors undermined this attempt. First, the presence of large numbers of agency staff, not employed by TCS, meant that the organization could not apply its policies on pay, performance management, and discipline to about half the workers on-site. Second, the diverse nature of the work on the different client contracts meant that the work experience of the CSRs, the skills they required and the pressures they faced varied widely from one client contract to another. In these circumstances the TCS core values had not ensured a consistency in the management of staff throughout the whole site. However, significantly, even without these pressures, neither could the TCS core values in the TCS-L site match long-standing values of public service. In the Airport case, the airlines' strong bargaining power over the handling firms and the perceived 'common' goal of providing good quality service to passengers have led to the employing organization taking a back seat *vis-à-vis* the non-employer client firms' hands-on role in managing the (commitment of the) workforce. The power of contractors is therefore important when exploring organizational commitment in multi-employer and multi-client sites as employees are all too aware that their job security depends on whether the next contract will be signed. This also raises the question whether the same strategy would work in a context of skill shortage and tight labour markets.

The case-study evidence reveals the paradox at the centre of changing organizational forms as employees are both simultaneously powerful and powerless. The organizations using fragmented systems are dependent more than ever on workers performing and negotiating their work in ways that smooth over inter-organizational relations. Yet, while this would appear to put employees in a powerful position, in fact they have little choice but to comply. Those who were transferred had little say in the process and were left to negotiate the contradictory cultures at work in PPPs, while those in the airport and the multi-client call centre in positions of job insecurity have little choice but to manage the realities of complex client–contractor relations on the ground. While both employers and non-employers appear to be obtaining the desired outcomes from employees, it is motivations of doing a good job, working towards a common goal or service and collegial loyalty, rather than commitment to the firm as such, that produce these outcomes.

9

Changing Boundaries, Shaping Skills: The Fragmented Organizational Form and Employee Skills

IRENA GRUGULIS AND STEVEN VINCENT

9.1 Introduction

This chapter aims to explore the impact that changing organizational forms have on skill. As both Littler (1982) and Cockburn (1983) have argued, skill is the result of a complex interplay between the expertise and experience of individuals; the way that work is designed and controlled; and the status and labour market power that these individuals (or the groups they belong to) are deemed to possess. The relationship is not a static one, and skill will be affected by changes in the functions carried out, changes in ways of performing those functions, changes in the division of labour, products, services, technologies, management strategy and work design (Rose et al. 1994).

The role of the employer is particularly pivotal (see, for example, the contributors to Rubery and Wilkinson 1994; Cappelli 1999). In traditional bureaucratic firms with internal labour markets, skills are developed over a working lifetime with commitment and loyalty exchanged for job security and the possibility of progression. When these organizational forms are fragmented and the employment relationship 'marketised' (Cappelli 1995), both the skills that are exercised and the mechanisms in place to develop them may change. This can have advantages, privileging skills such as creativity, innovation, and entrepreneurship that are not necessarily valued within bureaucracies or advantaging groups such as women or minorities. According to Albert and Bradley (1997) it is the need for these skills, coupled with workers' desire to preserve control over their own activities that will drive some forms of organizational restructuring. Assuming that there will be a dramatic growth in the number of 'knowledge workers' (though see also Thompson et al. 2001), they argue that expertise requires discretion (Fox 1974) and, even when outsourced, expert work cannot be rigidly controlled. So the small, artist-run studios in Hollywood, AT&T's lists of internal experts and employment agencies in

London that provide accountants with temporary placements effectively liberate those who work for them from the burdens of bureaucracy without adding on different forms of control (which would invalidate the workers' expertise). The experts are 'catalysts' (Albert and Bradley 1997: 98) in this restructuring and 'the casualization of expert employees is more adequately explained by the desire of specific individuals to gain discretion over their work rather than the demands generated by specific organizations' (ibid.: 5).

Nor will these high discretion networks be restricted to experts. Other employees, aware of the advantages such fragmented forms can bring, will compete to be hired on 'at will' contracts and 'expert employees, their opportunities and their choices will alter and create institutions' (ibid.: 99).

Other evidence supports the idea that moving away from traditional employers can advantage those whose skills give them power in the labour markets. In Harvey and Kanwal's (2000) account of self-employed IT workers, the contractors enjoyed and appreciated the freedoms that their new status provided; pressures to return to full-time permanent contracts tended to come from employers. Similarly, the US-respondents to Kunda et al.'s (2002) survey might fear the financial consequences of their independence, but appreciated the advantages too much to relinquish them.

So, new organizational forms can support 'skill in the job' by providing levels of discretion not found in more traditional organizations. They may also support individual skills by providing access to networks of experts and information about more formal training opportunities (Kunda et al. 2002). Interestingly, in Finegold's (1999) account of work in Silicon Valley, California, it is the mobility of the workforce that fosters the development of a 'high skills ecosystem'. This would actively damage a firm's skills base from more traditional perspectives yet here, because there are so many experts in the 'ecosystem', mobility encourages communication, extends personal networks, and shares practices. These, coupled with the cutting edge tasks that workers are engaged in, the proximity and involvement of universities, and the existence of professional associations, maintain and extend expert skills. In this context, contracting supports the development of skills.

However, restructuring organizations can also create problems for skills development. Even when there are market premiums to be gained from higher skills, individuals on contract can and do prioritize gaining work over maintaining expertise (Mallon and Duberley 2002). The positive effects felt by the IT workers studied by Harvey and Kanwal (2000) and Kunda et al. (2002) need to be set against the stresses and insecurity restructuring can cause in others (Sparrow 2001). Moreover, as Cappelli (2001) argues, market-based relations may not be the most appropriate mechanism for sustaining and controlling particular occupations. Managerial and skilled work presents a very complicated challenge in terms of workplace performance. When workers are no longer provided with long-term job security in exchange for loyalty and commitment, their approach to employment may change.

Such contradictory pressures exist in inter-firm networks as well. Different organizations may have privileged access to particular forms of expertise (Matsuick and Hill 1998) and sharing this can help all of the firms in a supply chain (Brown 2001) though the advantages may not be evenly divided (Hunter et al. 1996). However, these networks are, as Rubery et al. (2002) argue, no longer single employers with shared interests and this may present problems (Scarbrough 2000) and result in exploitation, rather than partnership (Rainnie 1988; Blyton and Turnbull 1998; Thompson and McHugh 2002).

Fragmenting organizational forms presents particular pressures in the United Kingdom where outside the professions, few intermediary organizations exist and the responsibility for vocational education and training has traditionally rested with the individual firm. In the past this has resulted in a polarized division of skills with pockets of excellent practice (that fails to 'trickle down', Lloyd 2002) set against the existence of large numbers of jobs that demand neither skills nor qualifications of the workers who carry them out (Felstead et al. 2002). This 'low skills equilibrium' (Finegold and Soskice 1988) is both a cause and a consequence of the tight control systems that are imposed. As Clarke and Hermann's (2001) research demonstrates, the lack of skills among British construction workers leads to their jobs being far more tightly monitored than their counterparts in Germany, Denmark, and the Netherlands.

This chapter explores the way that the development and control of skills changed in several of the case-study companies and assesses the impact of inter-organizational relationships. It considers the mechanisms in place for reproducing skills as well as the changes and continuities in the way that jobs were designed and the impact that this had on work. It also highlights changes in the *types* of skills that were developed and valued: particularly the switch of emphasis from 'technical' to 'soft' skills.

This shift is part of an increasingly general change both in the skills that are considered important and in the way that the word 'skill' is used. Service sector work now dominates the economy and working in the service sector demands very different skills to those required in manufacturing. When the process of being served is as much a part of the sale as any physical products that may be involved, the way workers feel and the feelings they produce in others are important. Flight attendants are required to make passengers feel good, debt collectors 'create alarm' to persuade debtors to pay, call centre workers must establish rapport then, just as quickly, emotionally disengage. People working in the most prosaic jobs, from bank clerks and waitresses to language tutors and bar staff must demonstrate the 'right' emotional orientation, look, and sound (see, among others, Hochschild 1983; Trethewey 1999; Korczynski 2001; Nickson et al. 2001; Grugulis 2002; Noon and Blyton 2002). In all of these instances, the product being sold includes some part of the employees. So now, gaining employment is about appearing and feeling as much as it is about doing and the effort bargain is extended to aesthetics and emotions (Noon and Blyton 2002).

An emphasis on human feelings can be a highly pleasurable experience for the workers involved (Leidner 1993; Wharton 1996). But that is not its central aim: Work is not redesigned to accommodate employees' emotions, rather employees are redesigned to fit what is deemed necessary at work (Putnam and Mumby 1993). Such redesign may also have negative consequences, including high levels of stress and employee turnover, burnout, increased pressure, and an inability to engage with the emotion in its uncommodified form (Hochschild 1983; Korczynski 2001).

There are also wider issues to consider when emotions, aesthetics, and personal attributes are relabelled as skills (Payne 1999, 2000; Keep 2001). Establishing a managerial prerogative over feelings is very different to the monitoring of technical abilities; employees may lose the freedom to exercise control over their own emotions and have lesser (or no) rights to courtesy, consideration, and respect in interactions (Goffman 1959; Paules 1991). Judgements over these factors are far more likely to incorporate stereotypical assumptions on gender and race since, when skills are embodied these may be the most visible elements of 'skill'. Nor is this skewed ledger necessarily evened by a wage (Hochschild 1983); soft skills, regardless of their desirability or complexity rarely give individuals labour market power when unaccompanied by technical expertise (Bolton 2004). Part of the reason for this is that, as here, the skills and attributes required are local ones; qualities valued and rewarded in one environment may not be equally favoured in another. In these case studies a 'private sector' and 'customer focused' approach was valued (and often influenced the way that the organization was structured). But loyalty to the new management was also highly prized and often explicitly rewarded over and above technical skills.

This chapter explores the effect that inter-organizational relationships had on skill in the widest sense as well as reviewing the impact of an increasing emphasis on soft skills. It argues that, although relational partnerships and high trust knowledge exchange were often desired, the risks inherent in networks resulted in a significant increase in performance monitoring. This was often needed to check that tasks had been completed or regulatory requirements met, but it also meant that the skills employees could exercise were limited and devalued. Such a context was rarely conducive to an exchange of expertise and completing the (often redefined and narrower) task took precedence over skill development.

9.2   Skill in the job

Since skill is located in the job as well as in the individual, the way that work is designed and the way that it is controlled can impact on skill levels. Networks of organizations may seek to draw advantage from this. The partnership between FutureTech and Govco in which FutureTech took over the running and administration of Govco's computer services was intended to provide Govco with access to more expertise than its in-house operation could offer as well as providing staff with a greater choice of career paths. The work itself (that of programming, developing, and maintaining computer systems) was highly skilled and remained largely the same; but outsourcing changed the way that it was controlled.

Before the contract had been set up, the government department had conducted an audit of the tasks undertaken by their computing staff. These extensive investigations attempted to codify the work so that FutureTech knew what was required, the government department knew what it was contracting out and the whole process could be readily checked by national auditors. Each contractual specification required a 'business case', based on the cheapest way to achieve whatever computing service was requested, so employees spent considerable amounts of time on audit. These management systems also affected the expertise that Govco was given access to. Tight budgetary controls meant that staff had less freedom to pursue technological innovations and experiment with new software. Once outsourced, software development was restricted to cheaper (and arguably less suitable) pre-tested technologies.

The supply teachers working for TeacherTemp were also engaged in the same tasks but subject to a slightly different control system than their permanent colleagues. This was often welcomed since it gave them an opportunity to *teach* rather than participate in the paperwork and administration involved in running a school (Albert and Bradley 1997; Grimshaw et al. 2001). Most viewed this as liberation from an onerous burden, but the price generally paid was the loss of the ability to control what was taught. Part of the paperwork that teachers were required to complete was lesson plans. Supply teachers, unless on long-term contracts, rarely had to write these up but, since lesson plans must both exist and be followed, they were required to conform to plans drawn up by others. Since learning outcomes tend to be written in general terms they can be very difficult to interpret and, for many, much of the pleasure of class contact was lost:

I thought I would have more freedom to [do] certain things. I thought, I will be able to decide I am here for a day and we will do a project on that and at the end of the day we would have produced a book about so-and-so and they would go home thinking, right it has been a whole day with a different person who has been really nice to us . . . and you cannot do that. So that is a bit disappointing. (TeacherTemp, supply teacher 18, female)

In TCS-L caseworkers' jobs were redesigned (Marchington et al. 2003). Housing benefit staff had previously been responsible for seeing an entire claim through from start to finish. Under TCS processing was reorganized so that caseworkers 'specialized' in one part of the claims process:

The nature of the job has changed a lot. From being able to assess a claim from A to Z they go to a system where you can only go up to a certain phase and then leave it suspended and hand it over to somebody else to check. It's not a satisfying job. (Council X, caseworker 1, female)

In addition to this, because the Council could not delegate its authority to pay, caseworkers lost the power to make decisions on claims. Minor omissions could no longer be condoned and simple changes, such as rent increases, which had been dealt with on the basis of a telephone call when the operation was in-house, now required benefit to be suspended pending approval. Every form processed was sent over to the Council where a team of about twenty determination officers checked that they had been completed correctly. Since TCS was financially penalized for mistakes a system of internal monitoring was introduced to supplement this. Forms with errors were returned to TCS's Service Excellence Team which recorded the reason for rejection (and occasionally contested this with the Council's staff) then sent back to the caseworkers, a process which, as one caseworker noted, could take weeks:

It's like with backdating decisions. I might agree that this person has proved their case. I can't do it straight away. I have to put a letter together, send it upstairs, wait a couple of weeks and they send it back and say you can send it and then any backdated money you can pay—but I can't pay it until I get the OK from them. Or they say, sorry, I don't agree with your decisions so they can override me. So I have to go by what they say so all those powers have been taken away from me. It is deskilling, that is why so many people have left over the years. (TCS-L, caseworker 3, female)

This constant checking was also a source of irritation:

It's just, what irritates staff is the inconsistency and the picky bits like, oh, for God's sake yes, that is 10p out but let it go. (TCS-L, Manager 4, female)

To make the process more efficient, two specialist sections were introduced, a call centre (with fifteen staff) and a reception area (with twenty). Workers taking on these roles performed only a narrow range of tasks and staff could be on call centre work for periods of six months (see also Chapter 11). Housing benefit is a complex area and regulations are subject to change. In the period in which this fieldwork was conducted, eighty-eight changes (of varying degrees of magnitude) were made in the applications procedure. Staff were no longer aware of changes that occurred outside their own narrow remit. Refresher training was promised to those working in the call centre, but never materialized.

In FutureTech, TCS, and TeacherTemp, work was skilled and, for the first two organizations, workers' terms and conditions protected by TUPE. When jobs required less obvious individual expertise the decline in discretion was more dramatic and often accompanied by reduced wages (Holly et al. 2001; Rainbird and Munro 2003). Efficiency gains from Compulsory Competitive Tendering (CCT) have largely come from work intensification, through increasing standards (Vincent 1997; see also Boyne 1998); doing the same work with fewer staff (Cutler and Wayne 1994) and increasing workloads (McIntosh and Broderick 1996). At Scotchem, where workers nearing retirement could be transferred to security jobs in the firm's Gatehouse, outsourcing was intended to achieve cost savings. The Gatehouse was responsible for letting vehicles and visitors on and off of the site, out-of-hours telephony duties and special duties in the event of emergencies. The old security staff, who were given early retirement, had a wealth of local knowledge and enjoyed a great deal of autonomy in completing these tasks. The new agency workers, supplied by Securiforce were more tightly regulated. They lost the power to coordinate deliveries with the warehouse (a useful activity when lorries arrived early) and were required to answer telephone calls with reference to a script, a practice which was much resented.

The changes in the control systems that restructuring required impacted on the way skills could be deployed and reduced the discretion that individual employees could exercise. To a certain extent this was an inevitable part of the contracting process; tasks may be contracted out, but responsibility remains with the original organization and inspection could not always be waived. According to one senior manager at Council X, other authorities that had outsourced their claims processing had attempted to sample completed forms rather than checking each individual one. The benefit fraud inspectorate, supported by the government and the Council's auditors, had prevented them from doing this. Schools were subject to inspection and needed to ensure that lesson plans were drawn up and followed. Scotchem needed to conform to health and safety legislation. Even where these regulatory requirements did not exist, as at Govco, mechanisms needed to be in place to ensure that FutureTech had provided the services specified. These necessarily reduced the discretion that individual employees could exercise.

9.3   Developing skills

Fragmenting organizational forms increased risk and increased risk resulted in a dependency on written contracts and performance monitoring. These reduced skill in the job by limiting employees' discretion, but their impact on individual skills was more complex. These were affected by the control systems imposed but, contrary to Cappelli (1995), might also be supported by the introduction of formal training mechanisms.

In TCS-L a six-week training course was introduced to teach new hires how to process housing benefit claims. These recruits were far less well qualified then the trainee caseworkers hired by Council X, since TCS hoped to discourage turnover. The course put on for them met a mixed response. It was far shorter, and far more limited than the old 13-week course that had been run by the council, but that course had not run for five years and, when the contract had been transferred, no system was in place to train recruits. Experience of mentoring on the job varied from section to section. In the call centre, a team coach helped with queries and one experienced caseworker was formally appointed to be her deputy. Elsewhere, caseworkers objected to being regularly asked to assist colleagues, particularly since these interruptions were not formally acknowledged as part of their workload and prevented them meeting their own targets.

In the Post Office attempts were made to ensure that all staff received training, regardless of the type of outlet they were employed by. New recruits to Crown Offices received three weeks' residential training in Post Office procedures before being shadowed by (and shadowing) more experienced colleagues on the tills, though this was much reduced from the six weeks training given previously. Franchise staff had to attend these courses too, and this often presented franchisees with logistical problems. In sub-post offices provision was less formal; the contract holder received the full residential training and was responsible for passing their knowledge on to anyone they hired. In addition to this, in all Post Office outlets there was a new emphasis on sales training, with Crown Offices obliged and franchise and sub-Post Offices advised, to hold regular training sessions to encourage the cross-selling of related products.

In FutureTech graduate trainees, hired to replace more expensive (and experienced) contractors (Grimshaw et al. 2002; Vincent and Grugulis 2004), were trained in programming and applications. This was reinforced and developed at a three-week residential induction in the United States of America and was supposed to be further developed through on the job training. In practice, however (as noted below), short-term business needs predominated and this aspect was often neglected.

The existence of such formal provision in each of these organizations is welcome and counters fears that employees on 'marketized' contracts would be less likely to receive training (Cappelli 1995). However, as Rainbird and Munro (2003) observe in their study of cleaning contractors, formal training had actually increased (and record keeping was much improved) but the form that it took was narrower, more task-focused, and less developmental.

Other workers, particularly agency staff, fared less well in terms of formal provision. Supply teachers who were quite often doing work that they were not qualified for, were almost never included in school development activities and there was little incentive to provide even individual feedback and coaching with schools responding to unsatisfactory performance simply by asking the agency to send someone else next time. The security guards also fell through the net, despite pressure from Scotchem managers:

It's not the boys in the gatehouse, it's not them we are not happy about. We put the guys under a lot of pressure and they are certainly not getting the backup from Securiforce, to come down and give them any training whatsoever. (Scotchem, Manager 8, male)

This was particularly worrying, given the extent to which some of the organizations relied on temporary staff. In TCS-L agency staff formed a significant minority (twenty from a workforce of 120; with an additional twenty later employed in a site in the north-west to work on clearing the backlog of claims). The managerial view was that these workers had been hired on the basis that they could perform a task but few of their colleagues agreed.

9.4   Skill development and 'learning networks'

While the pressures of contracting and control often reduced employees' skills there were examples of cooperation in networks where the establishment of social relations for technical exchange was central to the labour process. In Scotchem, while agency staff for security and cleaning were tightly controlled and had few opportunities for development, relations with some raw material suppliers and customers involved much mutual learning. These cooperative networks existed with only a few carefully chosen partners, typically those involving large quantities of materials of significance to both parties and where relationships had built up over time. Other less important, or more competitive, purchases and sales were managed through external agents and Multichem's internal web of selling organizations. Goods purchased from and supplied to competitors tended to be in small quantities (see Chapter 4) and information on production processes was heavily guarded. In contrast to this, relations with Acidchem, a production facility in the north of England and Scandichem, a Danish company, involved far higher levels of trust. Contracts were loosely specified and it was assumed that relationships would continue indefinitely. There were periodic negotiations over price and discussions about quantities, but in both cases the relationship was more important than any individual contracts so when market changes meant that one party would be disadvantaged, quantities were never contractually enforced.

In terms of skill and product development it was the non-contractual elements of these relationships that were most interesting. Acidchem encouraged close personal links between its staff and employees at Scotchem at a variety of levels, including sales and purchasing managers, plant managers, and research chemists:

What we try and do is foster different links at different levels in different functions. For example, there was some interest on the part of Scotchem's research and development people to understand pigment shading. So we had a joint research group involving my senior chemist and the research and development group up at Scotchem. (Acidchem, Director 1, male)

This exchange contributed to a variety of joint problem solving groups and mutually beneficial innovations. Changes were made to the way that chemicals were packaged and transported, there was extensive investment in plant equipment at both sites and experiments involved both shop floor staff and researchers.

Collaborations could go further than this. When Scotchem opened a new plant facility with Scandichem, the latter benefited from having a supplier closer to home, reducing transportation costs, and making supply more flexible, while Scotchem wished to use the new plant to penetrate new markets. There was an extensive exchange of information before the plant was established, covering production processes, qualities required in the products, and projections of demand. Several people commented that the plant's success depended on both sides' generosity with information.

In the new plant the demarcation lines between process, engineering, and testing were more blurred than on the rest of the site. Process operators did 'asset care' work, looking after equipment, doing checks, and carrying out minor maintenance, while the engineering workers spent about 25 per cent of their time on process work. Process operators also had responsibility for quality assurance that would fall to qualified chemists elsewhere and groups had more autonomy in deciding how work was done:

We've been left with quite a free role to prioritize ourselves, and sort our own team out, what we do and who does it, left to our own responsibility for that. . . . We know our responsibilities, we organize ourselves. I think the ownership has come because we understand the business and the needs of the business. (Scotchem, operative 3, male)

Different teams have different ways of operating. I don't mind so long as they go from this position here to that position there before the end of the shift. (Scotchem, Manager 10, male)

Here, the use of networks encouraged the development of both firm specific knowledge and inter-organizational trust. FutureTech's 'partnership' with Govco was also intended to be as collaborative as these networks. In it managers were given specific duties in relation to knowledge development and innovation; collaborative groups worked to assess new technologies or considered how technology might be used to save money for Govco, and senior managers in both organizations worked closely together. However, here much of the local knowledge that might have been shared by the programmers had been lost. Staff had taken redundancy when the work had been contracted out, leaving for work that offered more money or better prospects or simply retired. Govco's internal systems were extremely complicated and changes to one area could impact on many others. According to one programmer, even after working on one of the larger IT systems for two years 'you can only scratch the surface of being useful to the team because of the business knowledge'. But the number of people who possessed this knowledge was declining: 'When we joined there was a lot of expertise that's gone now, wasn't there?' (FutureTech, programmer 3, male).

Graduates working on new systems took a great deal of pleasure in their work but those engaged in maintaining or developing the existing programmes were less satisfied. Lack of local knowledge and pressures of work meant that they were often required to do repetitive tasks for prolonged periods:

at the end of the day [career development] boils down to what business needs dictate so . . . whatever you want comes second place to what FutureTech wants, which is perhaps fair enough because they pay your wages. (FutureTech, Manager 28, male)

Many moved on, taking advantage of the greater career opportunities elsewhere in FutureTech or going to work for other companies and turnover among the programmers increased from just over 2 to 9 per cent. This caused problems for Govco and managers worried that their work was being run by a 'B-team' (particularly when some ex-Govco staff, who had not been highly regarded internally, were promoted by FutureTech for their knowledge of Govco's internal systems). However, the contract measured work in technical 'function points' and, while these could be adjusted to cater for work that was straightforward or skilful or for which there was a high level of demand in the market place, it did not allow Govco to specify which individuals should carry out tasks. The input of individuals could and did make a real difference in the workplace, but this was not reflected in the system of measurement.

9.5 Changing skills

In many of the case studies the control systems introduced limited the opportunities employees had to exercise or develop technical skills; audit mechanisms and tighter managerial controls reduced the scope for discretion at work; and financial constraints often limited the activities workers could engage in. At the same time other 'soft' skills were actively encouraged. New 'partners' sought to bring 'private sector' attitudes into public sector work, and also ensure that employees were loyal to them and observed their priorities. This shift was particularly marked, for different reasons, in TCS and Post Office Counters.

In the customer service case the TCS-L general manager was keen to eliminate what he condemned as the '9 to 5 local government mentality'; seeking staff who had customer focus, attitude, flexibility, and (interestingly) 'endurance':

There's no point in having the skills to do benefits casework if you haven't got the attitude to go with it. And they're both as important as each other. (TCS-L, General Manager, male)

This focus on attitude was new and attracted both praise and condemnation. Several staff still working for the council were sympathetic to the fact that TCS had some 'difficult' staff. Others were less pleased. One local authority manager estimated that TCS had lost some of the best and most experienced workers and two caseworkers who had been transferred over expressed concern that workers had been 'encouraged' to leave (an estimated thirty caseworkers either taking redundancy payments or moving on since the transfer). Messages about the 'right' attitude were conveyed in a range of ways. New recruits were carefully screened:

the staff that we're bringing in have got a different attitude and the recruitment process is definitely working because we had an awful lot of negative people that used to work with us and most of those have gone by now. And when we're doing the selection there's lots of tests that sort of test attitude and things like that. (TCS-L, Manager 4, female)

TCS's caseworker training course, which provided a basic introduction to the benefits system also placed a great deal of emphasis on behavioural skills, dealing with punctuality, an overbearing new recruit, one new hire's problem with BO and attitudes. Several interviewees welcomed the fact that poor performance was now disciplined in ways that it had not been under the council and good performance rewarded, but this good performance was often attitudinal rather than technical. In particular, it seemed that the role of manager had changed with less emphasis placed on being an experienced and expert benefits caseworker:

Team managers used to have skills, housing benefit related—backdating decisions, [you] used to be able to go to them and ask them for advice and discuss them. They don't have those skills now. All their skills are about doing statistics. You have to go round to people who have been here for a long time. Because no-one ever knows everything in this job, it's the type of job you will always be finding something new . . . TCS says you don't need to have those skills. (TCS-L, caseworker 3, female)

It seems that the 'new' managers were chosen on the basis of soft skills, personal attributes, and their commitment to TCS rather than on knowledge, experience, or awareness of housing benefit. Performance was monitored through statistics and one caseworker who occasionally acted as a manager protested that her caseworker skills conflicted with what she was expected to do there. It may have been that others also felt this way. During the fieldwork when a managerial post was advertised none of the experienced caseworkers applied and no candidate had more than 12 months exposure to benefits. This also had implications for the way skills were used in the workplace. Experienced caseworkers found that they were expected to deal with colleagues' problems as well as their own caseload and busy periods could no longer be resolved by 'everyone chipping in'. There were other worrying implications too; one trade union representative expressed concern at the 'surprising' under-representation of minority groups in management.

The soft skills demanded in the Post Office were different to those valued in TCS. There customer service skills and sales experience were emphasized over organizational commitment. This change of emphasis was the result of the change to the Post Office's product range: From 2003 it was due to lose its monopoly on benefit payments (from which it earned one-third of its income); utility companies and their customers were abandoning counter-based payments; and most postal services had been opened to competition. As a result, counter staff were required to increase sales and promote new products:

Cross selling that's called and that's the retail culture. . . . I went into my local branch office recently and said, 'Can I have a passport form please?' What I got was a passport form, a leaflet on travel insurance, a leaflet on currency and the clerk finished up by saying 'and we also offer a passport checking service as well for £3.50 and send it off for you'. Now that's cross selling. Branch staff do it automatically now, that's their culture. (NFSP, Manager 1, male)

Here, too, the switch in which skills were considered prestigious was most visible in recruitment and promotion. Previously Post Office work had been considered of higher status than 'mere' retail, attracting higher pay, more favourable terms and conditions and greater job security, in part at least because the work was considered more technically demanding. In larger offices staff might deal with up to 170 different types of transaction. During this research however, respondents tended to downplay the importance of this:

there's nothing you need to be a rocket scientist to do, it's all relatively simple, but you do need a huge volume of small detail knowledge about all of those. (SPO 3, Manager 1, male)

Others put even less stress on the technical side of counter work:

Almost anybody, realistically, could do the transactions over the counter. . . . But to do the other things, the selling and the customer care, it takes a certain kind of personality to do that. (POCL, HQ, Manager 5, female)

One of the Regional Network Managers contacted had been interviewing candidates for work on the counter earlier that day. She commented with surprise that a candidate with retail experience had been appointed in preference to one who had worked in a Post Office before. Ten years earlier such a decision would have been unheard of.

The smaller outlets, though equally keen to increase sales, were far less concerned with consciously recruiting attitude. While the Crown Offices worked from lists of recruitment criteria sent down from the central HR department that stressed personality and the ability to sell, franchise holders and sub-postmasters and mistresses spoke of recruiting experienced Post Office workers. One single franchise holder had waited 5 weeks for a suitably experienced candidate, covering the disruption to his business rather than compromise.

Interestingly, despite the emphasis on how 'natural' customer service skills were and the demand for a 'certain type of personality', the customer service side of Post Office work was designed to minimize employee input rather than harness the talents sought in recruitment (see also Callaghan and Thompson 2002). In all outlets, the form that these 'new' sales-oriented skills took was scripted and synthetic. According to the official checklist, employees were required to make eye contact with customers, give a polite greeting, serve the customer immediately, give them their full attention, offer other products, and make a pleasing closing statement. Name badges were worn and mystery shoppers monitored staff on scripts, product knowledge, and cross-selling. These formalized controls could and did cause problems. Several small sub-offices and franchises had received critical reports for not offering products specified by that day's mystery shopper checklist but which the Post Office would not let them sell and the scripts were widely resented. Some prompts secured such trivial increases in sales that they seemed designed simply to ensure obedience to the idea of cross selling. During this research, books of stamps were redesigned into groups of six and twelve rather than four and ten and staff were instructed to offer a book of twelve stamps to customers asking for ten. A Regional Network Manager, arguing that increasing sales was easy and could readily be incorporated into every transaction pointed out how little extra time it took for clerks to mention that stamps now came in books of twelve. A sub-postmaster, on the front line himself, was less positive and saw this exercise, 'for which you earn 0.00001p' (sub-postmaster (SPO) 3, male) as meaningless.

Post Office management also seemed to be changing. Just as TCS privileged skills other than technical caseworker ones in their promotion decisions, so too in the Post Office Regional Network Managers were expected to monitor sales and customer service performance in increasingly large areas, rather than acting as repositories of expertise for branches with queries. Technical work was managed through performance indicators and monitored by official statistics on sales, queues, and service quality which branches were required to collate (each day Crown Offices received a computer generated list of the times at which managers should monitor queues and the penalties for those who attempted to distort their data were harsh). External verification came from mystery shoppers. Senior staff monitored the overall statistics and aimed to increase sales:

Why would I be ringing up a branch manager on £25,000 a year, or whatever, and saying, 'what are you doing about so-on and so-on', with some minor niggle or whatever? That's what *they* are being paid to do. . . . I feel that I'm paid to go out there and make sure that the changes that need to take place to improve the service to the customer have been made. (POCL, HQ, Manager 5, female)

Technical queries were directed to specialist call centres, but these were often staffed by clerks who were themselves unfamiliar with systems and processes:

Before you had an area manager's office you could deal with, and in that office there will be a wealth of knowledge you could pick up on. Now it's a manager that is based further away and covers more offices. . . . If we ring our call centre for information nine times out often they won't give you the answer you want . . . so you know that you are probably not going to get the right answer and they have got to fend it off to somebody else. (SPO4, Manager 1, male)

And again 'I've reached the point that I try to avoid them [call centres]. They keep you hanging on for so long and you can be given the wrong information' (SPO3, Manager 3, male).

Ways of coping were devised. Post Office franchise holders solved their own problems or waited until call centre specialists had referred their question elsewhere and called them back, but few were pleased about the new arrangements.

This change in orientation is difficult to explain on the basis of job design alone. Technology and reorganization meant that fewer technical skills were required, but these had not been eliminated entirely, nor were they unimportant. Work has always demanded a combination of both technical and personal skills and these organizations were no exception. Even with the new Horizon computer system that provided prompts and assistance to counter clerks, Post Office sales were complicated and demanded a high level of product knowledge.

Very experienced sub-postmasters could still be confused by requests for unfamiliar services. Similarly, in benefits work, the reorganizations introduced by TCS did not eliminate the need for skilled caseworkers (though there was optimistic talk among the senior management of a computer system that might). In these organizations technically skilled staff were at a premium. Yet, in both the increasing emphasis on soft skills, customer service, and personal attributes was used to diminish the importance of technical skills. As will be seen in Chapter 10 this had implications (both positive and negative) for gender.

It is also interesting to note that the way these 'new' skills were introduced was not particularly 'skilful'. Just as employees' discretion over the technical aspects of their work was declining, so the form these soft skills could and should take was prescribed. In these organizations 'loyalty' was expressed and 'customer service' performed in specific, specified, and tightly controlled ways. Such control over the way that people inhabit their jobs contrasts with the traditional professional and managerial exchange of loyalty and commitment for trust (Fox 1974). Instead, it resembles Korczynski's (2001) 'Customer Oriented Bureaucracy' in which the emotional orientations required for service work are combined with high levels of (often Taylorist) formal control.

Moreover, while these particular 'skills' had a great deal of local relevance, it is doubtful whether they conferred any sort of external labour market power on the individuals who exercised them. Indeed, their internal power was precarious and heavily dependent on management favour. It may be, as Lafer (2004) argues, that relabelling attitudes as skills is actively unhelpful. The employment relationship is a fluid one in which control systems, job design, organizational structure, and immediate colleagues (among others) will affect the way that workers perform. Calling 'loyalty' or 'commitment' skills individualizes responsibility for them and ignores the fact that they are reciprocal, that workers may choose to give or withhold them depending on the way that they themselves are treated.

In part, this shift in emphasis from technical to social skills reflects the nature of service work itself. The Post Office, in particular, had moved from being a monopoly supplier of a range of (often specialist) goods and services to a position in which many of its most profitable work was being lost and others were open to competition. Under these circumstances the increasing redefinition of employees as salespeople was hardly surprising. But this transition was to a scripted and synthetic form of emotional labour with exchanges regulated and controlled by both management and machines (see also Korczynski 2001). It may have been this increasing control over the form that interactions with customers took that contributed to technical skills being devalued; if only because it would be difficult to regulate one area tightly while allowing workers discretion in another.

The way that these network organizations were structured also helps to explain the devaluation of technical skills. TCS-L and the FutureTech/Govco partnership in particular were seen as opportunities to harness private sector expertise rather than as a mutually advantageous collaboration (as Scotchem's networks were). In FutureTech, which genuinely possessed far greater organizational IT expertise, this asymmetry of power meant that local knowledge of Govco's computer systems was downplayed and formed no part of the system of function points that graded work, although it was necessary to implement changes. In TCS, where the company had had no experience of benefit work before the transfer, this meant that the skills most highly valued were those of attitude, commitment to the organization, and personal skills. Politically, this emphasis is easy to understand since, had TCS praised caseworker skills, their own contribution to the network might have been questioned. One trade union representative, who had been involved in the discussions between TCS and Council X pre-transfer had tried to convince TCS of the complexities of housing benefit work without success; their negotiators had repeatedly described the process with reference to the sort of business they were familiar with. '[T]hey used to try and say, answering a call about a [utility] bill is the same, we'd say 'no, it's not' (TCS-L, union rep., male).

It seems that, as Burchell et al. (1994) argued, managers tend to undervalue skills they are not familiar with. At the time they drew their conclusions, Burchell et al. raised concerns that this degradation of unfamiliar skills had implications for public sector work being taken into the private sector, conclusions that seem to be supported here. It is also likely that favouring particular types of skill and expertise affected the ways that these networks could function. When knowledge transfer is to take only one form and travel in only one direction there are limits to the extent that alliances can be collaborative.

This switch in emphasis was not a straightforward case of deskilling, although the ways in which individuals were expected to exercise the newly important skills were increasingly prescribed by others. It did, however, have a dramatic effect on the relative value placed on particular skills and the extent to which skilled workers could claim 'skill in the setting' (in marked contrast to Turner 1962 and Penn 1984). Here, despite the very real labour market power that the caseworkers in TCS possessed and the need for their skills in the workplace, technical skills were no longer valued in terms of prestige, recruitment, or promotion. Indeed, workers were encouraged to demonstrate the right orientation, attitudes and (presumably) endurance and the rewards for these depended on pleasing management.

9.6   Discussion and conclusions

Network organizations are often assumed to have the capacity to tap into different forms of advantage: in expertise and experience; in markets and hierarchy; in control mechanisms and work design. Factors that offer opportunities for learning, developing skills, and transferring knowledge. As Scotchem's experience has shown, such advantages are not illusory. Its relationship with both Scandichem and Acidchem gave workers the opportunity to share and develop work practices, a process that was actively encouraged by management. But these networks were alliances of specially selected partners who had dealt with one another over long periods of time in a market in which each was dependent on the other. Workers at Scotchem did not have to negotiate with multiple 'employers' or clients, they were employed directly by Scotchem, on permanent contracts and with the expectation of job security. Significantly too, the relational element of the network was not only extended to large numbers of workers, it was also valued above short-term market gains in the very real sense that contracts were not enforced when they materially disadvantaged 'partner' organizations.

This combination of circumstances is unusual and provides a high trust route for managing the various risks that every network faces. Elsewhere, the growth in both the perceived and the actual distribution of risk was controlled in rather different ways. Even in networks where relational aspects were considered important (and featured heavily in senior management accounts) the drive to cooperate and collaborate was muted by the existence of strict contractual requirements, which 'partners' would resort to when problems occurred.

Reintegrating the employment relationship into analyses of networks renders the difficulties of this mixture of contract and trust particularly visible. As Fox (1974) argues, high trust relationships are controlled in very different ways to low trust ones and rhetorical demands that employees should give trust in circumstances when they are not themselves trusted are seldom effective. While high trust relations support skill, low trust ones detract from it (see also Streeck 1987). Yet, here the contractual relations between the various parties almost demanded low trust forms of governance. In each of these organizations there was a growth in performance monitoring: processes that were needed to ensure that contracts had been fulfilled or regulatory demands complied with, but which changed the ways that people worked and, through this, impacted on the skills employees could demonstrate. At their most dramatic, tightly specified performance indicators not only excluded skill enhancement, but also de-skilled the work they controlled.

Such performance measures also necessarily de-personalize work, reducing it to a series of measurable tasks or outcomes. This disaggregation may be a helpful analytical device but it fails to capture the integrated complexity of meaningful work and has negative implications for skill development and career progression. It may also be counterproductive when judging performance. When the design of new computer applications affects existing systems, experienced programmers are badly needed; just as expertise in claims processing is required to deal with housing benefit work or knowledge of Post Office transactions is useful when serving customers. Yet, the systems of monitoring and management focused on statistics or function points, assessing tasks in isolation from the people employed to carry them out.

These forms of monitoring also re-shape the role that managers are expected to play as technical skills are degraded and devalued and judgements made against different criteria. So Regional Network Managers in the Post Office and line managers in TCS were no longer expected to provide technical support. Rather, they were required to have retail or 'customer focussed' skills, to control work through statistics and ensure targets had been met. The problems created by such 'rational' means of control are well documented (see, among others, Doray 1988; Power 1997). Nor is it clear, even in this narrow range of case studies, that soft skills are individual and generic rather than reciprocal and relational (Keep 2003; Grugulis et al. 2004; Lafer 2004). Indeed, many studies of managerial work argue that it is far from homogeneous and that local knowledge of people, processes and procedures is vitally important (Stewart 1963; Watson 1994; Keep and Rainbird 2000). In these case studies, changes to managerial practice may have been conscious attempts to alter the nature of the organizations by bringing in different forms of expertise. But on this evidence, it is difficult to argue the case for knowledge transfer. Moreover, it was interesting to note that in the smallest units, the franchised and sub-Post Offices, where employee performance was most visible, there was no attempt to devalue technical expertise and managers would actively go out of their way to seek it.

Nor does it seem that relational and transactional forms of contracting can be readily separated from one another (in contrast to Williamson 1985). Even the simplest jobs, such as the security staff at Scotchem, were broader and demanded more skills to be performed well than was assumed by the performance indicators set (see also Rainbird and Munro 2003). With more complex work, where relational elements were expected and encouraged, monitoring undermined broad skills and created problems for performance.

It was against this context of increased monitoring, an emphasis on the contractual aspects of the labour process and efforts to decrease risk that soft skills became a significant feature of work. Perhaps unsurprisingly, the form that they took was a regulated one. In contrast to the hopes of commentators such as Frenkel et al. (1999) who argue that emotion work is necessarily skilled, the organizations observed here could and did seek to deskill this process. Scripts and prompts, devised presumably in the hope of eliminating poor customer service, actually detracted from the interaction and were the focus of numerous complaints (see also Taylor et al. 2002).

It seems that, while networks can, in principle, be based on high trust relationships that support the development of skills and assist in knowledge transfer, in practice the process of fragmenting organizations creates new boundaries and the simple fact that more than one organization is involved in a task does not mean that expertise will be shared and mutual advantages harnessed. Tasks that are outsourced must still be controlled and, since externally contracted work may be seen as (and may actually be) of greater risk than that conducted internally, there are high compliance costs to be paid in terms of both skill and control.

10

Gender and New Organizational Forms

GAIL HEBSON AND IRENA GRUGULIS

10.1 Introduction

This chapter aims to explore changing organizational forms from a gendered perspective. New forms potentially offer opportunities to challenge the power relations—including masculine power relations—embedded in traditional bureaucratic organizations. Feminist critiques of traditional forms provide the backdrop for such optimism. These differ as to whether it is possible that bureaucracy can be 'reclaimed' for women. Kanter (1977) suggests that the gender inequality found in bureaucracies is an irrational blip, a flaw that must be rectified if organizations are to function properly. For Kanter the problems facing women are powerlessness, not sex, and once women achieve positions of power gender equality is possible. Others, such as Ferguson (1984), using a post-structuralist account of 'bureaucratic discourse', argue that bureaucracy is inherently patriarchal, built upon 'male' ways of being. According to this argument equality can be achieved through the development of parallel women-centred organizations that are participative and non-hierarchical, and more akin to feminine ways of being. Others, notably Pringle (1989) in her analysis of secretarial work, use a post-structuralist account of power, where sexuality is at the centre of organizations and is used by both men and women to structure gender relations. Masculinities and femininities are 'produced' within organizational contexts, and therefore can take a number of forms. She distinguishes between coercive and non-coercive heterosexuality in organizations and argues that non-coercive sexuality can be pleasurable for women and can even be used by women to redress gendered power relations based upon male rationality within organizations.

The critiques of these positions have been well rehearsed. Kanter's account fails to recognize how inequalities are built into gender relations, assuming that bureaucracy is neutral and is unconnected from broader social and historical processes (Witz and Savage 1992). More recent feminist work has emphasized that far from being neutral, bureaucratic structures are premised on male experience and masculine values; gender is embedded in organizations (Acker 1990). Methods of recruitment which disadvantage women and career ladders based on male patterns of work (the long-serving, continuous, and full-time career) all point to the 'structural form of male power in modern organizations' (Halford and Leonard 1999: 55). Male power is not simply a layer added on to bureaucracy but part of the make up of bureaucracy.

Ferguson has been criticized for giving an essentializing account of women (Witz and Savage 1992). Although her starting point is that masculine power is embedded within the organization she is unable to establish why this would lead to women acting differently to men and her prescription that women should not embark on bureaucratic careers denies the reality that many do so and do it rather well.

Pringle's account has been criticized for underplaying the structured nature of power relations embedded in organizations (Witz and Savage 1992). Indeed, it is difficult to reconcile the emphasis upon the constructed nature of femininities and masculinities, and the fluidity this suggests, with the stubborn regularity of gendered power relations within organizations. However, this does not deflect from the importance of Pringle's work in illuminating the ways women are not merely passive victims of gendered power, but actively negotiate this is their daily working lives.

These past accounts of the gendering of organizations have all critiqued traditional bureaucratic structures. When they are used to reflect upon the gendered implications of new organizational forms, the reasons for many of the optimistic discourses become clear. New structures may mark a departure from rigid hierarchies based upon seniority and age (Acker 1992). This move may, in theory, offer opportunities for women who no longer have to conform to the full-time continuous bureaucratic career (Arthur and Rousseau 1996). There are interesting sectoral dimensions in this argument. Schmid (1991), for example, argues that the over-representation of women in public sector employment may be redressed if private sector organizations restructure and introduce less rigid hierarchies. Furthermore, these new organizational forms are associated with the 'feminisation' of management qualities and a growth of managerial specialist occupations in which women are better represented (Peters 1990).

Yet, empirical studies of organizational restructuring show this potential has not come to fruition. Instead, restructuring has contradictory implications for gender inequality in employment, often increasing the quantity of opportunities, rather than their quality. Flexibilization strategies relied on women to fill part-time jobs that were often low paid and low status (Pollert 1991). The increasing number of jobs in service work provides an opportunity for many women to enter paid employment, but develop skills that provide little access to other work. Even the rise in representation at management level is problematic in that it reflects a business rationale rather than one of equality of opportunity (Coyle 1995). Furthermore, the nature of these new managerial positions has changed. Crompton's (1995) research on banking is typical, finding that although women in banking may be infiltrating positions such as branch manager this has coincided with the downgrading of these positions. Thus, an influx of women cannot be assumed to give them organizational power and women are often confined to gendered niches (Reskin and Roos 1990; Savage 1992; Crompton 1995; see also Halford et al. 1997).

Furthermore, the move to flatter hierarchies erodes middle management positions that have been important for women's occupational success and the introduction of individualized payment systems also opens the way for gender discrimination (Coyle 1995; Rubery 1995; Grimshaw and Rubery 2001). Women are still excluded from power-broking informal networks (Edwards et al. 1996, 1999) at a time when these are increasingly important in building careers. Indeed, it may be that organizational restructuring actively disadvantages women since most equal opportunities policies presume a Fordist system of employment and are based upon bureaucratic structures in specific employment establishments (Walby 1997), such as the public sector where, according to Davidson and Cooper (1992), women are most likely to find supportive structures. Changes here mean that 'fewer women than ever will be in the type of employment where organization-based equal opportunities policies have any relevance' (Coyle 1995: 61). These studies suggest the need to revisit the feminist critiques of bureaucracy. Was the assumption too readily made that forms of organization other than bureaucratic would necessarily be better for women? Furthermore, are there equal opportunities strategies in place that are adequate to combat the more opaque, but nonetheless discriminatory, practices of new organizational structures?

An analysis of changing organizational forms from a gendered perspective will need to take a different stance from the feminist critiques of bureaucratic structures that slipped into the 'sameness', 'difference', and 'social constructionist' accounts of gender. Current analyses of gender now take the view that there is a need to accommodate both sameness and difference (e.g. Cockburn 1991). As Crompton (2000: 33) argues 'biological sex is in fact only a proxy for "gender", which is a system of social *relations* constructed at all levels of society'. The biological differences between men and women cannot be dismissed, but crucially it is not necessarily these in themselves but the meanings attributed to them that perpetrate inequality. This more nuanced approach to difference has gone hand in hand with attempts to theorize accounts of gendered power which can accommodate the heterogeneity of gender relations. The concept of patriarchy has been found to be lacking the explanatory power needed to account for the complexity of gendered relations as they are lived (Bradley 1989; Pollert 1996; Crompton 1999) and there has been a move towards a 'gender systems' approach which recognizes that gender relations are socially constructed and variable. This has been used to establish the interconnections between the macro, meso, and individual level (Connell 1987; O'Reilly and Fagan 1995; Rubery et al. 1998; Crompton 1999). Building upon such an approach recent accounts of gender at work have aimed to explore both the gendered nature of employment structures and focus upon how both men and women 'do' gender at work (McDowell 1997; Crompton 1999), blending post-structuralist insights around identity and narrative with the recognition that gendered inequality is structured. This approach allows us to recognize the historical specificity of organizational forms and that 'structures are negotiated and interpreted by changing and flexible gendered subjects' (Crompton 1999: 7–8).

This chapter will, therefore, explore the nature of the work men and women perform in these new organizational contexts to reflect upon the gendered implications of the more flexible forms of our case study organizations. The first section discusses whether fluid organizational boundaries challenge gender segregation by identifying the differential impacts new organizational forms have upon women and men's jobs and whether there is any evidence of women and men entering non-traditional forms of work. In the second section there will be a focus specifically upon the 'relational' work that is required in new organizational forms and whether this is gendered work (see also Chapter 8). This is a concept developed by Barley and Kunda (2001) as they break down roles performed in organizations into non-relational (tasks) and relational (the social interactions necessary to carry out the role). A central finding of our study is that in increasingly complex organizational realities the relational aspects of roles become key in shaping organizational contexts. This section explores the gendered nature of this work, and therefore places gender relations at the centre of new organizational forms. The third section will provide an analysis of gendered cultures and identities in our case study organizations building upon Acker's (1990, 1992) account of the gendering of organizations which highlights the myriad of ways that gender divisions are created in organizations, including the creation of symbols, images, and forms of consciousness that explicate and justify gender divisions; interactions between individuals; and the internal mental work of individuals as they consciously construct their gendered understandings and identities within the structure of work and opportunities available (ibid. 1992: 252–253). This suggests the need for a gendered analysis of new organizational forms to account for both gendered structures and gendered cultures and appreciate how these are shaped by men and women within organizational contexts.

Data from across six of the case study sites will be drawn upon. Women's dominance in public sector employment means there will also be a specific focus upon the impact of changes in the public sector upon gender relations. The aims of this chapter are to explore the potential of changing organizational forms to challenge traditional gender divisions. There will be a focus upon continuities and changes in the position of men and women within these organizations as well as the processes by which new organizational forms build upon or challenge existing gendered relations. The chapter will explore whether changing organizations necessarily mean changing jobs for men and women and questions the extent to which the permeable structure of the organizations translates into more fluid gender relations at work. It also takes an approach to gendering that puts gendered agents at the centre of change and stasis;

a change in organizational form does not necessarily mean a change in gender relations will ensue. There will be an emphasis upon how individual men and women and their gendered understandings can shape organizations and in this respect there is a move away from a top down approach to the control of the employment relationship.

10.2 Gender segregation and new organizational forms

Debates around the wider restructuring of the economy have focused upon the increasing 'feminisation' of employment. Those who emphasize change focus upon women's increased participation in managerial and professional occupations as evidence of a decline in vertical segregation (see Walby 1997). Such progress has been explained by changing legal frameworks, such as the equal pay legislation and equal opportunities policies, and perhaps more crucially the increasing levels of academic and vocational qualifications obtained by young women (Crompton and Le Feuvre 1992; Walby 1997). However, there is little evidence that women's increased participation in the labour market is eroding the occupational segregation, that is the difference in the kinds of work men and women do, that has been central in feminist explanations of continuing gender inequality (Hakim 1979).[1] Only 30 per cent of managers in Britain are women and managerial jobs remain strongly segregated with women comprising the majority of personnel, training and industrial relations managers, but less than one in five ICT managers (LFS 2001). As noted earlier, the managerial positions women are entering through restructuring are relatively low paid in comparison to those traditionally occupied by men (Rubery and Fagan 1995); in 2001, there was a gender pay gap of 24 per cent between men and women managers (LFS 2001).

Furthermore, and particularly relevant to this study which focuses upon many low paid jobs, at the level of horizontal segregation there appears to be little change with a growing polarization between educated women in professional occupations and those that dominate low paid manual and service work. Wilkinson (1998) estimates that in 1998 between 1.9 and 2.4 million employees in the United Kingdom aged 18 and over earned below the National Minimum Wage (NMW) rates. Seven out of ten of these were women (most of whom worked part-time) and just under a quarter (24 per cent) were employed in wholesale and retail. Employees were most likely to be working below the NMW in hotels and restaurants, an industry in which women comprised 62 per cent of employees.

It is, therefore, important to explore whether fluid organizational boundaries can challenge gender segregation. Did the nature and quality of jobs women and men do change in anyway to mark a distinct shift in gendered power relations and did changing structures allow women and men to move into non-traditional areas of work?

A focus upon the low skilled jobs performed by women and men in the case studies suggests new organizational forms may, in fact, reinforce gender segregation. Across the case-study organizations there was evidence of women's continuing concentration in part-time and temporary work with gender segregation reinforced by some of the new practices. New forms of working in the Post Office disproportionately affected women. Women had always been well represented in the directly run Crown Offices, making up some 70 per cent of all staff (and 90 per cent of part-time staff). This work had traditionally been seen as more prestigious than shop work and attracted better terms and conditions. With the move to increased numbers of franchises and sub-offices, as well as the introduction of a 'new' rate for those starting work in Crown Offices, this well compensated option was no longer available. Elsewhere in the Post Office network, franchisees were free to set whatever pay and conditions they chose; in practice non-Crown offices paid approximately half the hourly rate of Crown Offices and could offer less job security. Few men were employed on the counter in non-Crown offices. No central database of these employees exist, but in our interviews we came across only one male counter worker, and that by repute. This was not the product of direct discrimination by the franchisees. Rather, as one of the interviewees commented, it was because few men were prepared to work for £4 an hour (ConvenienceCo, Manager 1, male). When restructuring results in the reduction in pay rates, in predominantly mixed occupations, the likely outcome is greater gender segregation (see Grimshaw and Rubery 2001).

Crucially, the fragmentation of organizational structures inevitably involves the restructuring of risks which, from our case-study evidence, leaves women's work particularly vulnerable. This could be seen clearly in the public sector where gender segregation was embedded in processes of organizational change and the restructuring of jobs. The public sector workforce has become increasingly feminized (EOC 2000). Previous research into public sector restructuring has shown that those in part-time manual occupations, which are most often women, are vulnerable to work intensification, job insecurity, and poorer pay (Escott and Whitfield 1995). While these studies were conducted in the context of Compulsory Competitive Tendering our focus is upon the restructuring towards more permeable organizations in the public sector and we have found in the newer 'partnership' arrangements many of these patterns re-emerge.

The Private Finance Initiative (PFI) case study illustrates the way in which the fragmentation of the employment relationship affects men and women in different ways and how the possibilities of challenging occupational segregation were not realized. The rationalization of two hospitals into one meant many domestic employees (who were largely part-time, women workers) were facing job insecurity and the prospect of cuts in hours. Other groups of workers, such as porters—a predominantly male group with only one woman porter–also faced changes in their working conditions and felt insecure but because they worked full time the number of hours they worked could not be changed. Furthermore, the porters effectively resisted pressure to apply for the new role of Patient Services Assistants (PSAs), that integrated cleaning, catering, and portering, while domestics were told they would be effectively resigning if they did not take up these jobs. This resistance by the porters was a rejection of low pay, but it was also based on their reluctance to perform 'women's work':

Yeah, the food yeah, I'd enjoy that, but not the domestic, I'm a very proud man, that would weigh in my decision in the end. (Hotel Services Company, porter 3, male)

In this case study, therefore, it was not only that women's jobs were the ones amenable to change, but also that women working part time were less likely to be able to challenge these changes. In contrast the porters argued more effectively against changes introduced by the Hotel Services Company, both because they were full time and also, significantly, because they were willing to use the union to challenge the employer. The UNISON shop steward argued that the porters could not be forced to take on the PSA role:

They even sent us [UNISON] a letter because they're struggling with it [getting volunteers for the PSA role]. I think they are putting pressure on the domestics, cutting their hours down so they put in for that. . . . The domestics are going through worse. They can't do to us what they're doing to them because they can't cut our hours. Our hours are set and they've already been agreed. (Hotel Services Company, porter, union rep. 2, male)

The shop steward also organized an unofficial ballot with porters working at the hospital due to close to protest against working with other porters from the new hospital who were paid higher shift bonuses. All porters voted to ban overtime and although the ballot was unofficial it was effective as the Hotel Services Company agreed to pay all porters the same shift bonuses.

The limitations of the TUPE regulations for those working part time, who are most likely to be women, were apparent (Cooke et al. 2004). Although in theory the PSA role could have provided an example of the way new organizational forms can bring new ways of working that challenge rigid occupational segregation, the seriousness of this challenge was always in doubt because of the low wage on offer. The job redesign that is possible to introduce under the TUPE regulations is more often than not put into effect to introduce poorer terms and conditions and work intensification (Colling 1993). It was women's labour that was to be used as a resource to create new ways of working that allowed this to happen. These new 'mixed' jobs were in fact targeted at women by the 'female' wages on offer, and therefore any degendering potential was sacrificed to the ultimate aim to reduce costs. The above is an example of how the fragmentation of employment allows the restructuring of risks to be concentrated on female segments of the workforce. This is not to argue that the porters in the above case did not also face risks, particularly that of job insecurity, but the women were particularly vulnerable to these as their hours of work and lack of unionization meant they were not in the same position to resist.

However, it is important to note that the limited evidence of regendering in the case studies could also lead to the deconstruction of male shelters and left men exposed to the risks typically faced by women. For example, in the Post Office, the increasing emphasis on customer care affected both men and women and, although women were overwhelmingly represented in part-time work, high levels of unemployment in some areas led to many men accepting part-time jobs, despite the fact that they were 'not particularly happy about it' (POCL, Manager 5, female). The same retail network manager felt that the part-time women workers would also prefer full-time jobs. It seems that regendering in new organizational forms can often involve men 'downgrading' to the terms and conditions of women's employment rather than women 'upgrading' to those of men's.

However, the key arguments made in relation to regendering and changing organizations generally focus upon women infiltrating the managerial positions that men once dominated. In theory, the move away from traditional bureaucratic organizations may allow women without traditional, continuous career paths to progress. This is partly because the organizational structures allow this and partly because these fragmented organizations are associated with the 'feminisation' of management qualities and a growth of managerial specialist occupations in which women are better represented (Peters 1990).

The case studies provided particularly interesting insights into whether permeable organizations do in fact create new managerial spaces for women. In the TCS-NW site nineteen of the thirty team leaders on the site were women. All had experienced very quick progression, rising through the ranks from customer service representative to team coach and then team manager, one reaching the position of section manager (there were two section managers, one male and one female). The section manager for Catalogco describes her trajectory:

I was going to try and go back to university and do a PhD. I was just working on the telephone in here and then saw the opportunities and the progression I could do and thought well I will leave that and put it on hold so that is what happened. The structure you can see is that I have moved around from water to electricity over to here (Catalogco), the new business. (TCS-NW, Catalogco, Manager, female)

However these managerial roles take a very specific form that often perpetuates traditional gendered stereotypes. These roles were central in smoothing inter-organizational relationships (see also Chapter 6) and involved two central aspects; reconciling the different cultures and interests at play on a multi-employer site (maintaining the identity of the client while imparting the TCS values as an overarching framework); and managing groups of workers on very different terms and conditions. The site had agency and permanent workers as well as those working for different clients, which demanded very different measures of performance. The women team managers' strategy in this environment was to emphasize the values of TCS; these were the 'soft' values of communication, priority to the customer, team work, empowering others, and responsibility for performance. They emphasized the 'culture' of TCS to a far greater extent than the male team managers that were interviewed and this would suggest that women are playing a critical role in new organizational forms by emphasizing 'traditional' feminine attributes.

While the language of company culture is a useful device for women managers to show commitment, men emphasized more competitive values, including responsibility and ownership of performance. We cannot say that there were fewer men in these team manager roles because of this. However, it certainly did not hinder men's progression higher up in the organization, as they dominated the senior levels of the organizations, with women concentrated in human resources, training, and general middle management positions, such as team and section manager.

In these multilayered organizations middle management positions are crucial to success, particularly in the juggling of the interests of various customers and different sets of employees. Therefore to describe them as 'expert niches' (see Crompton 1995) underplays their significance. However, it remains to be seen whether these roles are valued or lead to senior positions (Belt 2002) and it may be that the new managerial roles that require typically 'feminine' attributes can only get women so far.

It must also be noted that in other case-study organizations the possibility of quick progression for women is hindered. In the Post Office, when most offices had been Crown Offices, long-standing members of staff were usually promoted when managers left or retired. Since most workers were women this meant that some women secured managerial roles. By contrast, franchises and sub-offices tended to be small with relatively flat hierarchies (most were owner-managed). The women employed in these outlets had no opportunities for progression. These contradictory effects on women's potential to progress will be explored further in discussions of gendered cultures within these changing organizations but this alerts us to the importance of the specificity of new organizational forms, particularly in relation to the degree of fragmentation involved. This fragmentation of Post Office structures takes away opportunities for progression for both women and men but within organizational contexts of increasing competition for fewer senior positions women generally fare badly (Wajcman 1998). However, a different organizational context in TCS was found where the increased number of managerial positions due to the increased number of clients offered new opportunities for women's progression, albeit on the condition that they displayed typically gendered behaviours. The next section will focus specifically upon the gendered nature of jobs in more detail.

10.3   Gendered relational work

The above section has discussed the differential impact of new organizational forms upon women and men's work showing a general trend towards reinforcing rather than challenging patterns of gender segregation. However, this is coupled with possibilities for women to enter new managerial spaces which was directly related to the increased need for relational work in these organizations (Barley and Kunda 2001). This section will develop this by connecting the changing nature of jobs, in particular the increase in relational work, to the inter-organizational relationships that are central to the new organizational forms of our case studies. There will be a focus upon the changing nature of the jobs men and women perform and whether these transgress gender boundaries or entrench gendered assumptions further.

To a certain extent, the idea of skill is socially constructed (Penn 1984; Gallie 1994) with the status and labour market power of job holders influencing the way their skills are perceived (Rubery and Wilkinson 1994a, b). In practice this means that women's work, even when technically and objectively more complex than men's, tends to be undervalued (Phillips and Taylor 1986), a finding which, as Bolton (2004) argues, is particularly true of 'soft' skills. Despite repeated reports that these are in short supply, when unaccompanied by technical expertise, they seldom attract wage premiums, perhaps because, in women at least, they are considered 'natural'. However, in our case studies such skills take on a new significance as the relationships that are forged in an increasingly complex set of internal and external relations shape the nature and success of the organizational forms.

This is particularly the case in the reconstruction of public services as we found the use of gendered forms of work at the centre of the shift to Public–Private Partnerships (PPPs). The increasing emphasis upon customer work entrenches traditional notions of women's skill. In TCS-L the new inter-organizational relationships created segregation that had previously not existed by constructing the new need for customer focused work as 'women's work'. At the TCS-L site, work had been divided between a backroom, a reception area, and a call centre. Women were particularly concentrated in the reception area (sixteen of the twenty employees) which meant they were particularly vulnerable to de-skilling as they moved away from assessing cases to customer service work. As was noted in Chapter 9, TCS reorganized claims processing so that caseworkers 'specialised' in one part of the operation with the result that most lost touch with the skills needed in the rest of the process. This problem was particularly acute for workers on reception who simply acted as a 'post box', checking the documentation and diverting queries. As elsewhere in service work, recruitment was consciously gendered (Taylor and Tyler 2000). According to the manager

I'm getting into trouble from my staff about this . . . . It is because all of the agency staff we have recruited of late have been women. I actually find that their customer service skills are far better than the men's are. Some of the men I have had in have either quit quite quickly or I have had to get rid of. I have only sacked one agency staff who has been female, the others have all been male. If a customer comes over aggressive they (the guys) tend to respond aggressively. (TCS-L, Manager 8, male)

Significantly, the manager's recruitment policy came in the context of increased managerial discretion and the need to keep costs down while tackling TCS underperformance in terms of service delivery. The manager's focus was upon meeting new performance targets and hiring the people he felt could help deliver these. This increased managerial discretion in the public sector allows the hiring practices of managers to entrench gender stereotypes rather than opening new opportunities to challenge gender divisions.

Crucially, this was perpetuating a process of de-skilling and curtailing future opportunities for women's progression. The manager of the reception admitted that the people (mostly women) in the reception were feeling de-skilled and yet the gendered nature of this process was not recognized. TCS was forcing down pay for 'new entrants' by hiring pre-assessors instead of fully qualified assessment officers. These (predominantly women) workers would not have the opportunities to build upon their pre-assessor skills and become fully qualified.

Not only was this relational work seen as 'women's work', it was also extensively and rigidly monitored (see also Hochschild 1983; Taylor and Tyler 2000) and the new organizational forms created new outlets for management control over this form of work. In the airport the (mainly female) check-in agents working for the four airlines in the study were monitored on how they performed emotional labour, with a checklist of 'dos and don'ts':

We have three or four different forms in which we look at different things: did the agent smile at the passengers, did she say 'good morning'; did she address the passenger's name; did she wish them 'have a nice holiday'; did she have eye contact with the passenger; did she check the right questions . . . Each team manager measures the mistakes of each handling agent. Each mistake is logged in a daily log and it is reported to the senior manager's office. (FH, Manager 5, female)

Agents were also expected to act differently depending on which airline they were representing on that day. Significantly, and in contrast to this intense monitoring, the work of predominantly male groups, such as aircraft cleaners, and ramp and baggage handlers, was harder to pin down in performance measures and the often chaotic organization of work meant it was easier to deflect blame if anything went wrong. In this sense the detailed monitoring applied to women was not applied to the jobs of men. The relational aspects of these women's jobs becomes ever more crucial in these new organizational forms and yet, this did not alter power relations between men and women or lead to a re-evaluation of these skills.

But men too were required to develop these relational roles. Male customer service representatives worked in the call centre and in the PFI the maintenance workers had to perform supposed 'soft' skills to deal with the hospital's (often women) staff. Tact and diplomacy across organizational boundaries was one of the key characteristics men had to display if they were to be reappointed (all maintenance workers had to re-apply for their jobs to determine who was to be made redundant). As a manager responsible for recruitment commented, it was essential men could 'pacify' the nursing staff and for one joiner quoted below this relational aspect of his role had become the key part of his job:

With being in a hospital environment there's always cash constraints . . . One of the questions I have to ask when I take people on is how they react to adverse conditions because you do get irate sisters, you must try to pacify them. (Estates Company, Manager 3, male)

It's a sore point with a lot of the nurses, especially the sister. That's one of the main reasons I've been transferred to the new hospital because . . . I've got to say yes you can have that and no you can't have that. If you want it it's going to cost you this much whereas before it would never cost them anything. . . . You've got to be very diplomatic. (Estates Company, maintenance worker 5, male Joiner)

In the new organizational form these maintenance workers were on the frontline of managing relationships between the private and public sector and it was the trust they were able to build with public sector staff, rather than trust between managers as such, that smoothed over inter-organizational relationships. Therefore, this relational work was not only a specific skill performed by women and these changing organizations did open possibilities of degendering jobs by encompassing soft skills in traditional men's work. However, the ease with which these (older) men performed these roles was based upon the past relationships they had already built up in the public sector and the combination of this work alongside their traditional manual roles. In contrast, in the TCS-NW call centre site, the evidence of the regendering of 'customer' work was generally confined to younger men, who appeared to be more willing to be 'feminised' than older men, who dominated the back office work where there was no contact with customers. The young men spoke of the few alternatives available for unqualified men in the region and were conscious that call centre work was not typical 'men's' work:

There's a lot more women do call centre work than what men do. Men don't feel as well sitting in a room all day with headsets on. People don't see that as a man, if you know what I mean, they'd rather be out building walls or digging up holes. (TCS-NW, Phoneco, CSR agency worker, male)

Men negotiated these new roles in various ways. In the call centre, although all of these roles required 'emotional labour' different clients asked for different 'types' of emotional labour. While certain contracts emphasized rapport and had no limits on call time (Phoneco) others imposed tight limits or required workers to sell products (e.g. Gambleco and Catalogco). The majority of contracts were dominated by women, particularly where there was no limit upon call time and the client preferred permanent workers.

Furthermore, although all workers stressed the need to manage the emotions of the customers, men and women described this labour in very different ways. In the call centre for example, women talked about the need to be 'chirpy' and talk on the phone with 'a smile on your face'. Both men and women emphasized patience but male Customer Service Representatives (CSRs) (who were predominantly young) also talked of the need for confidence and being conscious of rigid time targets:

I think you need to be quite confident really on the phone. You can't be shy or retiring. You need to be able to listen to what they're saying and understand what they're saying, be patient and as helpful as you possibly can and clear and concise as to what your answer would be . . . . I think to be customer focused really. To make sure that you put the customer first and you can handle the calls and also to be aware of the wall charts, and to be taking calls when there's calls waiting, be ready to take a call. Try and wrap up your call time. (TCS-NW, Phoneco, CSR agency worker, male)

Crucially, men did not feel emasculated doing this work because they imbued this work with skill. This is in sharp contrast to the women who maintained that the qualities needed were 'natural'. It seems that, even when engaged on the same tasks, men and women interpret work in different ways (Leidner 1993). The contrasting ways two caseworkers at TCS-L spoke about their work in the reception illuminates this:

I think I take a lot as common sense. You need to be respectful. You need to understand the position they're [the clients'] in . . . Personally I don't know if these are skills, for myself I think these are common sense things, human being things, you need to be able to put yourself in their position but I don't know if they are skills. I don't know how you would be trained and where you would go to acquire these skills. (TCS-L, caseworker 5, female)

Certain things we have to do, we are all professional and we have to be seen as professional in the eyes of the customers because every day somebody will lose their rag, they will bang the counter, they might be having a bad day but we are the soft target and they take it out on us . . . So as well as controlling ourselves we've got to control our customer because we've got to take what they have got to give without giving what we want to give. (TCS-L, agency caseworker 3, male)

The processes of regendering skills were particularly revealing in showing the ways in which people live out and shape the institutional arrangements of new organizational forms. These studies demonstrate how men and women redefine their own ways of performing 'relationship' work and that people are not passive in these processes. Significantly, although the increase in relational work in these new organizational forms does present opportunities for degendering to some extent, men and women construct and perform these roles in gendered ways to ensure the values attached to the work men and women perform continue to be differentiated. How men and women shape the organizational form, in both gendered and non-gendered ways, is the focus of the next section.

10.4   New gendered cultures and identities

Critiques of bureaucratic structures from a feminist perspective have particularly highlighted the role of patriarchal cultures in perpetuating gender inequality within organizations (Acker 1992). Changing organizational forms and the emphasis upon valuing 'feminine' managerial skills and relational work might, therefore, be expected to challenge these traditions. At one level there is evidence of this and the formal culture, in TCS at least, was increasingly spoken about in so-called 'feminine' language. This was intended to secure competitive advantage by reassuring organizations that 'their people' would be cared for if they were to outsource (TCS-L, Office Manager, female). The company had changed its logo to reflect this:

I think the old logo (which was red and black) was seen as very 70s, very harsh not high-lighting what TCS feel is the importance of the people kind of thing. I think that the blue is a much softer image, more people focused and that was the impression, the message we are trying to put across to people really. (TCS-L, Manager 7, female)

More significantly, as noted above in both the call centre and TCS-L, it was the women workers who put greatest emphasis on the company's values and there is no doubt that this had aided many in their quick progression. Crucially, it was not just a career strategy but also a set of values these women had internalized and identified with. Gendered agents are at the centre of new organizational forms, as they draw upon aspects of gendered cultures that fit with their own agendas and values. However, as noted above, whether this challenges male power within organizations is unclear. It is significant that in interviews with one of the most senior members of the case-study organization, the male general manager, there was no use of 'culture talk', even when this was specifically asked about; instead he spoke of job profiles, union agreements and payment systems (Carroll et al. 2001).

These rhetorically 'feminine' cultures were coupled with new organizational norms that again marked a move away from bureaucracy but without the presumed benefits for women. In FutureTech pay systems and grading structures were no longer transparent; wages were individually negotiated and conversations about them banned. It has been argued that this can pave the way for gender discrimination (Grimshaw and Rubery 2001) and significantly the more flexible and individualized structures in FutureTech make this difficult to ascertain. While FutureTech recruited women into positions of authority, which did at least signal the possibility of advancement, we have no evidence as to whether this challenged gendered power within the organization. This is particularly the case in relation to pay equality between men and women. Equal opportunities policies traditionally based upon transparency would appear to be futile in an organization where pay is a private matter.

Another apparently gender-neutral aspect of PPPs was the generation of a 'long hours culture'. Hopes for promotion, insecurity about the transfer, and the desire to impress new employers all combined to foster this. The imposition of contractual deadlines also contributed:

We end up needing more people working on it or we're going to need the people working on it to work longer hours and work weekends. Cutting quality isn't an option, that's drummed into us, there is no option to cut corners, it has to be done properly. So what's likely to happen is that people will end up working very long hours. (FutureTech, Manager 7, female)

The long hours culture promoted by the contractual relations could work against both women and men with family commitments and take away a key benefit of working in the public sector (Coyle 1995; Corby 1999). This shift to individualistic and competitive cultures was also found at the other two PPPs. At TCS-L and FutureTech new opportunities were stressed, but these were ones that were dependent upon pushing yourself forward (often in FutureTech requiring regional mobility), working long hours, and internalizing private sector values. Therefore, although in theory there were equal opportunities for women and men, these were dependent upon the ability to work in a competitive environment and conform to the long hours culture this involves. This, of course, was also the case for men but significantly men have more chance of internalizing the values *and* working the hours they needed to prove that they did so, as although men are no longer the primary breadwinner in many dual earner households, women continue to take prime responsibility for childcare. This confirms the ambiguous effect the new managerialism in the public sector has upon gender inequality. The potential of a break-away from established management practices is countered by a new form of organizational masculinity that the increased credentialism of women will be insufficient to offset (Halford and Savage 1995). This is based upon competitive values that appear to be at odds with the relational aspects of managerial work that women lower down the hierarchy are engaged in.

While the PPPs focused on traditionally 'masculine' ways of working, another of the new organizational forms, TeacherTemp, openly marketed itself as an opening for women teachers to attain the flexibility they needed to balance work and family life. At one level we found evidence to support this with mothers using agency work because of the lack of permanent part-time positions available in teaching. This was in contrast to men working in supply teaching who generally thought of it as a stopgap until they found permanent work. The lack of flexibility offered by the teaching profession is an example of the way the traditional bureaucratic career can disadvantage women at certain stages in the lifecycle and was recognized by teaching unions as a major reason why temporary agencies were flourishing. This would appear to support Albert and Bradley's (1998) contention that women professionals use temporary agencies to gain more control over their working lives.

However, women who were using agencies missed out on the vital ingredients needed for a teaching career, including training, appraisals, and a supportive professional community. Crucially, because of the need to work to earn money and particularly because of the lack of holiday pay, parents (both men and women), rarely used the flexibility that was theoretically on offer, raising questions about the control professionals using agencies can exercise and suggesting that existing debates fail to account for the constraints which may affect their choices. Both mothers and fathers recognized the contradictions:

For me, first and foremost . . . my family need the money so I will work wherever you send me. I will go and do it because I need the money . . . To me, flexibility is an advantage but it is not the most important thing. (TeacherTemp, supply teacher 11, male)

I like the flexibility even though you don't very often use it because trying to get a day off is quite difficult because they are so desperate for teachers. You could be made to feel very guilty if you took a day off. (TeacherTemp, supply teacher 6, female)

This is an example of the trade-offs people make on a daily basis as they negotiate the organizational cultures on offer and structure their working lives accordingly. The more flexible new organizational forms do not appear to offer a straightforward alternative to the patriarchal structures that have in the past perpetuated gender inequality.

Whereas the above discussion has shown the centrality of gender relations in understanding the new cultures of new organizational forms, we also want to identify a parallel trend that operates alongside the continuing 'gender stories' in these organizations; that the multi-employer sites central to these organizational forms often mean gender divisions become increasingly invisible but no less present.

In interviews with both men and women we found they were generally reluctant to use gendered explanations to understand their working life, despite their very different access to organizational power. In the call centre at TCS-NW the majority of employees said that there were equal numbers of men and women working in the call centre and that there was no difference in the roles they were employed in. Yet, all contracts apart from Truckco had a much higher proportion of women than men (as only fifteen people work on the contract, nine men and six women, it is hard to gauge whether this is a move to employ men on a more 'masculine' contract) and men dominated the senior positions.

This was also the case in the Post Office where employees appeared to feel uneasy that there was a gender imbalance, as though any admission of the gendered nature of work would implicate them. When asked, both men and women at varying levels of seniority went into great detail about a male colleague they had worked with in the past or stressed how difficult it was to get men to apply for jobs that paid comparatively low wages.

The airport case provides an insight into processes that can lead to the combination of the invisibility or denial of gender alongside its pervasiveness. It is here, where there is rigid occupational segregation, that we might have expected to find a gendered view of the world. However, in this multilayered organization where there is a fragmentation of work and the coordination of work becomes the focus there seems to be little room for utilizing or challenging gendered understandings. As we have seen in Chapter 8 the consciousness of similarities in employment status led to cross-organizational cooperation (see also Rubery et al. 2002). However, this often disguised gender divisions. A striking example of this was the introduction of the airline representative by

Airline C. This new group of twelve workers were predominantly women who could directly challenge the work of people not under their managerial control, often the male dispatchers. Dispatchers were, of course, threatened and frustrated by this but this was never expressed in gendered terms; instead there was a frustration with the airline monitoring their work rather than their own employer. However, gendered centres were more evident in other parts of the organization where the continuing use of gendered terminology was used to show a united front. For example, baggage handlers constantly referred to helping the other 'lads' out, an expression of male as well as worker solidarity.

This does not necessarily signify that gendered understandings of work are now obsolete, and indeed such understandings have and will always vary according to specific historical, organizational, and occupational contexts. However, it may be the case that more than ever other divisions become more important in the daily experience of work, particularly in the case of divisions between employees of different employers. The introduction of women managers to TCS-L is a good example of how this manifests itself. An ex-Council employee, now transferred to TCS, argued that the people who progress are those who are 'TCS' people. The reasons given as to why TCS brought a new woman in to manage the call centre are described in relation to the nepotism usually reserved for explaining male power; 'Jobs for the boys' (TCS-L, caseworker 4, female). This is a very revealing way to use a traditional gendered understanding of the world of work showing one way divisions between men and women may no longer be as visible as those between the range of employers and non-employers in these new multi-employer sites.

10.5 Discussion

This chapter has challenged the assumption that changing organizational forms might provide an opportunity to break down traditional gender relations within organizations. Although feminist critiques of traditional bureaucracy argue for less hierarchical and rigid structures, our case-study evidence casts doubt on the premise that the move towards these new permeable organizations promotes more fluid gendering of work. In practice, these forms have far more diverse and nuanced implications for gender inequality at work. Table 10.1 summarizes not only the opportunity but also the risks that may come with changing organizational forms.

In particular, an analysis of gender segregation in the context of new organizational forms does not show an erosion of gender divisions but a reorienting of risks that becomes concentrated on low paid female segments of the workforce. A more contradictory picture emerges for women higher up in the hierarchy. The new 'feminine' discourses surrounding network forms are prevalent, but whether this translates into a challenge to gendered power relations is less clear. The reduced hierarchy certainly aids women's progression into middle

Table 10.1. Gender equality and new organizational forms:
opportunities and risk

New opportunities	New risks
Influx of women managers	Invisibility of male power
Performance-related pay	Openings for discrimination
Flexible working time	Long hours culture
Customer service skills/cultures	Danger of stereotyping
Men entering female-dominated sectors	Downgrading of men's work rather than upgrading of women's

managerial positions and in new organizational forms these roles are crucial in managing the inter-organizational relationships in, for example, multi-employer sites. These women often describe their roles in relation to traditional feminine attributes which suggests new spaces for women managers at this level. However, there is no evidence that the value of this is recognized in terms of rewards and future prospects as men continue to dominate the positions of organizational power. A parallel trend of restricted opportunities, particularly because of the fragmentation of workplaces and the lack of opportunities an overarching structure can bring, was also found.

We also found that the regendering of men's work was often related to the downgrading of men's jobs rather than the upgrading of women's as it came in a context of either job insecurity or a lack of alternatives for men in low-skilled work. Although some men were able to preserve their status we also found that regendering involved men facing the risks associated with women's work. In fact, Glucksmann (1995) argues that it is only because men's work is now starting to mirror that of women's that the fragmented nature of work and the blurring of boundaries is on the agenda. More specifically, it is low paid men who feel the brunt of this 'regendering-downgrading' relationship as they experience acute job insecurity and work intensification and move into the less protected and rewarded jobs offered in customer service work.

The gendered implications of PPPs have been a particular area of discussion. This chapter has shown that these changes may threaten the gains women have made in the public sector and challenge its 'good employer' status in relation to equal opportunities. The shift to customer service work in the delivery of public services meant women became concentrated in these areas and were vulnerable to low pay and processes of de-skilling and control. A long hours and individualistic culture now prevalent in the public sector could also serve to disadvantage women in an environment where they have traditionally thrived (Davidson and Cooper 1992). Structures and cultures of bureaucracy at least made transparent the processes of gendering which could then be addressed via equal opportunities policies (Du Gay 1996). However, our case study evidence of PPPs supports the general concern that in the context of public sector reform equal opportunities initiatives are taking a back seat as public sector organizations struggle to make sense of new agendas and perhaps more importantly, men and women focus upon making sense of increasingly complex organizational contexts. The line managers who now have the responsibility for equal opportunities may feel they have more important issues to cope with (Coyle 1995; Newman 1995; Walby 1997). Indeed, in one of our case studies, FutureTech, it would be difficult to monitor equal opportunities in a culture where pay is a taboo subject.

However, the paradox emerges that the increase in relational work and the 'soft' skills usually defined as 'women's work' is becoming increasingly central. Our case studies have shown that such skills take on a new significance as the relationships that are forged in an increasingly complex set of internal and external relations shape the nature and success of the organizational forms. This goes beyond the extension of customer service work that has been shown to perpetuate gender inequality in the labour market. Rather, the relationship work that women predominantly perform defines the nature of organizational relationships, particularly because they are often responsible for forging inter-organizational trust (see Chapter 6). This cuts across sectors and hierarchical positions; it ranged from women in team manager roles in TCS North West, caseworkers in the reception at TCS/London, to the check-in agents in the airport. As Barley and Kunda (2001) argue:

Any modification in an organization's structure must be grounded in changes that occur at the level of dyadic encounters. Alterations in dyadic relations may induce structural changes as the reformulation of cliques, the weakening of bridges between sectors of a network, or the differentiation of statuses. Such changes may occur because new forms of work reduce or create new dependencies, because they require interactions among people who did not previously interact, or because they alter the tenor of supervision, collaboration, and other social relationships. (2001: 90)

The relational aspects of these women's jobs becomes ever more crucial in new organizational forms and yet this did not alter power relations between men and women or lead to a re-evaluation of these skills. Significantly, this is related to the ways the 'internal mental work' (Acker 1992) of gendered subjects shape the nature of work in changing organizational forms, again emphasizing the need to recognize the importance of those living the employment relationship rather than taking a simple top-down approach to changing organizational forms. The men and women who performed these roles constructed the skills involved in these jobs in gendered ways, so even when men did perform these roles a shift in gendered power relations did not occur. As Halford and Savage (1995: 102) argue, restructuring does not simply 'happen' to people but is 'tied up with re-defining the characteristics people bring to organizations and the ways in which these are deployed inside organizations'. This approach shows how people contest and shape organizations and is specifically useful in understanding processes of regendering and resistance to this.

It also shows the importance of putting employment at the centre of the analysis if we are to move beyond assumptions about gender and different models of organizations. By using the employment relationship as the vehicle by which to explore new organizational forms we found that despite its continuing impact gender may not be experienced as a key marker of differentiation in men and women's understanding of employment. Other sources of unity and division, that cut across gender divides and build upon a common labour market position, are more likely to be forged in a context where increased cooperation is called for between workers across organizational boundaries. New alliances are made and, crucially, it is individual men and women experiencing the employment relationship who are deciding what is important. In this new context of change, divisions by gender are often downplayed and this supports wider debates in feminist theorizing which stress the complexity of gender relations. This is coupled with a lack of transparency and cultures of performance which puts the emphasis upon the individual and may further disguise gender divisions.

It is, therefore, an opportune moment to re-assess the advantages of bureaucratic forms of organizations, perhaps debunking many of the assumptions made by feminist critics. Overall, there is a need to recognize these new organizational forms will mean very different things for men and women and as the employment relationship becomes ever more crucial in shaping these new forms so too will the gendered subjects experiencing it. Crompton and Le Feuvre (1992) argued in relation to traditional feminist accounts of organizations that one approach cannot tell the whole story and it is in empirical studies of how men and women 'live' organizations that we see the need for a plurality of theoretical approaches to understand the gendering of organizations. This is even more pertinent in the study of new organizational forms that have remnants of past structures and cultures combined with newer patterns of structuring the employment relationship where the gendered implications are less well known.

What has become clear is that the tools that have been used to analyse gendered organizational life in the past are still central in exploring the gendering of new organizational forms. However, the contradiction is that the structure and cultures of new organizational forms may conjure up the feeling of the invisibility of gender while often building upon existing gendered power relations and leaving women feeling the brunt of organizational change. New organizational forms may represent a break with bureaucracy which has, in the past, offered little to women. However, the break with traditional bureaucratic structures is not because of the pervasiveness of inequalities and an attempt to address these, but rather because bureaucracy is not seen as able to accommodate new business opportunities and competitive pressures. The danger here is that this opens the path to new forms of inequalities and exploitation that simply build upon existing gender divisions which are now less visible, but still as present as they were in the past.

Note

1. It is recognized that the distinctions between horizontal and vertical segregation simplify gendered patterns of inequality in the labour market. For example in Scandinavian countries women's dominance in the caring professions is evidence of segregation but these are often well-paid jobs and therefore this form of segregation actually narrows the gender pay gap in these countries (Crompton 1999). As Crompton (1999: 44) sums up 'as far as women's equality is concerned, for practical purposes the problem is not occupational segregation but that women are poorly paid for what they do'.

11

Prospects for Worker Voice Across Organizational Boundaries

MICK MARCHINGTON, JILL RUBERY, AND FANG LEE COOKE

11.1 Introduction

The landscape of British industrial relations has changed markedly during the last 25 years from its collectivist highpoint in 1979. Since then, union density and the coverage of collective bargaining have almost halved (Cully et al. 1999; Edwards 2003), and even where pay is still determined by collective bargaining, its scope is typically much narrower (Kelly 1997; Towers 1997). The problem is particularly marked in 'new' establishments, where it has proved very difficult for unions to gain recognition and the experience of being a trade union member is increasingly rare (Machin 2000; Waddington 2003). Although joint consultative committees and union–management (or employee–management) partnerships are now a more important part of the agenda (Bacon and Storey 2000; Guest and Peccei 2001; Marchington 2001; Terry 2003), they are less able than collective bargaining to provide workers with an independent voice. Indeed, JCCS are only found in just over one-quarter of establishments (Cully et al. 1999). In short, because the UK system developed through voluntary arrangements at establishment or enterprise level, rather than through the creation of legal supports at national level as in much of mainland Europe, workers' rights are particularly vulnerable to a loss in trade union power.

Most readers will find nothing new in this short résumé of changes in UK industrial relations. However, as we saw in Chapter 3, this analysis is based on an important and implicit assumption about how the subject is defined, one which is constrained by a focus on the relationship between a single employer and its employees. Because most commentators have been focusing on the extent to which employees working for a *particular* employer have 'lost their voice', they have overlooked the fact that many organizations now choose to use subcontracted labour rather than employ people direct. This has been particularly apparent in the public sector where large swathes of work have been transferred to the private sector via Compulsory Competitive Tendering (CCT), Best Value, and Private Finance Initiatives (PFIs). Private sector firms have also cut back on work such as catering, cleaning, haulage, and security to focus on what they see as core activities. Some have gone even further by contracting out lower value-added manufacturing operations so as to concentrate on customer service work. In other words, the 'typical' employer of today is very different from 25 years ago, and many of what were characterized as standard, internalized jobs are now undertaken by subcontractors, agency workers, or the self-employed. Moreover, there are numerous situations in which workers employed by different organizations, or by agencies, work alongside each other at the same workplace, often employed on quite different terms and conditions. Some are likely to be union members while others are not, some will find that previous alliances with other union members at the same workplace have now fragmented or disintegrated, and yet others will be denied the opportunity to join unions by hostile employers. Here, we are particularly interested in analysing whether and how workers are able to make their voice heard when organizational boundaries are redrawn.

There are few studies that conceive of industrial relations beyond organizational boundaries (Rubery et al. 2003). Heery and Abbott (2000) argue that trade unions must move away from their traditional, relatively narrow agenda of specifically defending the rights of their own members and adopt a wider concern with workers as a whole. They suggest (2000: 167) that, 'putting it crudely, the trade union movement has to decide whether it will speak primarily for the economic "insiders", many of whom feel embattled, or whether it will accept a broader representative remit which encompasses the substantial proportion of employees with non-standard working arrangements'. Following on from this, Heery et al. (2002: 13) examine what trade unions have been doing in order to represent four sets of 'contingent workers'—part-timers, workers on fixed term contracts, agency staff, and freelancers. Based on a postal survey of fifty-six trade unions, they find (2002: 13) there has been rather more progress in relation to part-time workers than any other group, but overall most unions do not invest in dedicated recruitment activities for contingent workers. There have been some attempts to set up specialist branches for agency workers or provide them with a dedicated full-time officer, but this is limited to unions facing sizeable problems in this regard—for example, NUMAST and the CWU. In conclusion, Heery et al. (2001: 29) argue for a 'form of trade unionism that breaks with the dominant workplace model and seeks to represent workers "beyond the enterprise" '.

In this chapter we address the concept of worker voice and representation, as well as the forms they take, in the context of inter-organizational relationships. In these situations, we have to rely on alternative and more complex conceptions of employment and organizational relationships that allow for influences from 'non-employers' over the nature of work, as well as focus on the problems workers face in trying to express their voice beyond organizational boundaries. This requires us to examine the ways in which inter-organizational contracting changes existing mechanisms for voice or makes it difficult for some workers to express their opinions. For example, agency workers might feel excluded from the channels available to other staff or find it difficult to develop close relations with union members working for different employers there. Workers who are employed by the same firm on contracts at one workplace could experience major problems forging links with their colleagues at other workplaces, even if they are in the same union. Yet other workers might have little chance to join unions and find voice only through a managerially dominated consultation system. In short, the blurring of organizational boundaries has major implications for worker voice.

Four cases are examined here, including two different parts of the Customer Service network, and the principal points about each case are summarized in Table 11.1. This is developed from Willman et al. (2003), and it differentiates between (a) employees' propensity to join a union, (b) the union's propensity to organize a workplace, and (c) the employer's propensity to deal with a union. This is useful because it demonstrates clearly how patterns of voice are dependent on the attitudes and behaviours of a range of different actors and the interplay between them. It is often assumed that employers represent the major stumbling block for unions trying to recruit new members but it is also clear that some groups of workers are not especially interested in joining unions either. Rather less common, but nevertheless important, is the situation where unions do not consider it cost-effective aiming to recruit new members due to workplace size, perceived employer hostility, or worker indifference. Useful though this framework is however, it ignores the fact that more than one employer may have an influence on employment relations at a particular workplace, either as a client or as a major employer at the same place of work. It also ignores the role of the union prior to contracting, a factor that is especially important if transfers have taken place between organizations or if permanent and agency staff—perhaps employed on different terms and conditions—work alongside each other and interact at work. Indeed, by treating each actor as if it were a single, unified agent, major simplifications have to be made when analysing voice across organizational boundaries. Accordingly, in Table 11.1 we attempt to incorporate the attitudes of employers and clients as well as between historical union traditions and those of workers employed by different organizations at the same workplace. Moreover, we believe it is crucial to examine patterns of worker representation both within organizations and across organizational boundaries.

Although precise developments in each case differed, depending on the interplay of different forces, the common theme was a reduction in worker voice following changes in contracting arrangements. One of the major consequences had been to displace risk from one organization to another, and in

Table 11.1. Voice across organizational boundaries

Case	Employers' propensity to deal with unions	Unions' propensity to organize a workplace	Workers' propensity to join unions
Chemicals	Scotchem has strong traditions of working closely and positively with unions. Securiforce has no traditions of working with unions.	The unions represented at Scotchem allowed the work of security guards to be contracted out and have shown no interest in wanting to organize them, and no other unions have approached Securiforce.	Manual workers at Scotchem are heavily unionized, as are sections of the white-collar staff. The security guards appear to show little interest in unions.
Teacher Supply	Schools accept the principle that most staff will be in unions and work with them. TeacherTemp has no tradition of negotiating with unions but accepts their presence.	All the teaching unions are interested in recruiting teachers, including those on supply. They have made no attempt to set up recognition deals with the agencies.	Most teachers, including supply teachers, join unions either at college or thereafter for professional or instrumental reasons. Competition between the major unions for members leads to some tensions.
Airport	Airportco had strong traditions of working with unions but was concerned about union militancy,	The unions continue to recruit new members working for Airportco, FH, and BH at the	Most workers at the airport automatically became union members in the past, and most

	especially at the fire station. BH has a partnership approach with the unions and supports their presence as partners. FH is neutral/mildly supportive.	airport. There are some tensions between union representatives at the different companies and a desire to work with their own employer to the detriment of union members in other firms.	still do. There are tensions between union members at different firms and between those employed on different terms and conditions by the same employer—the three-tier workforce.
Customer Service (housing benefits)	Council X has strong traditions of working with unions. TCS takes a pragmatic stance in relation to unions and deals with unions at the housing benefits operation.	The union is keen to organize workers now employed by TCS and has loose links between these members and those working elsewhere at Council X.	Most workers at TCS (L) were union members at the time of the transfer, and most remain so. New workers and agency staff are less likely to join.
Customer Service (call centre)	TCS takes a pragmatic stance in relation to unions but neither TCS nor the agency recognizes them at the call centre and has made no attempt to deal with them.	The union is interested in extending membership within TCS but has not yet tried to organize at the call centre.	Most workers at TCS (NW) and at the agency show little overt interest in joining the union.

particular to groups of workers who were less able to articulate their views and resist the changes imposed on them. Their lack of power resulted in worse terms and conditions, either in terms of lower pay, less employment security, and limited career development—as we have already seen in earlier chapters. So, for example, the security staff who worked for an agency but employed at the Scotchem site were *disenfranchised* from any form of meaningful voice because not only did the agency fail to involve them, they were also ignored by the unions at the site where they worked. While the supply teachers generally retained their union membership, they had little opportunity to become involved in union activities at the schools and felt their voice was *fractured* from traditional channels both at the school and at the agency. Industrial relations at the airport had become *fragmented* following the requirement to end monopoly provision of services and instead seek these from a series of different contractors. Even though workers remained in the same unions and membership levels were sustained, conflicts arose repeatedly between those working for different firms and on different conditions. Finally, voice in the customer service case was *disconnected*, partly due to geographical distance and multiple sites but also due to sharply contrasting union traditions and the disparate nature of inter-organizational relations on different contracts. In each case, therefore, interrelationships between different employers, unions, and workers had major consequences for worker voice. In effect, opportunities were limited in contexts where work (and sometimes workers) was transferred to new employers, where organizational boundaries were blurred and work was fragmented. In the following analysis, we consider each of these cases in turn.

11.2   Disenfranchised voice

There were strong traditions of trade unionism at Scotchem (Marchington 2001; Marchington et al. 1992) and ample evidence that management had adopted a de facto partnership approach since the 1990s. The company recognized several unions (GMB, TGWU, and AEEU), membership levels were high, and senior shop stewards had access to management through a range of consultative and bargaining mechanisms at establishment level. For the most part the unions worked well together, although there have been some tensions between craft and process workers. During the research period, a new communications group had been set up comprising the senior managers and senior stewards, and additional training sessions had taken place for this group under the auspices of a local trade union college. Both sides viewed management–union relations at plant level in a generally positive light: 'I talk with them (the senior stewards) about the manufacturing plan for the next month and what the issues are. It gives them a chance to express one or two of their concerns about the future' (Scotchem, Director 1, male).

In the late 1990s, Scotchem decided to outsource various aspects of its work, including security, to external contractors. Prior to this, security work had been undertaken by manual workers who were finding it increasingly difficult to cope with the physical demands of working on the plant, and they were redeployed to this work in the run-up to retirement. They were retained on the main negotiated rates for chemical workers, and the move to security work was regarded as recognition for long-term service. As part of a worldwide drive to control costs in Multichem, senior management at Scotchem decided it was no longer cost-effective to continue with existing arrangements and people working on the gatehouse were offered relatively generous early retirement packages. The contract was won by Securiforce, which brought in its own staff to run the system. The trade unions went along with this largely because they feared cuts elsewhere, and instead devoted their energies to negotiating severance terms and developing strategies to help make the plant more viable in the future.

The task of providing security work was therefore undertaken by a quite different set of people from those previously employed by Scotchem, and they had no links with other staff on the site. Securiforce did not recognize trade unions, and since most people working for the agency were ex-service personnel they lacked any union traditions. Pay levels were much lower than for other Scotchem workers and for those who previously worked in the gatehouse, largely because most Securiforce workers already received pensions from their previous work. Moreover, they were employed on a short-term basis, rarely if ever met up with other agency staff, and had limited contact with management. As one of the security staff noted:

It's not a job, career-wise, that anybody would consider, but if you wanted to fill a gap for six or seven months you could certainly do worse. (Securiforce, guard 1, male)

In such a situation, it was unlikely trade unionism could flourish, and indeed it did not. The security guards felt isolated from the rest of the workforce, they were not invited to social or communications events with Scotchem workers and they felt there was little interest in them or their needs. Indeed, given the fact that their employment effectively closed off a potential future job for Scotchem workers, they felt resented and marginalized. The site unions did not feel any responsibility to speak for this group either, and the de facto partnership agreement did not include Securiforce workers because they were not covered by the terms of collective agreements. In short, the lack of representative machinery both with the agency and within the Scotchem regime rendered staff in the gatehouse almost totally voiceless. At best, they had limited communications with Scotchem's Administration Manager. While Scotchem management were positive towards unions for their own employees, this did not extend to those working for other companies on the site and, given the lack of interest at Securiforce and among the agency workers they employed, channels for voice were absent. The contracting arrangement effectively disenfranchised the people employed on security work.

11.3 Fractured voice

The teacher supply case contrasted sharply with this, largely because union membership was relatively high among supply teachers and at similar levels to staff employed on permanent contracts. According to the main teacher unions at least 30,000 supply teachers were on their books (about 75 per cent of those employed in this capacity) and numbers grew sizeably during the last few years. Subscriptions for supply teachers were on reduced rates, recognizing they are not likely to be employed as many days as permanent staff, but benefits were similar and the NUT, the NASUWT, and the ATL all argued this indicated unions were equally committed to both groups. Even though they may spend only a few days at each school, supply teachers were generally union members because many had been employed on permanent contracts in the past and/or saw it as valuable for professional or instrumental reasons. Indeed, among the sample of supply teachers interviewed only one said that they were not in a union, with the remainder split between the three mentioned above. The unions were in an ambivalent position about agencies because while they wished to recruit members involved in this work, they were also concerned that agency work could undermine the terms and conditions of permanent staff. However, none of the unions had negotiated a deal with the agencies, so union membership was both individualized and distanced from their legal employer, the agency. Nevertheless, no distinctions were made between members:

Once they have subscribed and been accepted for membership they are members and we don't differentiate between a supply teacher and a full-time (sic) teacher. We don't say you can only hold branch office, for example, because of this. (ATL, union rep. 2, female)

While there may be high levels of union membership among supply teachers, opportunities to exercise voice were fractured for several reasons. First, under the 'old' system Local Education Authorities (LEAs) kept a register of interested teachers who, like permanent staff, were on nationally negotiated pay scales and had similar levels of holiday pay. Now that supply teachers came through agencies, they could not claim parity with their colleagues employed by the schools where seniority was rewarded by additional pay increments. They were paid a flat rate as a Newly Qualified Teacher (NQT) although this rose for teachers with more than five years' experience, and it may also be supplemented on an individual basis at the discretion of the agency (Grimshaw et al. 2003). There was no collective route to the agencies to determine pay, thus making it difficult to improve terms and conditions for the whole group.

Second, they were marginal both to the schools and the agencies. In the case of the former, teachers were typically employed on short-term contracts that made it hard to establish close and trusting relations with other union members at the schools, and there was less incentive to stay behind to attend union meetings because of the temporary nature of their work. Union activism was problematic given the lack of a base in a particular school and the fact that there were a number of competing unions in the sector. The dominant union tended to vary depending upon region and whether the school was primary or secondary, and even if an agency supply teacher was a member of a large union there was no guarantee it would have sizeable representation in the schools where they worked. There were also problems in getting their voice heard at the agency because, although there were regular contacts to offer work, and in some cases check how things were progressing at a school, there was no formal mechanism for supply teachers to meet up and discuss issues related to work. This meant their voice was unlikely to be heard unless things went wrong. Raising a grievance was not easy either. Four of the supply teachers that were interviewed (out of twenty-four) claimed to have been assaulted by pupils—because they were regarded as 'easy game'—but only one felt confident to challenge the school and they gained support from the agency rather than the union. Most felt powerless if there were grievances because the school did not owe them anything and 'making waves' could jeopardize chances of a permanent post at the school (Grimshaw et al. 2003: 276). Another respondent (TeacherTemp, supply teacher 11, male) said he would be reticent to take up a grievance either with the Head or the agency for fear of being blacklisted by the school or by the agency. Yet, another saw no point in being in a union:

All the union would have done would be to cause problems between myself and the school and indirectly that would have caused problems between the agency and myself. It wouldn't have done my employment opportunities much good. (TeacherTemp, supply teacher 13, male)

Third, there were often tensions between permanent staff and agency teachers that made it difficult to establish a common stance. Quite a few permanent staff that were interviewed expressed resentment about supply teachers, arguing they were not committed to the school, the pupils or the teaching profession. For example, two said:

Most supply teachers come in with their newspaper, their coats, umbrella and expect every lesson to be sorted out for them . . . if they arrive at a classroom and there is no work set they won't do anything. (School B, senior teacher 3, male)

No, they don't come to parents' evenings, they don't write reports, they don't do break duties . . . The head of department would prepare their work and say to the supply teacher 'this is what you are teaching in this lesson, go in there and deliver it.' (School A, ATL union rep. 1, male)

In these circumstances, it was highly unlikely that union representatives in the schools, who were usually permanent teachers, would have much incentive to progress supply teachers' grievances or would be able to generate support from the rest of the membership. Even if they did, by the time the issue came out in the formal arena, in most cases the supply teacher would have moved on. In short, therefore, despite this group of agency workers having high levels of union membership, there were a number of major obstacles—multi-unionism, lack of bargaining opportunities with the agency, and tensions in the schools—that caused their voice to be fractured.

11.4 Fragmented voice

At first sight, the airport case might appear quite simple because all activity took place on one site and the majority of the workers, although employed by different firms, were in the same union (the TGWU). However, the historical context for this case is critically important to understand how the processes of contracting and recontracting led to divisions between workers and the fragmentation of voice. Airportco had high levels of union membership, a long history of management–union relations based upon local authority agreements and the routine involvement of councillors. Industrial relations had traditionally been characterized by conflict, especially in those areas where workers were prepared to use their power, as in the fire station or among baggage handlers at times of high throughput, and militant union traditions had been bolstered by the adoption of a no redundancy policy by the airport, in line with that of the local authorities. This tradition developed when airport operations were relatively integrated, but in the early 1990s application of competition legislation required various airport activities to be put out to tender. This enforced fragmentation was also used by management at the airport to implement major changes to the employment relationship, by limiting coverage of the 'no redundancy' policy and by using the threat of competitive tendering to force the union to accept lower pay rates for new hires.

The restructuring of industrial relations involved several interrelated developments. First, to meet the competition requirements, Airportco set up a wholly owned baggage handling subsidiary (BH) with an independent management system and lower rates of pay so it could tender successfully for work against the existing handling company (FH). Existing staff were redeployed under the no compulsory redundancy policy to other jobs within Airportco but employment security for new staff was explicitly tied to securing contracts from the airlines. This brought some operations at Airportco into direct competition with the private sector. The same union had traditionally represented both airport and FH staff[1] but the creation of BH led to direct competition between the operations; now the same union represented workers from Airportco as well as BH and FH staff. Second, management at Airportco used its new-found confidence associated with the establishment of BH on lower terms and conditions to apply the same logic to its internal operations and pushed for changes to existing employment arrangements. The threat of future competition was used to introduce the so-called market rates for all areas, thereby creating a two-tier system of wages depending upon date of recruitment and not skill level. Furthermore, failure to secure change at the fire station led to the establishment of an independent subsidiary that hired new staff for a second shift on worse terms and conditions. In this case, therefore, the fragmentation of the industrial relations and employment system was brought about both by the involvement of new private sector organizations and by the creation of subsidiaries owned by the airport itself. Moreover, because Airportco retained its no compulsory redundancy policy under the influence of the local authority, a third tier to the workforce was introduced comprising temporary and seasonal workers, often provided by agencies, who were on part-time contracts to meet peak demands.

Given this much more fragmented and divided employment system, it was perhaps surprising that union membership remained high among staff at Airportco, in BH and in FH, all of which recognized the same union. In principle high union density might be expected to enhance the likelihood of effective site-wide representation so as to avoid damaging internecine conflicts. However, for a number of reasons, this did not happen and worker voice and representation was fragmented across organizations at this multi-employer site. While some of this can be attributed to a failure of union imagination and perspective, to a large extent the problems reflected the legacy of previous industrial relations and the rather cumbersome and divisive way in which this system was changed. Instead of producing a strong solidaristic system of trade union organization—as it did in the past—the current arrangements tended to please no one. Long-serving employees either resented the loss of union power or blamed the union for its continuing and unhelpful militant stance. New recruits blamed the union for failing to prevent them being employed on inferior market rates, while the third tier of temporary, seasonal workers remained excluded from representation. Blame appeared to be allocated evenly between management who were felt to use unreasonable threats to force through market rates and the union that was perceived as lacking commitment to new staff:

'They (the management) keep threatening us, "you will do this or we will lose the contract." ' (Airportco, union rep. 1, female). 'The union only represents the ex-airport personnel and older people, and not the new people'. (Airportco, supervisor 1, male)

This was particularly evident among security staff where the union agreed to the hire of new staff at market rates that involved a pay rate 40 per cent lower than for existing staff. However, the union continued to oppose the deployment of market-rate staff on gate duty, insisting that their pay should be increased to the old rates. New staff felt this action was blocking their access to progression within the company. A security officer hired on market rates named one of her main grievances against the union:

Not giving any information to ourselves about what exactly market related pay involves and why we can't progress. (Airportco, security officer 1, female)

Many permanent staff, both at BH and airport security, were not convinced the union was taking a sufficiently proactive stance to protect the interests of temporary workers, focusing instead on enforcing job demarcations or getting time off for union duties rather than the bigger questions of market rates and the share of permanent jobs. This led to disillusionment among staff:

I can't be really bothered about the union. They seem to fight over petty little things like rosters . . . they're not fighting for permanent jobs. (BH, baggage handler 1, male)

It was clear the union had not made a very successful transition from representing a largely integrated workforce to adopt new approaches that protected members from, rather than exposed them to, being used as part of a process of inter-organizational competition that had the effect—in part by design—of weakening worker voice. Not only did the union fail to find an effective way of regulating and moving towards harmonization across the three-tier workforce, but it also adopted a narrow, sectionalist stance to inter-organizational competition. It was clear from interviews at BH and FH that union representatives in both organizations encouraged management to take a more aggressive stance *vis-à-vis* the other handling company even though the baggage handlers in both organizations were represented by the same union and were competing for the same volume of work. According to the BH General Manager, the union was leading a general staff reluctance to cooperate with FH staff when dealing with an airline contract that BH had just lost. FH management also appeared willing to take advantage of the hostility between representatives in the two firms as the union had

distanced itself from the grievances of the part-time workforce because (it) supported FH management's plans to expand its business into Terminal X—which had been the traditional sphere of BH. (FH, Manager 3, male)

However, while the union can be criticized for its failure to adapt to new conditions, the opportunity to develop a more progressive response was undoubtedly hampered by shifts in management policies and practices—both at Airportco and elsewhere. The approach at the airport had changed a number of times over the past decade; several managers and workers referred to a policy in the early 1990s called variously 'excellence through partnership' or 'quality through partnership'. There was general agreement that this experiment had been abandoned, but for different reasons; for some managers it had just led to a loss of control and a further deterioration of industrial relations. For union representatives, the abandonment of partnership signalled the change to a hard-line stance by managers at Airportco, associated with the drive for market rates and the move away from regular fortnightly joint meetings with the union to quarterly meetings. Not all managers were convinced of the wisdom of this approach, feeling the new market rate system was divisive and unfair, and may even have pushed rates too low and had an adverse effect:

You have people virtually doing the same job . . . on a substantial amount of money less than somebody else . . . You then get somebody who's on market-rated pay doing a bloody good job and they're standing next to somebody who's not doing quite as well as they are, and they're being paid a lot more money. (Airportco, Manager 3, male)

At BH there was evidence of a closer partnership between management and the union, a policy that had worked well according to top management and involved regular formal meetings between management and the shop stewards, up to twice monthly, along with frequent informal contact. The unions were represented by a full-time convenor and eleven other shop stewards. The Managing Director spoke warmly about the quality of the relationship:

We do have a close working relationship with the trade union and we are proud of that. Without that relationship we would not have been able to achieve some of the successes we have achieved in the five or six years since I've been with the organization. We've not had a major industrial dispute, we've not had any major operational disruptions and we've been able to negotiate some quite significant restructuring proposals . . . We have introduced market pay. We have, because of the commercial realities, seen staff wages fall quite substantially. (BH, Managing Director, male)

However, middle management appeared less impressed and felt the union was restricting initiatives. One suggested that

although there are lots of meetings going on, the union is not necessarily co-operative . . . initiatives are not implemented because the union does not like them. (BH, Manager 3, male)

These conflicting accounts of industrial relations at BH depend on the point of comparison; relations were more cooperative and harmonious than at Airportco but the union at BH had considerably more operational control than at other organizations which had never been part of the main airport—for example, FH and CleanCo. Engagement with the union at these firms was more arm's length and there were fewer positive and fewer negative comments on the industrial relations climate, as well as more diverse views about what the union should do to represent its members more effectively.

Thus, despite having high membership density within the same union, workers lost immediate and ongoing contact with colleagues in other organizations. As we have seen, tensions arose between workers at BH and FH due to battles for a set amount of work from the airlines. One of the terminal supervisors at BH noted:

The unions are very disintegrated. Each department and group looks after its own interests no matter what happens to other departments or groups. If the Indians fight amongst themselves, the Chiefs can sit back and laugh. (BH, supervisor 1, male)

These inter-organizational divisions reinforced those between the three tiers of the workforce, leading to a fragmented and divided system of worker representation. A telling example of this was the failure of union representatives to keep each other informed about developments. The two female shop stewards representing the new market-rate staff in security felt excluded from the inner circle of the union:

There is a lot going on, on both sides (TU and management), but some TU reps who have been to the meetings would not tell other reps what was going on. We (TU reps) all go separate ways. The other lady shop steward and I have not been kept informed of what has been going on. (Airportco, union rep. 1, female)

The airport case illustrates clearly the problems faced by unions in a system where groups of workers, albeit in the same union, were placed in direct competition with each other after organizational restructuring and the intro-duction of new management initiatives. Not only were there potential tensions between workers employed by different firms as they fought for work, there were also divisions and contradictions between different types of worker (permanent versus temporary; men versus women; established and market rates) employed by the same company. In such circumstances, there was little chance that a coherent and unified voice could develop across the airport, even for members of the same union. Instead, because the system relied on cost-cutting and finan-cial gains through contracting and recontracting, voice became fragmented.

11.5 Disconnected voice

The final case assesses voice in the customer service case where there were mul-tiple links between TCS and its clients. In its early days, TCS was known to be anti-union and keen to break away from what was seen by management as tra-ditional bureaucratic values. Under its first managing director this approach was pursued with vigour, UNISON was derecognized across the company and, while membership levels held up reasonably well (about 40 per cent) at the site with the strongest traditions, at others it plummeted. Towards the end of the 1990s, however, a series of changes at board level led to a shift in management attitudes and the reopening of discussions with UNISON. New Labour's interest in part-nership convinced senior managers there was little point trying to avoid unions and that greater benefits could be gained by restructuring industrial relations around a cooperative agenda. However, it was not agreed to recognize unions at all sites, and the company adopted an essentially pragmatic stance. For example, the Company Handbook made it clear that TCS 'recognizes the fundamental right of individuals to join, or not to join, a trade union' and to engage in collec-tive bargaining where 'the culture of the particular business determines that (it) is appropriate'. This shows how, irrespective of corporate views promoting part-nership in principle, decisions about the implementation of voice were devolved to unit level. Given the diverse range of contracting in which TCS was involved, as well as the widespread use of agency staff, this had the effect of disconnecting workers' voice within and across organizational boundaries.

The convenor responsible for developing partnership acknowledged the difficulties involved in trying to extend union membership across all sites. To some extent, this was a matter of union priorities as the need to service existing members and recruit new members at sites where there was already recognition was a more valuable use of limited resources. The union was fully aware that TCS did not want to upset clients:

They are comfortable with the public sector because they are pro-union and to some extent so are some of the private sector employers, but there is a sort of wariness amongst what can be described as the enterprize companies. So that is where the difficulty lies. (TCS union official 1, male)

Following the creation of the new management team, UNISON was re-recognized at the 'oldest' and most unionized site, and a partnership deal was accepted following a majority vote in favour. Moreover, a series of membership drives at other sites (especially call centres) has led to a renewed and revitalized union movement at TCS (Bain and Taylor 2001). Since then, UNISON and TCS have worked closely together making joint presentations to publicize partnership. It was also appreciated that, should TCS wish to tender for more contracts with the public sector, this approach could help in negotiations whereas outright opposition could lead to major difficulties. The UNISON representatives were convinced this had helped TCS gain more contracts:

They see partnership as a business plus. They took the view because it worked well they can go into bids for contracts and say 'look, we are successful at working with our staff and our trade unions, look at this wonderful partnership', and they can go confidently and bid for contracts and say 'compare us with other contractors'. (TCS-NW, union official 1, male)

The guiding principles behind the original partnership agreement between TCS and UNISON emphasized the usual factors noted by the IPA: mutual trust and cooperation; common interest in business success; flexibility and employment security (see Coupar and Stevens 1998; Guest and Peccei 2001). In addition, there were specific clauses requiring union representatives to reflect the views of all staff, not just union members, and to accept there should be space both for consultative and negotiating forums. Perhaps, because of this, partnership has developed in a somewhat patchy and uneven manner across the company, faring best at the site with the strongest and most historically embedded systems for employee representation as well as the longest standing relationships between UNISON and TCS.

Voice at the call centre

The call centre was set up as a green-field site in the late 1990s, TCS gaining contracts with a number of organizations for the provision of different sorts of services, each of which varied in terms of the proportion of permanent to agency staff. At the time of our initial interviews, there were five clients from very different markets (see glossary for details), yet just two years later several of these contracts had come to an end and some new contracts had been introduced instead. Of the 950 people working across the site as a whole, about 60 per cent were supplied by agencies while the remainder were on permanent or temporary employment contracts with TCS. Shift-working was the norm with operating hours varying—depending on the client—between 15 hours each day to all round the clock. Recruitment was outsourced to Beststaff, an agency that had an office on site and placed job adverts in the local paper each week. Successful applicants were given a six-month contract with the possibility they might be recruited onto a permanent contract with TCS at the end of the period. All staff worked in teams, usually containing both permanent and agency staff alongside one another. In other words, each contract was staffed by a range of different types of workers, but generally none had much experience of unions.

Most of the clients were from the private service sector. Some had no tradition of unionization while others dealt with unions at their main site but may have viewed TCS as an opportunity to evade union controls on in-house operations.[2] The clients did not exert any pressure on TCS to deal with unions and the company was therefore able to divert any approach by referring to its 'culture'. The general manager was aware there had been attempts by the GMB to get access to staff and it was also clear that UNISON was keen to recruit members. Indeed, union representatives had started making presentations to agency staff during their induction course at some other sites, and whilst the union did not yet have any recognition deals with agencies, it had 'come close' on one occasion (TCS union rep. 2, female).

Customer representatives made no mention of unions during our interviews, although they did know about the staff forums that were the principal channel for communication and consultation at TCS-NW—both for TCS employees and for agency staff. Although it had proved difficult to maintain interest, with meetings being cancelled or run intermittently, the forums remained in existence and the Regional HR manager was seeking to 'reenergize' them. According to her (TCS-NW, Manager 5, female) the forums were 'part business, part local driven', and each meeting included a business update from one of the management team, as well as discussions about canteen facilities that were available to all customer service representatives across all the contracts, including agency workers. The forums were attended by up to seven managers, including the Regional Manager, and twelve representatives elected by customer service personnel—drawn from the range of business contracts— roughly on a ratio of 1:50 as specified in the agreement. In principle, the forums were not meant to deal with issues related to agency staff but the question of pay differentials between permanent and temporary staff had been taken up in the forum and two agency workers started to attend the forum towards the end of the research period.

The forums were seen as a channel for workers, both TCS and agency staff, to raise issues that were affecting the site as a whole. Some workers pointed to gains that had accrued from the forums, such as the location of a new canteen at the center of the building. Though such issues are often regarded as trivial—and indeed they are in relation to wider business decisions about the future of contracts—this was an important factor for shift workers. One said very positively:

If there are any problems there is a meeting very regularly, and it's voiced there and discussed. Any solutions are made there and we get feedback from that. So, if you've got a problem, it does get sorted. (TCS-NW Truckco, CSR, female)

Despite this, it was also admitted (Phoneco, CSR1, female) there were hardly any connections between staff on different contracts unless they already knew someone working elsewhere. In other words, there was little common identity across the contracts even for people employed by TCS. For agency workers it was even worse: 'I think there's one girl who deals with complaints but I'm not sure' (TCS-NW UtilityCo, CSR agency worker 1, female).

Furthermore, high levels of labour turnover and a range of different working hours and contracts all limited the extent to which workers—or their representatives on the forums—were able to build up expertise or any embedded collective awareness of issues. Even though they worked in the same building and shared a canteen, factors that may have facilitated some degree of collective identity, this did not seem to have materialized. One of the CSRs explained:

We don't necessarily mix. Even though they are just down there, there's not really much mixing, only if you've got a friend (on one of the other contracts). We don't really get to know the people who work on them. (TCS-NW Phoneco, CSR2, female)

Working time arrangements varied across contracts while terms and conditions differed between permanent and agency staff, both of which could have led to unrest had there been a union presence at the site. In addition, pay rates were lower here than at the other two sites we examined. The complexities of representation in a multi-employer environment and having to go through multiple channels, however, was also very apparent for the agency staff as shown by the following quote from a member of the forum:

The issues raised in Gambleco are seen to by our managers and then they're raised with us as representatives. We take it to the TCS people, it goes through the forum. (TCS-NW Gambleco, CSR, female)

In summary, although TCS had publicized its commitment to partnership through employee forums, these were hardly central to employee experiences or to management strategy at the north-west site. In the absence of union recognition, the forum represented the sole opportunity for workers employed by TCS and agency staff to express their voice. It was clear this provided few connections, but the forum continued to function and a majority of respondents knew something about them. On the other hand, it would be hard to claim they filled a 'representation gap'.

Union activity and representation at the London site

TCS won the contract with Council X after beating off competition from three other outsourcing companies. According to one of the Council's senior managers, while it was recognized that TCS lacked knowledge of how to operate a housing benefits service, the company's experience in customer service management and its preparedness to invest in IT so as to establish a call centre was precisely what was needed. The senior union representative at the London site attended the presentation by each of the companies and, despite knowing of TCS's previous anti-union stance, he was nevertheless impressed by its willingness to work with UNISON. He felt this was the most beneficial bid for his members and the future of the service in comparison with the authoritarian attitudes displayed by the others. He argued:

At the end of the day, we decided they were the least worst option of the four because we got a recognition deal out of them. We got guarantees about terms and conditions, guarantees as far as we could about avoiding compulsory redundancies, and as its panned out we've had none. (TCS-L, union rep. 2, male)

About seventy workers were transferred across from the council to TCS, about thirty left under a voluntary redundancy deal while the remainder decided to stay with the Council. Given the TUPE regulations, transferred staff retained their existing terms and conditions, including membership of UNISON. TCS-L continued with collective negotiations for these staff, the vast majority of whom were union members, although the bargaining unit was now different—comprising just TCS staff rather than all Council employees. The TCS-L Staff Handbook made specific mention of the recognition agreement between TCS and UNISON, and union representatives were given access to new recruits. During the first few years of the contract further recruitment took numbers employed up to about 120, twenty of whom were agency workers. Despite some of the original staff leaving, union density dropped only slightly to 80 per cent of permanent staff, but agency workers were not covered by collective bargaining—and were less likely to be union members unless they had retained membership from their previous service in housing benefits (rather like the supply teachers discussed in Section 11.3). Interestingly, the TCS-L HR Manager site told us a high proportion of new recruits going through the training programme had joined UNISON, attributing this to the strong local government ethos among housing benefit officers:

You wonder if they have been indoctrinated into the local government culture we have here . . . You still have a hard core of people like that and people can be sucked into that way of working or not feeling strong enough to stand away from the crowd. (TCS-L, Manager 6, male)

The contract between TCS and Council X was complicated by the fact that staff working for TCS communicated with the claimants and prepared cases for payment, but then had to send their estimates and draft letters for approval by a team of housing benefit officers employed by the Council. Many of the people employed by TCS used to work for the Council before they were transferred, and indeed were workmates of the people who checked they had estimated benefits correctly. While this could encourage shared identity across organizational boundaries, and thus make it easier to establish a collective ethos (Hebson et al. 2003), tensions between workers prevented connections from developing. Several of the housing benefit officers now working for TCS regarded their former colleagues in such a negative light that this inhibited any chance of UNISON members working for TCS and Council X combining together.

Although union membership remained high, the role of union representatives and the experience of union membership changed significantly. Housing benefits staff had a history of militancy prior to the Public–Private Partnership (PPP) and they played a particularly active part in the UNISON branch according to the Council X Branch Secretary, but following the transfer it was difficult to maintain links. None of the branch officials came from those employed by TCS, which is hardly surprising given that the whole branch had over 2,000 members, and in addition it became increasingly difficult for the shop stewards at TCS to take time off to attend meetings. Indeed, it was felt the branch was no longer interested in members working for TCS:

You have seen a weakening of their position. Union representatives used to have the support of local branch officers but they no longer have that as they work in a private industry. The branch officer is the branch officer for Council X members and has nothing to do with TCS. (Council X, Manager 2, male)

This situation was further complicated because of UNISON's ambivalent views about public–private contracts. One of the caseworkers felt that given their isolation from the membership in Council X and in TCS more broadly, TCS shop stewards had done a good job in representing them to local management. The primary concerns of union members at TCS were different from those working for the council, and branch meetings were arranged at times when it was hard for staff working at TCS to attend. Moreover, despite offering support for the union in principle, TCS did not specifically allow time off to attend branch meetings. Another of the caseworkers said:

Before (the PPP) I would be at every single meeting. Now I pick and choose. I look at the staffing situation and if there is not enough staff I won't go to the meeting. (TCS-L, caseworker 5, female)

This lessening of collective identity with local authority staff was probably inevitable after the transfer, reinforced by a growing recognition that their futures were more intimately tied into the success of the contract, and perhaps more broadly the fortunes of TCS. Moreover, management at the site was keen to involve individual workers instead of relying on collective channels. The TCS-L HR manager laid great emphasis on the importance of having frequent meetings with all workers, not just union representatives, stressing that the union should not be granted any special favours:

We try to be inclusive with the trade union but we also try to be inclusive with all staff. We've opened it wider and I will happily discuss issues with staff without any trade unions being around. (TCS-L, Manager 6, male)

Despite trying to encourage worker commitment to TCS by publicizing its core values and conducting organization-wide attitude surveys, most employment issues were dealt with at local level. There was some discussion among

UNISON representatives about the possibility of a TCS branch of the union—representing workers across all TCS sites—but that had not come to fruition, partly because of the geographical spread of the company, but also because of the widely differing levels of union membership and representation. This case illustrates the difficulties unions face in trying to organize not only across organizational boundaries, but also within a highly decentralized and differentiated employment system. A good example of this was the absence of partnership at the London site. Union representatives had been suspicious of the company's intentions and made sure they filled all the seats on the forum in the first instance. The UNISON convenor at TCS-L explained that the draft agreement originally included a clause allowing for a staff forum:

As far as we were concerned this was an attempt to undermine collective bargaining. The way we countered that was by making sure that all the reps were from UNISON, so effectively we had two opportunities to discuss things with them rather than one. (TCS-L, union rep. 2, male)

In short, worker voice at TCS-L was weakened by the lack of links with UNISON members working for Council X as well as the failure to develop links with workers on TCS contracts at other locations. Not surprisingly, in this situation, worker voice was highly disconnected, adapting to the circumstances of diverse workplaces with varying levels of union membership and traditions. Moreover, it was also apparent that union commitment had been at least partially undermined by the increasing numbers of agency workers.

11.6   Discussion and conclusions

There are two sets of points to make in the conclusions to this chapter. First, though the Willman et al. categorization is useful in directing analysis to how the propensities of different sets of actors (employers, unions, and employees) shape industrial relations outcomes, it inevitably simplifies the situation. It is rare for managers, unions, or employees to be unified in their attitudes and behaviours at any single workplace, so once we go beyond the boundaries of the organization, processes are much more complex and multifaceted. For example, the influence of more than one employer was apparent at every case we examined here, ranging from the relatively straightforward situation in the chemicals case, where just two employers played a part in marginalizing voice for security workers, through to the airport case where a range of historical traditions and changes in organizational forms had splintered employment across a wide range of firms. Similarly, it was hard to conceive of a cohesive union position in any of the cases, most obviously where several different unions were recognized and worker voice was fragmented rather than focused on a common cause. In multi-employer workplaces however, it was even harder for unions to build coalitions between groups of workers who were engaged on different parts of the contract; for example, in the customer service case, despite being members of the same union and in the same branch, hostilities between housing benefit workers employed by the Council and TCS made it very difficult to establish and sustain a shared identity. Moreover, there was no evidence that union representatives had combined together across TCS, and in some cases (e.g. the call centre) UNISON appeared to accept it was unlikely to gain recognition in the short term—though other unions have elsewhere (Bain and Taylor 2001). To some extent this was due to the fact that the workers themselves showed little interest in joining unions, and for agency workers in particular there was little knowledge of what unions did. However, this was not universal and the agency workers in teaching and housing benefits administration had a much greater propensity to join unions, either for professional or instrumental reasons. Accordingly, just like employers and unions, it is unlikely that workers attitudes can be simply classified as positive or negative; much depends on their occupational allegiances and their employment status (temporary or permanent, first or second tier in the workforce).

Second, while worker voice was marginalized in each case, the precise form that this took varied depending on circumstances. The security workers were disenfranchised because neither their own employer nor the unions showed much interest in helping them articulate their views, even though Scotchem workers at the same site were able to take advantage of a wide range of EI practices. The outcome for the supply teachers was different in that they tended to have reasonably high levels of union membership, but their voice was fractured across organizational boundaries. Previously, supply teachers tended to come from a local authority pool, where they were both subject to similar sets of conditions to other teachers employed by the same LEA and covered by the same bargaining arrangements. Now that supply teachers were provided by agencies and they could work in schools across a number of LEAs, they found it much harder to become involved in union activities at the schools. Moreover, their employer (Teacher Supply) did not recognize unions and there was a feeling that future work prospects would be harmed if they raised grievances either with the agency or with Heads in the schools. The whole airport system had been fragmented following anti-monopoly legislation such that workers, even though they might still be in the same union, were divided in terms of what they saw as their best interests, and there were examples of shop stewards at one company urging their managers not to cooperate with other companies even though their fellow members' jobs might be at risk because of this. Furthermore, there were tensions across different groups of workers, in particular between those on historically determined (higher) rates of pay and those on lower, market-rated pay. In short, the reorganization of business systems had helped to fragment worker solidarity. Given the wide range of sites and types of business contracts involved in the customer service case, worker voice was disconnected both within TCS as well as across organizational boundaries. This was apparent in the divisions between union members working for Council X and for TCS in the housing benefits case, and between TCS and agency workers at the call centre.

Each of these cases illustrates well the problems workers face when trying to establish or maintain voice in the context of inter-organizational contracting. The transfer of risk from one employer to another, and then on to the individuals who provide the service, is starkly apparent when temporary contracts are not extended or the demand for labour declines—as is now the case with supply teachers following reduction in school budgets. Other cases are less dramatic but nevertheless demonstrate the consequences of inter-organizational contracting for workers' wages and conditions, as well as their career development, when they no longer have a strong countervailing source of power at work through trade unions. In short, while workers employed by some organizations in the network might have clearly defined channels for voice in order to articulate their grievances and protect their conditions, those employed on precarious contracts across organizational boundaries lack the collective strength to make their voice heard.

Notes

1. A different union represented the passenger handling check-in staff.
2. For example, one of the firms had a partnership agreement with unions at its in-house operations while another had no union recognition at its main site.

12

Conclusion: Redrawing Boundaries, Reflecting on Practice and Policy

DAMIAN GRIMSHAW, MICK MARCHINGTON, JILL RUBERY,
AND HUGH WILLMOTT

12.1 Introduction

In this chapter we draw together the main threads of the book. Our focus has been upon the development and operation of inter-organizational relationships in the context of broader institutional changes, including the closer collaboration of public and private sectors. Our cases have been drawn from across these sectors and have included examples of their intersection through partnerships and the use of agency workers. The blurring of organizational boundaries and the fragmentation of work and employment have been central themes, exploring how established, standardized, and unified forms of organization and employment have been disrupted. They have been disordered as hybrids; less singular and integrated arrangements have been constructed to address perceived shortcomings—of cost, performance, or innovation. Our central argument has been that understanding the dynamics of inter-organizational relationships requires recognition of the critical significance of employment relationships beyond the boundaries of the single organization. This requires the development of a framework that is attentive to how organizations are embedded within wider institutional structures and how their strategies are shaped, at least in part, by legislation and industry-wide norms and regulations.

We question accounts of change that assume the rational pursuit of more efficient and/or effective organizations, and instead find substantial evidence of fragmentation as an outcome of complex, institutionally anchored, political processes of negotiation over the form of organizations and employment relationships. Rationality is routinely invoked as a means of articulating and justifying the claimed 'need' for change and the reasonableness of the means of its implementation. However, what is claimed to be 'rational' or self-evidently logical by one party is frequently viewed as partial and/or self-serving by others. Politics are inescapably present as those engaged in negotiating and maintaining the nature and boundaries of intra- and inter-organizational activity exist in a relation of interdependence to each other. Each party is engaged in a struggle to preserve or reform these relations in order to affirm or legitimize a collective and/or individual sense of identity and reality. A relationship of trust and transparency may, in principle, be favoured by all parties, yet this ethos may be underpinned and, on occasion, subverted, by the mutual knowledge that one or more of the collaborating organizations has the option of supplementing such trust with the use of credible, punitive sanctions.

Collectively and individually, those commanding greater resources, and who have other options, occupy a comparatively advantageous position when negotiating their preferred outcomes. They may mobilize resources to reduce their costs and/or to enhance their benefits by striving to shift risk to other parties. In this process, the accountability of more powerful groups may be diluted or obscured, yet they remain vulnerable. They are not omniscient about processes of negotiation, and they are ultimately dependent upon the cooperation of others who may deploy restricted capabilities highly effectively in the pursuit of their own claims, in the augmentation of their limited resources or even in shifting the definition of valued resources. In this sense, power mediates their relationships; the elimination of risk is elusive; and the construction of trust presents an appealing means of containing risk and gaining benefits.

We begin by revisiting our recurrent motif of 'fragmenting work', recalling the diverse ways in which our study has explored its manifestations. This leads us to reflect upon a number of key concepts—risk/power, trust, and identity—that, in combination, have proved valuable in analysing the different ways in which work, organization, and employment is fragmenting.

12.2 Fragmenting work

The metaphors of 'fragmentation' and 'disorder' have been used throughout this book in order to characterize changes in organization and employment. We have argued that established models of organization and employment, based upon the assumption of a single employer and a unified organization, have diminishing relevance and value where standardized employment conditions based upon full-time, permanent contracts with a single employer are accompanied and supplanted by a plurality of other forms and arrangements. Despite some signs of continuity, many jobs are now less permanent and secure, more people work for agencies supplying temporary workers, and organizations increasingly outsource activities that were previously undertaken in-house and considered integral to their operation. In short, work is fragmenting and boundaries between organizations are blurring, no more so than at the interface of the public and private sectors.

Such 'fragmentation' is, of course, relative to stability and integration. Prior to the establishment of large, vertically integrated organizations, employment relations lacked the structures that were acquired during the late development of advanced capitalist societies. During this period, from the late 1940s to the mid-1970s, there was steady demand for industrially produced goods accompanied by limited international competition. That changed when the oil shock, which led governments and companies to reassess their commitments, was accompanied by the growing penetration of new competitors, together with alternative organizational, employment and regulatory structures, into established markets. For a variety of reasons, this effect was felt strongly in the United Kingdom where comparatively protected markets and the exceptional contribution of the City of London concealed the lack of re-investment in both 'old' and 'new' manufacturing industries. The outcome was a series of crises during the 1970s and 1980s, both of currency and labour relations, which were symptomatic of Britain's status as the 'sick man of Europe'.

The medicine administered to this ailing economy was monetarism supplemented by privatization. Thatcherism declared that enterprise must be liberated from the state and private sector disciplines—such as competitive tendering—were mobilized to revive its residual responsibilities. In the event, the vision was imperfectly realized but its effect has been to challenge and 'shake-up' established monopolies of all varieties—albeit that this spawned the contradictory creation of private monopolies either directly (e.g. Railtrack) or indirectly through allowing for the concentration of ownership (e.g. the privately acquired ex-public utilities). However, just as important as the withdrawal of subsidies, the championing of a discourse of enterprise encouraged both public and private sector organizations to reassess their obligations and commitments. The paternalist idea that employers have a social responsibility towards their employees has been widely supplanted by the entrepreneurial doctrine that nobody is owed a living and that future employment depends upon more flexible and fragmented arrangements. People could no longer expect, as of right, to have permanent, secure jobs. Instead, they must now recognize that employment is a burden and risk for organizations, and that their capacity to compete (or provide value-for-money public services) depends upon minimizing this liability—the substitution of franchises for direct employment at the Post Office being a prime example of this shift. In the calculations of shareholder value and 'financialization' more generally (see Chapter 1), only a privileged minority of workers can expect secure jobs with company pensions. An increasing number of workers are required to accept part-time, temporary, and insecure forms of employment, take greater responsibility for their future employment, and recognize that retraining is a recurrent obligation.[1] In the public sector, this transformation has occurred through stealth; the discipline of 'market-testing' is applied to the provision of public services where private sector providers are hired to undertake the work previously undertaken by public sector employees, with the latter being faced with redundancy or accepting a transfer to a private sector company—such as FutureTech or TCS.

As a means of securing profitable growth (or efficiency savings within the public sector), the erosion of employment security has been accompanied by efforts to identify, harness, and exploit previously untapped sources of innovation, revenue enhancement, or other means of cost reduction. The construction of inter-organizational synergies through vertical disaggregation offers one such strategy. Rejecting the conventional wisdom that *vertical integration* provides an effective means of improving control in addition to reducing transaction costs, and thereby enhances competitiveness, the new 'network' thinking suggests that organizations have specialist, core competencies; and that the *horizontal meshing* of specialization is a source of competitive advantage (or improved value-for-money). Mutually beneficial relationships may be the aspiration of network thinking and, where it is undertaken across organizations employing staff with shared value systems and priorities, there may be a good prospect of anticipated benefits materializing. The chemicals case provides an example of such mutually beneficial meshing of specialist capabilities, although it should be noted that in most cases the dominant partner, Scotchem, has applied its market muscle to influence supplier practices (see Chapter 4). There may, however, be considerable resistance to attempts to translate supposed complementary strengths into everyday working relationships that are experienced as 'mutually beneficial'. Several of our cases (e.g. ceramics) highlighted significant, and perhaps intractable, 'political' difficulties involved in translating abstract economic principles into effective organizational and employment practices.

It is audacious to assume that relations between organizations within a network are inevitably effective just because their respective competences are complementary; it is equally plausible to characterize these relationships as ones of mutual exploitation and accommodation. As we saw in various chapters, the scope for fragmentation, prompted by the process of vertical disaggregation, is extensive. For example, in the customer service and teacher supply cases, tensions arose from the employment of agency staff, on different terms and conditions, working alongside staff employed by other organizations. Moreover, comparatively clear lines of reporting and responsibility have become disjointed, the final resort being to invoke the terms of the contract and ultimately pose the threat of legal redress (see Chapter 7). In principle, there is a shared responsibility for ensuring that the interface between purchaser and provider is effectively managed. Yet, in practice, as we saw in Chapter 5, the primary responsibility of the private sector manager is to the shareholders of the company, not to the public sector purchaser or the ultimate customer (e.g. hospital patient, school child, benefit claimant).

In summary, forces of change are manifest in the fragmentation of established organizational and employment relationships. Vertical disaggregation and horizontal meshing characterize the shift in organizational forms; and employment relationships are also fragmenting as the internalized worker (full time or part time) is supplemented, if not supplanted, by externalized, temporary, and self-employed workers.

12.3 Reflections on practice

A recurrent theme of our analysis is that network forms or inter-organizational relations are embedded within wider social structures and relations that include local communities and established norms, the involvement of trade unions, legislative requirements, and changes in product, labour, and capital markets. By exploring diverse dimensions of inter-organizational relations, we have shown how they are conditioned by dynamic distributions of power and risk, shifting degrees of suspicion and trust, and the redrawing of organizational and occupational identities.

Dynamic distributions of power and risk

Our analysis has been premised upon the understanding that relations of power and assessments of risk mediate decisions to participate in the development and operation of networks. Instead of assuming that exchanges between network members are entered without coercion or constraint, and are fair and equal in their operation, we understand these processes to be shaped by the balance of power between members. Scotchem's purchasing power, for example, enabled it to be highly selective in its choice of haulage suppliers, and to shape their behaviour by requiring them to abide by a code of conduct in order to minimize reputational risk. Similarly, as we saw in Chapter 6, while some schools were able to exert pressure on TeacherTemp to provide them with 'good' teachers, schools in more deprived areas had little option but to accept whom they were sent. While a major advantage of outsourcing is externalization of the responsibility and liabilities associated with vertical integration, it also involves a loss of control and associated risk that is then managed through a combination of (formal) service level agreements and (informal) efforts to engender relations of trust, as in the case of CleanCo's relational contract with Airportco or that between Council X and TCS.

The power of network members is exercised in the avoidance and shifting of risk to their partners. For example, FH and BH workers recognized they had to meet the demands of certain airlines, even if they appeared ridiculous, because of their purchasing power. Moreover, as we saw in Chapter 8, temporary and agency workers at the TCS-NW call centre knew that future job prospects depended on how well they were viewed by the client for whom they worked. A good example of shifting risk was seen in the ceramics case, where Domestic China mitigated the threat of receiving faulty product by favouring manufacturers with very low labour costs where rigorous inspection of product quality, often resulting in high wastage rates, was comparatively costless to the supplier. It is worth noting, however, that outsourcing is less straightforward where there is low substitutability of suppliers. For public sector bodies bidding for large contracts—such as the IT contract awarded by Govco to FutureTech—there is invariably a limited choice of suppliers big enough to make a credible bid; and the costs of putting together consortia of smaller suppliers inhibits wider participation. Moreover, once a purchaser has invested in a provider, there is the risk of 'lock in'—not only because the relationship becomes established and institutionalized, but also because the likelihood of the contract being renewed deters credible, well-researched (and therefore very costly) bids being assembled by alternative suppliers. The awarding of a contract to an alternative supplier could be interpreted as an admission of a failure, either in selecting a suitable supplier in the first instance or in acknowledging the contract has not been managed effectively.

In most cases, especially where there are substantial cost implications associated with a change of provider, the preferred option is to influence how the service is delivered—for example, by shaping the supplier's employment and human resource policies. This was most noticeable, as we saw in Chapter 7, in the airport and customer service cases. Here, there were interventions by clients to shape patterns of work, the implementation of different pay structures and rates, and varying proportions of temporary staff employed on different contracts, all of which led to a blurring of boundaries between employers as well as the emergence of more fragmented systems of employment. This also occurs at a collective level; in Chapter 11 we illustrated how workers were struggling to achieve or maintain their voice across organizational boundaries. In some cases, voice was disconnected or fragmented, while in others workers found they were effectively disenfranchised as the employer subcontracted work to a third party—as with security staff in the chemicals case and with some contracts in the customer service case. Indeed these and other examples show clearly how imbalances in power between clients and suppliers within inter-organizational relationships routinely re-emerge as increased risks for workers.

This risk extends to the difficulties encountered by in-house bidders who lack experience in assembling and negotiating contracts, unlike their private sector competitors who have a wealth of experience (and credibility) in winning contracts. Fragmentation becomes institutionalized and virtually impossible to reverse for those lacking the power and resources to compete with large private sector companies. Similar outcomes were apparent in the housing benefits and Private Finance Initiatives (PFI) cases. In the former, the in-house bid was rejected at an early stage by the Council, only for TCS later to appoint an ex-local authority manager to run the service after their own internally appointed managers experienced problems due to a lack of housing benefits expertise. It surprised local authority managers that private companies were reliant on public sector knowledge when they had been led to expect modernization through the introduction of private sector disciplines and skills (see Chapter 9). The team that put together the specification for the PPP in the health service case was disbanded soon after the completion of its work, and specialist and experienced staff were transferred to the private sector consortium. Indeed, the very demand for privatization of public services and the formation of Public–Private Partnerships (PPPs) is stimulated by the running down of public services, including—in the IT case—the severe difficulty of recruiting specialist staff on civil service pay scales. In short, the weakened capacity of in-house staff to compete for future contracts is symptomatic of the malady for which contracting out was commended as a remedy.

In contrast to the risk of 'lock-in' with the Govco–FutureTech partnership, the teacher supply case indicates the possibility that the purchaser might benefit by drawing temporary staff from agencies rather than relying upon a list vetted and provided by the local authority. In theory, schools can mobilize their purchasing power to extend the supply of teachers and shift the risk to agencies that undertake the time-consuming and politically charged process of recruiting and dismissing temporary staff. Against this benefit, however, schools were vulnerable to being harassed by agencies eager to provide them with teachers— often teachers that other schools were not willing to re-employ. Given that supply teachers are cheaper than permanent staff in the long run, this makes them increasingly attractive to schools that are struggling to reduce costs, yet the increased use of temps, especially by the most disadvantaged schools, renders children vulnerable to an inferior education and further undermines the reputation of such schools.

In all these situations, service failure tends to be attributed to the public sector purchaser rather than the private sector provider. In the IT case, for example, FutureTech's failure to deliver robust systems resulted in national press coverage over several days, but Govco's service came in for sustained public criticism; there was little or no mention in media interviews that these services were delivered by a private sector contractor. Similarly, although it is widely known that many 'hotel' services within hospitals are provided by private sector firms, it is the hospitals rather than the providers that are issued with 'stars' to signify their level of (in)adequacy. The risk of failing to honour service level agreements is carried by the public sector, with minimal impact on the reputation of the private sector provider (see Chapter 5).

The structure and operation of power relations within a network is influenced by the employment situation preceding the establishment of inter-organizational relations, and it is also a condition of their development. In the Post Office case, the capacity to introduce agency and franchising arrangements was complicated by the comparatively advantageous terms and conditions enjoyed by employees who had previously worked in Crown Offices. One response has been to establish the grade of Customer Service Advisor (CSA) on a level of pay about half that enjoyed by established staff so that CSAs can be more readily transferred to future franchisees. In other cases, particularly those that involved transfers from the public to the private sector, lingering attachments to a public sector ethos were interwoven with influences from their new employers in a way that reflects changes to the balance of power in these workplaces (see Chapters 8 and 11) and shapes assessments of risk and opportunity in their new circumstances. In general, the institutional context in which employment relationships are embedded necessarily enables the development of practices that are consistent with its features just as it constrains practices that deviate from it. For example, in the ceramics case, the use of overseas rather than local suppliers was tolerated by workers so long as they believed the company was fully committed to avoiding redundancies and protecting their future employment.

To sum up, we have highlighted the centrality of power relations in the establishment and operation of inter-organizational relations, both in terms of employer–employer linkages and in employer–worker relationships. For the most part, one of the organizations in each case-study network was in a weaker position, and it was commonplace for these weaknesses to be passed on in the form of higher risks for workers. However, given the contradictory dynamics of capital–labour relations, it ought to be no surprise that we also found evidence of risk being displaced even in organizations in a stronger position in the network relationship (e.g. in the private sector providers in the Private Finance Initiative (PFI) case, see Chapter 5). Of course, there were examples of greater equality in power relations and instances where individual workers were able to develop their careers more effectively following a transfer to the private sector, but the general picture was one of inequalities in the distribution of power and the allocation of risk.

Shifting degrees of suspicion and trust

Given the imbalances of power and risk identified above, it is hardly surprising that trust and suspicion manifested themselves both in inter-organizational relations and employment relations, either on an individual or a collective basis. Of course, as we have repeatedly argued, employment relations and inter-organizational relations can not be analysed separately; close and trusting relations between organizations at the most senior levels may well—but not necessarily—spill over into relations between employers and employees, in particular if there are long-term relations that allow for greater levels of employment security or a partnership arrangement with trade unions. Conversely, the implications of a low-trust relationship between organizations may lead boundary spanning agents working for the client to monitor the performance of the supplier—and its workers—more carefully.

Chapters 4 and 5 provided examples at an organizational level of variations in the degree to which private–private relations or public–private relations were built upon trust and suspicion, and it was apparent that trusting relations were more likely the longer the contract (or repeat contracts) had existed. Forces beyond the level of the organization—such as trade association rules, regional ties or legislation—were also influential in shaping the degree of trust or suspicion characterizing inter-organizational relations. For example, the broadly relational contract between Scotchem and Acidchem was bolstered by the Chemical Industries Association (CIA) codes of practice, cultural similarities between the firms, and mutual dependence on each other in a highly competitive world market comprising a few major companies. Others, such as those between BH and FH at the airport, were largely extensions of prior informal practices that were insecure and subject to change as competitive pressures dictated. Yet others, such as contracts at the call centre or some of the schools, were typically of short duration with clients changing suppliers as new opportunities or pressures arose. There is little doubt, however, that the level of trust and suspicion in inter-organizational relations had major implications for employment relations. For example, if clients made no effort to hide the transactional nature of contracts this merely served to reinforce the precarious nature of employment, or continual questioning by the client might lead workers to have lower levels of job satisfaction and notions of self-worth. Moreover, in the absence of long-term trusting relations between firms it is highly unlikely that employers can see advantage in trying to establish partnership relations with trade unions and workers, even more so if the majority of workers are agency temps or have relatively short periods of service (see Chapter 11).

High trust relations may be pursued because both purchasers and providers are frustrated by the difficulties encountered and costs incurred by a low trust reliance on the contract. For purchasers, an ability to trust the provider—as in the case of CleanCo at the airport—minimized the costs of closely monitoring the contract and remedying underperformance. For providers, increased trust allowed them to innovate in service delivery without fear that divergence from strict performance criteria would immediately be interpreted as a failure to comply with the contract. Yet, time is often required to enable this degree of cooperation to develop, and there needs to be leeway in interpretation of the contract by the client if recriminations are not to dominate the relationship. Conversely, trust tends to be undermined if it becomes apparent that the supplier is solely interested in making profits out of the contract. This was particularly apparent in the chemicals case where Securiforce could extract a profit from the contract only through its breach—behaviour that did not concern the company as it had no desire to win further business from Scotchem. In the teacher supply case, many head teachers were suspicious about claims made by agencies regarding the quality of the teachers on their books because they recognized the agency needed to extract a profit from their business. Accordingly, efforts were made to establish 'trust' relationships with particular agencies from whom the schools hoped to receive preferential treatment. Moreover, depending on the degree of trust in their relationships with consultants at TeacherTemp, some teachers were repeatedly placed at schools they wanted whereas others always found themselves working at schools with discipline problems and/or a lack of resources.

Where imbalances of power and risk allow one party to exploit its position of comparative advantage, the establishment of trust may be impeded. Trust may also be constrained where key performance measures are applied to monitor service delivery. In each case, it is a matter of how such arrangements are interpreted: do they signal a lack of confidence in less formal control mechanisms, or are they understood as part and parcel of an inevitable but largely ceremonial control apparatus with which each party is obliged to comply? The difficulty is that there is often no clear-cut or agreed answer to such questions. In the IT case, there was a mutual understanding at the most senior levels about the need for performance measures, but these were not viewed as ceremonial, if only because their publication and interrogation by the Public Accounts Committee had major implications for the reputations of FutureTech and Govco and the career prospects of those held responsible for managing the contract. Other cases were not so public as this, but external assessments of performance still occurred, most obviously where public money was involved—such as TCS-L, which was the subject of a consultancy report commissioned by Council X. Concern in many of the private–private networks focused more specifically on cost reduction, either in terms of cheaper goods as in the Ceramics case, or lower labour costs (and also lower wages as well) in the Airport or Post Office cases. As we saw in Chapter 7, contracting out in these situations offered a perfect opportunity to establish inferior terms and conditions for new recruits.

Despite, or perhaps because of, the importance attached to key performance measures there were often close personal relationships between the most senior managers (boundary spanning agents—see Chapter 6) on each side of the contract. This undoubtedly facilitated a process of give-and-take when the contract entered areas of conflict—for example, over late deliveries, failure to provide adequate advance notice of changed specifications, or the replacement of staff. Open discussion of problems is often identified as an indicator of a trusting relationship, such that instead of denying problems or blaming another party, they are candidly presented and explored. At the very least, this leads to a greater awareness of the difficulties under which each organization or individual is labouring; and, in the context of a partnership or relational contract, there may be an opportunity to explore how the problems may be jointly addressed, or at least worked-around. This may then feed through to particular operational issues; for example, assistance might be offered if bags drop off a trailer at the time of plane turnarounds; drivers might be allowed on site if they arrive early and there is a slot available; or teachers may be allocated to particular schools due to the nature of relations between the boundary spanners at the school and TeacherTemp. However, trust building moves may equally be interpreted as ways of buying time and sympathy, rather than encouraging a process of mutual learning, or they may be seen as a tactic on the part of suppliers to enhance their profits by 'softening' up the client; for example, there was a feeling that relations between Govco and FutureTech were too cosy, and indeed there are dangers that sweet-talking the purchaser around key issues of performance effectively distracts attention from the detail of contractual obligations.

More generally, we have questioned whether the institutional ethos of individualism, distance and confrontation within the UK economy is conducive to the establishment of network forms based upon trust rather than mutual exploitation. In this context, the open discussion of problems can be seen as threatening, since it requires a reciprocity that disrupts habitual patterns of distance and secrecy, albeit that these are cloaked in superficial friendliness. In the public sector, this difficulty is compounded by widespread suspicion of private sector practices and priorities. Greater familiarity and face-to-face contact may mitigate these tendencies but they are unlikely to remove the underlying tensions associated with relations of dependency and risk or provide greater employment protection for workers.

Redrawing organizational and occupational identities

We have seen that the established identities of organizations, employers, workers, and trade union members are disrupted and redefined by the blurring of boundaries associated with the rise of network forms. This is most immediately apparent when there are changes in organizational forms and structures—such as the Post Office franchises and PPPs—as well as in the emergence of multi-employer workplaces where workers from several organizations work alongside and often in collaboration with one another—such as at the airport or the TCS-NW call centre. In other cases, such as the chemicals and ceramics networks, changes to organizational forms and structures are less radical, with outsourcing of work—such as security and cleaning—to other organizations and growing efforts to develop closer relations with both suppliers and clients. In the ceramics case boundary-spanners maintained and nurtured relationships with competitors to arrange for outsourcing of work so as to smooth peaks in demand for their products. In the teacher supply case, head teachers became direct purchasers of temporary teachers, and their previous hierarchical relationship with the local authority was replaced by a market relationship with several agencies to form a web of possible suppliers. In these cases, however, there was minimal blurring of organizational boundaries or work activities, notably because clients exerted little influence upon the internal operations of other organizations.

However, long-standing identities were disrupted in several cases, especially where privately supplied services were introduced into public sector organizations. POCL has been shifting its operations out of Crown Offices to become integrated with other retail outlets in larger units and extending the range of merchandise sold by its staff that have been incentivized to generate revenue by cross-selling goods and services. Along with lower rates of pay for workers in these units, their identity has been transformed from quasi-public servant to shop worker. The outcome is a messy set of compromises that disordered existing organizational forms into a complex and fragmented set of businesses with multiple and competing identities. Employees of the Post Office and workers at its agency and franchise outlets are being retrained or recruited for their soft skills in selling to customers, and technical queries are directed to call centres, with massive implications for questions of skill (see Chapter 9). Similarly, major shifts of identity and identification have occurred at the three PPPs, particularly where staff had been transferred from a public to a private sector employer and the result was a complex and confusing set of different terms and conditions—as we saw in Chapter 7. Many workers found difficulty in identifying with a specialist service provider and even more so with a private company as they had previously regarded themselves as working for the NHS, a local authority or a branch of the Civil Service. Of course, for some employees— such as many of those who transferred from Govco to FutureTech—this change was welcomed as an opportunity to extend their skills, broaden the scope of their careers and work for a multinational company on a much wider range of projects requiring the development of new social and technical competencies. Balanced against this, however, was the fact that Govco employees had chosen to work in the public sector, and to remain within the sector even though jobs with much better pay and career prospects had been widely available in private sector firms. Not surprisingly, therefore, some ex-Govco employees continued to identify with their former organization rather than with FutureTech, even referring to their current employer as 'them' rather than 'us'.

   Confused organizational and occupational identities were apparent in several cases, most obviously at the airport and in the TCS-NW call centre. Operations at the airport were fragmented following requirements to break up the previous monopoly and set up a subsidiary to provide baggage-handling capability in competition with other established private sector firms. Airport operations are such that staff regularly wear the uniforms of another employer in their customer-facing activities, and the whole system operates through disordered systems of contracting and recontracting. In these circumstances, individual identities become blurred (see Chapters 8 and 10). Staff who are subcontracted to other organizations become aware of competing goals, contrasting styles of management and mission statements, and different patterns of working; on some occasions they are seduced by the glamour of working for the other organization. This causes problems when they return to their own employer or move back to agency work. Similar contradictions were apparent at the call centre; for example, an agency worker employed by Beststaff can work on a contract for a company such as Gambleco alongside workers who are employed by TCS on different terms and conditions. Multiple identities and commitments are, therefore, the unexceptional outcome of such a confused situation. We have already alluded to the retention of public sector values after workers have transferred to the private sector, and in some cases this stretches to an almost complete rejection of private sector goals. In this situation, as we saw in Chapters 5 and 8, other commitments may be much deeper—to an under-privileged group or hospital patient rather than to a company or even a public sector organization—and this can result in immense efforts to ensure these people are well served even if it means breaching company rules or working longer hours.

Identities and commitments were also disrupted and challenged on grounds of gender stereotyping and allegiance to trade unions. The former was most overt in cases where men and women were segregated into different types of jobs or men undertook work that was traditionally seen as the preserve of women; in the customer service case, as we saw in Chapter 10, some of the managers preferred to hire women for jobs which were defined as those requiring female qualities but men also undertook these sorts of tasks. This caused some men to joke about the kinds of work they were expected to do, but it was apparent that any re-gendering of men's work was due to downgrading their jobs rather than upgrading women's work. More positively, given the problems that women have had to confront in male-dominated bureaucracies, there are hopes that 'new' forms of work and permeable organization might provide further career opportunities for women. Unfortunately, our research found little evidence that these hopes can be realized as women were being exposed to new forms of inequality that are perhaps less visible than under previous regimes. If the prospects for women are not particularly rosy, those for trade union commitment and organization are perhaps yet more challenging. We found evidence of workers/union members, whose jobs have been fragmented across organizational boundaries, such as at the airport or at TCS, blaming their unions or their fellow workers rather than employers for deteriorating terms and conditions. Also, many transferred workers blamed ex-employers, rather than their current employers, for problems of work intensification and performance monitoring (especially in the PFI case). Unions have always faced problems in trying to mobilize workers from the same union but at different places of work, but the sheer complexity of new organizational forms, and the transient nature of many jobs, makes it even more difficult to develop and maintain union commitment and identity. The situation for temporary workers is particularly problematic given their disconnections from a single and an ongoing place of work, though there was some evidence from other TCS sites that unions were being recognized and that workers were joining or rejoining unions. Overall, it is clear the fragmentation of work across organizational boundaries has disordered existing patterns of identity and commitment.

12.4 Rethinking policy

The fragmentation of work and organization demands a rethinking of conventional policy fields and policy approaches. Pressures towards fragmentation and the shifting of risk have concentrated power away from centralized locations where there are opportunities to establish effective institutions of countervailing power (Galbraith 1963). Accordingly, policy initiatives aimed at providing protection for the worker, as well as the citizen, may need to rebuild connections and re-establish lines of accountability. By default, if not by design, the legal and policy framework often frustrates individuals and groups who seek to mount an effective opposition to corporate agendas as it prevents ready identification of the agents who are responsible, and thus frustrates the process of bringing them to account. If effective countervailing power is to be exercised, policies must be developed that reduce opportunities for risk shifting and fragmentation or, if this is not considered a feasible political option, the customary and legal boundaries to the fields of policy formation require redrawing.

It is frequently the least powerful who are most at risk from the fragmentation of work, yet the current system may also be damaging the interests of capitalists and producers. Research on varieties of capitalism has demonstrated that a more coordinated or orderly form of industrial organization can generate an environment more conducive to innovation and growth than less coordinated or unconstrained versions of market capitalism. However, history also suggests that many investors and managers are disinclined to acknowledge or anticipate such benefits, and therefore tend to oppose constraints on their actions (Jacoby 1984). Countervailing power is needed not only to protect the interests of citizens when engaging directly with corporate power as workers or consumers, but also to guard against the destructive impact of unfettered competition on the innovatory capacities of capitalism (Gray 1998).

To explore these policy issues further, the following section considers two main areas of policy reform—the governance of contracting relations and employment policy. Our concern is not to present specific policy prescriptions but to indicate the changes in policy orientation required—particularly changes in the formation of communities of interests necessary to match changes in the organization of work and production. We take an agnostic approach as to whether the development of new policy approaches would act primarily as pressure towards the re-integration of systems of production; we do not see the trends towards the so-called network firm or the 'free', independent worker as an inevitable aspect of twenty-first-century capitalism for many of the reasons we have outlined above. Our argument is that the outcome of fragmentation—in terms of both productive performance and distributional justice—is highly contingent. The policy framework, therefore, provides one element in the process of determining the scale and direction of trends towards integration or non-integration. Our concern is not to outline methods for opposing all forms of fragmentation, but to identify how a more even balance of power, and some strengthened forms of democratic lines of accountability and control, could be introduced. The focus is on the countervailing power that can be provided through government policy and legislation and by forms of worker representation. We do not address the roles of citizens as consumers, except in so far as this is discussed in relation to public services. This omission reflects the focus of our study on the workplace and does not imply any denial of the power of consumer and other groups to act as counterweights to forces for change.

Governing contracting relations

Ideas and exhortations about improved modes of corporate governance have been a feature of contemporary discourse on employing organizations within both public and private sectors. In the public sector, the focus has been upon internal means of eliminating inefficiency and waste, with the remedy often taking the form of introducing private sector expertise and disciplines, including the 'market testing' of services. In the private sector, attention has been focused upon external accountabilities, spurred on by corporate failures and an emphasis upon the value delivered to shareholders. Somewhat overshadowed by these issues, there has been an undercurrent of discontent and concern about the adequacy of established thinking about the nature and scope of corporate governance—not least a questioning of shareholder value as a dominant philosophy of corporate governance. This concern extends to considerations of the broader, institutional infrastructure in which thinking and reforms of corporate governance develop. The challenge, as we see it, is to develop modes of corporate governance that are better aligned to changes in organizational form and inter-organizational relationships. Our research suggests three areas for policy development: multi-stakeholders and new performance indicators; the limits of the 'smart client'; and greater clarity on what constitutes inter-organizational synergies.

Multi-stakeholders and new performance indicators. Present and proposed modes of governance are too narrowly conceived. The claims of some stakeholders are privileged while the less powerful or well organized—ranging from small investors to citizens affected by the environmental impacts of big business—are marginalized or excluded. Our conception of corporate governance stretches beyond internal checks and balances (e.g. the role of non-executive directors) to encompass the wider social responsibility of public and private corporations with respect to the lives of consumers, pensioners, suppliers, and disadvantaged groups.

It is not just shareholders, or even organized sections of their workforces, but many other parties that are affected by, and dependent upon, the effective, cooperative operations of organizations. An institutional infrastructure, including corporate governance policy that includes a concern for the interests of diverse stakeholders, is more likely to be perceived as legitimate and to be supported by the wider community; and this increased legitimacy may prove more conducive to establishing and maintaining the conditions of stability necessary to foster economic prosperity.

Any move in this direction involves the building and supporting of institutions that enable the multiple constituencies to give voice to, and exert an influence over, all aspects of corporate governance—from the appointment of board members to the recognition of the rights of workers who are not direct employees of the core organization. In this, legislation can play a role, but it needs to be accompanied by opinion leadership by politicians and senior executives, as well as trade union leaders who spearhead efforts to modernize the institutions and day-to-day realities of corporate governance.

One way to extend corporate governance so that it becomes more socially inclusive of other constituencies would be to reform annual reports and related modes of accountability so that information is made available in a form that has direct relevance to a plurality of stakeholders. Key performance indicators need not be restricted to measures of profitability and growth but can be extended to demonstrate the record on issues of pollution and community service, as well as employment and working conditions. One step in this direction could be the proposed requirement to introduce human capital reporting into corporate accounts (Accounting for People Task-Force 2003). A publicly visible and broadly based assessment of performance would begin to rebalance the erosion of countervailing power that has been a major consequence of the fragmentation of work. It would stimulate organizations to review their operations, and to introduce governance changes that would demonstrate their attentiveness to their wider constituencies and social responsibilities. Tax breaks or additional funding for organizations that can show significant innovation and improvement in their governance may be required to make such systems effective.

Within the debate on public–private contracting, it is especially important that measures of value for money incorporate an assessment of whether citizens' rights are being upheld. According to Crouch (2003a, b), these rights are challenged by the new triangular structure of public services provision: each citizen has a democratic link to government, the government has a contractual link with the private sector supplier but the citizen, following privatization, has lost his or her link to the supplier. The problem, Crouch argues, is that government has pursued its outsourcing agenda without first clarifying what ought to be the 'core activities' that are retained in-house, including those associated with the distinctive place of citizenship. Instead, they have defined the core as narrowly as possible in order to liberate government from the messy tasks of service delivery:

Indeed, if we follow the logic of commercialisation to its conclusion, one can envisage the emergence of a quite different idea of politics. By distancing itself from service delivery through lengthy contract chains, government could imitate a discovery of the really smart firms of the 1990s: get rid of the core business itself. ... How much easier would the work of governments be if they needed to cultivate only their brand and image, and were not directly responsible for the actual quality of their policy products! (Crouch 2003b: 23)

New solutions are required to meet citizens' demands for improved public services but contracting for services with private sector firms does not provide a panacea. Instead reforms to make public sector organizations more participative and consultative need to be developed within the framework of a social democracy, and not through the substitution of market principles for citizenship rights.

The limits of the 'smart client'. The ability of both public and private sector organizations to benefit from inter-organizational contracting is very contingent upon the expertise of the client (or purchasing) organization in designing and monitoring the contract for services provision. In government circles, the importance of this was only appreciated by the end of the 1990s. Time and again, government reports and evidence given to the Public Sector Accounts Committee stressed the failure of many public sector organizations—NHS Trusts, government departments, and others—to act as a 'smart client' in their dealings with more experienced private sector contractors. In 1999, a government commissioned report on public–private contracting concluded that many features essential for proper contractual relations were lacking on the public sector side. In particular it found there was no coordination among different agencies and bodies involved with procurement, no standardized process for managing large, complex, or novel procurements, no common data base of information about private sector suppliers, no good common systems for measuring the true costs of procurement transactions and the year on year value added, and insufficient skill and expertise among staff in the government procurement agencies (with a 'serious situation' regarding the high turnover of the more qualified staff to the private sector) (Gershon 1999).

The government has responded to some of these issues, but problems have persisted. At one of the government's Public Sector Accounts Committee meetings in 2002, it was reported that almost one in four public sector clients experienced a decline in value for money during the life of a PFI project, 'with high prices for additional services an area of concern' (House of Commons 2002); that only half of contracts surveyed had appropriate mechanisms in place to ensure value for money (benchmarking, open book accounting, etc.) and very few (just 15 per cent) had put in place mechanisms to share in refinancing profits[2] (ibid.: 1–2); and that many organizations suffer from a 'loss of memory' due to quits among the management team involved in negotiating the original partnership agreement (ibid.).

Policy reforms continue, albeit at a very slow pace, with efforts to standardize procurement approaches, to reduce contracting costs, to systematize a value-for-money appraisal process and to improve capabilities of public sector client personnel (HM Treasury 2003). Our research suggests that a narrow policy focus on improving client expertise will prove insufficient to restore countervailing power. In many areas of services provision, the private sector base of suppliers is becoming increasingly concentrated, resulting in problems of overdependency on two or three powerful conglomerate firms, as the government's 1999 review suggests:

A significant number of senior level government inputs identified concern about the potential level of dependence on a small number of key suppliers in areas of strategic importance and the inability to collectively identify this level of dependence without asking the suppliers for the data. (Gershon 1999: 6)

Trade unions have also become increasingly critical of the power of a handful of multinational firms to shape the quality of public services. UNISON found that just six firms handled 60 per cent of outsourced services in the NHS. Moreover, these firms were moving away from the previous practice of specializing in say catering, or grounds maintenance, and were offering combined services (UNISON 2003a).[3] Even the best efforts to increase client capabilities may not, therefore, be sufficient to match the extra clout enjoyed by increasingly powerful private sector suppliers. More needs to be done to discourage concentration in services provision.

Re-assessing inter-organizational synergies. Even if the key performance indicators used to assess inter-organizational relationships are broadened, as we propose, there remains the very real problem of how those benefits, or synergies which are effectively intangible are to be measured. The pooling of capabilities, or knowledge, between organizations is often claimed to benefit all organizational partners, but these effects may be difficult to identify or measure. A particular problem is the absence of counterfactual information. In practice, studies that have researched the performance attributes of various inter-organizational contracting arrangements tend to rely on relatively subjective perceptions of client managers who have a vested interest in making a favourable assessment, and sweeping embarrassing findings under the collaborative carpet (House of Commons 2002). While there can be no laboratory-type test for assessing performance, more can be done to ensure that clients and suppliers establish well-informed expectations of both the tangible and the intangible benefits (and risks) from entering into contracting arrangements.

A particular concern is with the claim that private sector companies add management expertise. In practice, many private sector suppliers appear to have positioned themselves as specialists in the art of government contracting, often by poaching skilled personnel from public sector organizations and then contracting back their services. Pools of private sector expertise may lie mainly in the practice of winning and overseeing contracts, not necessarily in adding of value or service quality (see also, Crouch 2003b).

Our research evidence suggests that many managers believe in the need to establish strong trusting relations to secure many of the intangible benefits of inter-organizational contracting. In practice, however, trusting relations were often undermined by a lack of shared understanding of agreed codes of conduct, of standards of services provision, and of what was defined in the contract. A rebuilding and strengthening of trade associations, active intervention by trade unions and proposals from government regarding procurement rules all represent measures which would usefully complement trust-building between organizations and reduce the risk of inter-organizational arrangements being plagued by opportunistic behaviour and the oppressive exercise of power.

Employment policy

In the realm of employment law and employment policy much of the framework remains predicated on the notion of a single employer and allows responsibility and accountability at the organization level to be limited to the actions of the legal entity. As organizational boundaries become more blurred and work fragments, the question of where responsibility lies for poor working conditions, poor customer service or inefficiency, and waste of resources is increasingly ambiguous. The following discussion considers three areas: training policy; employment rights; and trade union renewal.

Training policy in a context of fragmentation. Training is a key area of state policy, in large part because of the acknowledged problems of market failure in this area. Inter-organizational contracting may intensify such problems as responsibilities for training become even more ambiguous. The client may distance itself from the process of renewal and replacement of skills and shift the responsibility to the market, in practice placing the burden on the supplier. Training requires organizations to take a long-term perspective but the risks that contracts will not be renewed reduces the capacity of, and incentives for, suppliers to provide training, particularly in specific product-related knowledge. The tendency to train in more generic skills may not generate the same quality of service or product, nor offer the same opportunities for employee skill development. The scope for upskilling may be further reduced if, in order to minimize the risks of contracting, jobs are designed to limit the level of discretion. Research has shown that the effectiveness of training depends upon opportunities to utilize skills and knowledge in a challenging work context (Eraut et al. 2000). If contracting leads to a reduction in job tenure, there is the additional risk of skill loss unless current skills are certified and recognized, so that they can be deployed in a new employment context.

As our research evidence demonstrates, the extent to which fragmentation leads to reduced skills level is in part an empirical issue, contingent upon, for example, the training requirements built into the contracts or the involvement by clients in training provision. Training may actually increase in a context of labour supply shortage, or where workers are transferred into more specialized organizations. However, even though not all changes to the boundaries of organizations result in negative impacts on skills or training opportunities, the increased diffusion of responsibility for skill development poses additional problems for the achievement of a high skill economy within the UK's voluntarist, employer-driven training model.

These concerns suggest a need to rethink training policy. The increased risk is that under inter-organizational contracting, responsibility for training will be shifted between parties without resolution. This adds weight to the case that universal levies should be made on all companies to promote investment in training. However, the government has set itself against extending to all sectors the Industrial Training Boards that are still operating on the basis of statutory levies in engineering and construction: 'while the statutory levy approach may suit some industries, it is unlikely to be a solution for many' (National Skills Strategy September 2003: 58).

One mechanism that could improve the skill base is to extend 'licence to practice' requirements since these provide information on skill levels and offer the individual employee a marketable skill. The government is not prepared to use direct regulation except in the context of 'overwhelming market failure' (The Cabinet Office's Regulatory Impact unit—quoted in SKOPE 2002); the 2003 National Skills Strategy fails to mention extending certification or licence to practice arrangements. Instead the government favours voluntary measures or self-regulation, reinforced by minimum training requirements specified in subcontracting agreements. For example, the Strategic Rail Authority has been allowed by the government to 'establish minimum training levels across the industry by setting higher thresholds through the franchising mechanisms' and the Learning and Skills Council has encouraged contractors in the gas industry to 'exercise purchasing power by setting minimum standards which firms tendering for contracts must meet (subject to procurement law)' (Learning and Skills Council 2002). Here, we find a paradox: the very same arrangements that are causing risks of under-training are being adopted as a vehicle for the diffusion of good practice in the training area.

These developments could, however, be regarded as far too weak a response to the training problem. Not only are the schemes partial—applying only to some sectors, regions or even specific supply chains—but there is no intention to generalize these to all sectors. Moreover, even the new schemes are unambitious in design; in construction the United Kingdom is aiming for NVQ level 1 or 2 while other northern European countries would be training more to level 3 (Green 2001; Bosch and Phillips 2002). The overall skills strategy still focuses on sectors without any detailed analysis of how sectors or occupations are to be defined within a context of increasing fragmentation. Where the boundaries around sectors should be drawn, and whether these now define relevant communities of interest, needs to be seriously addressed. Similarly, we need to question whether the solution to low productivity and performance within the UK economy lies mainly in remedying training deficiencies or in countering the tendency for inter-organizational contracting to favour systems of work organization which minimize the scope for discretion and the full development of productive skills.

Employment rights in a context of fragmentation and the presence of multi-agencies. The single employer framework for employment law and employment protection is increasingly being called into question by cases coming before the courts involving 'multi-agency' situations—that is, where an employee provides services for, or works under the control of, more than one employing organization. Case law based on the existing framework is likely to lead to further ambiguities as, at the time of drafting the legislation, the question of how to provide protections and rights to those working under such conditions was not generally taken into account. Under the influence of European law, some employee rights have been extended to workers, thereby blurring the boundary between employees and the self-employed. Further change is now required to take into account the ambiguities in the concept of the single employer.

Protection for employees in the workplace is being compromised by a number of ambiguities in the employment relationship that relate to the presence of multi-agencies. The first problem in focusing on the legal employer as the basis for the protection of employees is that there are limitations to their legal employer's liability for the actions of other agents or their employees. Second, this focus deflects attention from the influence of clients and other agents on the actions of the employer; for example, currently a dismissal can be deemed fair, even if not based on substantiated evidence, if an employer is placed under pressure by a third party such as a client to dismiss or not deploy a member of staff. Particular problems arise when workers employed by different organizations are found working side-by-side in the same workplace, cooperating in the same labour process. Here, for example, the restriction of liability for equal pay to the 'single employer' prevents the use of comparators drawn from the same workplace if they happen to work for a different organization. Indeed, in some cases, the legal separation of entities may be used explicitly in order to evade the responsibilities and risks associated with the role of employer.

A number of ways forward suggest themselves. First, there is the possibility of developing the notion of joint employer responsibilities to reduce incentives for using the single employer concept in order to avoid employment responsibilities: for example, employers would not be able to use repeated subcontracting instead of direct employment to evade responsibility for personal injury claims by employees. A 'joint employer' doctrine is used in the United States in relation to the National Labour Relations Board and the concept of a 'statutory employer' is also used for workers' compensation schemes. In the United Kingdom, the only similar example is found in S23 of the Employment Relations Act 1999, under which any order by government may 'make provision as to who are to be regarded as the employers' of individuals, thereby extending 'employee' rights to groups of workers currently excluded.

It may, however, be desirable to determine who is the responsible employer in relation to the question being posed. For instance, if an employee has been injured at work, the person who should be deemed to be the employer is the one who has the greater control over the working environment. In other areas of employment law, the appropriate approach may be to increase the obligations of the legal employer rather than to enhance the role of third parties. For example, an employee should have the right not to be disciplined on the basis of the claims of a third party unless these have been subject to investigation and verification by their own employer. An alternative approach could be to make more use of legal fictions which would place obligations on the non-employer for a restricted period or a restricted purpose, in circumstances where it is the non-employer who is exercising the employer functions of control and supervision.[4] However, again such fictions should not permit the legal employer to evade responsibility to its own employees.

There is also a case for extending the remit of certain rights and obligations beyond the immediate employer. An existing example is the extension of the duty not to discriminate unlawfully to the agency to whom contract workers are made available for work. Contract compliance clauses and other mechanisms could be used to diffuse protection though a supply chain or network organization. The need to extend notions of fair employment conditions to include consistency between workers in the same workplace is explicit in the European Commission's proposal for a directive on the working conditions of temporary (agency) workers (DTI 2002).

A case can also be made for extending the field for comparison under the Equal Pay Act to cover situations in which there is perceived inequity of treatment between similarly placed workers, even if they do not share the same legal employer. The increased use of contracting out in the public sector, in particular, places in jeopardy the commitment to establish gender sensitive job grading for all workforce groups (Kingsmill 2001). The presence of employees of different organizations in the same workplace also poses problems for legislation relating to employee voice. The Employment Relations Act (1999) bases the rights for workers to be accompanied by a trade union official (or work colleague) and for trade unions to be recognized for collective bargaining on achieving a 40 per cent or more votes of those in the workplace unit in favour. However, employees of other organizations cannot be included within the bargaining unit. While it might be difficult in practice to make more than one employer a party to the bargaining unit—and might indeed reduce the chance of reaching agreement on recognition or on subsequent bargains—it might be possible and desirable to consider extending the terms and conditions negotiated through the bargaining unit to some groups of non-employees such as agency workers. This would continue the trend towards extending of the scope of worker protection beyond the boundaries of the legal employer.

There are two main legal mechanisms that can be used to reduce the risk of downgrading pay and employment conditions as a consequence of inter-organizational contracting. The first is the establishment of a set of minimum employment rights that provide an effective floor to employment protection that is not dependent on the particular employer, such as minimum wages. The second is to protect the rights of transferred workers—as is currently provided for by the TUPE regulations. The present system protects the terms and conditions of transferred workers but freezes them in time with no procedures laid down for either upgrading terms and conditions, or for harmonizing them in some way with those of the new organization. At least for unionized workplaces some use could be made of the concept of derogation, where it may be acceptable to bring in new terms and conditions provided these are both acceptable to the unions and can be shown to be equally favourable to those prior to the TUPE transfer.

Policies for trade union renewal in a context of fragmented organizations. The main response of trade unions to the fragmenting of work and organizations has been to seek to reorganize and renew their influence within the model of the single autonomous employer (see Chapter 11), and indeed there is some evidence of limited success with this approach at Scottish call centres (Bain and Taylor 2001). But unions have also become more aware of the weaknesses of relying on company-specific bargaining. This realization has led to major changes in UK trade unions' attitude towards legal employment rights—from one of agnosticism, or even hostility, to strong support for developing cross-national institutions for collective bargaining and voice for multinational companies. The main force galvanizing interest in issues of inter-organizational relations has been the growth of public–private contracting since this carries with it the danger of reduced protection for employees and the creation of a two-tier workforce. Trade unions are now demanding a role in public–private contracting, in particular in the process of selecting the private sector contractor.[5] They have also mounted a general campaign against a two-tier workforce that enjoyed an apparently major victory in the early part of 2003 when a new statutory code of practice governing transfers to the private sector in local government was agreed. This code provides protection for new recruits as well as transferred staff that they will receive terms and conditions no less favourable than those of non-transferred staff in the public sector—and this time to include pension provisions.[6] However, this code has yet to be extended to other parts of the public sector. Elsewhere, in the health service, a campaign by UNISON has led to an interim solution, known as the 'retention of employment' model, whereby in PFI schemes signed off after June 2001, most non-supervisory ancillary staff will not transfer to the private sector provider but remain NHS employees, albeit managed by the private sector partner. However, supervisory and managerial roles still transfer to the private sector (UNISON 2003*b*).[7]

The risks to the trade union movement of the process of fragmentation is much greater in the United Kingdom than elsewhere in Europe, where systems of collective bargaining and union protection still apply across the majority of the workforce, often to non signatory employers. As such it makes more sense to look to the United States, where the system of confining collective bargaining to single organizations has a longer history, reinforced by regulation, than in the United Kingdom. Perhaps surprisingly there is more evidence that the unions and other social reformers have woken up to the bankruptcy of existing modes of intervening in the economy. The so-called social movement unionism in the United States has identified two problems to be faced in order to renew trade union organization in a context of fragmented capital. First, unions have to find new ways to bring workers into unions, and second they have to develop countervailing power that strikes where the power in the employment relationship actually lies. Amy Dean, from the South Bay AFL-CIO in California, characterizes the issue as follows:

We know that I may go to work under one roof, sitting next to somebody who is employed through some kind of intermediary institution. Although we are all under the same roof, we have multiple employers. People may be working for the same employer but spread out across the world. Therefore, redefining what constitutes legitimate communities of interests for the purpose of bargaining collectively, whether we work individually or we work under one roof, is an important reform. (Dean 2002: 148)

The union strategy in the United States has been to mobilize groups disenfranchised by the old system of unionization—the immigrant Latino workers in particular—and to found the campaign on the wider issue of social justice, not upon narrow workplace objectives. Another novel aspect is the lobbying of client organizations. The Justice for Janitors campaign in California sought to persuade clients not to employ non-union contracting companies (Johnston 1994; Zabin et al. 2001; Erickson et al. 2002). Social movement unionism has also been influential in its support of living wage campaigns. Over the 1990s, various US states have enacted living wage laws requiring all those organizations receiving government funds to pay living wage levels—that is, minimum wages set much higher than either the Federal or the state minimum wages (Figart et al. 2002). These living wage ordinances have been gradually extended to more and more organizations, providing a labour market, rather than a firm level, basis for promoting improved terms and conditions.[8]

In the United Kingdom there has also been some momentum behind a living wage campaign. The East London Community Organization (TELCO) launched a campaign in 2001 with support from UNISON and some thirty-seven local political, religious, and community groups to persuade public sector hospitals, schools, universities, and local authorities to introduce a 'fair wage clause' into their market tenders for contracting. Also, since many of the companies which contract with the public sector also have contracts with the large corporate firms in East London, a second target of the campaign has been to demand a living wage from the private banks and financial services companies in Canary Wharf (Grimshaw 2004). However, while there have been some successes at individual organizations,[9] it is more difficult in the United Kingdom than in the more decentralized US to get acceptance of higher minimum wages at a local or regional level. Indeed the unions supporting local living wage campaigns are wary of the effect that these local campaigns may have on the system of national collective bargaining in the public sector.

12.5 Conclusion: reconnecting employment and organization

The main argument we have made in this study of fragmenting work is that new or renewed connections need to be made across a variety of boundaries. The first connection is between inter-organizational relations and the organization of work and employment. Too often, the importance of work has been neglected in studies of inter-organizational relations, which assume that synergies and mutual gains are inevitably associated with the revival of network forms of organization. Work, we have argued, is becoming more fragmented, through the subdivision and contracting out of processes, but at the same time it is being reconfigured through inter-organizational mechanisms of collaboration and control. By focusing on the complexities of work in the context of inter-organizational relations, we have exposed the limitations of approaches that divided inter-organizational relationships into those which are market-mediated and others that are cooperative and relational contracts. Our findings demonstrate relations within and across boundaries contain elements of the cooperation/ conflict dilemma that also lies at the heart of both employment relationships and inter-organizational relationships. We need to appreciate the dual layers of cooperative and control relations that are apparent across both organizational boundaries and the management/ labour divide.

A second (re)connection places the employment relationship within the wider context of changing patterns of inter-organizational relations. In strict legal terms, the employment contract itself remains confined within the box of the single employer–employee relationship, yet the experience of the employment relationship for a growing number of workers may be very different. It is not just external customers that exert influence and pressure on workers—as has been recognized in the service work literature (Leidner 1993; Korcynzski 2001; Sturdy et al. 2001)—but also the clients, subcontractors, franchisers, and partners of the employer. As the focus for understanding the employment relationship becomes broader, so too does the need to develop a wider understanding of a range of employment issues. Limiting the focus to the legal employing organization—whether for understanding commitment and efficiency issues or for concerns over employment rights and voice—is becoming increasingly indefensible and inappropriate. By looking at the intersections between organizations and their impact on employment relations, we have identified the need to reconnect the study of employment to the institutional organization of the wider societal system and environment in a way that invites consideration of the formation of communities of interests and modes of social organization that can foster the effective development of new forms of countervailing power.

This brings us to the third connection, which is perhaps at the heart of our endeavour. Effort is required to make new connections between disciplinary subjects in order to achieve a more integrated analysis in which discussion of the changes explored in this book moves beyond the boundaries of single academic disciplines and narrow, internal debates. These academic divisions allow policy-makers to separate out economic or efficiency considerations from broader social and community interests. They also allows practitioners to embrace new forms of organization without considering wider ramifications concerned with imbalances in power relations that occur through contracting or the effects of the new forms of organization on the actions and motivations of workers—even though their impact remains critical in determining productivity and performance outcomes. A clearer and more holistic understanding of the changes taking place in organizations and in employment will emerge only if we can build bridges across traditional academic divides.

A more holistic approach to analysis would, in our view, lead to a rethinking of lines of accountability to be capable of offsetting trends in inter-organizational relations that diffuse responsibility and obscure power relations. This concern underlines the focus on the policy implications of our study, and was implicit in the discussion of our empirical material on which this book is based. There are two main themes to this issue of accountability. First, we have to find ways of countering severance of the democratic link between citizens and the providers of public services that tends to occur when public sector reforms result in the outsourcing of activities to third parties. Second, and more generally, we have to move beyond the consideration of organizations and employers as standalone, independent entities. This approach has allowed accountability and responsibility to be passed down the contracting chain in ways that have tended to inhibit employee voice by excluding workers or their representatives from engagement in the design and operation of the inter-organizational contracting arrangements which shape the terms and conditions under which their work and employment is organized. Our research has shown repeatedly that the fragmenting of employment and organization raises major problems for workers in terms of fair treatment. Rather than employers and policy-makers being sanguine about such developments, we believe they ought to be equally, if not more, concerned about the effects of losing workers' skills, commitment, and voice for the long-term performance of both individual organizations and the economy as a whole.

Notes

1. Several studies of job insecurity identify the role of mergers and takeovers (Burchell et al. 2002) and 'environmental factors' such as the greater exposure of the workforce to market forces (Doogan 2001). Our evidence demonstrates that it is not the 'blind force' of the market which shapes insecurity but employer strategy in adapting the boundaries of their organizations, thus leading to transformations in labour market structure.
2. The need to share in refinancing profits arises from the practice among private sector contractors to negotiate the PFI contract on the basis of high risks at the early stage (with high interest borrowing rates), but subsequently to refinance loans at lower rates of interest as the income flows come in.
3. For example, one firm, ISS, controls 18 per cent of all outsourced services in the NHS and a good part of this reflects its success in winning PFI contracts; ISS has a 14 per cent share of all PFI facilities management services in the NHS (UNISON 2003a: 2).
4. For example, the control factor has been used to allow drivers supplied by temporary work agencies to be regarded as 'deemed temporary servants' of the client for whom

they were working (*Interlink Express Parcels Ltd* v. *Night Trunkers Ltd* [2001] EWCA Civ 360, a case concerning the Goods Vehicle (Licensing of Operators) Act 1995).

5. There is less evidence of trade union pressure for involvement in private sector mergers and takeovers but the Transport and General Workers' Union in its intervention over the competitive bidding for Safeway supermarkets, argued in favour of Sainsburys on the basis of its support for the food and farming industries through its treatment of suppliers (T&G 2003).

6. The 2003 Queen's speech suggests that the pension bill will include improved protection for pensions under TUPE transfers more generally (*The Guardian* 29 November 2003).

7. Estates and maintenance staff are excluded from the ROE model. Also, some ancillary services are not automatically covered by the ROE model, but instead have to make a value for money case. These are switchboard and patient reception services, central sterile supply service departments, medical/patient records and IT systems/payroll (UNISON 2003*b*: 5).

8. These high minimum standards have the advantage of extending protection to all employers in a supply chain and cannot be avoided through fragmentation. For example, in San Francisco the living wage in 2001 was $10 an hour or $11.25 if no medical insurance was provided compared to $6.25 at the state level and $5.15 as the Federal minimum. At San Francisco airport, a site with over 100 employers, the living wage requirement was implemented across all the employers, coordinated by the SF Airport Commission. The SF Airport Commission was also able to use the higher minimum wages to improve on quality standards at the airport as turnover rates among pre-board screeners dropped from 110 per cent in 1999 to 25 per cent in 2001 (Reich et al. 2001).

9. One major success resulting from the TELCO living wage campaign was the agreement in 2003 by the north-east London Strategic Health Authority that all private sector contractors providing services to the local hospitals (around fifteen in total) should pay their staff equivalent terms and conditions to collectively bargained rates for NHS staff, allowing contractors to phase in changes by April 2006 (Grimshaw 2004).

REFERENCES

ACKER, J. (1990), 'Hierarchies, jobs, bodies: a theory of gendered organizations', *Gender and Society*, 4(2): 139–58.

—— (1992), 'Gendering Organizational Theory', in A. Mills and P. Tancred (eds.), *Gendering Organizational Analysis*, London: Sage.

ACKROYD, S. (2002), *The Organization of Business: Applying Organizational Theory to Contemporary Change*, Oxford: Oxford University Press.

—— and Procter, S. (1998), 'British manufacturing organization and workplace industrial relations: some attributes of the new flexible firm', *British Journal of Industrial Relations*, 36(2): 163–83.

ADLER, P. (2001), 'Market, hierarchy, and trust: the knowledge economy and the future of capitalism', *Organization Science*, 12(2): 214–34.

ALBERT, S. and BRADLEY, K. (1997), *Managing Knowledge: Experts, Agencies and Organizations*, Cambridge: Cambridge University Press.

—— and —— (1998), 'Professional temporary agencies, women and professional discretion: implications for organizations and management', *British Journal of Management*, 9: 261–72.

ARGYRIS, C. (1960), *Understanding Organizational Behaviour*, Homewood, IL: Dorsey Press.

ARRIGHETTI, A., BACHMANN, R., and DEAKIN, S. (1997), 'Contract law, social norms and inter-firm cooperation', *Cambridge Journal of Economics*, 21(2): 171–95.

ARTHUR ANDERSEN (2000), *Value for Money Drivers in the Private Finance Initiative*, A report by Arthur Andersen and Enterprise LSE commissioned by The Treasury Taskforce.

ARTHUR, M. and ROUSSEAU, D. (eds.) (1996), *The Boundaryless Career: A New Employment Principle for a New Organizational Era*, Oxford: Oxford University Press.

ASHKENAS, R., ULRICH, D., JICK, T., and KERR, S. (1995), *The Boundaryless Organization*, San Francisco: Jossey-Bass.

ATKINSON, J. (1984), 'Manpower strategies for flexible organizations', *Personnel Management*, 16(8): 28–31.

BACHMANN, R. (1999), *Trust, Power and Culture in Trans-Organizational Relations*, ESRC Centre for Business Research, Working Paper Series 129.

—— (2001), 'Trust, power and control in trans-organizational relations', *Organization Studies*, 22(2): 337–65.

BACON, N. and STOREY, J. (2000), 'New employee relations strategies in Britain: towards individualism or partnership?' *British Journal of Industrial Relations*, 38(3): 407–27.

BAIN, P. and TAYLOR, P. (2001), 'Seizing the time? Union recruitment potential in Scottish call centres', *Scottish Affairs*, Autumn 37: 104–28.

BAKER, W. E. (1992), 'The network organization in theory and practice', in N. Nohria and R. Eccles (eds.), *Networks and Organization: Structure, Form and Action*, Boston, MA: Harvard Business School Press.

BAKER, G., GIBBONS, R., and MURPHY, K. J. (2002), 'Relational contracts and the theory of the firm', *Quarterly Journal of Economics*, 117: 38–84.

BARLEY, S. R. and KUNDA, G. (2001), 'Bringing work back in', *Organization Science*, 12(1): 76–95.

BARLIN, D. and HALLGARTEN, J. (2001), *Supply Teachers: Symptom of the Problem or Part of the Solution?* London: Institute for Public Policy Research.

BARNEY, J. (1991), 'Firm resources and sustained comparative advantage', *Journal of Management*, 17(1): 99–120.

—— and HANSEN, M. (1994), 'Trustworthiness as a Source of Competitive Advantage', *Strategic Management Journal*, 15: 175–90.

BARON, J. N. and KREPS, D. M. (1999), *Strategic Human Resources: Frameworks for General Managers*, New York: John Wiley and Sons.

BARTEL, C. (2001), 'Social comparison in boundary-spanning work: effects of community outreach on members' organizational identity and identification', *Administrative Science Quarterly*, 46(3): 379–413.

BEAUMONT, P. B., HUNTER, L. C., and SINCLAIR, D. (1996), 'Customer-supplier relations and the diffusion of employee relations changes', *Employee Relations*, 18(1): 9–19.

BECKER, C. (1996), 'Labor law outside the employment relations', *Texas Law Review*, 75: 1527–62.

BELT, V. (2002), 'A female ghetto? Women's careers in call centres', *Human Resource Management Journal*, 12(4): 51–66.

BEYNON, H., GRIMSHAW, D., RUBERY, J., and WARD, K. (2002), *Managing Employment Change: the New Realities of Work*, Oxford: Oxford University Press.

BLOIS, K. (2002), 'Business to business exchanges: a rich descriptive apparatus derived from MacNeil's and Menger's analyses', *Journal of Management Studies*, 39(4): 523–51.

BLYTON, P. and TURNBULL, P. (1998), *The Dynamics of Employee Relations* (2nd edn), London: Macmillan.

BOLTON, S. (2004), 'Conceptual confusions: emotion work as skilled work', in C. Warhurst, E. Keep, and I. Grugulis (eds.), *Skill Matters*, London: Palgrave.

BORYS, B. and JEMISON, D. B. (1989), 'Hybrid arrangements as strategic alliances: theoretical issues in organizational combinations', *Academy of Management Review*, 14: 234–49.

BOSCH, G. and PHILLIPS, P. (eds.) (2002), *Building Chaos: An International Comparison of Deregulation in the Construction Industry*, London: Routledge.

BOXALL, P. (1998), 'Achieving competitive advantage through human resource strategy: towards a theory of industry dynamics', *Human Resource Management Review*, 8(3): 265–88.

—— and PURCELL, J. (2003), *Strategy and Human Resource Management*, Basingstoke: Palgrave.

—— and STEENEVELD, M. (1999), 'Human resource strategy and competitive advantage: a longitudinal study of engineering consultancies', *Journal of Management Studies*, 36(4): 443–63.

BOYNE, G. A. (1998), 'Competitive tendering in local government: a review of theory and evidence', *Public Administration*, 76: 695–712.

BRADLEY, H. (1989), *Men's Work, Women's Work*, Cambridge: Polity Press.

BRERETON, M. and TEMPLE, M. (1999), 'The new public service ethos: An ethical environment for governance', *Public Administration*, 77(3): 455–74.

BROADBENT, J., HASLAM, C., and LAUGHLIN, R. (2000), 'The origins and operation of the Private Finance Initiative', in P. Robinson, J. Hawksworth, J. Broadbent, R. Laughlin, and C. Haslam (eds.), *The Private Finance Initiative: Saviour, Villain or Irrelevance?* IPPR, A Working Paper from the Commission on Public Private Partnerships.

BROWN, A. (2001), 'Supporting learning in advanced supply systems in automotive and aerospace industries', *Paper presented at a joint Network/SKOPE/TLPRP international workshop*. University College Northampton, 8th–10th November.

BRUSCO, S. (1982), 'The Emilian model', *Cambridge Journal of Economics*, 6: 167–84.

—— (1986), 'Small firms and industrial districts: the experience of Italy', in D. Keeble and E. Wever (eds.), *New Firms and Regional Development in Europe*, London: Croom Helm.

BUCKLEY, P. J. and CASSON, M. (1996), 'Joint ventures', in P. J. Buckley and J. Michie (eds.), *Firms, Organizations and Contracts: A Reader in Industrial Organization*, Oxford: Oxford University Press.

—— and CHAPMAN, M. (1997), 'The perception and measurement of transaction costs', *Cambridge Journal of Economics*, 21(2): 127–45.

BURAWOY, M. (1985), *The Politics of Production*, London: Verso.

BURCHELL, B. and WILKINSON, F. (1997), 'Trust, business relationships and the contractual environment', *Cambridge Journal of Economics*, 21(2): 217–37.

—— ELLIOT, J., RUBERY, J., and WILKINSON, F. (1994), 'Management and employee perceptions of skill', in R. Penn, M. Rose, and J. Rubery (eds.), *Skill and Occupational Change*, Oxford: Oxford University Press.

—— LADIPO, D., and WILKINSON, F. (eds.) (2002), *Job Security and Work Intensification*, London: Routledge.

CALLAGHAN, G. and THOMPSON, P. (2002), 'We recruit attitude: the selection and shaping of routine call centre labour', *Journal of Management Studies*, 39(2): 233–54.

CAPPELLI, P. (1995), 'Rethinking employment', *British Journal of Industrial Relations*, 33(4): 563–602.

—— (ed.) (1999), *Employment Practices and Business Strategy*, New York and Oxford: Oxford University Press.

—— (2001), 'The new deal with employees and its implications for business strategy', in J. Gual and J. E. Ricart (eds.), *Strategy, Organization and the Changing Nature of Work*, Cheltenham and Massachusetts: Edward Elgar.

CAPPELLI, L., BASSI, H., KATZ, D., KNOKE, P., OSTERMAN, P., and USEEM, M. (1997a), *Change at Work*, New York: Oxford University Press Inc.

—— —— —— —— and —— (1997b), *Change at Work*, New York: Oxford University Press, Inc.

CARROLL, M., COOKE, F. L., GRUGULIS, I., RUBERY, J., AND EARNSHAW, J. (2001), 'Analysing Diversity in the Management of Human Resources in Call Centres', *Human Resource Management Journal Sponsored Conference, Call Centres and Beyond: the HRM Implications*, King's College, University of London, November.

CARROLL, M., COOKE, F. L., HASSARD, J., and MARCHINGTON, M. (2002), 'The strategic management of outsourcing in the ceramic tableware industry', *Competition and Change*, 6(4): 327–43.

CASTELLS, M. (1996), *The Information Age: Economy, Society and Culture, Volume 1. The Rise of the Network Society*, Oxford: Blackwell.

CHILD, J. and FAULKNER, D. (1998), *Strategies of Co-operation: Managing Alliances, Networks and Joint Ventures*, Oxford: Oxford University Press.

—— and McGRATH, G. (2001), 'Organizational form in an information-intensive economy', *In Academy of Management Journal*; Briarcliff Manor, 44(6): 1135–48.

CLARKE, L. and HERMANN, G. (2001), 'Cost versus production: disparities in construction labour processes in Europe', *Paper presented at the 19th Annual Labour Process Conference*. Royal Holloway, University of London, 26th–28th March.

CLEGG, H. (1970), *The System of Industrial Relations in Great Britain*, Oxford: Blackwell.

Cm4310 (1999), 'Modernising Government', London: HMSO.

COASE, R. (1937), 'The nature of the firm', *Economica*, 4(4): 386–405.

COCKBURN, C. (1983), *Brothers: Male Dominance and Technological Change*, London: Pluto Press.

—— (1991), *In the Way of Women*, London: Macmillan.

COLLING, T. (1993), 'Contracting public services: the management of compulsory competitive tendering in two county councils', *Human Resource Management Journal*, 3(4): 1–15.

—— (2000), 'Personnel management in the extended organization', in K. Sisson (ed.), *Personnel Management: A Comprehensive Guide to Theory and Practice*, Oxford: Blackwell.

CONNELL, R. (1987), *Gender and Power*, Cambridge: Polity Press.

COOKE, F. L. (2001), 'Human resource strategy to improve organizational performance: a route for firms in Britain?', *International Journal of Management Reviews*, 3(4): 321–340.

—— (2003), 'Maintaining change: the maintenance function and the change process', *New Technology, Work and Employment*, 18(1): 35–49.

COOKE, F. L., EARNSHAW, J., MARCHINGTON, M., and RUBERY, J. (2004), 'For better and for worse: transfer of undertaking and the reshaping of employment relations', *International Journal of Human Resource Management*, 15(2): 276–94.

COOMBS, J. G. and KETCHEN, D. J. (1999), 'Explaining interfirm co-operation and performance: toward a reconciliation of predictions from the RBV and organizational economics', *Strategic Management Journal*, 20: 867–88.

COOMBS, R. and BATTAGLIA, P. (1998), *Outsourcing of business services and the boundaries of the firm*, University of Manchester: Centre for Research on Innovation and Competition (CRIC), Working Papers Series.

CORBY, S. (1999), 'Equal opportunities: fair shares for all?', in S. Corby and G. White (eds.), *Employee Relations in the Public Services: Themes and Issues*, London: Routledge.

—— and WHITE, G. (eds.) (1999), *Employee Relations in the Public Services: Themes and Issues*, London: Routledge.

COUPAR, W. and STEVENS, B. (1998), 'Towards a new model of industrial partnership: beyond the 'HRM versus industrial relations' argument', in P. Sparrow and M. Marchington (eds.), *Human Resource Management: The New Agenda*, London: FT/Pitman.

COYLE, A. (1995), *Women and Organisational Change*, Manchester Equal Opportunities Commission.

CROMPTON, R. (1995), 'Women's employment and the "middle class"', in T. Butler and M. Savage (eds.), *Social Change and the Middle Classes*, London: UCL Press.

—— (1999), *Restructuring Gender Relations and Employment*, Oxford: Oxford University Press.

—— (2000), 'Changing Gender Boundaries in Employment and Households', in K. Purcell (ed.) *Changing Boundaries in Employment*, Bristol: Bristol Academic Press.

—— and LE FEUVRE, N. (1992), 'Gender and bureaucracy: women in finance in Britain and France', in M. Savage and A. Witz (eds.), *Gender and Bureaucracy*, Oxford: Blackwell.

—— and SANDERSON, K. (1990), *Gendered Jobs and Social Change*, London: Unwin Hyman.

CROUCH, C. (1997), 'Skills-based full employment: the latest Philosopher's Stone', *British Journal of Industrial Relations*, 35(3): 367–91.

—— (2003a), 'The state: economic management and incomes policy', in P. Edwards (ed.), *Industrial Relations: Theory and Practice* (2nd edn), Oxford: Blackwell Publishing Ltd.

—— (2003b), *Commercialisation or Citizenship: Education Policy and the Future of Public Services*, London: Fabian Society.

CULLY, M., WOODLAND, S., O'REILLY, A., and DIX, G. (1999), *Britain at Work*, London: Routledge.

CUTLER, T. and WAINE, B. (1994), *Managing the Welfare State: The Politics of Public Sector Management*, Oxford: Berg Publishers.

D'AVENI, R. A. (1994), *Hypercompetition: Managing the Dynamics of Strategic Maneouvering*, New York: The Free Press.

DAVIDOW, W. H. and MALONE, M. S. (1992), 'The virtual corporation', *California Business*, 27(11): 34–40.

DAVIDSON, M. and COOPER, C. (1992), *Shattering the Glass Ceiling; The Woman Manager*, London: Paul Chapman.

DAY, M., BURNETT, J., FORRESTER, L., and HASSARD, J. (2000), 'Britain's last industrial district? A case study of ceramics production', *International Journal of Production Economics*, 65: 5–15.

DEAKIN, N. and WALSH, K. (1996), 'The enabling state: the role of markets and contracts', *Public Administration*, 74: 33–48.

—— GOODWIN, T., and HUGHES, A. (1997), 'Cooperation and trust in inter-firm relations: beyond competition policy?' in S. Deakin and J. Michie (eds.), *Contracts, Cooperation and Competition. Studies in Economics, Management and Law*, Oxford: Oxford University Press.

DEAN, A. (2002), 'The view from silicon valley', in P. Auer and C. Daniel (eds.), *The Future of Work, Employment and Social Protection*, International Institute for Labour Studies.

DESS, G. and SHAW, J. D. (2001), 'Voluntary turnover, social capital, and organizational performance', *Academy of Management Review*, 26(3): 446–57.

DIMAGGIO, P. (2001), *The Twenty-first-Century Firm: Changing Economic Organization in International Perspective*, Princeton, NJ: Princeton University Press.

—— and —— (1991), 'The iron cage revisited: institutional isomorphism and collective rationality in organizational fields', in W. Powell and P. DiMaggio (eds.), *The New Institutionalism in Organizational Analysis*, Chicago and London: The Chicago University Press.

DOMBERGER, S. (1998), *The Contracting Organization: A Strategic Guide to Outsourcing*, Oxford: Oxford University Press.

DOOGAN, K. (2001), 'Insecurity and long-term employment', *Work, Employment and Society*, 15(3): 419–42.

DORAY, B. (1988), *From Taylorism to Fordism, A Rational Madness*, London: Free Association Books.

DORE, R. (1986), *Flexible rigidities: industrial policy and structural adjustment in the Japanese Economy, 1970–1980*, Stanford, CA: Stanford University Press.

—— (1996), 'Goodwill and the spirit of market capitalism', in P. Buckley and J. Michie (eds.), *Firms, Organizations and Contracts: A Reader in Industrial Organization*, Oxford: Oxford University Press.

DTI (2002), Commission Proposal for a Directive on Agency Work, http://www.dti.gov.uk/er/agency/directive.htm.

Du Gay, P. (1996), *Consumption and Identity at Work*, London: Sage.

—— (2000), *In Praise of Bureaucracy*, London: Sage.

—— and Salmon, G. (1992), 'The cult[ure] of the customer', *Journal of Management Studies*, 29(5): 615–33.

Dyer, J. and Singh, H. (1998), 'The relational view: cooperative strategy and sources of interorganizational competitive advantage', *The Academy of Management Review*, 23(4): 660–79.

Earnshaw, J., Rubery, J., and Cooke, F. L. (2002), *Who is the Employer?* London: Institute for Employment Rights.

Edwards, C., Woodall, J., and Welchman, R. (1996), 'Organizational change and women managers' careers: The Restructuring of Disadvantage?' *Employee Relations*, 18(5): 25–45.

—— Robinson, O., Welchman, R., and Woodall, J. (1999), 'Lost opportunities? Organizational restructuring and women managers', *Human Resource Management Journal*, 9(1): 55–64.

Edwards, P. (ed.) (2003), *Industrial Relations: Theory and Practice*, Oxford: Blackwell.

Equal Opportunities Commission (EOC) (2000), *Women and Men in Britain: The Labour Market*, Manchester: EOC.

Eraut, M., Alderton, J., Cole, G., and Senker, P. (2000), 'The development of knowledge and skills at work', in F. Coffield (ed.), *Differing visions of a Learning Society* (Vol. I), Bristol: Policy Press.

Erickson, C., Fisk, C., Milkman, R., Mitchell, D., and Wong, K. (2002), 'Justice for janitors in Los Angeles: lessons from three rounds of negotiations', *British Journal of Industrial Relations*, 40(3): 543–67.

Escott, K. and Whitfield, D. (1995), *The Gender Impact of Compulsory Competitive Tendering in Local Government*, Manchester: EOC.

Ezzamel, M., Willmott, H., and Worthington, F. (2001), 'Power, control and resistance in "the factory that time forgot" ', *Journal of Management Studies*, 38(8): 1053–79.

Felstead, A. (1991), 'The social organization of the franchise: a case of "controlled self-employment" ', *Work, Employment and Society*, 5(1): 37–57.

—— (1993), *The Corporate Paradox: Power and Control in the Business Franchise*, London: Routledge.

—— and Jewson, N. (1999), *Global Trends in Flexible Labour*, Basingstoke: MacMillan.

—— Gallie, D., and Green, F. (2002), *Work Skills in Britain 1986–2002*, Nottingham: DfES Publications.

Fenton, E. and Pettigrew, A. M. (eds.) (2000), *The Innovating Organization*. London: Sage.

Ferguson, K. E. (1984), *The Feminist Case Against Bureaucracy*, Philadelphia: Temple University Press.

Figart, D., Mutari, E., and Power, M. (2002), *Living Wages, Equal Wages: Gender and Labour Market Policies in the US*, New York: Routledge.

Finegold, D. (1999), 'Creating self-sustaining, high-skill ecosystems', *Oxford Review of Economic Policy*, 15(1): 60–81.

—— and Soskice, D. (1988), 'The failure of training in Britain: Analysis and Prescription', *Oxford Review of Economic Policy*, 4(3): 21–43.

Fleming, P. and Spicer, A. (2003), 'Working at a cynical distance: implications for power, subjectivity and resistance', *Organization*, 10(1): 157–79.

Foray, D. and Lundvall, B. A. (1996), 'The knowledge-based economics of knowledge to the learning economy', in D. Foray and B. A. Lundvall (eds.), *Employment and Growth in the Knowledge-Based Economy*, Paris: OECD.

Fox, A. (1974), *Beyond Contract: Work, Power and Trust Relations*, London: Faber and Faber.

Frenkel, S., Korczynski, M., Shire, K. A., and Tam, M. (1999), *On the Front Line: Organization of Work in the Information Economy*, Ithaca and London: Cornell University Press.

Friedman, A. (1977), *Industry and Labor*, London: MacMillan.

Froud, J., Haslam, C., Johal, S., and Williams, K. (2000), 'Shareholder value and financialization: consultancy promises, management moves', *Economy and Society*, 29(1): 80–111.

Fry, B. R. (1989), *Mastering Public Administration: From Max Weber to Dwight Waldo*, Chatham, NJ: Chatham House Publishers.

Fryxell, G., Dooley, R., and Vryza, M. (2002), 'After the ink dries: the interaction of trust and control in US-based international joint ventures', *Journal of Management Studies*, 39(6): 865–86.

Galbraith, J. K. (1963), *American Capitalism: the Concept of Countervailing Power*, Middlesex: Penguin Books Ltd.

Gallie, D. (1994), 'Patterns of skill change: upskilling, deskilling or polarization?', in R. Penn, M. Rose, and J. Rubery (eds.), *Skill and Occupational Change*, Oxford: Oxford University Press.

——, White, M., Cheng, Y., and Tomlinson, M. (1998), *Restructuring the Employment Relationship*, Oxford: Oxford University Press.

Gasteen, A. and Sewell, J. (1994), 'The Aberdeen off-shore oil industry: core and periphery', in J. Rubery and F. Wilkinson (eds.), *Employer Strategy and the Labour Market*, Oxford: Oxford University Press.

Geary, J. (1992), 'Employment flexibility and human resource management', *Work, Employment and Society*, 6(2): 251–70.

Gershon, P. (1999), *Review of Civil Procurement in Central Government*, www.ogc.gov.uk/ gershon/pgfinalr.htm.

Gilder, G. (1989), *Microcosm: The Quantum Revolution in Economics and Technology*, New York: Simon and Schuster.

Glucksmann, M. (1995), ' "Why Work"? Gender and the Total Social Organization of Labour' *Gender, Work and Organization*, 2(2): 63–73.

Goffman, E. (1959), *The Presentation of Self in Everyday Life*, Harmondsworth: Penguin.

Gottfried, H. (1994), 'Learning the score: the duality of control and everyday resistance in the temporary-help service industry', in J. Jermier, D. Knight, and W. Nora (eds.), *Resistance and Power in Organizations*, London: Routledge.

Grabher, G. (1993), 'The weakness of strong ties: the lock-in of regional development in the Ruhr area', in G. Grabher (ed.), *The Embedded Firm: on the Socio-Economics of Industrial Networks*, London: Routledge.

Granovetter, M. S. (1985), 'Economic action and social structure: the problem of embeddedness', *American Journal of Sociology*, 91(3): 481–510.

Gray, J. (1998), *False Dawn*, London: Granta Books.

Green, A. (2001), *Construction Industry Skills and the Impact of Occupational Regulation*, Draft report on SKOPE project, London: Institute of Education.

Grey, R. (1994), 'Career as a project of the self and labour process discipline', *Sociology*, 28(2): 479–98.

Grimshaw, D. (2004), 'Living wage and low pay campaigns in the UK', in D. Figart (ed.), *Global Living Wage Movements*, New York: Routledge, forthcoming.

—— and Rubery, J. (1998), 'Integrating the internal and external labour markets', *Cambridge Journal of Economics*, 22(2): 199–220.

GRIMSHAW, D. and RUBERY, J. (2001), *The Gender Pay Gap: A Research Review*, Manchester: Equal Opportunities Commission.

—— WILLMOTT, H., and VINCENT, S. (2002a), 'Going Privately: Partnership and Outsourcing in UK Public Services', *Public Administration*, 80(3): 475–502.

—— COOKE, F. L., GRUGULIS, I., and VINCENT, S. (2000b), 'New technology and changing organizational forms: implications for managerial control and skills', *New Technology, Work and Employment* (Special Issue: The Future of Work), 17(3): 186–203.

—— and RUBERY, J. (2003), 'Intercapital Relations and the Network Organisation: Redefining the Issues Concerning Work and Employment', Paper presented at the University of Cambridge Conference on 'Economics for the Future' (September).

—— EARNSHAW, J., and HEBSON, G. (2003), 'Private sector provision of supply teachers: a case of legal swings and professional roundabouts', *Journal of Education Policy*, 18(3): 267–88.

GROUT, P. (1997), 'The economics of the private finance initiative', *Oxford Review of Economic Policy*, 13(4): 53–66.

GRUGULIS, I. (2002), *Emotions and Aesthetics for Work and Labour: The Pleasures and Pains of the Changing Nature of Work*, School of Management, Salford University Working Paper No. 2.

—— KEEP, E., and WARHURST, C. (2004), 'Whatever happened to skill?' in C. Warhurst, E. Keep, and I. Grugulis (eds.), *The Skills that Matter*, Basingstoke: Palgrave.

GUEST, D. (1987), 'Human Resource Management and Industrial Relations', *Journal of Management Studies*, 24(5): 503–21.

—— (1998a), 'Is the psychological contract worth taking seriously?' *Journal of Organizational Behaviour*, 19: 649–64.

—— (1998b), 'Beyond HRM: commitment and the contract culture', in P. Sparrow and M. Marchington (eds.), *Human Resource Management: the New Agenda*, London: Pitman.

—— and PECCEI, R. (2001), 'Partnership at Work: mutuality and the balance of advantage', *British Journal of Industrial Relations*, 39(1): 207–36.

—— MICHIE, J., CONWAY, N., and SHEEHAN, M. (2003), 'Human Resource Management and Corporate Performance in the UK', *British Journal of Industrial Relations*, 41(2): 291–314.

GULATI, R. (1995), 'Does familiarity breed trust? The implications of repeated ties for contractual choice in alliances', *Academy of Management Journal*, 38(1): 85–112.

GUY, F. (2000), 'Technology planning, bargaining and the growth of inequality since 1980', mimeo. London: Department of Management, Birbeck College.

HAGEDOORN, J. and DUYSTERS, G. (2002), 'External sources of innovative capabilities; the preference for strategic alliances or mergers and acquisitions', *Journal of Management Studies*, 39(2): 167–88.

HAKIM, C. (1979), *Occupational Segregation: A Comparative Study of the Degree and Pattern of*, London: Department of Employment, Research Paper no. 9.

HALFORD, S. and LEONARD, P. (1999), *Gender, Power and Organizations*, Hampshire: Palgrave.

—— and SAVAGE, M. (1995), 'Restructuring organizations, changing people: gender and restructuring in banking and local government', *Work, Employment and Society*, 9(1): 97–122.

—— —— and WITZ, A. (1997), *Gender, Career and Organizations: Current Developments in Banking, Nursing and Local Government*, Basingstoke: Macmillan.

HANDY, C. (1985), *The Future of Work*, Oxford: Basil Blackwell Ltd.

HARRISON, B. (1994), *Lean and Mean*, London: The Guilford Press.

HARVEY, C. and KANWAL, S. (2000), 'Self-employed IT knowledge workers and the experience of flexibility: evidence from the United Kingdom', in K. Purcell (ed.), *Changing Boundaries in Employment*, Bristol: Bristol Academic Press.

HEBSON, G., GRIMSHAW, D., and MARCHINGTON, M. (2003), 'PPPs and the changing public sector ethos: case-study evidence from the health and local authority sectors', *Work Employment and Society*, 17(3): 483–503.

HEERY, E. (2002), 'Partnership versus organizing: alternative futures for British trade unionism', *Industrial Relations Journal*, 33(1), 20–35.

—— and ABBOTT, B. (2000), 'Trade unions and the insecure workforce', in E. Heery and J. Salmon (eds.), *The Insecure Workforce*, London: Routledge.

—— CONLEY, H., DELBRIDG, R., and STEWART, P. (2001), *Beyond the Enterprise? Trade Unions and the Representation of Contingent Workers*, ESRC Future of Work Working Paper No 7, London.

—— SIMMS, M., CONLEY, H., DELBRIDGE, R., and STEWART, P. (2002), *Trade Unions and the Flexible Workforce: A Survey Analysis of Union Policy and Practice*, ESRC Future of Work Working Paper No 22, London.

Her Majesty's Stationery Office (HMSO). (1991), *Competing for Quality*, London: HMSO.

HM Treasury (2003), *PFI: Meeting the Investment Challenge*, London: The Stationary Office.

HOCHSCHILD, A. R. (1983), *The Managed Heart: The Commercialisation of Human Feeling*, Berkeley: University of California Press.

HODGSON, G. M. (1999), *Economics and Utopia*, London: Routledge.

HOLLY, L., RAINBIRD, H., MUNRO, A., and LEISTEN, R. (2001), 'Delivering public services that are high quality and efficient: the rhetoric and reality of delivering quality public services', *Paper presented at the 16th Annual Cardiff Business School Conference*.

House of Commons Committee of Public Accounts (2002), *Managing the Relationship to Secure a Successful Partnership in PFI Projects*, Forty-second Report of Session 2001–02, London: The Stationery Office Ltd.

—— (2003), *Delivering Better Value for Money from the Private Finance Initiative*, Twenty-eighth Report of Session 2002–03, London: The Stationery Office Ltd.

HUNTER, L., BEAUMONT, P., and SINCLAIR, D. (1996), 'A "partnership" route to human resource management', *Journal of Management Studies*, 33(2): 235–57.

HUXHAM, C. (ed.) (1996), *Creating Collaborative Advantage*, London: Sage.

HYMAN, R. (1975), *Industrial Relations: A Marxist Introduction*, London: Macmillan.

ILINITCH, A. Y., D'AVENI, R. A., and LEWIN, A. Y. (1996), 'New Organizational Forms and Strategies for Managing in Hypercompetitive Environments', *Organization Science*, 7(3): 211–20.

IMAI, M. (1986), *Kaizen*, Cambridge, MA: McGraw-Hill.

Institute for Public Policy Research (IPPR) (2001), *Building Better Partnerships: The Final Report of the Commission on Public Private Partnerships*, London: IPPR.

IRONSIDE, M. and SEIFERT, R. (1995), *Industrial Relations in Schools*, London: Routledge.

JACOB, S. (1984), 'The development of internal labour markets in American manufacturing firms', in P. Osterman (ed.), *Internal Labour Markets*, Cambridge, MA: MIT Press.

JARILLO, J. C. (1988), 'On strategic networks', *Strategic Management Journal*, 9: 31–41.

JEFFRIES, F. and REED, R. (2000), 'Trust and adaptation in relational contracting', *The Academy of Management Review*, 25(4): 873–82.

JOHNSTON, P. (1994), *Success While Others Fail: Social Movement Unionism and the Public Workplace*, Ithaca: ILR Press.

JOHNSON, N. (1983), 'Management in government', in M. J. Earl (ed.), *Perspectives on Management*, Oxford: OUP.

KANTER, R. M. (1977), *Men and Women of the Corporation*, New York: Basic Books.

KAUFMAN, A., WOOD, C., and THEYEL, G. (2000), 'Collaboration and technology linkages: a strategic supplier typology', *Strategic Management Journal*, 21: 649–63.

KEEP, E. (2001), 'If it Moves, It's a skill', Paper presented at an ESRC Seminar on the changing nature of skill and knowledge, Manchester 3rd–4th September.

—— and RAINBIRD, H. (2000), 'Towards the learning organization?' in S. Bach and K. Sisson (eds.), *Personnel Management: A Comprehensive Guide to Theory and Practice* (3rd edn), Oxford: Blackwell.

KELLY, J. (1997), 'Industrial relations: Looking to the future', *British Journal of Industrial Relations*, 35(3): 393–8.

KERR, D. (1998), 'The private finance initiative and the changing governance of the built environment', *Urban Studies*, 35(12): 22–77.

KICKERT, W., KLIJN, E.-H., KOPPENJAN, J. (eds.) (1997), *Managing Complex Networks: Strategies for the Public Sector*, London: Sage.

KINGSMILL, D. (2001), *The Kingsmill Review of Women's Employment and Pay*, www.kingsmillreview.gov.uk.

KINNIE, N., PURCELL, J., and HUTCHINSON, S. (2000), 'Managing the employment relationship in telephone call centres', in K. Purcell (ed.), *Changing Boundaries in Employment*, Bristol: Bristol Academic Press.

KOGUT, B. (2000), 'The network as knowledge: generative rules and the emergence of structure', *Strategic Management Journal*, 21: 405–25.

KORCZYNSKI, M. (2001), 'The contradictions of service work: call centre as customer-oriented bureaucracy', in A. Sturdy, I. Grugulis, and H. Willmott (eds.), *Customer Service: Empowerment and Entrapment*, London: Palgrave.

KOTTER, J. P. (1973), 'The psychological contract: managing the joining up process', *California Management Review*, 15(3): 91–99.

KREPPS, D. M. (1990), 'Corporate culture and economic theory', in J. E. Alt and K. A. Shepsle (eds.), *Perspectives on Positive Political Economy*, Cambridge: Cambridge University Press.

KUNDA, G., BARLEY, S. R., and EVANS, J. (2002), 'Why do contractors contract? The experience of highly skilled technical professionals in a contingent labour market', *Industrial and Labor Relations Review*, 55(2): 234–60.

Labour Force Survey (LFS) (2001), Spring, Office for National Statistics.

LACLAU, E. and MOUFFE, C. (1985), *Hegemony and Socialist Strategy: Towards a Radical Democractic Politics*, London: Verso.

LAFER, G. (2004), 'What is skill?', in C. Warhurst, I. Grugulis, and E. Keep (eds.) *The Skills that Matter*. Basingstoke: Palgrave Macmillan.

LANE, C. and BACHMANN, R. (1997), 'Co-operation in inter-firm relations in Britain and Germany: the role of social institutions', *British Journal of Sociology*, 48(2): 226–54.

—— and —— (eds.) (1998), *Trust Within and Between Organizations: Conceptual Issues and Empirical Applications*, Oxford: OUP.

LANE, J. E. (2000), *New Public Management*, London: Routledge.

LAWLER, E. E. (1990), *Strategic Pay. Aligning Organizational Strategies and Pay Systems*, San Francisco: Jossey Bass.

—— (1995), 'The new pay: a strategic approach', *Compensation and Benefits Review*, July–August: 46–54.

LAZONICK, W. and O'SULLIVAN, M. (1996), 'Organization, finance and international competition', *Industrial and Corporate Change*, 5(1): 1–49.

LEANA, C. and VAN BUREN III, H. (1999), 'Organizational social capital and employment practices', *The Academy of Management Review*, 24(3): 538–55.

Learning and Skills Council (2002), Draft Workforce Development Strategy to 2002–2005.

LEGGE, K. (1989), 'Human resource management: a critical analysis', in J. Storey (ed.), *New Perspectives on Human Resource Management*, London: Routledge.

—— (1995), *Human Resource Management: Rhetorics and Realities*, London: Macmillan Press Ltd.

LEIDNER, R. (1993), *Fast Food, Fast Talk: Service Work and the Routinization of Everyday Life*, Berkeley and Los Angeles: University of California Press.

LEPAK, D. and SNELL, S. (1999), 'The human resource architecture: towards a theory of human capital allocation and development', *The Academy of Management Review*, 24(1): 31–48.

LINCOLN, J., GERLACH, M., and TAKAHASHI, P. (1992), 'Keiretsu networks in the Japanese economy: A dyad analysis of intercorporate ties', *American Sociological Review*, 57: 561–85.

LITTLER, C. (1982), *The Development of the Labour Process in Capitalist Societies*, London: Heinemann.

LLOYD, C. (2002), 'Training and development deficiencies in "high skills" sectors', *Human Resource Management Journal*, 12(2): 64–81.

LORENZ, E. (1988), 'Neither Friends nor strangers: informal networks of sub-contracting in French industry', in D. Gambetta (ed.), *Trust: Making and Breaking Co-operative Relations*, Oxford: Blackwell.

—— (2003), 'Inter-organizational trust, boundary spanners and communities of practice', in B. Burchell, S. Deakin, J. Michie, and J. Rubery (eds.), *Systems of Production: Markets, Organizations and Performance*, London: Routledge.

LORENZONI, G. and LIPPARINI, A. (1999), 'The leveraging of interfirm relationships as a distinctive organizational capability: a longitudinal study', *Strategic Management Journal*, 20: 317–38.

LUHMANN, N. (1988), 'Familiarity, confidence, trust: problems and alternatives', in D. Gambetta (ed.), *Trust: Making and Breaking Co-operative Relations*, Oxford: Blackwell.

MACAULAY, S. (1963), 'Non-contractual relations in business: a preliminary study', *American Sociological Review*, 28: 55–67.

MACHIN, S (2000), 'Union decline in Britain', *British Journal of Industrial Relations*, 38(4): 631–45.

MACKENZIE, R. (2000), 'Subcontracting and the reregulation of the employment relationship: a case study from the telecommunications industry', *Work, Employment and Society*, 14(4): 707–26.

MACNEIL, I. (1974), 'The many futures of contracts', *Southern California Law Review*, 47: 696–816.

MAILLY, R. (1986), 'The impact of contracting out in the NHS', *Employee Relations*, 8(1): 10–16.

MALECKI, E. (1997), *Technology and Economic Development* (2nd edn), Harlow: Longman.

MALLON, M. and DUBERLEY, J. (2002), 'Managers and professionals in the contingent workforce', *Human Resource Management Journal*, 10(1): 33–47.

MARCH, J. and SIMON, H. (1958), *Organizations*, New York: Wiley.

MARCHINGTON, M. (2001), 'Employee involvement at work', in J. Storey (ed.), *Human Resource Management: A Critical Text* (2nd edn), London: Thomson Learning.

—— and GRUGULIS, I. (2000), ' "Best practice" human resource management: perfect opportunity or dangerous illusion?', *International Journal of Human Resource Management*, 11(6): 1104–24.

—— and VINCENT, S. (2004) 'Analysing the influence of institutional, organizational and interpersonal forces in shaping inter-organizational relations', *Journal of Management Studies*, 41(6), 1029–56.

—— COOKE, F., and HEBSON, G. (2003), 'Performing for the 'customer': managing housing benefit operations across organizational boundaries', *Local Government Studies*, 29(1): 51–74.

—— GOODMAN, J., WILKINSON, A., and ACKERS, P. (1992), *New Developments in Employee Involvement*, London: CIPD.

MARGLIN, S. (1974), 'What do bosses do?' in A. Gorz (ed.), *The Division of Labour: The Labour Process and Class Struggle in Modern Capitalism*, Sussex: Harvester Press.

MARSDEN, D. (1999), *A Theory of Employment Systems: Microfoundations of Societal Diversity*, Oxford: Oxford University Press.

MATHIESON, H. and CORBY, S. (1999), 'Trade unions: the challenge of individualism', in S. Corby and G. White (eds.), *Employee Relations in Public Services*, London: Routledge.

MATUSIK, S. and HILL, C. (1998), 'The utilization of contingent work, knowledge creation, and competitive advantage', *Academy of Management Review*, 23(4): 680–97.

McCLEAN PARKS, J., KIDDER, D., and GALLAGHER, D. (1998), 'Fitting square pegs into round holes: mapping the domain of contingent work arrangements onto the psychological contract', *Journal of Organizational Behaviour*, 19: 697–730.

McDOWELL, L. (1997), *Capital Culture: Gender at Work in the City*, Oxford: Blackwell.

McINTOSH, I. and BRODERICK, J. (1996), 'Neither one thing nor the other: compulsory tendering and Southborough Cleansing Services', *Work, Employment and Society*, 10: 413–30.

MILBURN, A. (1999), Speech at the IPPR Launch of the Commission on Public Private Partnerships, 20 September.

MILES, R. E. and SNOW, C. (1984), 'Fit, failure, and the Hall of Fame', *California Management Review*, XXVI: 10–28.

—— and —— (1986), 'Organizations: New Concepts for New Forms', *California Management Review*, XXVIII(3): 62–73.

—— and —— (1996), 'Twenty-first century careers', in M. B. Arthur and D. M. Rousseau (eds.), *The Boundaryless Career: A New Employment Principle for a New Organizational Era*, Oxford: Oxford University Press.

MIOZZO, M., GRIMSHAW, D., and RAMIREZ, P. (2002), 'Contracting for knowledge: IT outsourcing and the limits to performance gains', *Paper presented at the European Association for Evolutionary Political Economy Conference*. Aix-en-Provence: November.

MORGAN, G. (1990), *Organizations in Society*, Basingstoke: MacMillan Press Ltd.

MYTELKA, L. K. (1991), 'States, Strategic Alliances, and International Oligopolies: The European ESPRIT Programme', in L. K. Mytelka (ed.), *Strategic Partnerships, States, Firms and International Competition*, London: Pinter.

National Skills Strategy (2003), '21st century skills. Realising our potential', White paper presented to Parliament by the Secretary of State for Educational and Skills, July 2003.

NEATHEY, F. and HURSTFIELD, J. (1995), *Flexibility in Practice—Women's Employment and Pay in Retail and Finance*, Manchester: Equal Opportunities Commission.

NEDO (1986), *Changing Working Patterns: How Companies Achieve Flexibility to Meet New Needs*. London: NEDO.

NEWMAN, J. (1995), 'Gender and culture change', in C. Itzin and J. Newman (ed.), *Gender, Culture and Organizational Change; Putting Theory into Practice*. London: Routledge.

NICKSON, D., WARHURST, C., WITZ, A., and CULLEN, A. M. (2001), 'The importance of being aesthetic: work, employment and service organization', in A. Sturdy, I. Grugulis, and H. Willmott (eds.), *Customer Service: Empowerment and Entrapment*, Basingstoke: Palgrave.

NOON, M. and BLYTON, P. (2002), *The Realities of Work* (2nd edn), Basingstoke: Palgrave.

NOHRIA, N. and ECCLES, R. (1992*a*), 'Face-to-face: making network organizations work', in N. Nohria and R. Eccles (eds.), *Networks and Organizations*, Boston, MA: Harvard Business School Press.

—— and —— (eds.) (1992*b*), *Networks and Organizations*, Boston, MA: Harvard Business School Press.

O'CONNOR, J. (1973), *The Fiscal Crisis of the State*, New York: St. Martin's Press.

O'REILLY, J. and FAGAN, C. (ed.) (1995), *Part-Time Prospects: An International Comparison of Part-Time Work in Europe, North America and the Pacific Rim*, London: Routledge.

O'TOOLE, B. J. (1993), 'The loss of purity: the corruption of public service in Britain', *Public Policy and Administration*, 8(2): 1–6.

—— (2000), 'The Public Interest: A Political and Administrative Convenience', in R. Chapman (ed.), *Ethics in Public Service for the New Millennium*, Aldershot: Ashgate.

OECD (1997), 'Benchmarking, evaluation and strategic management in the public sector', *OECD Working Papers*, Vol. 5, No. 67, Paris: OECD.

OPSR (Office of Public Services Reform) (2002), 'Reforming our public services: Principles into Practice', The Prime Minister's Office of Public Services Reform. www. pm.gov.uk/files/pdf/Principles.pdf.

PARRY, I. and TRANFIELD, D. (1998), 'Leadership in the front line: the changing nature of supervision in UK manufacturing', in R. Delbridge and J. Lowe (eds.), *Manufacturing in Transition*, London: Routledge.

PAULES, G. F. (1991), *Dishing it Out: Power and Resistance Among Waitresses in a New Jersey Restaurant*, Philadelphia: Temple University Press.

PAYNE, J. (1999), *All Things to all People: Changing Perceptions of 'Skill' Among Britain's Policymakers Since the 1950s and Their Implications*, SKOPE Research Paper No. 1, Oxford and Warwick Universities.

—— (2000), 'The unbearable lightness of skill: the changing meaning of skill in UK policy discourses and some implications for education and training', *Journal of Education Policy*, 15(3): 353–69.

PEARCE, J. (1993), 'Toward an organizational behaviour of contract labourers: their psychological involvement and effect on co-workers', *Academy of Management Journal*, 36: 1082–96.

PENN, R. (1984), *Skilled Workers in the Class Structure*, Cambridge: Cambridge University Press.

PETERS, T. (1990), 'The best new managers will listen, motivate, support: isn't that just like a woman?' *Working Woman*, September, 142(3): 216–17.

PETTIGREW, A. M. and FENTON, E. M. (eds.) (2000), *The Innovating Organization*, London: Sage.

PETTIGREW, A. M., WHITTINGTON, R., MELIN, L., RUNCLE, C. S., VAN DEN BOSCH, S. A. J., RUIGROK, W., and NUMAGANI, T. (2003) *Innovative forms of Organizing: International Perspectives*, London: Sage.

PFEFFER, J. (1998), *The Human Equation: Building Profits by Putting People First*, Boston: Harvard Business School.

PHILLIPS, A. and TAYLOR, B. (1986), 'Sex and skill', *Feminist Review*, 6: 79–83.

PIORE, M. H. and SABEL, C. F. (1984), *The Second Industrial Divide: Possibilities For Prosperity*, New York: Basic Books.

POLLERT, A. (1996), 'Gender and class revisited; or, the poverty of "patriarchy" ', *Sociology*, 30(4): 639–59.

—— (ed.) (1991), *Farewell to Flexibility?* Oxford: Basil Blackwell.

POLLOCK, A., SHAOUL, J., ROWLAND, D., and PLAYER, S. (2001), 'Public services and the private sector: a response to the IPPR', *Catalyst Working Paper*, London: Catalyst.

POPPO, L. and ZENGER, T. (2002), 'Do formal contracts and relational governance function as substitutes or complements?' *Strategic Management Journal*, 23: 707–25.

POWELL, W. W. (1990), 'Neither market nor hierarchy: network forms of organization', *Research in Organizational Behaviour*, 12: 295–336.

—— (2001), 'The capitalist firm in the 21st century: emerging patterns in Western enterprise', in P. DiMaggio (ed.), *The Twenty-First-Century Firm: Changing Economic Organization in International Perspective*, Princeton: Princeton University Press, pp. 33–68.

POWELL, W., KOPUT, K., and SMITH-DOERR, L. (1996), 'Interorganizational collaboration and the locus of innovation: networks of learning in biotechnology', *Administrative Science Quarterly*, 41(1): 116–45.

POWER, M. (1997), *The Audit Society*, Oxford: Oxford University Press.

PRAHALAD, C. K. and HAMEL, G. (1990), 'The core competence of the corporation', *Harvard Business Review*, 68(3) May–June: 79–91.

PRATCHETT, L. and WINGFIELD, M. (1996), 'Petty bureaucracy and woolly minded liberalism? The changing ethos of local government officers', *Public Administration*, 74: 639–56.

PRIEM, R. and BUTLER, J. (2001), 'Is the resource-based "view" a useful perspective for strategic management research?' *The Academy of Management Review*, 26(1): 22–40.

PRINGLE, R. (1989), *Secretaries Talk*, London: Verso.

Private Finance Quarterly (1996), 'Editorial: The end of the road?', Winter: 32.

PSPRU (Public Services Privatisation Research Unit) (1998), 'Alternative models of public private partnership', www.unison.org.uk/pfi/pppcon.htm. London: UNISON.

PURCELL, J. (1989), 'The impact of corporate strategy on human resource management', in J. Storey (ed.), *New Perspectives on Human Resource Management*, London: Routledge.

—— (1999), 'Best practice and best fit: Chimera or cul-de-sac?' *Human Resource Management Journal*, 9(3): 26–41.

—— and ALHSTRAND, B. (1994), *Human Resource Management in the Multi-divisional Company*, Oxford: Oxford University Press.

PURCELL, K. and PURCELL, J. (1999), 'Insourcing, outsourcing and the growth of contingent labour as evidence of flexible employment strategies', *Bulletin of Comparative Labour Relations*, 35: 163–181.

PUTNAM, L. and MUMBY, D. K. (1993), 'Organizations, emotions and the myth of rationality', in S. Fineman (ed.), *Emotion in Organizations*, London: Sage.

RAINBIRD, H. and MUNRO, A. (2003), 'Workplace learning and the employment relationship in the public sector', *Human Resource Management Journal*, 13(2): 30–44.

RAINNIE, A. (1988), *Employment Relations in the Small Firm*, London: Routledge and Kegan Paul.

—— (1991), 'Just-in-time, sub-contracting and the small firm', *Work, Employment and Society*, 5(3): 353–375.

—— (1992), 'The reorganization of large firm contracting: myth and reality', *Capital and Class*, 49: 53–75.

REICH, M., HALL, P., and JACOBS, K. (2001), 'Living wages and airport security', Occasional paper no. 3. Institute for Labour and Employment, University of California, Los Angeles.

REICH, R. B. (1991), *The Work of Nations: Preparing Ourselves for 21st Century Capitalism*, London: Simon & Schuster Ltd.

RESKIN, B. F. and ROOS, P. A. (1990), *Job Queues, Gender Queues: Explaining Women's Inroads into Male Occupations*, Philadelphia: Temple University Press.

Rifkin, J. (1995), *The End of Work: The Decline of the Global Labor Force and the Dawn of the Post-market Era*, New York: G. P. Putnam's Son.

RING, P. S. and VAN DE VEN, A. H. (1994), 'Developmental processes of cooperative interorganizational relationships', *Academy of Management Review*, 19(1): 90–118.

ROBINSON, P., HAWKSWORTH, J., BROADBENT, J., LAUGHLIN, R., and HASLAM, C. (eds.) (2000), *The Private Finance Initiative: Saviour, Villain or Irrelevance?* IPPR, A Working Paper from the Commission on Public Private Partnerships.

ROGERS, J. (1995), 'Just a temp: experience and structure of alienation in temporary clerical employment', *Work and Occupations*, 22: 137–66.

ROPER, I., PRABHU, V., and VAN ZWANDENBERG, N. (1997), 'Only just-in-time: Japanization and the "non-learning" firm', *Work, Employment and Society*, 11(1): 27–46.

ROSE, M., PENN, R., and RUBERY, J. (1994), 'Introduction, the SCELI skill findings', in R. Penn, M. Rose, and J. Rubery (eds.), *Skill and Occupational Change*, Oxford: Oxford University Press.

RUBERY, J. (1978), 'Structured labour markets, worker organization and low pay', *Cambridge Journal of Economics*, 2(1): 17–37.

—— (1995), 'Performance related pay and the prospects for gender pay equity', *Journal of Management Studies*, 32(5): 637–54.

—— (1998), 'Women in the labour market: a gender equality perspective', Paper prepared for the conference: Changing Labour Market and Gender Equality: the role of policy, held in Oslo, 12–13 October 1998.

—— and FAGAN, C. (1995), 'Gender segregation in societal context', *Work Employment and Society*, 9(2): 213–40.

—— and GRIMSHAW, D. (2001), 'ICTs and employment: the problem of job quality', *International Labour Review*, 140(2): 165–92.

—— and WILKINSON, F. (1994a), 'Introduction', in J. Rubery and F. Wilkinson (eds.), *Employer Strategy and the Labour Market*, Oxford: Oxford University Press.

—— and —— (eds.) (1994b), *Employer Strategy and the Labour Market*, Oxford: Oxford University Press.

—— SMITH, M., and FAGAN, C. (1998). *Women's Employment in Europe*, London: Routledge.

—— EARNSHAW, J., MARCHINGTON, M., COOKE, F. L., and VINCENT, S. (2002), 'Changing organizational forms and the employment relationship', *Journal of Management Studies*, 39(5): 645–72.

RUBERY, J., COOKE, F. L., EARNSHAW, J., and MARCHINGTON, M. (2003), 'Contracts, co-operation and employment relationships: working in a multi-employer environment', *British Journal of Industrial Relations*, 41(2): 265–89.

—— CARROLL, M., COOKE, F. L., GRUGULIS, I., and EARNSHAW, J. (2004), 'Human resource management and the permeable organization: the case of the multi-client call centre', *Journal of Management Studies*, forthcoming.

RUBIN, P. (1990), *Managing Business Transactions*, New York: Free Press.

SACHDEV, S. (2001), *Contracting Culture: from CCT to PPPs*, A report for UNISON, November.

SAKO, M. (1992), *Prices, Quality and Trust: Inter-firm relations in Britain and Japan*, Cambridge University Press.

SAVAGE, M. (1992), 'Women's expertise, men's authority: gendered organization and the contemporary middle classes', in M. Savage and A. Witz (eds.), *Gender and Bureaucracy*, Oxford: Blackwell.

SAXENIAN, A. (1994), *Regional Advantage: Culture and Competition in Silicon Valley and Route 128*, Cambridge, MA: Harvard University Press.

—— (1996), 'Beyond boundaries: open labour markets and learning in Silicon Valley', in M. B. Arthur and D. M. Rousseau (eds.), *The Boundaryless Career: A New Employment Principle for a new Organizational Era*, Oxford: Oxford University Press.

SAYER, A. (1986), 'New developments in manufacturing: the just-in-time system', *Capital and Class*, 30: 43–72.

—— and WALKER, R. (1992), *The Social Economy: Reworking The Division of Labor*, Oxford: Blackwell.

SCARBROUGH, H. (2000), 'The HR implications of supply chain relationships', *Human Resource Management Journal*, 10(1): 5–17.

SCHMID, G. (1991), *Women in the Public Sector*, Paris: OECD.

SEMLINGER, K. (1991a), 'New developments in subcontracting: mixing market and hierarchy', in A. Amin, and M. Dietrich, (eds.), *Towards a New Europe*, Cheltenham: Edward Elgar.

—— (1991b), 'Small firms in big subcontracting', in N. Altmann, C. Köhler, and P. Meil (eds.), *Technology and Work in German Industry*, New York: Campus.

SENNETT, R. (1998), *The Corrosion of Character*, New York: W. W. Norton.

SIMON, H. A. (1976), *Administrative Behaviour* (3rd edn), New York: Free Press.

SMITH, T. (2000), *Technology and Capital in the Age of Lean Production*, Albany: University of New York Press.

SPARROW, P. R. (2001), 'The new employment relationships: the dilemmas of a post-downsized, socially excluded and low trust future', in J. Gual and J. E. Ricart (eds.), *Strategy, Organization and the Changing Nature of Work*, Cheltenham and Massachusetts: Edward Elgar.

STEWART, R. (1963), *The Reality of Management*, London: Heinemann.

STIGLITZ, J. E. (1989), 'On the economic role of the state', in A. Heertje (ed.), *The Economic Role of the State*, Oxford: Basil Blackwell.

STREECK, W. (1987), 'The uncertainties of management in the management of uncertainty: employers, labour relations and industrial adjustment in the 1980s', *Work, Employment and Society*, 1(3): 281–308.

STURDY, A., KNIGHTS, D., and WILMOTT, H. (eds.) (1992), *Skill and Consent in the Labour Process*, London: Macmillan.

—— GRUGULIS, I., and WILLMOTT, H. (eds.) (2001), *Customer Service: Empowerment or Entrapment?* Basingstoke: Palgrave.

SUPIOT, A. (2001), *Beyond Employment: Changes in Work and the Future of Labour Law in Europe*, Oxford: Oxford University Press.

SWART, J. and KINNIE, N. (2003), 'Knowledge intensive firms: the influence of the client on HR systems', *Human Resource Management Journal*, 13(3): 37–55.

SYDOW, J. and WINDELER, A. (1998), 'Organizing and evaluating interfirm networks: a structurationist perspective on network processes and effectiveness', *Organization Science*, 9(3): 265–84.

TAKEISHI, A. (2001), 'Bridging inter- and intra-firm boundaries: management of supplier involvement in automobile product development', *Strategic Management Journal*, 2: 403–433.

TAYLOR, P., MULVEY, G., HYMAN, J., and BAIN, P. (2002), 'Work organization, control and the experience of work in call centres', *Work, Employment and Society*, 16(1): 133–50.

TAYLOR, R. (2002), *The Future of Employment Relations*, ESRC Future of Work Programme Seminar Series, Number 1.

TAYLOR, S. and TYLER, M. (2000), 'Emotional labour and sexual difference in the airline industry', *Work Employment and Society*, 14(1): 77–95.

TEECE, D. J. (1986), 'Firm boundaries, technological innovation and strategic management', in L. G. Thomas (ed.), *The Economics of Strategic Planning*. Lexington, MA: D. C. Heath.

TERRY, M. (2003), 'Employee representation: shop stewards and the new legal framework', in P. Edwards (ed.), *Industrial Relations: Theory and Practice*, Oxford: Blackwell.

The Cabinet Office's Regulatory Impact Unit (2002), SKOPE (ESRC Centre on Skills, Knowledge and Organisational Performance), Mid-term Review submission to the ESRC, October 2002.

T&G. (2003), 'Back Sainsbury's bod, say T&G' news release 30.4.2003, www.tgwu.org.uk/newsrelease/2003/03153.htm.

The Guardian (2003), 'Glimmer of hope over the pensions loophole', *The Guardian*, 29 November 2003.

THOMPSON, P. and MCHUGH, D. (2002), *Work Organizations* (3rd edn), Basingstoke: Palgrave.

—— WARHURST, C., and CALLAGHAN, G. (2001), 'Ignorant theory and knowledgeable workers: interrogating the connections between knowledge, skills and services', *Journal of Management Studies*, November 38(7): 923–42.

TOWERS, B. (1997), *The Representation Gap: Change and Reform in British and American Workplaces*, Oxford: Oxford University Press.

TOYNBEE, P. (2003), *Hard Work: Life in Low-Pay Britain*, London: Bloomsbury Publishing.

TRETHEWEY, A. (1999), 'Disciplined bodies: women's embodied identities at work', *Organization Studies*, 20(3): 423–50.

TURNBULL, P., DELBRIDGE, R., OLIVER, N., and WILKINSON, B. (1993), 'Winners and losers—the "tiering" of components suppliers in the UK automotive industry', *Journal of General Management*, 19(1): 48–63.

TURNER, H. A. (1962), *Trade Union Growth, Structure and Policy*, London: Allen and Unwin.

UNISON (2001), *Public Services, Private Finance: Accountability, Affordability and the Two-Tier Workforce*, Report for UNISON by Health Services and Health Policy Research Unit, University College London.

UNISON (2002), 'Best value and the two-tier workforce in local government'. *Best Value Intelligence Unit*, UNISON www.unison.org.uk/acrobat/B318.pdf.

—— (2003*a*), 'UNISON bargaining support', April.

—— (2003*b*), 'The private finance initiative: the retention of employment model, a UNISON briefing and negotiating guide', UNISON Health Care.

UZZI, B. (1997), 'Social structure and competition in Interfirm Networks: The paradox of embeddedness', *Administrative Science Quarterly*, 42(1): 35–67.

VICTOR, B. and STEPHENS, C. (1994), 'The dark side of the new organizational forms: an editorial essay', *Organization Science*, 5(4): 479–482.

VINCENT, S. (1997), *The Increasing Significance of the Contracting Form of Labour: A Case Study of Contract Management*, University of Manchester Sociology Working Paper, Number 4.

—— and GRUGULIS, I. (2004), 'Strategy, contracts and control in the management of government IT work', in P. Stewart (ed.), *Organizational Change and the Future of Work*, Basingstoke: Palgrave-MacMillan.

VON HIPPEL, E. (1987), 'Co-operation between rivals: informal know-how trading', *Research Policy*, 16: 291–302.

WADDINGTON, J. (2003), 'Trade Union Organization', in P. Edwards (ed.), *Industrial Relations: Theory and Practice*, Oxford: Blackwell.

WAJCMAN, J. (1998), *Managing Like a Man*, Cambridge: Polity Press.

WALBY, S. (1997), *Gender Transformations*, London: Routledge.

WARD, K., GRIMSHAW, D., RUBERY, J., and BEYNON, H. (2001), 'Dilemmas in the management of temporary work agency staff', *Human Resource Management Journal*, 11(4): 3–21.

WATSON, T. J. (1994), *In Search of Management*, London: Routledge.

WEST, M., BORRILL, C., DAWSON, J., SCULLY, J., CARTER, M., ANELAY, S. et al. (2002), 'The link between the management of employees and patient mortality in acute hospitals', *International Journal of Human Resource Management*, 13(8): 1299–1310.

WHARTON, A. S. (1996), 'Service with a smile: understanding the consequences of emotional labour', in C. L. Macdonald and C. Sirianni (eds.), *Working in the Service Society*, Philadelphia: Temple University Press.

WHITE, G. (2000), 'Determining pay', in G. White and J. Druker (eds.), *Reward Management: A Critical Text*, London: Routledge.

WILKINSON, D. (1998), 'Who are the low paid?' *Labour Market Trends*, 106(12): 617–22.

WILKINSON, F. (1983), 'Productive Systems', *Cambridge Journal of Economics*, 7: 413–429.

WILLIAMS, P. (2002), 'The competent boundary-spanner', *Public Administration*, 80(1): 103–124.

WILLIAMSON, O. E. (1975), *Markets and Hierarchies: Analysis and Antitrust Implications*, New York: Free Press.

WILLIAMSON, O. E. (1985), *The Economic Institutions of Capitalism: Firms, Markets, Relational Contracting*, New York: Free Press.

WILLIS, P. (2001), 'Letter from the liberal democrats shadow education secretary to the office of fair trading', Courtesy of the Liberal Democrats.

WILLMAN, P., BRYSON, A., and GOMEZ, R. (2003), *Why do Voice Regimes Differ?* Paper presented to the IIRA 13th World Congress, Berlin, September.

WILLMOTT, H. (1993), 'Strength is Ignorance; Slavery is Freedom: Managing Cultures in Modern Organizations', *Journal of Management Studies*, 30(4): 515–52.

WITZ, A. and Savage, M. (1992), 'The Gender of Organizations', in M. Savage and A. Witz (eds.), *Gender and Bureaucracy*, Oxford: Blackwell.

WRZESNIEWSKI, A. and DUTTON, J. (2001), 'Crafting a job: revisioning employees as active crafters of their work', *The Academy of Management Review*, 26(2): 179–201.

YOUNG, G., SMITH, K. G., and GRIMM, C. M. (1996), ' "Austrian" and industrial organization perspectives on firm-level competitive activity and performance', *Organization Science*, 7(3): 243–54.

ZABIN, C., QUAN, K., and DELP, L. (2001), 'Union organizing in California: challenges and opportunities', in P. Ong and J. Lincoln (eds.), *The State of California Labor*, Berkeley, CA: University of California Institute of Industrial Relations.

INDEX